# History of Egypt, Chaldea, Syria, Babylonia and Assyria

by Gaston Maspero and
A. H. Sayce
Volume 8

Translated by M. L. McCLURE, Member of the Committee of the Egypt Exploration Fund

ISBN: 978-1-63923-898-9

All Rights reserved. No part of this book maybe reproduced without written permission from the publishers, except by a reviewer who may quote brief passages in a review to be printed in a newspaper or magazine.

Printed: March 2023

Published and Distributed By:
Lushena Books
607 Country Club Drive, Unit E
Bensenville, IL 60106
www.lushenabks.com

ISBN: 978-1-63923-898-9

FRIEZE OF ARCHERS AT SUSA.

# CONTENTS

## CHAPTER I.

### SENNACHERIB (705–681 B.C.)

The Struggle of Sennacherib with Judæa and Egypt — Destruction of Babylon . . . . . . . . . . . . 3

## CHAPTER II.

### THE POWER OF ASSYRIA AT ITS ZENITH — ESARHADDON AND ASSUR-BANI-PAL

The Medes and Cimmerians: Lydia — The Conquest of Egypt, of Arabia, and of Elam . . . . . . . . . . . 81

## CHAPTER III.

### THE MEDES AND THE SECOND CHALDÆAN EMPIRE

The Fall of Nineveh and the Rise of the Chaldæan and Median Empires — The XXVIth Egyptian Dynasty: Cyaxares, Alyattes, and Nebuchadrezzar . . . . . . . . . . . 264

# LIST OF ILLUSTRATIONS

|  | PAGE |
|---|---|
| Frieze of Archers at Susa | *Frontispiece* |
| Clay seal with Cartouche of Sabaco | 11 |
| A Phœnician galley with two banks of oars | 17 |
| The Pass of Leguia, in Lebanon | 28 |
| Guard at the water-mill | 29 |
| Sennacherib receiving the submission of the Jews in his camp before Lachish | 31 |
| A raid among the woods and mountains | 43 |
| The fleet of Sennacherib on the Nar-Marratum | 49 |
| A skirmish in the marshes | 52 |
| The horse of Nergal-Ushezîb falling in the battle | 54 |
| The mounds of Nineveh seen from the terrace of a house in Mosul | 63 |
| King Sennacherib watching the transport of a colossal statue | 65 |
| Assyrian bas-reliefs at Bavian | 66 |
| Unknown subjects painted in the Fifth Tomb of the Eastern Kings | 68 |
| Great Assyrian Stele at Bavian | 69 |
| An Assyrian cavalry raid through the woods | 73 |
| Transport of a winged bull on a sledge | 74 |
| Sennacherib | 79 |
| One of the Egyptian ivories found in Assyria | 83 |
| Stone lion at Hamadân | 87 |
| View of Hamadân and Mount Elvend in winter | 88 |
| Monument commemorative of Midas | 95 |
| A Phrygian god | 96 |
| The mother-goddess between lions | 97 |
| The mother-goddess and Atys | 98 |
| The god-men associated with the sun and other deities | 99 |
| The steep banks of the Halys failed to arrest them | 104 |
| View over the plain of Sardes | 105 |
| A conflict with two griffins | 110 |
| Scythians armed for war | 111 |
| Inhabited caves on the banks of the Halys | 115 |
| The town of Kharkhar with its triple rampart | 131 |

## LIST OF ILLUSTRATIONS

|  | PAGE |
|---|---|
| Shabîtoku, King of Egypt | 137 |
| Tabarqa and his Queen Dikahîtamanu | 139 |
| The Column of Taharqa at Karnak | 142 |
| The Hemispeos of Hâthor and Bisû, at Gebel-Barkal | 143 |
| Entrance to the Hemispeos of Bîsû (Bes) at Gebel-Barkal | 144 |
| Taharqa | 145 |
| Southern promontory at the mouth of the Nahr-el-Kelb | 156 |
| Stele of Esarhaddon at the Nahr-el-Kelb | 157 |
| Stele of Zinjirli | 158 |
| Assyrian Sphinx in Egyptian style supporting the base of a column | 161 |
| Assur-Bani-Pal as a bearer of offerings | 168 |
| Shamash Shumukîn as a bearer of offerings | 169 |
| Montumihâît, Prince of Thebes | 174 |
| Psammetichus | 175 |
| Lydian Horsemen | 181 |
| Assur-Bani-Pal | 187 |
| Mural decorations from the grottos | 190 |
| King Tanuatamanu in adoration before the gods of Thebes | 191 |
| A lion issuing from its cage | 198 |
| Ituni breaks his bow with a blow of his sword, and gives himself up to the executioner | 206 |
| The Battle of Tullîz | 207 |
| Urtaku, cousin of Tiummân, surrendering to an Assyrian | 209 |
| The last arrow of Tiummân and his son | 210 |
| Death of Tiummân and his son | 211 |
| Khumban-Igash acclaimed as king after the Battle of Tullîz | 213 |
| The head of Tiummân sent to Nineveh | 215 |
| Assur-Bani-Pal banqueting with his queen | 216 |
| Two Elamite chiefs flayed alive after the Battle of Tullîz | 217 |
| Psammetichus I. | 235 |
| Battle of the Cimmerians against the Greeks accompanied by their dogs | 240 |
| Moorish-Arab Façade | 243 |
| Statues of the gods carried off by Assyrian soldiery | 251 |
| The Great Tumulus of Susa | 253 |
| Scythians lassoing horses | 265 |
| Nisæan horses harnessed to a royal chariot | 279 |
| Scene in the mountains of Persia | 283 |
| Head of a Persian archer | 285 |
| A Persian | 287 |
| A herd of wild goats — a bas-relief of the time of Assur-Bani-Pal | 290 |
| Illustrated manuscripts on papyrus in hieroglyphics | 291 |

## LIST OF ILLUSTRATIONS

|  | PAGE |
|---|---|
| Remains of Assur-Bani-Pal's wall at Nippur | 294 |
| Medic and Persian foot-soldiers | 297 |
| A Medic horseman | 298 |
| Part of the Fosse at Nineveh | 302 |
| Scythians tending their wounded | 308 |
| Iranian soldiers fighting against the Scythians | 311 |
| Three Hoplites in action | 335 |
| Statue of a Theban queen | 338 |
| The Saite fortress of Daphnæ | 347 |
| Egyptian Greek | 348 |
| Chamber and Sarcophagus of an Apis | 355 |
| The great Gallery of the Serapeum | 356 |
| Memphite bas-relief of the Saite Epoch | 359 |
| The ruins of Sais | 361 |
| A view in the mountains of the Messogis | 390 |
| The site of Priênê | 391 |
| The ruins of Pteria | 396 |
| The entrance to the sanctuary of Pteria | 397 |
| One of the processions in the ravine of Pteria | 398 |
| An Egyptian vessel of the Saite period | 404 |
| The ancient head of the Red Sea, now the northern extremity of the Bitter Lakes | 405 |
| The façade of the Great Temple of Abu-Simbel | 417 |
| Apries, from a Sphinx in the Louvre | 422 |
| Stele of Nebuchadrezzar | 423 |
| Prisoners under torture having their tongues torn out | 427 |
| A King putting out the eyes of a prisoner | 428 |
| A people carried away into captivity with their household goods and cattle | 431 |
| Bronze lion of Bohbaît | 436 |
| The small obelisk in the Piazza Della Minerva at Rome | 437 |
| The Oasis of Amon and the Spring of the Sun | 440 |
| A portion of the ruins of Cyrene, the Necropolis | 441 |
| Weighing silphium in presence of King Arkesilas | 444 |
| City defended by a triple wall | 456 |
| Probable section of the triple wall of Babylon | 457 |
| Fragment of a Babylonian bas-relief | 458 |
| Ruins of the Ziggurât of the temple of Bel | 459 |
| The stone lion of Babylon | 460 |

# SENNACHERIB (705-681 B.C.).

THE STRUGGLE OF SENNACHERIB WITH JUDÆA AND EGYPT—DESTRUCTION
OF BABYLON

*The upheaval of the entire Eastern world on the accession of Sennacherib— Revolt of Babylon: return of Merodach-baladan and his efforts to form a coalition against Assyria; the battle of Kish (703 B.C.)—Belibni, King of Babylon (702-699 B.C.)—Sabaco, King of Egypt, Amenertas and Pionkhi, Shabi-toku—Tyre and its kings after Ethbaal II.: Phœnician colonisation in Libya and the foundation of Carthage—The kingdom of Tyre in the time of Tiglath-pileser III. and Sargon: Elulai—Judah and the reforms of Hezekiah; alliance of Judah and Tyre with Egypt, the downfall of the Tyrian kingdom (702 B.C.)—The battle of Altaku and the siege of Jerusalem: Sennacherib encamped before Lachish, his Egyptian expedition, the disaster at Pelusium.*

*Renewed revolt of Babylon and the Tabal (699 B.C.): flight of the people of Bit-Yakin into Elamite territory; Sennacherib's fleet and descent on Nagitu (697-696 B.C.)—Khalludush invades Karduniash (695 B.C.); Nirgal-ushezib and Mushesib-marduk at Babylon (693-689 B.C.)—Sennacherib invades Elam (693 B.C.): battle of Khalulê (692 B.C.), siege and destruction of Babylon (689 B.C.)—Buildings of Sennacherib at Nineveh: his palace at Kouyunjik; its decoration with battle, hunting, and building scenes.*

# CHAPTER I

## SENNACHERIB (705-681 B.C.)

*The struggle of Sennacherib with Judæa and Egypt—Destruction of Babylon.*

SENNACHERIB either failed to inherit his father's good fortune, or lacked his ability.[1] He was not deficient in military genius, nor in the energy necessary to withstand the various enemies who rose against him at widely removed points of his frontier, but he had neither the adaptability of character nor the delicate tact required to manage successfully the heterogeneous elements combined under his sway. He lacked the wisdom to conciliate the vanquished, or opportunely to check his own repressive measures; he destroyed towns, massacred entire tribes, and laid whole tracts of country waste, and by failing to repeople these with captive exiles from other nations, or to import colonists in sufficient numbers, he found himself towards the end of his reign ruling over a sparsely

---

[1] The two principal documents for the reign of Sennacherib are engraved on cylinders: the *Taylor Cylinder* and the *Bellino Cylinder,* duplicates of which, more or less perfect, exist in the collections of the British Museum. The *Taylor Cylinder,* found at **Kouyunjik or** Nebi-Yunus, contains the history of the first eight years of this reign; the *Bellino Cylinder* treats of the two first years of the reign.

inhabited desert where his father had bequeathed to him flourishing provinces and populous cities. His was the system of the first Assyrian conquerors, Shalmaneser III. and Assur-nazir-pal, substituted for that of Tiglath-pileser III. and Sargon. The assimilation of the conquered peoples to their conquerors was retarded, tribute was no longer paid regularly, and the loss of revenue under this head was not compensated by the uncertain increase in the spoils obtained by war; the recruiting of the army, rendered more difficult by the depopulation of revolted districts, weighed heavier still on those which remained faithful, and began, as in former times, to exhaust the nation. The news of Sargon's murder, published throughout the Eastern world, had rekindled hope in the countries recently subjugated by Assyria, as well as in those hostile to her. Phœnicia, Egypt, Media, and Elam roused themselves from their lethargy and anxiously awaited the turn which events should take at Nineveh and Babylon. Sennacherib did not consider it to his interest to assume the crown of Chaldæa, and to treat on a footing of absolute equality a country which had been subdued by force of arms: he relegated it to the rank of a vassal state, and while reserving the suzerainty for himself, sent thither one of his brothers to rule as king.[1] The Babylonians were

[1] The events which took place at Babylon at the beginning of Sennacherib's reign are known to us from the fragments of Berosus, compared with the Canon of Ptolemy and Pinches' Babylonian Canon. The first interregnum in the Canon of Ptolemy (704–702 B.C.) is filled in Pinches' Canon by three kings who are said to have reigned as follows: Sennacherib, two years; Marduk-zâkir-shumu, one month; Merodach-baladan, nine months. Berosus substitutes for Sennacherib one of his brothers, whose name apparently he

indignant at this slight. Accustomed to see their foreign ruler conform to their national customs, take the hands of Bel, and assume or receive from them a new throne-name, they could not resign themselves to descend to the level of mere tributaries: in less than two years they rebelled, assassinated the king who had been imposed upon them, and proclaimed in his stead Marduk-zâkir-shumu,[1] who was merely the son of a female slave (704 B.C.). This was the signal for a general insurrection in Chaldæa and the eastern part of the empire. Merodach-baladan, who had remained in hiding in the valleys on the Elamite frontier since his defeat in 709 B.C., suddenly issued forth with his adherents, and marched at once to Babylon; the very news of his approach caused a sedition, in the midst of which Marduk-zâkir-shumu perished, after having reigned for only one month. Merodach-baladan re-entered his former capital, and as soon as he was once more seated on the throne, he endeavoured to form alliances with all the princes, both small and great, who might create a diversion in his favour. His envoys obtained promises of help from Elam; other emissaries hastened to Syria to solicit the alliance of Hezekiah, and might have even proceeded to Egypt if their

did not know; and this is the version I have adopted, in agreement with most modern historians, as best tallying with the evident lack of affection for Babylon displayed by Sennacherib throughout his reign.

[1] The servile origin of this personage is indicated in Pinches' Babylonian Canon; he might, however, be connected through his father with a princely, or even a royal, family, and thereby be in a position to win popular support. Among modern Assyriologists, some suppose that the name Akises in Berosus is a corruption of [Marduk-]zâkir[shumu]; others consider Akises-Akishu as being the personal name of the king, and Marduk-zâkir-shumu his throne-name.

sovereign's good fortune had lasted long enough.¹ But Sennacherib did not waste his opportunities in lengthy preparations. The magnificent army left by Sargon was at his disposal, and summoning it at once into the field, he advanced on the town of Kîsh, where the Kaldâ monarch was entrenched with his Aramæan forces and the Elamite auxiliaries furnished by Shutruk-nakhunta. The battle issued in the complete rout of the confederate forces Merodach-baladan fled almost unattended, first to Guzum manu, and then to the marshes of the Tigris, where he found a temporary refuge ; the troops who were despatched in pursuit followed him for five days, and then, having failed to secure the fugitive, gave up the search.² His camp fell into the possession of the victor, with all its contents—chariots, horses, mules, camels, and herds cattle belonging to the commissariat department of the army : Babylon threw open its gates without resistance hoping, no doubt, that Sennacherib would at length resolve to imitate the precedent set by his father and retain the royal dignity for himself. He did, indeed, consent to remit the punishment for this first insurrection, and contented himself with pillaging the royal treasury and palace, but he did not deign to assume the crown conferring it on Belibni, a Babylonian of noble birth, who had been taken, when quite a child, to Nineveh and

¹ 2 *Kings* xx. **12–19 ;** *Isa.* xxxix. The embassy to Hezekiah has been assigned to the first reign of Merodach-baladan, under Sargon. In accordance with the information obtained from the Assyrian monuments, it seems to me that it could only have taken place during his second reign, in 703 B.C.

² The detail is furnished by the *Bellino Cylinder.* Berosus affirmed that Merodach-baladan was put to death by Belibni.

educated there under the eyes of Sargon.[1] While he was thus reorganising the government, his generals were bringing the campaign to a close: they sacked, one after another, eighty-nine strongholds and eight hundred and twenty villages of the Kaldâ; they drove out the Arabian and Aramæan garrisons which Merodach-baladan had placed in the cities of Karduniash, in Urak, Nipur, Kuta, and Kharshag-kalamma, and they re-established Assyrian supremacy over all the tribes on the east of the Tigris up to the frontiers of Elam, the Tumuna, the Ubudu, the Gambulu, and the Khindaru, as also over the Nabatæans and Hagarenes, who wandered over the deserts of Arabia to the west of the mouths of the Euphrates. The booty was enormous: 208,000 prisoners, both male and female, 7200 horses, 11,073 asses, 5230 camels, 80,100 oxen, 800,500 sheep, made their way like a gigantic horde of emigrants to Assyria under the escort of the victorious army. Meanwhile the Khirimmu remained defiant, and showed not the slightest intention to submit: their strongholds had to be attacked and the inhabitants annihilated before order could in any way be restored in the country. The second reign of Merodach-baladan had lasted barely nine months.

The blow which ruined Merodach-baladan broke up the coalition which he had tried to form against Assyria. Babylon was the only rallying-point where states so remote, and such entire strangers to each other as Judah and Elam, could enter into friendly relations and arrange a plan of combined action. Having lost Babylon as a centre,

[1] The name is transcribed Belibos in Greek, and it seems as if the Assyrian variants justify the pronunciation Belibush.

they were once more hopelessly isolated, and had no means of concerting measures against the common foe: they renounced all offensive action, and waited under arms to see how the conqueror would deal with each severally. The most threatening storm, however, was not that which was gathering over Palestine, even were Egypt to be drawn into open war: for a revolt of the western provinces, however serious, was never likely to lead to disastrous complications, and the distance from Pelusium to the Tigris was too great for a victory of the Pharaoh to compromise effectually the safety of the empire. On the other hand, should intervention on the part of Elam in the affairs of Babylon or Media be crowned with success, the most disastrous consequences might ensue: it would mean the loss of Karduniash, or of the frontier districts won with such difficulty by Tiglath-pileser III. and Sargon; it would entail permanent hostilities on the Tigris and the Zab, and perhaps the appearance of barbarian troops under the walls of Calah or of Nineveh. Elam had assisted Merodach-baladan, and its soldiers had fought on the plains of Kîsh. Months had elapsed since that battle, yet Shutruk-nakhunta showed no disposition to take the initiative: he accepted his defeat at all events for the time, but though he put off the day of reckoning till a more favourable opportunity, it argued neither weakness nor discouragement, and he was ready to give a fierce reception to any Assyrian monarch who should venture within his domain. Sennacherib, knowing both the character and resources of the Elamite king, did not attempt to meet him in the open field, but wreaked his resentment on the frontier tribes who had rebelled at the instigation of the Elamites, on the Cossæans, on Ellipi and its king Ishpabara. He pursued the inhabitants into the narrow valleys and forests of the Khoatras, where his chariots were unable to follow: proceeding with his troops, sometimes on horseback, at other times on foot, he reduced Bît-kilamzak, Khardishpi, and Bît-kubatti to ashes, and annexed the territories of the Cossæans and the Yasubigallâ to the prefecture of Arrapkha. Thence he entered Ellipi, where Ishpabara did not venture to come to close quarters with him in the open field, but led him on from town to town. He destroyed the two royal seats of Marubishti and Akkuddu, and thirty-four of their dependent strongholds; he took possession of Zizirtu, Kummalu, the district of Bitbarru, and the city of Elinzash, to which he gave the name Kar-Sennacherib,—the fortress of Sennacherib,—and annexed them to the government of Kharkhar. The distant Medes, disquieted at his advance, sent him presents, and renewed the assurances of devotion they had given to Sargon, but Sennacherib did not push forward into their territory as his predecessors had done: he was content to have maintained his authority as far as his outlying posts, and to have strengthened the Assyrian empire by acquiring some well-situated positions near the main routes which led from the Iranian table-land to the plains of Mesopotamia. Having accomplished this, he at once turned his attention towards the west, where the spirit of rebellion was still active in the countries bordering on the African frontier. Sabaco, now undisputed master of Egypt, was not content, like Piônkhi, to bring Egypt proper into a position of dependence, and govern it at a distance, by means of his generals. He took up his residence within it, at least during part of every year, and played the *rôle* of Pharaoh so well that his Egyptian subjects, both at Thebes and in the Delta, were obliged to acknowledge his sovereignty and recognise him as the founder of a new dynasty. He kept a close watch over the vassal princes, placing garrisons in Memphis and the other principal citadels, and throughout the country he took in hand public works which had been almost completely interrupted for more than a century owing to the civil wars: the highways were repaired, the canals cleaned out and enlarged, and the foundations of the towns raised above the level of the inundation. Bubastis especially profited under his rule, and regained the ascendency it had lost ever since the accession of the second Tanite dynasty; but this partiality was not to the detriment of other cities. Several of the temples at Memphis were restored, and the inscriptions effaced by time were re-engraved. Thebes, happy under the government of Amenertas and her husband Piônkhi, profited largely by the liberality of its Ethiopian rulers. At Luxor Sabaco restored the decoration of the principal gateway between the two pylons, and repaired several portions of the temple of Amon at Karnak. History subsequently related that, in order to obtain sufficient workmen, he substituted forced labour for the penalty of death: a policy which, beside being profitable, would win for him a reputation for clemency. Egypt, at length reduced to peace and order, began once more to flourish, and to display that inherent vitality of which she had so often given proof, and her reviving prosperity attracted as of old the attention of foreign powers. At the beginning of his reign, Sabaco had attempted to meddle in the intrigues of Syria, but the ease with which Sargon had quelled the revolt of Ashdod had inspired the Egyptian monarch with salutary distrust in his own power; he had sent presents to the conqueror and received gifts in exchange, which furnished him with a pretext for enrolling the Asiatic peoples among the tributary nations whose names he inscribed on his triumphal lists.¹ Since then he had had some diplomatic correspondence with his powerful neighbour, and a document bearing his name was laid up in the archives at Calah, where the clay seal once attached to it has been discovered. Peace had lasted for a dozen years, when he died about 703 B.C., and his son Shabîtoku ascended the throne.³ The temporary embarrassments in which the Babylonian revolution had plunged Sennacherib

CLAY SEAL WITH CARTOUCHE OF SABACO.²

---

¹ It was probably with reference to this exchange of presents that Sabaco caused the bas-relief at Karnak to be engraved, in which he represents himself as victorious over both Asiatics and Africans.

² Drawn by Faucher-Gudin, from a sketch by Layard.

³ One version of Manetho assigns twelve years to the reign of Sabaco, and this duration is confirmed by an inscription in Hammamât, dated in his twelfth year. Sabaco having succeeded to the throne in **716–715** B.C., his reign brings us down to 704 or 703 B.C., which obliges us to place the accession of Shabi-toku in the year following the death of Sargon.

must have offered a tempting opportunity for interference to this inexperienced king.

Tyre and Judah alone of all the Syrian states retained a sufficiently independent spirit to cherish any hope of deliverance from the foreign yoke. Tyre still maintained her supremacy over Southern Phœnicia, and her rulers were also kings of Sidon.[1] The long reign of Eth-baal and his alliance with the kings of Israel had gradually repaired the losses occasioned by civil discord, and had restored Tyre to the high degree of prosperity which it had enjoyed under Hiram. Few actual facts are known which can enlighten us as to the activity which prevailed under Eth baal: we know, however, that he rebuilt the small town of Botrys, which had been destroyed in the course of some civil war, and that he founded the city of Auza in Libyan territory, at the foot of the mountains of Aures, in one the richest mineral districts of modern Algeria.[2] In B.C. Assur-nazir-pal had crossed the Lebanon and skirted the shores of the Mediterranean: Eth-baal, naturally com pliant, had loaded him with gifts, and by this opportune submission had preserved his cities and country from the

---

[1] Eth-baal II., who, according to the testimony of the native historians belonged to the royal family of Tyre, is called King of the Sidonians in the Bible (1 *Kings* xvi. 31), and the Assyrian texts similarly call Elulai King of the Sidonians, while Menander mentions him as King of Tyre. It is probable that the King of Sidon, mentioned in the Annals of hal maneser III. side by side with the King of Tyre, was a vassal of the Ty ian monarch.

[2] The two facts are preserved in a passage of Menander. I admit the identity of the Auza mentioned in this fragment with the Auzea of Tacitus and with the *Colonia Septimia Aur. Auziensium* of the Roman inscriptions the present Aumale.

horrors of invasion.¹ Twenty years later Shalmaneser III had returned to Syria, and had come into conflict with Damascus. The northern Phœnicians formed a league with Ben-hadad (Adadidri) to withstand him, and drew upon themselves the penalty of their rashness; the Tyrians, faithful to their usual policy, preferred to submit voluntarily and purchase peace. Their conduct showed the greater wisdom in that, after the death of Eth-baal, internal troubles again broke out with renewed fierceness and with even more disastrous results. His immediate successor was Balezor (854–846 B.C.), followed by Mutton I. (845–821 B.C.), who flung himself at the feet of Shalmaneser III., in 842 B.C., in the camp at Baalirasi, and renewed his homage three years later, in 839 B.C. The legends concerning the foundation of Carthage blend with our slight knowledge of his history. They attribute to Mutton I. a daughter named Elissa, who was married to her uncle Sicharbal, high priest of Melkarth, and a young son named Pygmalion (820–774 B.C.). Sicharbal had been nominated by Mutton as regent during the minority of Pygmalion, but he was overthrown by the people, and some years later murdered by his ward. From that time forward Elissa's one aim was to avenge the murder of her husband. She formed a conspiracy which was joined by all the nobles, but being betrayed and threatened with death, she seized a fleet which lay ready to sail in the harbour, and embarking with all her adherents set sail for Africa, landing in the district

[1] The King of Tyre who sent gifts to Assur-nazir-pal is not named in the Assyrian documents: our knowledge of Tyrian chronology permits us with all probability to identify him with Eth-baal.

of Zeugitanê, where the Sidonians had already built Kambê. There she purchased a tract of land from Iarbas, chief of the Liby-phœnicians, and built on the ruins of the ancient factory a new town, Qart-hadshat, which the Greeks called Carchedo and the Romans Carthage. The genius of Virgil has rendered the name of Dido illustrious: but history fails to recognise in the narratives which form the basis of his tale anything beyond a legendary account fabricated after the actual origin (814-813 B.C.) of the great Punic city had been forgotten. Thus weakened, Tyre could less than ever think of opposing the ambitious designs of Assyria: Pygmalion took no part in the rebellions of the petty Syrian kings against Samsî-rammân, and in 803 B.C. he received his suzerain Rammân-nirâri with the accustomed gifts, when that king passed through Phœnicia before attacking Damascus. Pygmalion died about 774 B.C., and the names of his immediate successors are not known;[1] it may be supposed, however, that when the power of Nineveh temporarily declined, the ties which held Tyre to Assyria became naturally relaxed, and the city released herself from the burden of a tribute which had in the past been very irregularly paid. The yoke was reassumed half a century later, at the mere echo of the

---

[1] The fragment of Menander which has preserved for us the list of Tyrian kings from Abî-baal to Pygmalion, was only quoted by Josephus, because the seventh year of Pygmalion's reign corresponding to the date of the foundation of Carthage,—814-813 B.C. according to the chronological system of Timæus,—the Hebrew historian found in it a fixed date which seemed to permit of his establishing the chronology of the kings of Israel and Judah on a trustworthy basis between the reign of Pygmalion and Hiram I., the contemporary of David and Solomon.

first victories of Tiglath-pileser III.; and Hiram II., who then reigned in Tyre, hastened to carry to the camp at Arpad assurances of his fidelity (742 B.C.). He gave pledges of his allegiance once more in 738 B.C.; then he disappears, and Mutton II. takes his place about 736 B.C. This king cast off, unhappily for himself, his hereditary apathy, and as soon as a pretext offered itself, abandoned the policy of neutrality to which his ancestors had adhered so firmly. He entered into an alliance in 734 B.C. with Damascus, Israel and Philistia, secretly supported and probably instigated by Egypt; then, when Israel was conquered and Damascus overthrown, he delayed repairing his error till an Assyrian army appeared before Tyre: he had then to pay the price of his temerity by 120 talents of gold and many loads of merchandise (728 B.C.). The punishment was light and the loss inconsiderable in comparison with the accumulated wealth of the city, which its maritime trade was daily increasing:* Mutton thought the episode was closed,[1] but the peaceful policy of his house, having been twice interrupted, could not be resumed. Southern Phœnicia, having once launched on the stream of Asiatic politics, followed its fluctuations, and was compelled henceforth to employ in her own defence the forces which had hitherto been utilised in promoting her colonial enterprises.

But it was not due to the foolish caprice of ignorant

* [For a description of the trade carried on by Tyre, cf. *Ezek.* xxvi., xxvii., and xxviii.—Tr.]

[1] Pygmalion having died about 774 B.C., and Hiram II. not appearing till 742 B.C., it is probable that we should intercalate between these two kings at least one sovereign whose name is still unknown.

or rash sovereigns that Tyre renounced her former neutral policy: she was constrained to do so, almost perforce, by the changes which had taken place in Europe. The progress of the Greeks, and their triumph in the waters of the Ægean and Ionian Seas, and the rapid expansion of the Etruscan navy after the end of the ninth century, had gradually restricted the Phœnician merchantmen to the coasts of the Western Mediterranean and the Atlantic: they industriously exploited the mineral wealth of Africa and Spain, and traffic with the barbarous tribes of Morocco and Lusitania, as well as the discovery and working of the British tin mines, had largely compensated for the losses occasioned by the closing of the Greek and Italian markets. Their ships, obliged now to coast along the inhospitable cliffs of Northern Africa and to face the open sea, were more strongly and scientifically built than any vessels hitherto constructed. The Egyptian undecked galleys, with stem and stern curving inwards, were discarded as a build ill adapted to resist the attacks of wind or wave. The new Phœnician galley had a long, low, narrow, well-balanced hull, the stern raised and curving inwards above the steersman, as heretofore, but the bows pointed and furnished with a sharp ram projecting from the keel, equally serviceable to cleave the waves or to stave in the side of an enemy's ship. Motive power was supplied by two banks of oars, the upper ones resting in rowlocks on the gunwale, the lower ones in rowlocks pierced in the timbers of the vessel's side. An upper deck, supported by stout posts, ran from stem to stern, above the heads of the rowers, and was reserved for the soldiers and the rest of the crew: on a light railing surrounding it were hung the circular shields of the former, forming as it were a rampart on either side The mast, passing through both decks, was firmly fixed in the keel, and was supported by two stays made fast to stem and stern. The rectangular sail was attached to

A PHŒNICIAN GALLEY WITH TWO BANKS OF OARS.[1]

a yard which could be hoisted or lowered at will. The wealth which accrued to the Tyrians from their naval expeditions had rendered the superiority of Tyre over the neighbouring cities so manifest that they had nearly all become her vassals. Arvad and Northern Phœnicia were still independent, as also the sacred city of Bylos, but the entire coast from the Nahr-el-Kelb to the headland formed by Mount Carmel was directly subject to Tyre

[1] Drawn by Faucher-Gudin, from Layard. Sennacherib affirms that vessels of this type had been constructed by Syrian shipwrights, and were manned by Tyrian, Sidonian, and Ionian sailors.

[2] The kings of Arvad and Byblos are still found mentioned at the beginning of Sennacherib's reign.

comprising the two Sidons, Bit-ziti, and Sarepta, the country from Mahalliba to the fords of the Litâny, Ushu and its hinterland as far as Kana, Akzîb, Akko, and Dora; and this compact territory, partly protected by the range of Lebanon, and secured by the habitual pru

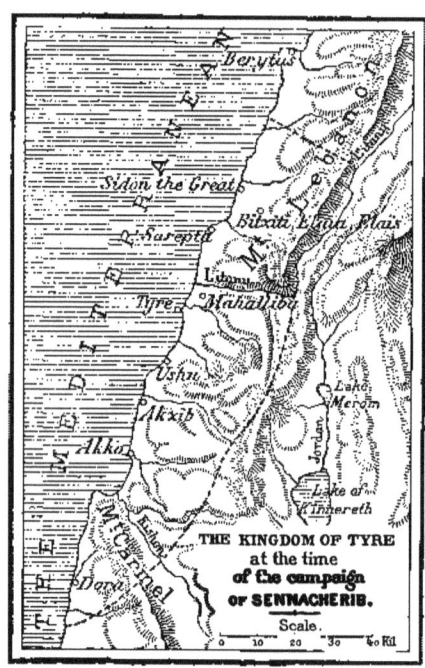

THE KINGDOM OF TYRE at the time of the campaign of SENNACHERIB.

dence of its rulers from the invasions which had desolated Syria, formed the most flourishing, and perhaps also the most populous, kingdom which still existed between the Euphrates and the Egyptian desert.[1] Besides these some parts of Cyprus were dependent on Tyre, though the Achæan colonies, continually reinforced by fresh immigrants, had absorbed most of the native population and driven the rest into the mountains. A hybrid civilisation had developed among these early Greek settlers amalgamating the customs, religions, and arts of the ancient eastern world of Egypt, Syria, and Chaldæa in

---

[1] The extent of the kingdom of Tyre is indicated by the passage in which Sennacherib enumerated the cities which he had taken from Elulai. To these must be added Dor, to the south of Carmel, which was always regarded as belonging to the Tyrians, and whose isolated position between the headland, the sea, and the forest might cause the Assyrians to leave it unmolested.

variable proportions : their script was probably derived from one of the Asianic systems whose monuments are still but partly known, and it consisted of a syllabary awkwardly adapted to a language for which it had not been designed. A dozen petty kings, of whom the majority were Greeks, disputed possession of the northern and eastern parts of the island, at Idalion, Khytros, Paphos, Soli, Kourion, Tamassos, and Ledron. The Phœnicians had given way at first before the invaders, and had grouped themselves in the eastern plain round Kition; they had, however, subsequently assumed the offensive, and endeavoured to regain the territory they had lost. Kition, which had been destroyed in one of their wars, had been rebuilt, and thus obtained the name of Qart-hadshat, "the new city."[1] Mutton's successor, Elulai, continued, as we know, the work of defence and conquest: perhaps it was with a view to checking his advance that seven kings of Cyprus sent an embassy, in 709 B.C., to his suzerain, Sargon, and placed themselves under the protection of Assyria. If this was actually the case, and Elulai was compelled to suspend hostilities against these hereditary foes, one can understand that this grievance, added to the reasons for uneasiness inspired by the

[1] The name of this city, at first read as Amtikhadashti, and identified with Ammokhostos or with Amathous,—*Amti-Khadashti* would in this case be equivalent to *New Amathous*,—is really Karti-Khadashti, as is proved by the variant reading discovered by Schrader, and this is identical with the native name of Carthage in Africa. This new city must have been of some antiquity by the time of Elulai, for it is mentioned on a fragment of a bronze vase found in Cyprus itself : this fragment belonged to a King Hiram, who according to some authorities would be Hiram II., according to others, Hiram I.

situation of his continental dominions, may have given him the desire to rid himself of the yoke of Assyria and contributed to his resolution to ally himself with the powers which were taking up arms against her. The constant intercourse of his subjects with the Delta, and his natural anxiety to avoid anything which might close one of the richest markets of the world to the Tyrian trade, inclined him to receive favourably the overtures of the Pharaoh: the emissaries of Shabîtoku found him as much disposed as Hezekiah himself to begin the struggle. The latter monarch, who had ascended the throne while still very young, had at first shown no ambition beyond the carrying out of religious reforms His father Ahaz had been far from orthodox, in spite the influence exerted over him by Isaiah. During visit to Tiglath-pileser at Damascus (729 B.C.) he had noticed an altar whose design pleased him. He sent description of it to the high priest Urijah, with orders to have a similar one constructed, and erected in the court of the temple at Jerusalem: this altar he appro priated to his personal use, and caused the priests to minister at it, instead of at the old altar, which he relegated to an inferior position. He also effected changes in the temple furniture, which doubtless appeared to him old-fashioned in comparison with the splendours of the Assyrian worship which he had witnessed, and he made some alterations in the approaches to the temple, wishing, as far as we can judge, that the King of Judah should henceforth, like his brother of Nineveh have a private means of access to his national god.

This was but the least of his offences : for had he not offered his own son as a holocaust at the moment he felt himself most menaced by the league of Israel and Damascus ? Among the people themselves there were many faint-hearted and faithless, who, doubting the power of the God of their forefathers, turned aside to the gods of the neighbouring nations, and besought from them the succour they despaired of receiving from any other source; the worship of Jahveh was confounded with that of Moloch in the valley of the children of Hinnom where there was a sanctuary or Tophet, at which the people celebrated the most horrible rites : a large and fierce pyre was kept continually burning there, to consume the children whose fathers brought them to offer in sacrifice.[1] Isaiah complains bitterly of these unbelievers who profaned the land with their idols, " worshipping the work of their own hands, that which their own fingers had made."[2] The new king, obedient to the divine command, renounced the errors of his father; he removed the fetishes with which the superstition of his predecessors had cumbered the temple, and which they had connec ted with the worship of Jahveh, and in his zeal even destroyed the ancient brazen serpent, the Nehushtan the origin of which was attributed to Moses.[3] On the occasion of the revolt of Yamani, Isaiah counselled

[1] *Isa.* xxx. 33, where the prophet describes the Tophet Jahveh's anger is preparing for Assyria.
[2] *Isa.* ii. 8.
[3] 2 *Kings* xviii. 4. I leave the account of this religious reformation in the place assigned to it in the Bible; other historians relegate it to a time subsequent to the invasion of Sennacherib

Hezekiah to remain neutral, and this prudence enabled him to look on in security at the ruin of the Philistines the hereditary foes of his race. Under his wise administration the kingdom of Judah, secured against annoyance from envious neighbours by the protection which Assur freely afforded to its obedient vassals, and revived by thirty years of peace, rose rapidly from the rank secondary importance which it had formerly been content to occupy. "Their land was full of silver and gold neither was there any end of their treasures; their land also was full of horses, neither was there any end of their chariots."[1] Now that the kingdom of Israel had been reduced to the condition of an Assyrian province, it was on Judah and its capital that the hopes of the whole Hebrew nation were centred.

Tyre and Jerusalem had hitherto formed the extreme outwork of the Syrian states; they were the only remaining barrier which separated the empires of Egypt and Assyria, and it was to the interest of the Pharaoh to purchase their alliance and increase their strength by every means in his power. Negotiations must have been going on for some time between the three powers, but up to the time of the death of Sargon and the return of Merodach baladan to Babylon their results had been unimportant and it was possible that the disasters which had befallen the Kaldâ would tend to cool the ardour of the allies An unforeseen circumstance opportunely

---

[1] *Isa.* ii 7, where the description applies better to the late years of Ahaz or the reign of Hezekiah than to the years preceding the war against Pekah and Rezin

rekindled their zeal, and determined them to try their fortune. The inhabitants of Ekron, dissatisfied with Padî, the chief whom the Assyrians had set over them, seized his person and sent him in chains to Hezekiah.[1] To accept the present was equivalent to open rebellion, and a declaration of war against the power of the suzerain. Isaiah, as

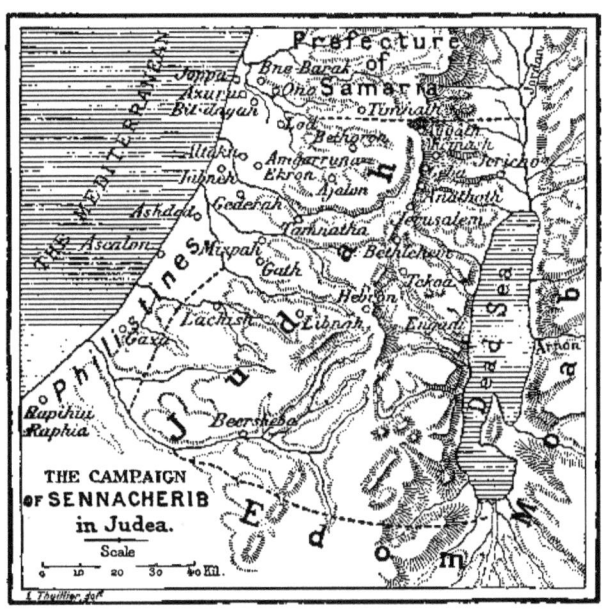

usual, wished Judah to rely on Jahveh alone, and preached against alliance with the Babylonians, for he foresaw that success would merely result in substituting the Kaldâ for the Ninevite monarch, and in aggravating the condition of Judah. "All that is in thine house," he said to Hezekiah, "and that which thy fathers have laid up in store unto this day, shall be carried to Babylon; nothing

[1] The name of the city, written Amgarruna, is really Akkaron-Ekron.

shall be left, saith the Lord. And of thy sons that shall issue from thee, which thou shalt beget, shall they take away; and they shall be eunuchs in the palace of the King of Babylon." Hezekiah did not pay much heed to the prediction, for, he reflected, " peace and truth shall be in my days," and the future troubled him little When the overthrow of Merodach-baladan had taken place the prophet still more earnestly urged the people not to incur the vengeance of Assyria without other help than that of Tyre or Ethiopia, and Eliakim, son of Hilkia spoke in the same strain; but Shebna, the prefect of palace, declaimed against this advice, and the latter s counsel prevailed with his master.² Hezekiah agreed to accept the sovereignty over Ekron which its inhabitants offered to him, but a remnant of prudence kept him from putting Padi to death, and he contented himself with casting him into prison. Isaiah, though temporarily out of favour with the king, ceased not to proclaim aloud in all quarters the will of the Almighty. "Woe to the rebellious children, saith the Lord, that take counsel, but not of Me ; and that cover with a covering (form alliances), but not of My spirit, that they may add sin to sin : that walk to go down into Egypt, and have not asked at My mouth, to strengthen themselves in the strength of Pharaoh, and to trust in the shadow of Egypt ! Therefore shall the strength of Pharaoh be your shame, and the trust in the shadow of Egypt your confusion. When your

¹ 2 Kings xx. 16–19.
² This follows from the terms in which the prophet compares the two men (Isa. xxii. 15–25).

princes shall be at Tanis, and your messengers shall come to Heracleopolis,* you shall all be ashamed of a people that cannot profit you. . . . For Egypt helpeth in vain, and to no purpose: therefore have I called her Rahab that sitteth still."[1] He returned, unwearied and with varying imagery, to his theme, contrasting the uncertainty and frailty of the expedients of worldly wisdom urged by the military party, with the steadfast will of Jahveh and the irresistible authority with which He invests His faithful servants. "The Egyptians are men, and not God; and their horses flesh, and not spirit; and when the Lord shall stretch out His hand, both he that helpeth shall stumble, and he that is holpen shall fall, and they shall all fail together. For thus saith the Lord unto me, Like as when the lion growleth, and the young lion over his prey, if a multitude of shepherds be called forth against him, he will not be dismayed at their voice, nor abase himself for the noise of them: so shall the Lord of hosts come down to fight upon Mount Zion, and upon the hill thereof. As birds flying, so will the Lord of hosts protect Jerusalem: He will protect and deliver it. Turn ye unto Him from whom ye have deeply revolted, O children of Israel."[2] No one, however, gave heed to his warnings, either king or people; but the example of Phœnicia soon proved that he was right. When Sennacherib bestirred himself, in the spring of

---

\* [Heb. Hanes.—Tr.]

[1] *Isa.* **xxx.** 1–5, 7. In verses **4, 5,** the original text employs the third person; I have restored the second person, to avoid confusion.

[2] *Isa.* xxxi. 3–6.

702 B.C., either the Ethiopians were not ready, or they dared not advance to encounter him in Cœle-Syria, and they left Elulai to get out of his difficulties as best he might. He had no army to risk in a pitched battle; but fondly imagined that his cities, long since fortified, and protected on the east by the range of Lebanon, would offer a resistance sufficiently stubborn to wear out the patience of his assailant. The Assyrians, however, disconcerted his plans. Instead of advancing against him by the pass of Nahr-el-Kebir, according to their usual custom, they attacked him in flank, descending into the very midst of his positions by the *col* of Legnia or one of the neighbouring passes.[1] They captured in succession the two Sidons, Bît-zîti, Sarepta, Mahalliba, Ushu, Akzîb, and Acco: Elulai, reduced to the possession of the island of Tyre alone, retreated to one of his colonies in Cyprus where he died some years later, without having set foot again on the continent. All his former possessions on the mainland were given to a certain Eth-baal, who chose Sidon for his seat of government, and Tyre lost by this one skirmish the rank of metropolis which she had enjoyed for centuries.[2]

This summary punishment decided all the Syrian princes who were not compromised beyond hope of pardon to humble themselves before the suzerain. Menahem of Samsi-muruna,[3] Abdiliti of Arvad, Uru-malik of Byblos

---

[1] This follows from the very order in which the cities were taken in the course of this campaign.

[2] The Assyrian text gives for the name of the King of Sidon a shortened form Tu-baal instead of Eth-baal, paralleled by Lulia for Elulai.

[3] Several of the early Assyriologists read Usi-muruna, and identified the

Puduîlu of Ammon, Chemosh-nadab of Moab, Malîk-rammu of Edom, Mitinti of Ashdod, all brought their tribute in person to the Assyrian camp before Ushu: Zedekiah of Ashkelon and Hezekiah of Judah alone persisted in their hostility. Egypt had at length been moved by the misfortunes of her allies, and the Ethiopian troops had advanced to the seat of war, but they did not arrive in time to save Zedekiah: Sennacherib razed to the ground all his strongholds one after another, Beth-dagon, Joppa, Bene-berak, and Hazor,[1] took him prisoner at Ascalon, and sent him with his family to Assyria, setting up Sharludarî, son of Rukibti, in his stead. Sennacherib then turned against Ekron, and was about to begin the siege of the city, when the long-expected Egyptians at length made their appearance. Shabîtoku did not command them in person, but he had sent his best troops—the contingents furnished by the petty kings of the Delta, and the sheikhs of the Sinaitic peninsula, who were vassals of Egypt. The encounter took place near Altaku,[2] and on this occasion again, as at Raphia,

city bearing this name with Samaria. The discovery of the reading Samsi-muruna on a fragment of the time of Assur-bani-pal no longer permits of this identification, and obliges us to look for the city in Phœnicia.

[1] These are the cities attributed to the tribes of Dan and Judah in *Josh.* xv. 25, 41; xix. 45. Beth-dagon is now Bêt-Dejân; Azurn is Yazûr, to the south-east of Joppa; Beni-barak is Ibn-Abrak, to the north-east of the same town.

[2] Altaku is certainly Eltekeh of Dan (*Josh.* xix. 44), as was seen from the outset; the site, however, of Eltekeh cannot be fixed with any certainty. It has been located at Bêt-Lukkieh, in the mountainous country north-west of Jerusalem, but this position in no way corresponds to the requirements of the Assyrian text, according to which the battle took place on a plain large enough for the evolutions of the Egyptian chariots, and situated between the

the scientific tactics of the Assyrians prevailed over the stereotyped organisation of Pharaoh's army: the Ethiopian generals left some of their chariots in the hands of the conqueror, and retreated with the remnants of their force beyond the Isthmus. Altaku capitulated, an example followed by the neighbouring fortress of Timnath, and subsequently by Ekron itself, all three being made to feel Sennacherib's vengeance. "The nobles and chiefs who had offended, I slew," he remarks, "and set up their corpses on stakes in a circle round the city; those of the inhabitants who had offended and committed crimes, I took them prisoners, and for the rest who had neither offended

THE PASS OF LEGNIA, IN LEBANON.[1]

group of towns formed by Beth-dagon, Joppa, Beni-barak, and Hazor, which Sennacherib had just captured, and the cities of Ekron, Timnath, and Eltekeh, which he took directly after his victory: a suitable locality must be looked for in the vicinity of Ramleh or Zernuka.

[1] Drawn by Boudier, from a photograph given in Lortet.

## HEZEKIAH PREPARES FOR A SIEGE

nor transgressed, I pardoned them." We may here pause to inquire how Hezekiah was occupied while his fate was being decided on the field of Altaku. He was fortifying Jerusalem, and storing within it munitions of war, and enrolling Jewish soldiers and mercenary troops from the Arab tribes of the desert. He had suddenly become aware that large portions of the wall of the city of David had crumbled away, and he set about demolishing the neighbouring houses to obtain materials for repairing these breaches: he hastily strengthened the weak points in his fortifications, stopped up the springs which flowed into the Gihon, and cut off the brook itself, constructing a reservoir between the inner and outer city walls to store up the waters of the ancient pool. These alterations[1] rendered the city, which from its natural position was well defended, so impregnable that Sennacherib decided not to attack it until the rest of the kingdom had been subjugated: with this object in view he pitched his camp before Lachish, whence he could keep a watch over the main routes from Egypt where they crossed the frontier, and then scattered his forces over the land of Judah, delivering it up to pillage in a systematic manner. He took forty-six walled towns, and numberless strongholds and villages, demolishing the walls and leading into captivity 200,150 persons of all ages and conditions, together with their household goods, their horses, asses, mules, camels, oxen, and sheep;[2] it was a war as

---

[1] *Isa.* xxii. 8–11.

[2] An allusion to the sojourn of Sennacherib near Lachish is found in 2 *Kings* xviii 14–17; xix 8, and in *Isa.* xxxvi 2; xxxvii 8

disastrous in its effects as that which terminated in the fall of Samaria, or which led to the final captivity in Babylon.[1] The work of destruction accomplished, the Rabshakeh brought up all his forces and threw up a complete circle of earthworks round Jerusalem: Hezekiah found himself shut up in his capital "like a bird in a cage." The inhabitants soon became accustomed to this isolated life, but Isaiah was indignant at seeing them indifferent to their calamities, and inveighed against them with angry eloquence: "What aileth thee now, that thou art wholly gone up to the housetops? O thou that art full of shoutings, a tumultuous city, a joyous town; thy slain are not slain with the sword, neither are they dead in battle. All thy rulers fled away together, they are made prisoners without drawing the bow; they are come hither from afar for safety, and all that meet together here shall be taken together."* The danger was urgent the Assyrians were massed in their entrenchments with their auxiliaries ranged behind them to support them "Elam bare the quiver with chariots of men and horsemen and Kir uncovered the shield (for the assault). And it came to pass that thy choicest valleys were full of chariots and the horsemen set themselves in array at thy gate and he took away the covering of Judah." In those days therefore, Jahveh, without pity for His people, called them to "weeping, and to mourning, and to baldness

[1] It seems that the Jewish historian Demetrios considered the captivities under Nebuchadrezzar and Sennacherib to be on the same footing.

* [The R.V. gives this passage as follows: "They were bound by the archers: all that were found of thee were bound together, they fled afar off."—TR.]

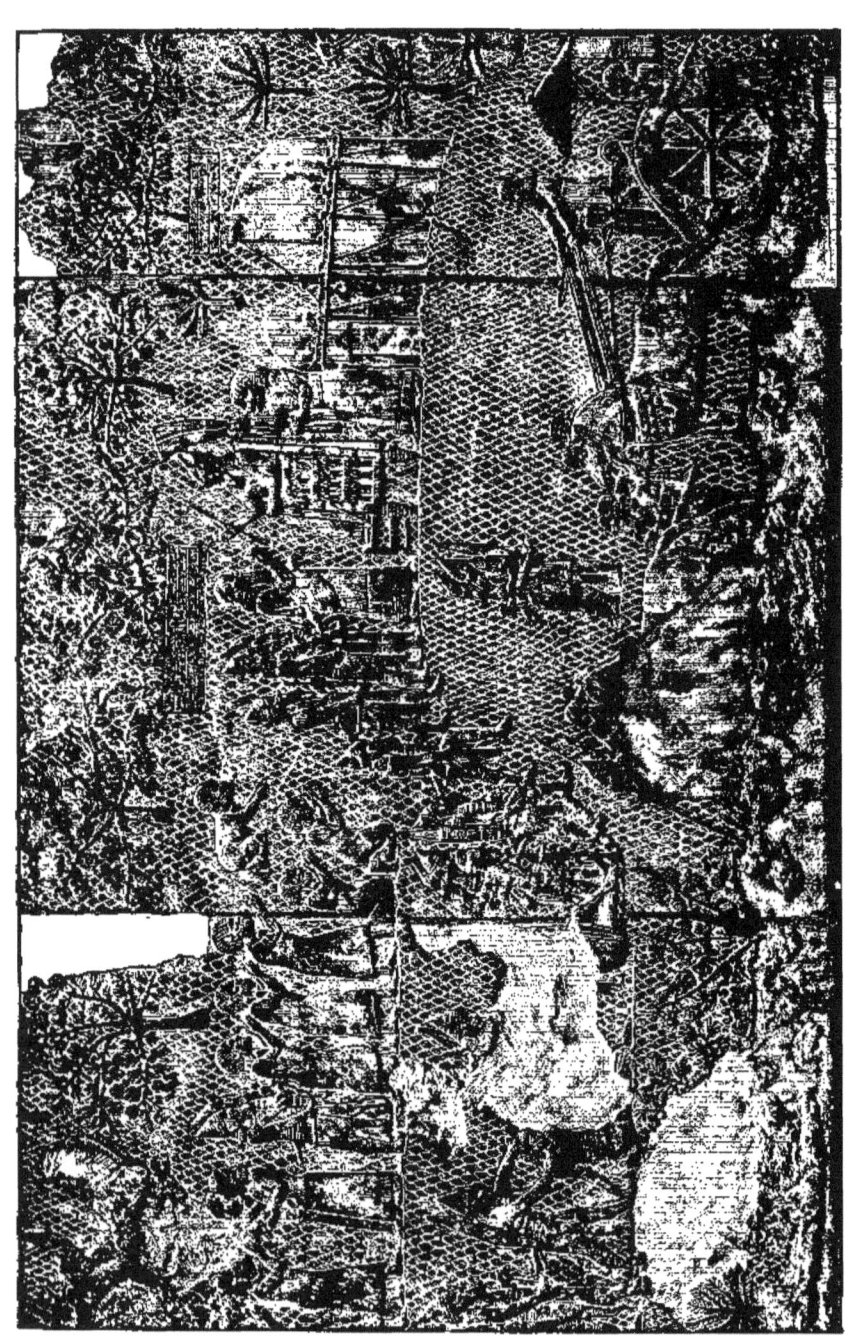

SENNACHERIB RECEIVING THE SUBMISSION OF THE JEWS IN HIS CAMP BEFORE LACHISH.

Drawn by Boudier, from LAYARD, *Monuments of Nineveh*, vol. ii. pl. 22.

and to girding with sackcloth: and behold, joy and gladness, slaying oxen and killing sheep, eating flesh and drinking wine: let us eat and drink, for to-morrow we shall die. And the Lord of hosts revealed Himself in mine ears, Surely this iniquity shall not be purged from you till ye die, saith the Lord, the Lord of Hosts."[1] The prophet threw the blame on the courtiers especially Shebna, who still hoped for succour from the Egyptians, and kept up the king's illusions on this point. He threatened him with the divine anger; he depicted him as seized by Jahveh, rolled and kneaded into a lump, "and tossed like a ball into a large country: there shalt thou die, and there shall be the chariots of thy glory, thou shame of thy lord's house. And I will thrust thee from thy office, and from thy station he shall pull thee down!"[2] Meanwhile, day after day elapsed, and Pharaoh did not hasten to the rescue. Hezekiah's eyes were opened; he dismissed Shebna, and degraded him to the position of scribe, and set Eliakim in his place in the Council of State.[3] Isaiah's influence revived, and he persuaded the king to sue for peace while yet there was time.

Sennacherib was encamped at Lachish; but the Tartan and his two lieutenants received the overtures of peace, and proposed a parley near the conduit of the upper pool, in the highway of the fuller's field. Hezekiah did not venture to go in person to the meeting-place; he sent

---

[1] *Isa.* xxii. 1–14.   [2] *Isa.* xxii. 15–19.

[3] In the duplicate narrative of these negotiations with the Assyrian generals, Shebna is in fact considered as a mere scribe, while Eliakim is the prefect of the king's house (2 K*ings* xviii. 18, 37; xix. **2**; *Isa.* xxxvi. **3, 22**; **xxxvii. 2**).

Eliakim, the new prefect of the palace, Shebna, and the chancellor Joah, the chief cupbearer, and tradition relates that the Assyrian addressed them in severe terms in his master's name: "Now on whom dost thou trust, that thou rebellest against me? Behold, thou trustest upon the staff of this bruised reed, even upon Egypt; whereon if a man lean, it will go into his hand and pierce it: so is Pharaoh, King of Egypt, to all that trust on him." Then, as he continued to declaim in a loud voice, so that the crowds gathered on the wall could hear him, the delegates besought him to speak in Aramaic, which they understood, but "speak not to us in the Jews' language, in the ears of the people that are on the wall!" Instead, however of granting their request, the Assyrian general advanced towards the spectators and addressed them in Hebrew "Hear ye the words of the great king, the King of Assyria Let not Hezekiah deceive you; for he shall not be able to deliver you: neither let Hezekiah make you trust in the Lord, saying, The Lord will surely deliver us: this city shall not be given into the hand of the King of Assyria. Hearken not to Hezekiah: for thus saith the King of Assyria, Make your peace with me, and come out to me; and eat ye every one of his vine, and every one of his fig tree, and drink ye every one the waters of his own cistern; until I come and take you away to a land like your own land, a land of corn and wine, a land of bread and vineyards. Beware lest Hezekiah persuade you saying, The Lord will deliver us!" The specified conditions were less hard than might have been feared[1] The

[1] The Hebrew version of these events is recorded in 2 Kings xviii 13-37;

Jewish king was to give up his wives and daughters as hostages, to pledge himself to pay a regular tribute, and disburse immediately a ransom of thirty talents of gold, and eight hundred talents of silver: he could only make up this large sum by emptying the royal and sacred treasuries, and taking down the plates of gold with which merely a short while before he had adorned the doors and lintels of the temple. Padî was released from his long captivity, reseated on his throne, and received several Jewish towns as an indemnity: other portions of territory were bestowed upon Mitinti of Ashdod and Zillibel of Gaza as a reward for their loyalty.[1] Hezekiah issued from the

---

xix., and in *Isa.* xxxvi., **xxxvii.**, with only one important divergence, namely, the absence from Isaiah of verses 14–16 of 2 Kings xviii. This particular passage, in which the name of the king has a peculiar form, is a detached fragment of an older document, perhaps the official annals of the kingdom, whose contents agreed with the facts recorded in the Assyrian text. The rest is borrowed from the cycle of prophetic narratives, and contains two different versions of the same events. The first comprises 2 Kings xviii. 13, 17–37; xix. 1–9a, 36b–37, where Sennacherib is represented as despatching a verbal message to Hezekiah by the Tartan and his captains. The second consists merely of 2 Kings xix. 9b–36a, and in this has been inserted a long prophecy of Isaiah's (xix. 21–31) which has but a vague connection with the rest of the narrative. In this Sennacherib defied Hezekiah in a letter, which the Jewish king spread before the Lord, and shortly afterwards received a reply through the prophet. The two versions were combined towards the end of the seventh or beginning of the sixth century, by the compiler of the *Book of Kings*, and passed thence into the collection of the prophecies attributed to Isaiah.

[1] The sequence of events is not very well observed in the Assyrian text, and the liberation of Padi is inserted in ll. 8–11, before the account of the war with Hezekiah. It seems very unlikely that the King of Judah would have released his prisoner before his treaty with Sennacherib; the Assyrian scribe, wishing to bring together all the facts relating to Ekron, anticipated this event. Hebrew tradition fixed the ransom at the lowest figure, 300

struggle with his territory curtailed and his kingdom devastated; the last obstacle which stood in the way the Assyrians' victorious advance fell with him, and Sennacherib could now push forward with perfect safety towards the Nile. He had, indeed, already planned an attack on Egypt, and had reached the isthmus, when a mysterious accident arrested his further progress. The conflict on the plains of Altaku had been severe; and the army, already seriously diminished by its victory, had been still further weakened during the campaign in Judæa, and possibly the excesses indulged in by the soldiery had developed in them the germs of one of those terrible epidemics which had devastated Western Asia several times in the course of the century: whatever may have been the cause, half the army was destroyed by pestilence before it reached the frontier of the Delta, and Sennacherib led back the shattered remnants of his force to Nineveh [1] The Hebrews did not hesitate to ascribe the event to the vengeance of Jahveh, and to make it a subject of

talents of silver instead of the 800 given in the Assyrian document (2 Kings xviii. 14), and authorities have tried to reconcile this divergence by speculating on the different values represented by a talent in different countries and epochs.

[1] The Assyrian texts are silent about this catastrophe, and the sacred books of the Hebrews seem to refer it to the camp at Libnah in Palestine (2 Kings xix. 8–35); the Egyptian legend related by Herodotus seems to prove that it took place near the Egyptian frontier. Josephus takes the king as far as Pelusium, and describes the destruction of the Assyrian army as taking place in the camp before this town. He may have been misled by the meaning "mud," which attaches to the name of Libnah as well as to that of Pelusium. Oppert upheld his opinion, and identified the Libnah of the biblical narrative with the Pelusium of Herodotus. It is probable that each of the two nations referred the scene of the miracle to a different locality.

thankfulness. They related that before their brutal conqueror quitted the country he had sent a parting message to Hezekiah: "Let not thy God in whom thou trustest deceive thee, saying, Jerusalem shall not be given into the hand of the King of Assyria. Behold, thou hast heard what the kings of Assyria have done to all lands, by destroying them utterly; and shalt thou be delivered? Have the gods of the nations delivered them which my fathers have destroyed, Gozan and Haran and Rezeph, and the children of Eden which were in Telassar? Where is the King of Hamath, and the King of Arpad, and the King of the city of Sepharvaim, of Hena, and Ivvah?" Hezekiah, having received this letter of defiance, laid it in the temple before Jahveh, and prostrated himself in prayer: the response came to him through the mouth of Isaiah. "Thus saith the Lord concerning the King of Assyria, He shall not come unto this city, nor shoot an arrow there, neither shall he come before it with a shield, nor cast a mount against it. By the way that he came, by the same shall he return, and he shall not come unto this city, saith the Lord. For I will defend this city to save it, for Mine own sake and for My servant David's sake. And it came to pass that night, that the angel of the Lord went forth, and smote in the camp of the Assyrians an hundred four-score and five thousand: and when men arose early in the morning, behold, they were all dead corpses."[1] The Egyptians considered the event

[1] 2 Kings xix. 8–35; Isa. xxxvii. 8–36; this is the second tradition of which mention has been made, but already amalgamated with the first to form the narrative as it now stands.

no less miraculous than did the Hebrews, and one of their popular tales ascribed the prodigy to Phtah, the god Memphis. Sethon, the high priest of Phtah, lived in a time of national distress, and the warrior class, whom he had deprived of some of its privileges, refused to take up arms in his behalf. He repaired, therefore, to the temple to implore divine assistance, and, falling asleep, was visited by a dream. The god appeared to him, and promised to send him some auxiliaries who should ensure him success. He enlisted such of the Egyptians as were willing to follow him, shopkeepers, fullers, and sutlers, and led them to Pelusium to resist the threatened invasion. In the night a legion of field-mice came forth, whence no one kne and, noiselessly spreading throughout the camp of Assyrians, gnawed the quivers, the bowstrings, and the straps of the bucklers in such a way that, on the morrow, the enemy, finding themselves disarmed, fled after a mere pretence at resistance, and suffered severe losses. A statue was long shown in the temple at Memphis portraying this Sethon: he was represented holding a mouse in his hand, and the inscription bade men reverence the god who had wrought this miracle.[1]

The disaster was a terrible one: Sennacherib's triumphant advance was suddenly checked, and he was forced to return to Asia when the goal of his ambition was

---

[1] The statue with which this legend has been connected, must have represented a king offering the image of a mouse crouching on a basket, like the cynocephalus on the hieroglyphic sign which denotes centuries, or frog of the goddess Hiqît. Historians have desired to recognise in Sethon King Zêt of the XXIII$^{rd}$ dynasty, or even Shabîtoku of the XXV$^{th}$ dynasty; Krall identified him with Satni in the demotic story of *Satni-Khâmoîs*.

almost reached. The loss of a single army, however much to be deplored, was not irreparable, since Assyria could furnish her sovereign with a second force as numerous as that which lay buried in the desert on the road to Egypt, but it was uncertain what effect the news of the calamity and the sight of the survivors might have on the minds of his subjects and rivals. The latter took no immediate action, and the secret joy which they must have experienced did not blind them to the real facts of the case; for though the power of Assyria was shaken, she was still stronger than any one of them severally, or even than all of them together, and to attack her or rebel against her now, was to court defeat with as much certainty as in past days. The Pharaoh kept himself behind his rivers; the military science and skill which had baffled his generals on the field of Altaku did not inspire him with any desire to reappear on the plains of Palestine. Hezekiah, King of Judah, had emptied his treasury to furnish his ransom, his strongholds had capitulated one by one, and his territory, diminished by the loss of some of the towns of the Shephelah, was little better than a waste of smoking ruins. He thought himself fortunate to have preserved his power under the suzerainty of Assyria, and his sole aim for many years was to refill his treasury, reconstitute his army, and re-establish his kingdom. The Philistine and Nabatæan princes, and the chiefs of Moab, Ammon, and Idumæa, had nothing to gain by war, being too feeble to have any chance of success without the help of Judah, Tyre, and Egypt. The Syrians maintained a peaceful attitude, which was certainly their wisest policy; and during the following quarter of a century they loyally obeyed their governors, and gave Sennacherib no cause to revisit them. It was fortunate for him that they did so, for the peoples of the North and East the Kaldâ, and, above all, the Elamites, were the cause of much trouble, and exclusively occupied his attention during several years. The inhabitants of Bît-Yakin, urged on either by their natural restlessness or by the news of the misfortune which had befallen their enemy, determined once more to try the fortunes of war. Incited by Marduk ushezîb,[1] one of their princes, and by Merodach-baladan these people of the marshes intrigued with the courts of Babylon and Susa, and were emboldened to turn against the Assyrian garrisons stationed in their midst to preserve order. Sennacherib's vengeance fell first on Marduk ushezîb, who fled from his stronghold of Bîttutu after sustaining a short siege. Merodach-baladan, deserted by his accomplice, put the statues of his gods and his royal treasures on board his fleet, and embarking with his followers, crossed the lagoon, and effected a landing in the district of Nagîtu, in Susian territory, beyond the mouth of the Ulai.[2] Sennacherib entered Bît-Yakîn without striking a blow, and completed the destruction of the half-deserted town; he next proceeded to demolish the other cities one after the other, carrying off into captivity all the men and cattle who fell in his way. The Elamites

[1] Three kings of Babylon at this period bore very similar names Marduk-ushezîb, Nergal-ushezîb, and Mushezîb-marduk. Nergal-ushezîb is the elder of the two whom the texts call Shuzub, and whom Assyriologists at first confused one with another.

[2] Nagitu was bounded by the Nar-Marratum and the Ulai, which allows us to identify it with the territory south of Edrisieh.

disconcerted by the rapidity of his action, allowed him to crush their allies unopposed; and as they had not openly intervened, the conqueror refrained from calling them to account for their intrigues. Babylon paid the penalty for all: its sovereign, Belibni, who had failed to make the sacred authority of the suzerain respected in the city, and who, perhaps, had taken some part in the conspiracy, was with his family deported to Nineveh, and his vacant throne was given to Assur-nadin-shumu, a younger son of Sargon (699 B.C.).[1] Order was once more restored in Karduniash, but Sennacherib felt that its submission would be neither sincere nor permanent, so long as Merodach-baladan was hovering on its frontier possessed of an army, a fleet, and a supply of treasure, and prepared to enter the lists as soon as circumstances seemed favourable to his cause. Sennacherib resolved, therefore, to cross the head of the Persian Gulf and deal him such a blow as would once for all end the contest; but troubles which broke out on the Urartian frontier as soon as he returned forced him to put off his project. The tribes of Tumurru, who had placed their strongholds like eyries among the peaks of Nipur, had been making frequent descents on the plains of the Tigris, which they had ravaged unchecked by any fear of Assyrian power. Sennacherib formed an entrenched camp at the foot of their

[1] Berosus, misled by the deposition of Belibni, thought that the expedition was directed against Babylon itself; he has likewise confounded Assur-nâdin-shumu with Esar-haddon, and he has given this latter, whom he calls Asordanes, as the immediate successor of Belibni. The date 699 B.C. for these events is indicated in *Pinches' Babylonian Chronicle*, which places them in the third year of Belibni.

mountain retreat, and there left the greater part of his army, while he set out on an adventurous expedition wi h a picked body of infantry and cavalry. Over ravines and torrents, up rough and difficult slopes, they made their way, the king himself being conveyed in a litter, as there were no roads practicable for his royal chariot; he even deigned to walk when the hillsides were too steep for his bearers to carry him; he climbed like a goat, slept on the bare rocks, drank putrid water from a leathern bottle, and after many hardships at length came up with the enemy He burnt their villages, and carried off herds of cattle and troops of captives; but this exploit was more a satisfactio of his vanity than a distinct advantage gained, for the pillaging of the plains of the Tigris probably recommenced as soon as the king had quitted the country. The same year he pushed as far as Dayaîni, here similar tactics were employed. Constructing a camp in the neighbour hood of Mount Anara and Mount Uppa, he forced his way to the capital, Ukki, traversing a complicated network of gorges and forests which had hitherto been considered impenetrable. The king, Manîya, fled; Ukki was taken by assault and pillaged, the spoil obtained from it slightly exceeding that from Tumurru (699 B.C.). Shortly afterwards the province of Tulgarimmê revolted in concert with the Tabal: Sennacherib overcame the allied forces, and led his victorious regiments through the defiles of the Taurus.[1] Greek pirates or colonists having ventured from

[1] The dates of and connection between these two wars are not determined with any certainty. Some authorities assign them both to the same year, somewhere between 699 and 696 B.C., while others assign them

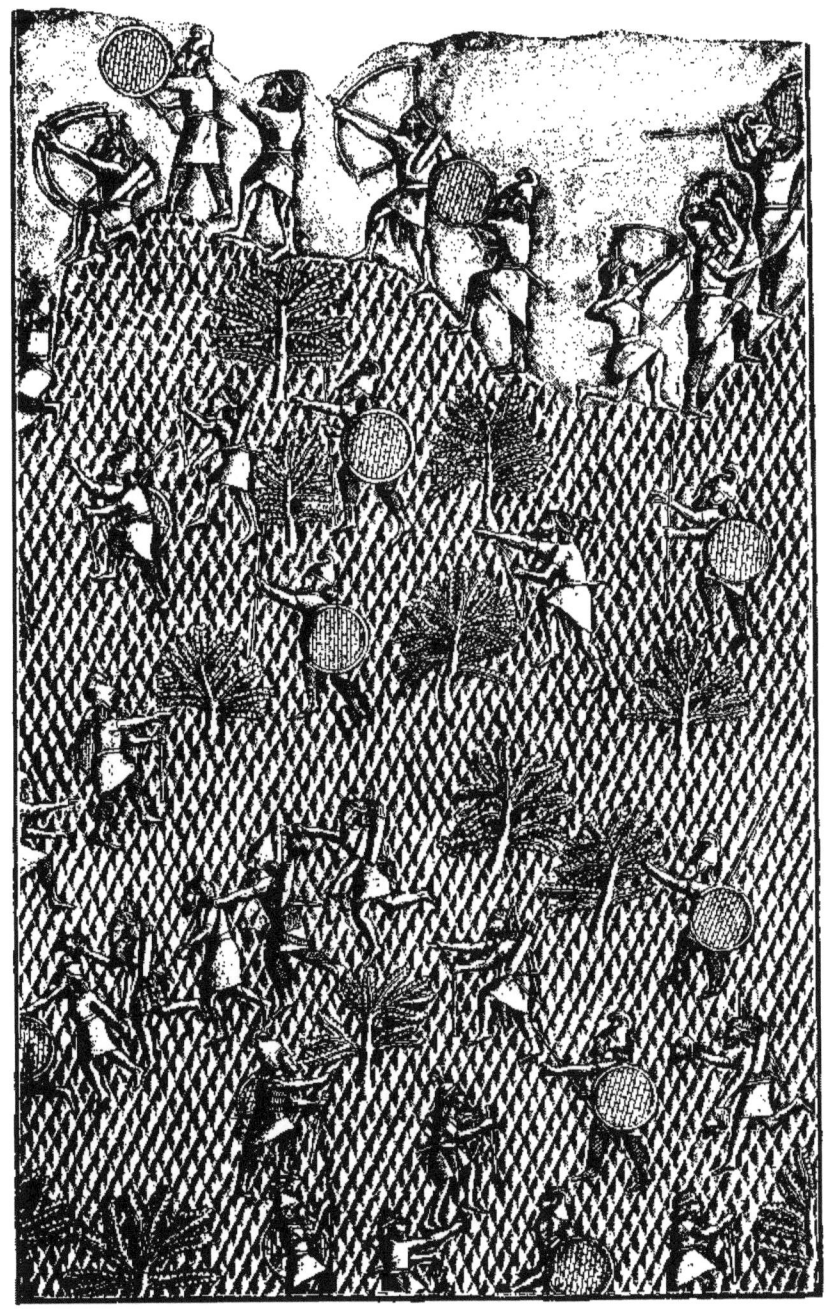

A RAID AMONG THE WOODS AND MOUNTAINS.
Drawn by Faucher-Gudin, from LAYARD, *Monuments of Nineveh*, vol. i. pl. 70.

time to time to ravage the seaboard, he destroyed one of their fleets near the mouth of the Saros, and took advantage of his sojourn in this region to fortify the two cities of Tarsus and Ankhialê, to defend his Cilician frontier against the peoples of Asia Minor.[1]

This was a necessary precaution, for the whole of Asia Minor was just then stirred by the inrush of new nations which were devastating the country, and the effect of these convulsions was beginning to be felt in the country to the south of the central plain, at the foot of the Taurus, and on the frontiers of the Assyrian empire. Barbarian hordes, attracted by the fame of the ancient Hittite sanctuaries in the upper basin of the Euphrates and the Araxes, had descended now and again to measure their strength against the advanced posts of Assyria or Urartu, but had subsequently withdrawn and disappeared beyond the Halys. Their movements may at this time have been so aggressive as to arouse serious anxiety in the minds of the Ninevite rulers; it is certain that Sennacherib, though apparently hindered by no revolt, delayed the execution of the projects he had formed against Merodach-baladan for three years; and it is possible his inaction may be attributed to the fear of some complication arising on his north-western frontier. He did not carry out his scheme till 695 B.C., when all

to two different years, the first to 699 or 696 B.C., the second to 698 or 695 B.C.

[1] The encounter of the Assyrians with the Greeks is only known to us from a fragment of Berosus. The foundation of Tarsus is definitely attributed to Sennacherib in the same passage; that of Ankhialê is referred to the fabulous Sardanapalus, but most historians with much probability attribute the foundation to Sennacherib.

danger in that quarter had passed away. The enterprise was a difficult one, for Nagîtu and the neighbouring districts were dependencies of Susa, and could not be reached by land without a violation of Elamite neutrality which would almost inevitably lead to a conflict. Shutruk-nakhunta was no longer alive. In the very year in which his rival had set up Assur-nâdin-shumu as King of Karduniash, a revolution had broken out in Elam, which was in all probability connected with the events then taking place in Babylon. His subjects were angry with him for having failed to send timely succour to his allies the Kaldâ, and for having allowed Bît-Yakîn to be stroyed: his own brother Khalludush sided with the malcontents, threw Shutruk-nakhunta into prison, and proclaimed himself king. This time the Ninevites, thinking that Elam was certain to intervene, sought how they might finally overpower Merodach-baladan before this interference could prove effectual. The feudal constitution of the Elamite monarchy rendered, as we know, the mobilisation of the army at the opening of a war a long and difficult task : weeks might easily elapse before the first and second grades of feudatory nobility could join the royal troops and form a combined army capable of striking an important blow. This was a cause of dangerous inferiority in a conflict with the Assyrians, the chief part of whose forces bivouacking close to the capital during the winter months could leave their quarters and set out on a campaign at little more than a day's notice; the kings of Elam mini mised the danger by keeping sufficient troops under arms on their northern and western frontiers to meet any emergency, but an attack by sea seemed to them so unlikely that they had not, for a long time past, thought of protecting their coast-line. The ancient Chaldæan cities, Uru, Lagash, Uruk, and Eridu had possessed fleets on the Persian Gulf; but the times were long past when they used to send to procure stone and wood from the countries of Magan and Melukhkha, and the seas which they had ruled were now traversed only by merchant vessels or fishing-boats. Besides this, the condition of the estuary seemed to prohibit all attack from that side. The space between Bit-Yakin and the long line of dunes or mud-banks which blocked the entrance to it was not so much a gulf as a lagoon of uncertain and shifting extent; the water flowed only in the middle, being stagnant near the shores; the whole expanse was irregularly dotted over with mud-banks, and its service was constantly altered by the alluvial soil brought down by the Tigris, the Euphrates, the Ulaî, and the Uknu. The navigation of this lagoon was dangerous, for the relative positions of the channels and shallows were constantly shifting, and vessels of deep draught often ran aground in passing from one end of it to the other.[1] Sennacherib decided to march his force to the

[1] The condition I describe here is very similar to what Alexander's admirals found 350 years later. Arrian has preserved for us the account of Nearchus' navigation in these waters, and his description shows such a well-defined condition of the estuary that its main outline must have remained unchanged for a considerable time; the only subsequent alterations which had taken place must have been in the internal configuration, where the deposit of alluvium must have necessarily reduced the area of the lake since the time of Sennacherib. The little map on the next page has no pretension to scientific exactitude; its only object is to show roughly what the estuary of the Euphrates was like, and to illustrate approximately the course of the Assyrian expedition.

mouth of the Euphrates, and, embarking it there, to bring it to bear suddenly on the portion of Elamite territory nearest to Nagîtu: if all went well, he would thus have time to crush the rising power of Merodach-baladan and regain his own port of departure before Khalludush could muster a sufficient army to render efficient succour to his vassal.

More than a year was consumed in preparations. The united cities of Chaldæa being unable to furnish the transports required to convey such a large host across the Nar-Marratum, it was necessary to construct a fleet, and to do so in such a way that the enemy should have no suspicion of danger. Sennacherib accordingly set up his dockyards at Tul-barsîp on the Euphrates and at Nineveh on the Tigris, and Syrian shipwrights built him a fleet of vessels after two distinct types. Some were galleys identical in build and equipment with those which the Mediterranean natives used for their traffic with distant lands. The others followed the old Babylonian model, with stem and stern both raised, the bows being sometimes distinguished by the carving of a horse's head, which justified the name of *sea-horse* given to a vessel of this kind. They had no masts, but propelling power was provided by two banks of oars one above the other, as in the galleys. The two divisions of the fleet were ready at the beginning of 694 B.C., and it was arranged that they should meet at Bit-Dakkuri, to the

THE NAR-MARRATUM in the time of SENNACHERIB

south of Babylon. The fleet from Tul-barsîp had merely to descend the Euphrates to reach the meeting-place,[1] but that from Nineveh had to make a more complicated

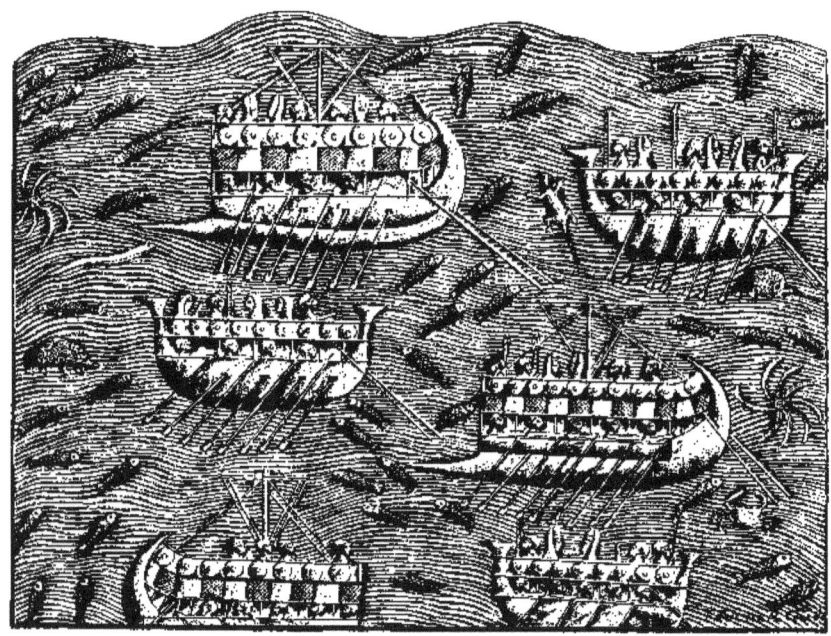

THE FLEET OF SENNACHERIB ON THE NAR-MARRATUM.[2]

journey. By following the course of the Tigris to its mouth it would have had to skirt the coast of Elam for

[1] The story of the preparations, as it has been transmitted to us in Sennacherib's inscriptions, is curiously similar to the accounts given by the Greek historians of the vessels Alexander had built at Babylon and Thapsacus by Phœnician workmen, which descended the Euphrates to join the fleet in the Persian Gulf. This fleet consisted of quinquiremes, according to Aristobulus, who was present at their construction: Quintus-Curtius makes them all vessels with seven banks of oars, but he evidently confuses the galleys built at Thapsacus with those which came in sections from Phœnicia and which Alexander had put together at Babylon.

[2] Drawn by Faucher-Gudin, from Layard.

a considerable distance, and would inevitably have aroused the suspicions of Khalludush; the passage of such a strong squadron must have revealed to him the importance the enterprise, and put him on his guard. The vessels therefore stayed their course at Upi, where they were drawn ashore and transported on rollers across the narrow isthmus which separates the Tigris from the Arakhtu canal on which they were then relaunched. Either the canal had not been well kept, or else it never had the necessary depth at certain places; but the crews managed to overcome all obstacles and rejoined their comrades in due time Sennacherib was ready waiting for them with all his troops—foot-soldiers, charioteers, and horsemen—and with supplies of food for the men, and of barley and oats for the horses; as soon as the last contingent had arrived he gave the signal for departure, and all advanced together the army marching along the southern bank, the fleet descending the current, to the little port of Bab-Salimeti, some twelve miles below the mouth of the river.[1] There they halted in order to proceed to the final embarcation but at the last moment their inexperience of the sea nearly compromised the success of the expedition. Even if they were not absolutely ignorant of the ebb and flow of the tide, they certainly did not know how dangerous the spring tide could prove at the equinox under the influence of a south wind. The rising tide then comes

[1] The mouth of the Euphrates being at that time not far from the site of Kornah, Bab-Salimeti, which was about twelve miles distant, must have been somewhere near the present village of Abu-Hatira, on the south bank of the river.

into conflict with the volume of water brought down by the stream, and in the encounter the banks are broken down, and sometimes large districts are inundated: this is what happened that year, to the terror of the Assyrians. Their camp was invaded and completely flooded by the waves; the king and his soldiers took refuge in haste on the galleys, where they were kept prisoners for five days "as in a huge cage." As soon as the waters abated, they completed their preparations and started on their voyage. At the point where the Euphrates enters the lagoon, Sennacherib pushed forward to the front of the line, and, standing in the bows of his flag-ship, offered a sacrifice to Eâ, the god of the Ocean. Having made a solemn libation, he threw into the water a gold model of a ship, a golden fish, and an image of the god himself, likewise in gold; this ceremony performed, he returned to the port of Bab-Salimeti with his guard, while the bulk of his forces continued their voyage eastward. The passage took place without mishap, but they could not disembark on the shore of the gulf itself, which was unapproachable by reason of the deposits of semi-liquid mud which girdled it; they therefore put into the mouth of the Ulaî, and ascended the river till they reached a spot where the slimy reed-beds gave place to firm ground, which permitted them to draw their ships to land.[1] The inhabitants assembled hastily at sight of the enemy, and the news, spreading through the neighbouring tribes,

[1] Billerbeck recognises in the narrative of Sennacherib the indication of two attempts at debarcation, of which the second only can have been successful; I can distinguish only one crossing.

brought together for their defence a confused crowd of archers, chariots, and horsemen. The Assyrians, leaping into the stream and climbing up the bank, easily over

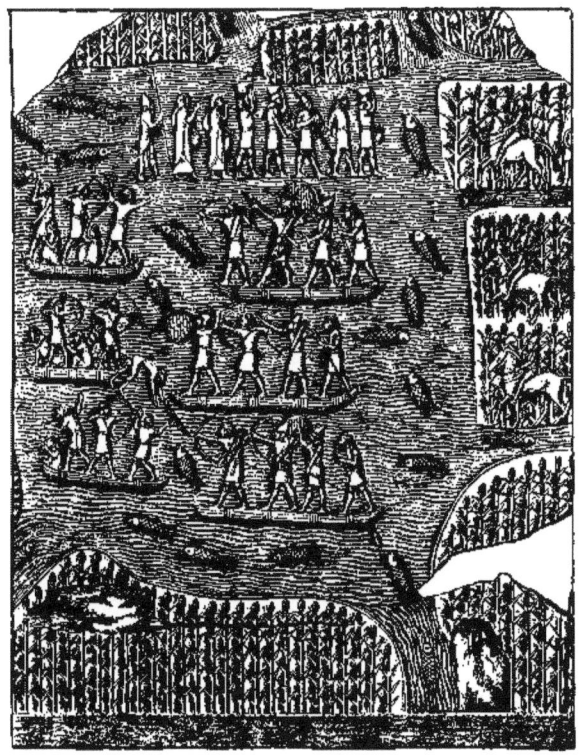

A SKIRMISH IN THE MARSHES.[1]

powered these undisciplined troops. They captured at the first onset Nagîtu, Nagîtu-Dibîna, Khilmu, Pillatu, and Khupapânu; and raiding the Kaldâ, forced them on board the fleet with their gods, their families, their flocks, and household possessions, and beat a hurried

[1] Drawn by Faucher-Gudin, from Layard.

retreat with their booty. Merodach-baladan himself and his children once more escaped their clutches, but the State he had tried to create was annihilated, and his power utterly crushed. Sennacherib received his generals with great demonstrations of joy at Bab-Salimeti, and carried the spoil in triumph to Nineveh. Khalludush, exasperated by the affront put upon him, instantly retaliated by invading Karduniash, where he pushed forward as far as Sippara, pillaging and destroying the inhabitants without opposition. The Babylonians who had accompanied Merodach-baladan into exile, returned in the train of the Elamites, and, secretly stealing back to their homes, stirred up a general revolt: Assur-nâdin-shumu, taken prisoner by his own subjects, was put in chains and despatched to Susa, his throne being bestowed on a Babylonian named Nergal-ushezîb,[1] who at once took the field (694 B.C.). His preliminary efforts were successful: he ravaged the frontier along the Turnât with the help of the Elamites, and took by assault the city of Nipur, which refused to desert the cause of Sennacherib (693 B.C.). Meanwhile the Assyrian generals had captured Uruk (Erech) on the 1st of Tisri, after the retreat of Khalludush; and having sacked the city, were retreating northwards with their spoil when they were defeated on the 7th near Nipur by Nergal-ushezîb. He had already rescued the statues of the gods and the treasure, when his horse fell in the midst of the fray, and he could not

---

[1] This is the prince whom the Assyrian documents name Shuzub, and whom we might call Shuzub the Babylonian, in contradistinction to Musheẑibmarduk, who is Shuzub the Kaldu

disengage himself His vanquished foes led him captive to Nineveh where Sennacherib exposed him in chains at the principal gateway of his palace the Babylonians who owed to him their latest success summoned a Kaldu prince, Mushezîb-marduk son of Gahul, to take command He hastened to comply and with the assistance of Elamite troops offered such a determined resistance to all attack that he was finally left in undisturbed possession of kingdom (692 B.C.): the actual result to Assyria therefore, of the ephemeral victory gained by the fleet had been the loss of Babylon A revolution

THE HORSE OF NERGAL-USHEZÎB FALLING IN THE BATTLE[1]

Elam speedily afforded Assyria an opportunity for revenge When Nergal-ushezîb was taken prisoner the people of Susa dissatisfied with the want of activity displayed by Khalludush, conspired to depose him on hearing there fore the news of the revolutions in Chaldæa, they rose in revolt on the 26th of Tisri and besieging him in his palace put him to death and elected a certain Kutur-nakhunta as his successor Sennacherib without a moment's hesitation crossed the frontier at Durîlu, before order was re-established at Susa and recovered

Drawn by Faucher-Gudin, from Layard

after very slight resistance, Raza and Bit-khairi which Shutruk-nakhunta had taken from Sargon. This preliminary success laid the lower plain of Susiana at his mercy, and he ravaged it pitilessly from Raza to Bît-bunaki. "Thirty-four strongholds and the townships depending on them, whose number is unequalled, I besieged and took by assault, their inhabitants I led into captivity, I demolished them and reduced them to ashes: I caused the smoke of their burning to rise into the wide heaven, like the smoke of one great sacrifice." Kutur-nakhunta, still insecurely seated on the throne of Susa, retreated with his army towards Khaîdalu, in the almost unexplored regions which bordered the Iranian plateau,[1] and entrenched himself strongly in the heart of the mountains. The season was already well advanced when the Assyrians set out on this expedition, and November set in while they were ravaging the plain: but the weather was still so fine that Sennacherib determined to take advantage of it to march upon Madaktu. Hardly had he scaled the heights when winter fell upon him with its accompaniment of cold and squally weather. "Violent storms broke out, it rained and snowed incessantly, the torrents and streams overflowed their banks," so that hostilities had to be suspended and the troops ordered back to Nineveh. The effect produced, however, by these bold measures was in no way diminished: though Kutur-nakhunta had not had the necessary time to prepare for the contest, he was nevertheless discredited among his subjects for failing to bring them out of it with glory, and three months after the retreat of the Assyrians he was

---

[1] Khaîdalu is very probably the present Dis Malkân.

assassinated in a riot on the 20th of Ab, 692 B.C.[1] His younger brother, Ummân-minânu, assumed the crown, and though his enemies disdainfully refused to credit him with either prudence or judgment, he soon restored his kingdom to such a formidable degree of power that Mushezîb-marduk thought the opportunity a favourable one for striking a blow at Assyria, from which she could never recover Elam had plenty of troops, but was deficient in the resources necessary to pay the men and their chiefs, and to induce the tribes of the table-land to furnish their contingents. Mushezîb-marduk, therefore, emptied the sacred treasury of Ê-sagilla, and sent the gold and silver of Bel and Zarpanit to Ummân-minânu with a message which ran thus: "Assemble thine army, and prepare thy camp, come to Babylon and strengthen our hands, for thou art our help." The Elamite asked nothing better than to avenge the provinces so cruelly harassed, and the cities consumed in the course of the last campaign: he summoned all his nobles, from the least to the greatest and enlisted the help of the troops of Parsuas, Ellipi, and Anzân, the Aramæan Puqudu and Gambulu of the Tigris as well as the Aramæans of the Euphrates, and the peoples of Bît-Adini and Bît-Amukkâni, who had rallied round Samuna, son of Merodach-baladan, and joined forces with the soldiers of Mushezîb-marduk in Babylon. "Like an invasion of countless locusts swooping down upon the land

---

[1] The Assyrian documents merely mention the death of Kutur-nakhunta less than three months after the return of Sennacherib to Nineveh. *Pinches' Babylonian Chronicle* only mentions the revolution in which he perished, and informs us that he had reigned ten months. It contracts Ummân-minânu, the name of the Elamite king, to Minânu.

they assembled, resolved to give me battle, and the dust of their feet rose before me, like a thick cloud which darkens the copper-coloured dome of the sky." The conflict took place near the township of Khalulê, on the banks of the Tigris, not far from the confluence of this river with the Turnât.[1] At this point the Turnât, flowing through the plain, divides into several branches, which ramify again and again, and form a kind of delta extending from the ruins of Nayân to those of Reshadeh. During the whole of the day the engagement between the two hosts raged on this unstable soil, and their leaders themselves sold their lives dearly in the struggle. Sennacherib invoked the help of Assur, Sin, Shamash, Nebo, Bel, Nergal, Ishtar of Nineveh, and Ishtar of Arbela, and the gods heard his prayers. "Like a lion I raged, I donned my harness, I covered my head with my casque, the badge of war; my powerful battle-chariot, which mows down the rebels, I ascended it in haste in the rage of my heart; the strong bow which Assur entrusted to me, I seized it, and the javelin, destroyer of life, I grasped it: the whole host of obdurate rebels I charged, shining like silver or like the day, and I roared as Rammân roareth." Khumba-undash, the Elamite general, was killed in one of the first encounters, and many of his officers perished

[1] Haupt attributes to the name the signification *holes, bogs*, and this interpretation agrees well enough with the state of the country round the mouths of the Diyala, in the low-lying district which separates that river from the Tigris; he compares it with the name **Haulâyeh,** quoted by Arab geographers in this neighbourhood, and with that of the canton of Hâleh, mentioned in Syrian texts as belonging to the district of **Râdhân,** between the Adhem and the Diyala.

around him, "of those who wore golden daggers at their belts, and bracelets of gold on their wrists." They fell one after the other, "like fat bulls chained" for the sacrifice or like sheep, and their blood flowed on the broad plain as the water after a violent storm: the horses plunged in it up to their knees, and the body of the royal chariot was reddened with it. A son of Merodach-baladan, Nabu shumishkun, was taken prisoner, but Ummân-minânu and Mushezîb-marduk escaped unhurt from the fatal field It seems as if fortune had at last decided in favour of the Assyrians, and they proclaimed the fact loudly, but their success was not so evident as to preclude their adversaries also claiming the victory with some show of truth. In any case, the losses on both sides were so considerable as to force the two belligerents to suspend operations; they returned each to his capital, and matters remained much as they had been before the battle took place.[1]

Years might have elapsed before Sennacherib could have ventured to recommence hostilities: he was not deluded by the exaggerated estimate of his victory in the accounts given by his court historians, and he recognised the fact that the issue of the struggle must be uncertain

---

[1] *Pinches' Babylonian Chronicle* attributes the victory to the Elamites and says that the year in which the battle was fought was unknown. The testimony of this chronicle is so often marred by partiality, that to prefer it always to that of the Ninevite inscriptions shows deficiency of critical ability the course of events seems to me to prove that the advantage remained with the Assyrians, though the victory was not decisive. The date, which necessarily falls between 692 and 689 B.C., has been decided by general considerations as 691 B.C., the very year in which the *Taylor Cylinder* was written.

as long as the alliance subsisted between Elam and Chaldæa. But fortune came to his aid sooner than he had expected. Ummân-minânu was not absolute in his dominions any more than his predecessors had been, and the losses he had sustained at Khalulê, without obtaining any compensating advantages in the form of prisoners or spoil, had lowered him in the estimation of his vassals; Mushezîb-marduk, on the other hand, had emptied his treasuries, and though Karduniash was wealthy, it was hardly able, after such a short interval, to provide further subsidies to purchase the assistance of the mountain tribes. Sennacherib's emissaries kept him well informed of all that occurred in the enemy's court, and he accordingly took the field again at the beginning of 689 B.C., and on this occasion circumstances seemed likely to combine to give him an easy victory.[1] Mushezîb-marduk shut himself up in Babylon, not doubting that the Elamites would hasten to his succour as soon as they should hear of his distress; but his expectation was not fulfilled. Ummân-minânu was struck down by apoplexy, on the 15th of Nisân, and though his illness did not at once terminate fatally, he was left paralysed with distorted mouth, and loss of speech, incapable of action, and almost unfit to govern. His seizure put a stop to his warlike preparations: and his ministers, preoccupied with the urgent question of the

[1] The Assyrian documents insert the account of the capture of Babylon directly after the battle of Khalulê, and modern historians therefore concluded that the two events took place within a few months of each other. The information afforded by *Pinches' Babylonian Chronicle* has enabled us to correct this mistake, and to bring down the date of the taking of Babylon to 689 B.C.

succession to the throne, had no desire to provoke a
conflict with Assyria, the issue of which could not be
foretold: they therefore left their ally to defend his own
interests as best he might. Babylon, reduced to rely
entirely on its own resources, does not seem to have held
out long, and perhaps the remembrance of the treatment it
had received on former occasions may account for the very
slight resistance it now offered. The Assyrian kings who
had from time to time conquered Babylon, had always
treated it with great consideration. They had looked upon
it as a sacred city, whose caprices and outbreaks must
always be pardoned; it was only with infinite precaution
that they had imposed their commands upon it, and eve
when they had felt that severity was desirable, they had
restrained themselves in using it, and humoured the
idiosyncrasies of the inhabitants. Tiglath-pileser III
Shalmaneser V., and Sargon had all preferred to be legally
crowned as sovereigns of Babylon instead of remaining
merely its masters by right of conquest, and though
Sennacherib had refused compliance with the traditions by
which his predecessors had submitted to be bound, he had
behaved with unwonted lenity after quelling the two
previous revolts. He now recognised that his clemency
had been shown in vain, and his small stock of patience
was completely exhausted just when fate threw the
rebellious city into his power. If the inhabitants had
expected to be once more let off easily, their illusions were
speedily dissipated: they were slain by the sword as if
they had been ordinary foes, such as Jews, Tibarenians, or
Kaldâ of Bit-Yakîn, and they were spared none of the

horrors which custom then permitted the stronger to inflict upon the weaker. For several days the pitiless massacre lasted. Young and old, all who fell into the hands of the soldiery, perished by the sword; piles of corpses filled the streets and the approaches to the temples, especially the avenue of winged bulls which led to Ê-sagilla, and, even after the first fury of carnage had been appeased, it was only to be succeeded by more organised pillage. Mushezîb-marduk was sent into exile with his family, and immense convoys of prisoners and spoil followed him. The treasures carried off from the royal palace, the temples, and the houses of the rich nobles were divided among the conquerors: they comprised gold, silver, precious stones, costly stuffs, and provisions of all sorts. The sacred edifices were sacked, the images hacked to pieces or carried off to Nineveh: Bel-Marduk, introduced into the sanctuary of Assur, became subordinate to the rival deity amid a crowd of strange gods. In the inmost recess of a chapel were discovered some ancient statues of Rammân and Shala of Ê-kallati, which Marduk-nâdin-akhê had carried off in the time of Tiglath-pileser I., and these were brought back in triumph to their own land, after an absence of four hundred and eighteen years. The buildings themselves suffered a like fate to that of their owners and their gods. " The city and its houses, from foundation to roof, I destroyed them, I demolished them, I burnt them with fire; walls, gateways, sacred chapels, and the towers of earth and tiles, I laid them all low and cast them into the Arakhtu." The incessant revolts of the people justified this wholesale destruction Babylon, as we have said before, was too powerful to be reduced for long to the second rank in a Mesopotamian empire : as soon as fate established the seat of empire in the districts bordering the Euphrates and the middle course of the Tigris, its well chosen situation, its size, its riches, the extent of its population, the number of its temples, and the beauty of its palaces, all conspired to make it the capital of the country In vain Assur, Calah, or Nineveh thrust themselves into the foremost rank, and by a strenuous effort made their princes rulers of Babylon; in a short time Babylon replenished her treasury, found allies, soldiers, and leaders and in spite of reverses of fortune soon regained the upper hand. The only treatment which could effectually destroy her ascendency was that of leaving in her not one brick upon another, thus preventing her from being re-peopled for several generations, since a new city could not at once spring up from the ashes of the old; until she had been utterly destroyed her conquerors had still reason to fear her This fact Sennacherib, or his councillors, knew well. If he merits any reproach, it is not for having seized the opportunity of destroying the city which Babylon offered him but rather for not having persevered in his design to the end, and reduced her to a mere name.

In the midst of these costly and absorbing wars, we may well wonder how Sennacherib found time and means to build villas or temples; yet he is nevertheless, among the kings of Assyria, the monarch who has left us the largest number of monuments. He restored a shrine of Nergal in the small town of Tarbizi; he fortified the village Alshi; and in 704 B.C. he founded a royal residence in the

fortress of Kakzi, which defended the approach to Calah
from the south east He did not reside much at Dur
Sharrukîn, neither did be complete the decoration of his
father s palace there his pride as a victorious warrior
suf ered when his surroundings reminded him of a more
successful conqueror than himself and Calah itself was too
full of memories of Tiglath-pileser III and the sovereigns
of the eighth century for him to desire to establish his
court there He preferred to reside at Nineveh which

THE MOUNDS OF NINEVEH SEEN FROM THE TERRACE OF A HOUSE IN MOSUL [1]

had been much neglected by his predecessors and where
the crumbling edifices merely recalled the memory of long
vanished splendours. He selected this city as his resi
dence at the very beginning of his reign, perhaps while he
was still only crown prince and began by repairing its
ancient fortifications later on, when the success of his
earlier campaigns had furnished him with a sufficient
supply of prisoners he undertook the restoration of the
whole city with its avenues streets canals quays gardens
and aqueducts the labour of all the captives brought
together from different quarters of his empire was pressed
into the execution of his plans—the Kaldâ, the Aramæans

Drawn by Boudler, from a lithograph in Layard.

the Manuai, the people of Kuî, the Cilicians, the Philistines, and the Tyrians; the provinces vied with each other in furnishing him with materials without stint,— precious woods were procured from Syria, marbles from Kapri-dargîla, alabaster from Balad, while Bît-Yakin provided the rushes to be laid between the courses of brick work. The river Tebilti, after causing the downfall of the royal mausolea and "displaying to the light of day the coffins which they concealed," had sapped the foundations of the palace of Assur-nazir-pal, and caused it to fall in a muddy pool now occupied the north-western quarter between the court of Ishtar and the lofty ziggurât of Assur This pool Sennacherib filled up, and regulated the course of the stream, providing against the recurrence of such accidents in future by building a substructure of masonry 454 cubits long by 289 wide, formed of large blocks of stone cemented together by bitumen. On this he erected a magnificent palace, a Bît-Khilâni in the Syrian style, with woodwork of fragrant cedar and cypress overlaid with gold and silver, panellings of sculptured marble and alabaster and friezes and cornices in glazed tiles of brilliant colouring: inspired by the goddess Nin-kurra, he caused winged bulls of white alabaster and limestone statues of the gods to be hewn in the quarries of Balad near Nineveh. He presided in person at all these operations—at the raising of the soil, the making of the substructures of the terrace the transport of the colossal statues or blocks and their subsequent erection; indeed, he was to be seen at every turn, standing in his ebony and ivory chariot, drawn by a team of men. When the building was finished, he was so delighted with its beauty that he named it " the incomparable palace," and his admiration was shared by his contemporaries; they were never wearied of extolling in glowing terms the twelve bronze lions, the twelve winged bulls, and the twenty-four statues of goddesses which kept watch

KING SENNACHERIB WATCHING THE TRANSPORT OF A COLOSSAL STATUE.[1]

over the entrance, and for the construction of which a new method of rapid casting had been invented. Formerly the erection of such edifices cost much in suffering to the artificers employed on them, but Sennacherib brought his great enterprise to a prompt completion without extravagant outlay or unnecessary hardship inflicted on his workmen. He proceeded to annex the neighbouring quarters of the

[1] Drawn by Faucher-Gudin, from Layard.

city, relegating the inhabitants to the suburbs while he laid out a great park on the land thus cleared; this park was well planted with trees, like the heights of Amanus, and in it flourished side by side all the forest growths indigenous

ASSYRIAN BAS-RELIEFS AT BAVIAN.[1]

to the Cilician mountains and the plains of Chaldæa. lake, fed by a canal leading from the Khuzur, supplied it with water, which was conducted in streams and rills through the thickets, keeping them always fresh and green Vines trained on trellises afforded a grateful shade during

[1] Drawn by Faucher-Gudin, from a sketch in Layard.

the sultry hours of the day; birds sang in the branches, herds of wild boar and deer roamed through the coverts, in order that the prince might enjoy the pleasures of the chase without quitting his own private grounds. The main part of these constructions was finished about 700 B.C., but many details were left incomplete, and the work was still proceeding after the court had long been in residence on the spot. Meanwhile a smaller palace, as well as barracks and a depôt for arms and provisions, sprang up elsewhere. Eighteen aqueducts, carried across the country, brought the water from the Muzri to the Khuzur, and secured an adequate supply to the city; the Ninevites, who had hitherto relied upon rain-water for the replenishing of their cisterns, awoke one day to find themselves released from all anxiety on this score. An ancient and semi-subterranean canal, which Assur-nazir-pal had constructed nearly two centuries before, but which, owing to the neglect of his successors, had become choked up, was cleaned out, enlarged and repaired, and made capable of bringing water to their doors from the springs of Mount Tas, in the same year as that in which the battle of Khalulê took place.[1] At a later date, magnificent bas-reliefs, carved on the rock by order of Esar-haddon, representing winged bulls, figures of the gods and of the king, with explanatory inscriptions, marked the site of the springs, and formed a kind of monumental façade to the ravine in which they took their rise.[2]

[1] Mount Tas is the group of hills enclosing the ravine of Bavian. These works were described in the Bavian inscription, of which they occupy the whole of the first part.

[2] The Bavian text speaks of six inscriptions and statues which the king had engraved on the Mount of Tas, at the source of the stream.

It would be hard to account for the rapidity with which these great works were completed, did one not remember that Sargon had previously carried out extensive architectural schemes, in which he must have employed all the available artists in his empire. The revolutions which had shattered the realm under the last descendants of Assur-nazir-pal, and the consequent impoverishment of the kingdom, had not been without a disastrous effect on the schools of Assyrian sculpture. Since the royal treasury alone was able to bear the expense of those vast compositions in which the artistic skill of the period could have free play, the closing of the royal workshops, owing to the misfortunes of the time, had the immediate effect of emptying the sculptors' studios. Even though the period of depression lasted for the space of two or three generations only, it became difficult to obtain artistic workmen; and those who were not discouraged from the pursuit of art by the uncertainty of employment, no longer possessed the high degree of skill attained by their predecessors, owing to lack of opportunity to cultivate it. Sculpture was at a very low ebb when Tiglath-pileser III. desired to emulate the royal builders of days gone by, and the awkwardness of composition noticeable in some of his bas-reliefs, and the almost barbaric style of the stelæ erected by persons of even so high a rank as Belharrân-beluzur, prove the lamentable deficiency of good artists at that epoch, and show that the king had no choice but to employ all the surviving members of the ancient guilds whether good, bad, or indifferent workmen. The increased demand however soon produced an

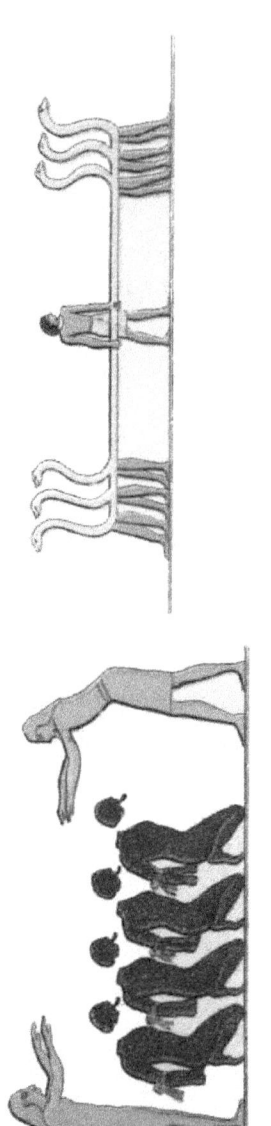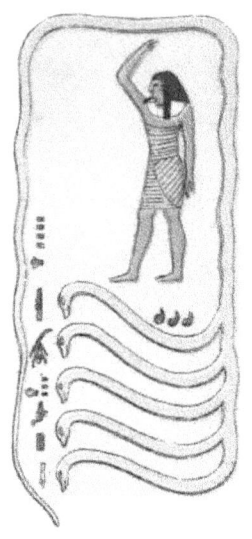

UNKNOWN SUBJECTS PAINTED IN THE FIFTH TOMB OF THE EASTERN KINGS.

GREAT ASSYRIAN STELE AT BAVIAN.
Drawn by Boudier, from Layard.

adequate supply of workers, and when Sargon ascended the throne, the royal guild of sculptors had been thoroughly reconstituted; the inefficient workmen on whom Tiglathpileser and Shalmaneser had been obliged to rely had been eliminated in course of time, and many of the sculptures which adorned the palace at Khorsabad display a purity of design and boldness of execution comparable to that of the best Egyptian art. The composition still shows traces of Chaldæan stiffness, and the exaggerated drawing of the muscles produces an occasionally unpleasing heaviness of outline, but none the less the work as a whole constitutes one of the richest and most ingenious schemes of decoration ever devised, which, while its colouring was still perfect, must have equalled in splendour the great triumphal battle-scenes at Ibsambul or Medinet-Habu. Sennacherib found ready to his hand a body of well-trained artists, whose number had considerably increased during the reign of Sargon, and he profited by the experience which they had acquired and the talent that many of them had developed." What immediately strikes the spectator in the series of pictures produced under his auspices, is the great skill with which his artists covered the whole surface at their disposal without overcrowding it. They no longer treated their subject, whether it were a warlike expedition, a hunting excursion, a sacrificial scene, or an episode of domestic life, as a simple juxtaposition of groups of almost equal importance ranged at the same elevation along the walls, the subject of each bas-relief being complete in itself and without any necessary connection with its neighbour. They now selected two or three principal incidents from the subjects proposed to them for representation, and round these they grouped such of the less important episodes as lent themselves best to picturesque treatment, and scattered sparingly over the rest of the field the minor accessories which seemed suitable to indicate more precisely the scene of the action. Under the auspices of this later school, Assyrian foot-soldiers are no longer depicted attacking the barbarians of Media **or** Elam on backgrounds of smooth stone, where no line marks the various levels, and where the remoter figures appear to be walking in the air without anything to support them. If the battle represented took place on a wooded slope crowned by a stronghold on the summit of the hill, the artist, in order to give an impression of the surroundings, covered his background with guilloche patterns by which to represent the rugged surface of the mountains; he placed here and there groups of various kinds of trees, especially the straight cypresses and firs which grew upon the slopes of the Iranian table-land: or he represented a body of lancers galloping in single file along the narrow woodland paths, and hastening to surprise a distant enemy, or again foot-soldiers chasing their foes through the forest or engaging them in single combat; while in the corners of the picture the wounded are being stabbed or otherwise despatched, fugitives are trying to escape through the undergrowth, and shepherds are pleading with the victors for their lives. It is the actual scene the sculptor sets himself to depict, and one is sometimes inclined to ask, while noting the precision with which the details of the battle are rendered, whether the picture was not drawn on the spot, and whether the conqueror did not carry artists in his train to make sketches for the decorators of the main features of the country traversed and of the victories won. The masses of infantry seem actually in

AN ASSYRIAN CAVALRY RAID THROUGH THE WOODS.[1]

motion, a troop of horsemen rush blindly over uneven ground, and the episodes of their raid are unfolded in all their confusion with unfailing animation. For the first time a spectator can realise Assyrian warfare with its striking contrasts of bravery and unbridled cruelty; he is no longer reduced to spell out laboriously a monotonous

[1] Drawn by Faucher-Gudin, from Layard.

narrative of a battle, for the battle takes place actually before his eyes. And after the return from the scene of

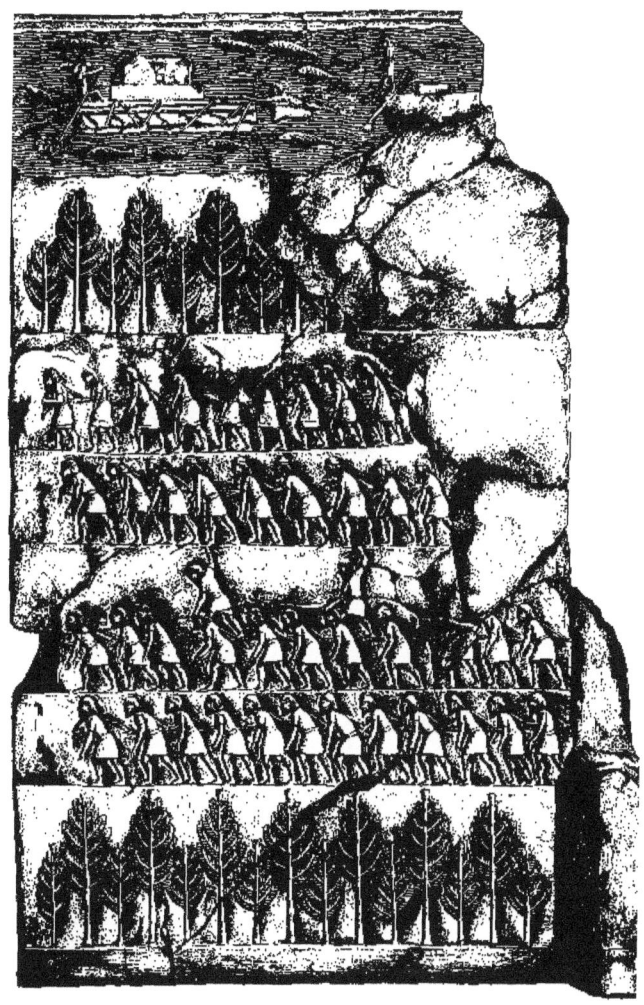

TRANSPORT OF A WINGED

action, when it is desired to show how the victor employed his prisoners for the greater honour of his gods and his own glory, the picture is no less detailed and realistic. There we see them, the noble and the great of all the conquered

BULL ON A SLEDGE.[1]

nations, Chaldæans and Elamites, inhabitants of Cilicia,

[1] Drawn by Faucher-Gudin, from Layard.

Phœnicia, and Judæa, harnessed to ropes and goaded by the whips of the overseers, dragging the colossal bull which is destined to mount guard at the gates of the palace: with bodies bent, pendant arms, and faces contorted with pain, they, who had been the chief men in their cities, now take the place of beasts of burden, while Sennacherib, erect on his state chariot, with steady glance and lips compressed, watches them as they pass slowly before him in their ignominy and misery.

After the destruction of Babylon there is a pause in the history of the conqueror, and with him in that of Assyria itself. It seems as if Nineveh had been exhausted by the greatness of her effort, and was stopping to take breath before setting out on a fresh career of conquest: the other nations also, as if overwhelmed by the magnitude of the catastrophe, appear to have henceforth despaired of their own security, and sought only how to avoid whatever might rouse against them the enmity of the master of the hour. His empire formed a compact and solid block in their midst, on which no human force seemed capable of making any impression. They had attacked it each in turn, or all at once, Elam in the east, Urartu in the north, Egypt in the south-west, and their efforts had not only miserably failed, but had for the most part drawn down upon them disastrous reprisals. The people of Urartu remained in gloomy inaction amidst their mountains, the Elamites had lost their supremacy over half the Aramæan tribes, and if Egypt was as yet inaccessible beyond the intervening deserts, she owed it less to the strength of her armies than to the mysterious fatality at Libnah. In one half-century the Assyrians had effectually and permanently disabled the first of these kingdoms, and inflicted on the others such serious injuries that they were slow in recovering from them. The fate of these proud nations had intimidated the inferior states — Arabs, Medes, tribes of Asia Minor, barbarous Cimmerians or Scythians,—all alike were careful to repress their natural inclinations to rapine and plunder. If occasionally their love of booty overpowered their prudence, and they hazarded a raid on some defenceless village in the neighbouring border territory, troops were hastily despatched from the nearest Assyrian garrison, who speedily drove them back across the frontier, and pursuing them into their own country, inflicted on them so severe a punishment that they remained for some considerable time paralysed by awe and terror. Assyria was the foremost kingdom of the East, and indeed of the whole world, and the hegemony which she exercised over all the countries within her reach cannot be accounted for solely by her military superiority. Not only did she excel in the art of conquest, as many before her had done— Babylonians, Elamites, Hittites, and Egyptians—but she did what none of them had been able to accomplish; she exacted lasting obedience from the conquered nations, ruling them with a firm hand, and accustoming them to live on good terms with one another in spite of diversity of race, and this with a light rein, with unfailing tact, and apparently with but little effort. The system of deportation so resolutely carried out by Tiglath-pileser III. and Sargon began to produce effect, and up to this time the most happy results only were discernible. colonies which had been planted throughout the empire from Palestine to Media, some of them two generations previously, others within recent years, were becoming more and more acclimatised to their new surroundings on which they were producing the effect desired by their conquerors; they were meant to hold in check the populations in whose midst they had been set down to act as a curb upon them, and also to break up their national unity and thus gradually prepare them for absorption into a wider fatherland, in which they would cease to be exclusively Damascenes, Samaritans, Hittites or Aramæans, since they would become Assyrians and fellow-citizens of a mighty empire. The provinces, brought at length under a regular system of government, protected against external dangers and internal discord by a well disciplined soldiery, and enjoying a peace and security they had rarely known in the days of their independence gradually became accustomed to live in concord under the rule of a common sovereign, and to feel themselves portions of a single empire. The speech of Assyria was their official language, the gods of Assyria were associated with their national gods in the prayers they offered up for the welfare of the sovereign, and foreign nations with whom they were brought into communication no longer distinguished between them and their conquerors, calling their country Assyria and regarding its inhabitants as Assyrians. As is invariably the case, domestic peace and good administration had caused a sudden development of wealth and commercial activity. Although Nineveh and Calah never became such centres of trade and industry as Babylon had been yet the presence of the court and the sovereign attracted thither merchants from all parts of the world The Medes reaching the capital by way of the passes of Rowândîz and Suleimaniyeh, brought in the lapis lazuli precious stones metals and woollen stuffs. of Central Asia and the farthest East while the Phœnicians and even Greeks who were already following in their foot steps came thither to sell in the bazaars of Assyria the most precious of the wares brought back by their merchant vessels from the shores of the Mediterranean the Atlantic and the farthest West The great cities of the triangle of Assyria were gradu

SENNACHERIB.[1]

ally supplanting all the capitals of the ancient world, not excepting Memphis and becoming the centres of universal trade unexcelled for centuries in the arts of war Assyria was in a fair way to become mistress also in the arts of peace A Jewish prophet thus described the empire at a later date "The Assyrian was a cedar in Lebanon with fair branches and with a shadowing shroud and of an high stature and his top was among the thick clouds The waters nourished him the deep made him grow therefore his stature was exalted above all the trees of the field and his boughs were multiplied and his branches became long by reason of many waters when he shot them forth All the fowls of the heaven made

Drawn by Faucher-Gudin, from Layard.

their nests in his boughs, and under his branches did all the beasts of the field bring forth their young, and under his shadow dwelt all great nations. Thus was he fair in his greatness, in the length of his branches: for his root was by many waters. The cedars in the garden of God could not hide him: the fir trees were not like his boughs, and the plane trees were not as his branches; nor was any tree like unto him in beauty: so that all the trees of Eden, that were in the garden of God, envied him " (*Ezek.* xxxi. 3–9).

# THE POWER OF ASSYRIA AT ITS ZENITH. ESARHADDON AND ASSUR-BANI-PAL

THE MEDES AND CIMMERIANS : LYDIA—THE CONQUEST OF EGYPT, OF ARABIA, AND OF ELAM.

*Last years of Sennacherib—New races appear upon the scene—The Medes: Deïokes and the foundation of Ecbatana, the Bît-Dayaukku and their origin—The races of Asia Minor—The Phrygians, their earliest rulers, their conquests, and their religion—Last of the Heraclidæ in Lydia, trade and constitution of their kingdom—The Tylonidæ and Mermnadæ—The Cimmerians driven back into Asia by the Scythians—The Treres.*

*Murder of Sennacherib and accession of Esarhaddon: defeat of Sharezer (681 B.C.)—Campaigns against the Kaldâ, the Cimmerians, the tribes of Cilicia, and against Sidon (680–679 B.C.); Cimmerian and Scythian invasions, revolt of the Mannai, and expeditions against the Medes; submission of the northern Arabs (678–676 B.C.)—Egyptian affairs; Taharqa (Tirhakah), his building operations, his Syrian policy—Disturbances on the frontiers of Elam and Urartu.*

VOL. VIII.                                                              G

*First invasion of Egypt and subjection of the country to Nineveh* (670 B.C.) —*Intrigues of rival claimants to the throne, and division of the Assyrian empire between Assur-bani-pal and Shamash shumukin* (668 B.C.)—*Revolt of Egypt and death of Esarhaddon* (668 B.C.); *accession of Assur-bani-pal; his campaign against Kirbît; defeat of Taharqa and reconstitution of the Egyptian province* (667 B.C.)—*Affairs of Asia Minor: Gyges* (693 B.C.), *his wars against the Greeks and Cimmerians; he sends ambassadors to Nineveh* (664 B.C.).

*Tanuatamanu reasserts the authority of Ethiopia in Egypt* (664 B.C.), *and Tammaritu of Elam invades Karduniash; reconquest of the Said and sack of Thebes—Psammetichus I. and the rise of the XXVI$^{th}$ dynasty—Disturbances among the Medes and Mannai—War against Teummân and the victory of Tulliz* (660 B.C.): *Elam yields to the Assyrians for the first time—Shamash-shumukin at Babylon; is at first on good terms with his brother, then becomes dissatisfied, and forms a coalition against the Ninevite supremacy.*

*The Uruk incident and outbreak of the war between Karduniash, Elam, and Assyria; Elam disabled by domestic discords—Siege and capture of Babylon; Assur-bani-pal ascends the throne under the name of Kandalanu* (648–646 B.C.) —*Revolt of Egypt: defeat and death of Gyges* (642 B.C.): *Ardys drives out the Cimmerians and Dugdamis is killed in Cilicia—Submission of Arabia.*

*Revolution in Elam—Attack on Indabigash—Tammaritu restored to power— Pillage and destruction of Susa—Campaign against the Arabs of Kedar and the Nabatæans: suppression of the Tyrian rebellion—Dying struggles of Elam— Capture of Madaktu and surrender of Khumbân-khaldash—The power of Assyria reaches its zenith.*

ONE OF THE EGYPTIAN IVORIES FOUND IN ASSYRIA.[1]

## CHAPTER II

### THE POWER OF ASSYRIA AT ITS ZENITH. ESARHADDON AND ASSUR-BANI-PAL

*The Medes and Cimmerians: Lydia—The conquest of Egypt, of Arabia, and of Elam.*

AS we have already seen, Sennacherib reigned for eight years after his triumph; eight years of tranquillity at home, and of peace with all his neighbours abroad. If we examine the contemporary monuments or the documents of a later period, and attempt to glean from them some details concerning the close of his career, we find that there is a complete absence of any record of national movement on the part of either

[1] Drawn by Faucher-Gudin, after Layard. The vignette, also by Faucher-Gudin, represents Tabarqa in a kneeling attitude, and is taken from a bronze statuette in the Macgregor collection.

Elam, Urartu, or Egypt. The only event of which any definite mention is made is a raid across the north of Arabia, in the course of which Hazael, King of Adumu, and chief among the princes of Kedar, was despoiled of the images of his gods. The older states of the Oriental world had, as we have pointed out, grown weary of warfare which brought them nothing but loss of men and treasure; but behind these states, on the distant horizon to the east and north-west, were rising up new nations whose growth and erratic movements assumed an importance that became daily more and more alarming. On the east, the Medes, till lately undistinguishable from the other tribes occupying the western corner of the Iranian table-land, had recently broken away from the main body, and, rallying round a single leader already gave promise of establishing an empire formidable alike by the energy of its people and the extent of its domain. A tradition afterwards accepted by them attributed their earlier successes to a certain Deïokes, son of Phraortes, a man wiser than his fellows, who first set himself to deal out justice in his own household. The men of his village observing his merits, chose him to be the arbiter of all their disputes, and, being secretly ambitious of sovereign power, he did his best to settle their differences on lines of the strictest equity and justice. "By these means he gained such credit with his fellow-citizens as to attract the attention of those who lived in the neighbouring villages, who had suffered from unjust judgments, so that when they heard of the singular uprightness of Deïokes and of the equity of his decisions they joyfully had recourse to him until at last they came to put confidence in no one else. The number of complaints brought before him continually increasing as people learnt more and more the justice of his judgments, Deïokes, finding himself now all-important, announced that he did not intend any longer to hear causes, and appeared no more in the seat in which he had been accustomed to sit and administer justice. 'It was not to his advantage,' he said, 'to spend the whole day in regulating other men's affairs to the neglect of his own.' Hereupon robbery and lawlessness broke out afresh and prevailed throughout the country even more than heretofore; wherefore the Medes assembled from all quarters and held a consultation on the state of affairs. The speakers, as I think, were chiefly friends of Deïokes. 'We cannot possibly,' they said, 'go on living in this country if things continue as they now are; let us, therefore, set a king over us, so that the land may be well governed, and we ourselves may be able to attend to our own affairs, and not be forced to quit our country on account of anarchy.' After speaking thus, they persuaded themselves that they desired a king, and forthwith debated whom they should choose. Deïokes was proposed and warmly praised by all, so they agreed to elect him." Whereupon Deïokes had a great palace built, and enrolled a bodyguard to attend upon him. He next called upon his subjects to leave their villages, and " the Medes, obedient to his orders, built the city now called Agbatana, the walls of which are of great size and strength, rising in circles one within the other. The walls are concentric, and so arranged that they rise one above the other by the height of their battlements. The nature of the ground, which is a gentle hill, favoured this arrangement. The number of the circles is seven, the royal palace and the treasuries standing within the last. The circuit of the outer wall is very nearly the same as that of Athens. Of this wall the battlements are white, of the next black of the third scarlet, of the fourth blue, of the fifth orange The two last have their battlements coated respectively with silver and gold. All these fortifications Deïokes caused to be raised for himself and his own palace; the people he required to dwell outside the citadel. When the town was finished, he established a rule that no one should have direct access to the king, but that all communications should pass through the hands of messengers. It was declared to be unseemly for any one to see the king face to face, or to laugh or spit in his presence. This ceremonial Deïokes established for his own security, fearing lest his compeers who had been brought up with him, and were of as good family and parts as he should be vexed at the sight of him and conspire against him: he thought that by rendering himself invisible to his vassals they would in time come to regard him as quite a different sort of being from themselves."

Two or three facts stand out from this legendary back ground. It is probable that Deïokes was an actual person that the empire of the Medes first took shape under his auspices; that he formed an important kingdom at the foot of Mount Elvend, and founded Ecbatana the Great, or, at at any rate, helped to raise it to the rank of a capital.[1] Its

---

[1] The existence of Deïokes has been called in question by Grote and by

site was happily chosen in a rich and fertile valley close to where the roads emerge which cross the Zagros chain of mountains and connect Irân with the valleys of the Tigris and Euphrates almost on the border of the salt desert which forms and renders sterile the central regions of the plateau  Mount Elvend shelters it and feeds with its snows the streams that irrigate it whose waters transform the whole country round into one vast orchard  The modern town has as it were swallowed up all traces of its

STONE LION AT HAMADÂN.[1]

predecessor  a stone lion overthrown and mutilated marks the site of the royal palace  The chronological reckoning of the native annalists as handed down to us by Herodotus credits Deïokes with a reign of fifty-three years which occupied almost the whole of the first half of the seventh century, *i.e.* from 709 to 656, or from 700 to 647 B.C.[2]  The

the Rawlinsons  Most recent historians, however, accept the story of this personage as true in its main facts  some believe him to have been merely the ancestor of the royal house which later on founded the united kingdom of the Medes

Drawn by Faucher-Gudin from Flandin and Coste

[2] Herodotus expressly attributes a reign of fifty-three years to his Deïokes, and the total of a hundred and fifty years which we obtain by adding together the number of years assigned by him to the four Median

records of Nineveh mention a certain Dayaukku who was governor of the Mannai, and an ally of the Assyrians in the days of Sargon, and was afterwards deported with his family to Hamath in 715; two years later reference is

VIEW OF HAMADÂN AND MOUNT ELVEND IN WINTER.[1]

made to an expedition across the territory of Bit-Dayaukku which is described as lying between Ellipi and Karalla,

kings (53 + 22 + 40 + 35) brings us back to 709–708, if we admit, as he does, that the year of the proclamation by Cyrus as King of Persia (559–558) was that in which **Astyages** was overthrown; we get 700–699 the date of **Deıokes'** accession, if we separate the two facts, as the monuments compel us to do, and reckon the hundred and fifty years of the Median empire from the fall of **Astyages** in 550–549.

[1] Drawn by **Boudier,** from a photograph by M. de Morgan.

thus corresponding to the modern province of Hamadân. It is quite within the bounds of possibility that the Dayaukku who gave his name to this district was identical with the Deïokes of later writers.[1] He was the official ancestor of a royal house, a fact proved by the way in which his conqueror uses the name to distinguish the country over which he had ruled; moreover, the epoch assigned to him by contemporary chroniclers coincides closely enough with that indicated by tradition in the case of Deïokes. He was never the august sovereign that posterity afterwards made him out to be, and his territory included barely half of what constituted the province of Media in classical times; he contrived, however—and it was this that gained him universal renown in later days—to create a central rallying-point for the Median tribes around which they henceforth grouped themselves. The work of concentration was merely in its initial stage during the lifetime of Sennacherib, and little or nothing was felt of its effects outside its immediate area of influence, but the pacific character ascribed to the worthy Deïokes by popular legends, is to a certain extent confirmed by the testimony of the monuments: they record only one expedition, in 702, against Ellipi and the neighbouring tribes, in the course of which some portions of the newly acquired territory were annexed to the province of Kharkhar, and after mentioning this the annals have nothing further to

[1] The form Deïokes, in place of Daïokes, is due to the Ionic dialect employed by Herodotus. Justi regards the name as an abbreviated form of the ancient Persian *Dahyaupati* = "the master of a province," with the suffix -*ka*.

relate during the rest of the reign. Sennacherib was too much taken up with his retaliatory measures against Babylon, or his disputes with Elam, to think of venturing on expeditions such as those which had brought Tiglath-pileser III. or Sargon within sight of Mount Bikni; while the Medes, on their part, had suffered so many reverses under these two monarchs that they probably thought twice before attacking any of the outposts scattered along the Assyrian frontier: nothing occurred to disturb their tranquillity during the early years of the seventh century and this peaceful interval probably enabled Deïokes to consolidate, if not to extend, his growing authority. But if matters were quiet, at all events on the surface, in this direction, the nations on the north and north-west had for some time past begun to adopt a more threatening attitude That migration of races between Europe and Asia, which had been in such active progress about the middle of the second millennium before our era, had increased twofold in intensity after the rise of the XX$^{th}$ Egyptian dynasty, and from thenceforward a wave of new races had gradually spread over the whole of Asia Minor, and had either driven the older peoples into the less fertile or more inaccessible districts, or else had overrun and absorbed them. Many of the nations that had fought against Ramses II. and Ramses III., such as the Uashasha, the Shagalasha, the Zakkali, the Danauna, and the Tursha, had disappeared but the Thracians, whose appearance on the scene caused such consternation in days gone by, had taken root in the very heart of the peninsula, and had, in the course of three or four generations, succeeded in establishing a thriving state. The legend which traced the descent of the royal line back to the fabulous hero Ascanius proves that at the outset the haughty tribe of the Ascanians must have taken precedence over their fellows;[1] it soon degenerated, however, and before long the Phrygian tribe gained the upper hand and gave its name to the whole nation. Phrygia proper, the country first colonised by them, lay between Mount Dindymus and the river Halys, in the valley of the Upper Sangarios and its affluents: it was there that the towns and strongholds of their most venerated leaders, such as Midaion, Dorylaion, Gordiaion, Tataion, and many others stood close together, perpetuating the memory of Midas, Dorylas, Gordios, and Tatas. Its climate was severe and liable to great extremes of temperature, being bitterly cold in winter and almost tropical during the summer months; forests of oak and pine, however, and fields of corn flourished, while the mountain slopes favoured the growth of the vine; it was, in short, an excellent and fertile country, well fitted for the development of a nation of vine-dressers and tillers of the soil. The slaying of an ox or the destruction of an agricultural implement was punishable by death, and legend relates that Gordios, the first Phrygian king, was a peasant by birth. His sole patrimony consisted of a single pair of oxen, and the waggon used by

---

[1] The name of this tribe was retained by a district afterwards included in the province of Bithynia, viz. Ascania, on the shores of the Ascanian lake: the distribution of place and personal names over the face of the country makes it seem extremely probable that Ascania and the early Ascanians occupied the whole of the region bounded on the north by the Propontis; in other words, the very country in which, according to Xanthus of Lydia, the Phrygians first established themselves after their arrival in Asia.

him in bringing home his sheaves after the harvest was afterwards placed as an offering in the temple of Cybele at Ancyra by his son Midas; there was a local tradition according to which the welfare of all Asia depended on the knot which bound the yoke to the pole being preserved intact. Midas did not imitate his father's simple habits and the poets, after crediting him with fabulous wealth tried also to make out that he was a conqueror. The kingdom expanded in all directions, and soon included the upper valley of the Mæander, with its primeval sanctuaries Kydrara, Colossæ, and Kylænæ, founded wherever exhala tions of steam and boiling springs betrayed the presence some supernatural power. The southern shores of the Hellespont, which formed part of the Troad, and was the former territory of the Ascania, belonged to it, as did also the majority of the peoples scattered along the coast of the Euxine between the mouth of the Sangarios and that of the Halys; those portions of the central steppe which border on Lake Tatta were also for a time subject to it Lydia was under its influence, and it is no exaggeration to say that in the tenth and eleventh centuries before our era there was a regular Phrygian empire which held sway almost without a rival, over the western half of Asia Minor.

It has left behind it so few relics of its existence, that we can only guess at what it must have been in the days its prosperity. Three or four ruined fortresses, a few votive stelæ, and a dozen bas-reliefs cut on the faces of cliffs in a style which at first recalls the Hittite and Asiatic carvings of the preceding age, and afterwards, as we come down to later times, betrays the influence of early Greek art. In the midst of one of their cemeteries we come upon a monument resembling the façade of a house or temple cut out of the virgin rock; it consists of a low triangular

MONUMENT COMMEMORATIVE OF MIDAS.[1]

pediment, surmounted by a double scroll, then a rectangle of greater length than height, framed between two pilasters and a horizontal string-course, the centre being decorated with a geometrical design of crosses in a way which suggests the pattern of a carpet; a recess is hollowed out on a level with the ground, and filled by a blind door with

[1] Drawn by Faucher-Gudin, from a plate in Perrot and Chipiez.

rebated doorposts. Is it a tomb? The inscription care fully engraved above one side of the pediment contains the name of Midas, and seems to show that we have before us a commemorative monument, piously dedicated by a certain Ates in honour of the Phrygian hero. Elsewhere we come upon the outlines of a draped female form sometimes alone, sometimes accompanied by two lions, or of a man clothed in a short tunic holding a sort of straight sceptre in his hand, and we fancy that we have the image of a god before our eyes, though we cannot say which of the deities handed down by tradition it may represent. The religion of the Phrygians is shrouded in the same mystery as their civilisation and their art, and presents a curious mixture European and Asianic elements. The old aboriginal races had worshipped from time immemorial a certain mothe goddess, Mâ, or Amma, the black earth, which brings forth without ceasing, and nourishes all living things. Her central place of worship seems, originally, to have been in the region of the Anti-taurus, and it was there that her

A PHRYGIAN GOD.[1]

[1] Drawn by Faucher-Gudin, from a sketch by Ramsay.

sacred cities Tyana, Venasa, and the Cappadocian Comana were to be found as late as Roman times in these towns her priests were regarded as kings and thousands of her priestesses spent lives of prostitution in her service but her sanctuaries with their special rites and regulations were scattered over the whole peninsula. She was sometimes worshipped under the form of a meteoric stone or betyle similar to those found in Canaan;[1] more frequently she was represented in female shape with attendant lions or placed erect on a lion in the attitude of walking. A moon-god Mên, shared divine honours with her and with a goddess Nana whose son Atys had been the only love of Mâ and the victim of her passion. We are told that she compelled him to emasculate himself in a fit of mad

THE MOTHER GODDESS BETWEEN LIONS

---

[1] *E.g.* at Mount Dindymus and at Pessinus, which latter place was supposed possess the oldest sanctuary of Cybele. The Pessinus stone which was carried off to Rome in 204 B.C., was small irregular in shape and of a dark colour. Another stone represented Ida

Drawn by Faucher-Gudin from a sketch by Ramsay

delirium, and then transformed him into a pine tree: thence forward her priests made the sacrifice of their virility with their own hands at the moment of dedicating themselves to the service of the goddess.[1] The gods introduced from Thrace by the Phrygians showed a close affinity with those of the purely Asiatic peoples. Precedence was universally given to a celestial divinity named Bagaios, Lord of the Oak, perhaps because he was worshipped under a gigantic sacred oak; he was king of go s and men, their father,[2] lord of the thunder and the lightning, the warrior who charges in his chariot. He

THE MOTHER-GODDESS AND ATYS.[3]

[1] Nana was made out to be the daughter of the river Sangarios. She is said to have conceived Atys by placing in her bosom the fruit of an almond tree which sprang from the hermaphrodite Agdistis. This was the form— extremely ancient in its main features—in which the legend was preserved at Pessinus.

[2] In this capacity he bore the surname Papas.

[3] Drawn by Faucher-Gudin, from a photograph by Chantre. One of the bas-reliefs at Iasilikiaia, to which we shall have occasion to refer later on in Chapter III. of the present volume.

doubtless, allowed a queen-regent of the earth to share his throne,[1] but Sauazios, another, and, at first, less venerable deity had thrown this august pair into the shade. The Greeks, finding this Sauazios at the head

THE GOD MÊN ASSOCIATED WITH THE SUN AND OTHER DEITIES.[2]

of the Phrygian Pantheon, identified him with their Zeus, or, less frequently, with the Sun; he was really

---

[1] The existence of such a goddess may be deduced from the passage in which Dionysius of Halicarnassus states that Manes, first king of the Phrygians, was the son of Zeus and Demeter.

[2] Drawn by Faucher-Gudin, from a photograph by Perdrizet. The last figure on the left is the god **Mên**; the **Sun** overlooks all the rest, and a god bearing an axe occupies the extreme right of the picture. The shapes of these ancient aboriginal deities have been modified by the influence of Græco-Roman syncretism, and I merely give these figures, as I do many others, for lack of better representations.

a variant of their Dionysos. He became torpid in the autumn and slept a death-like sleep all through the winter; but no sooner did he feel the warmth of the first breath of spring than he again awoke, glowing with youth and revelled during his summer in the heart of the forest or on the mountain side, leading a life of riot and intoxication, guarded by a band of Sauades, spirits of the springs and streams, the Sileni of Greek mythology. The resemblances detected by the new-comers between the orgies of Thrace and those of Asia quickly led to confusion between the different dogmas and divinities. The Phrygians adopted Mâ, and made her their queen, the Cybele who dwells in the hills, and takes her title from the mountain-tops which she inhabits—Dindymêne on Mount Dindymus, Sipylêne on Mount Sipylus. She is always the earth, but the earth untilled, and is seated in the midst of lions, or borne through her domain in a car drawn by lions, accompanied by a troop of Corybantes with dishevelled locks. Sauazios, identified with the Asianic Atys, became her lover and her priest, and Mên, transformed by popular etymology into Manes the good and beautiful, was looked upon as the giver of good luck, who protects men after death as well as in life. This religion, evolved from so many diverse elements possessed a character of sombre poetry and sensual fanaticism which appealed strongly to the Greek imagination ; they quickly adopted even its most barbarous mysteries, those celebrated in honour of the goddess and Atys, or of Sauazios. They tell us but little of the inner significance of the symbols and doctrines taught by its votaries, but have frequently described its outward manifestations. These consisted of aimless wanderings through the forests, in which the priest, incarnate representative of his god, led after him the ministers of the temple, who were identified with the Sauades and nymphs of the heavenly host. Men heard them passing in the night, heralded by the piercing notes of the flute provoking to frenzy, and by the clash of brazen cymbals, accompanied by the din of uproarious ecstasy: these sounds were broken at intervals by the bellowing of bulls and the roll of drums, like the rumbling of subterranean thunder.

A Midas followed a Gordios, and a Gordios a Midas, in alternate succession, and under their rule the Phrygian empire enjoyed a period of prosperous obscurity. Lydia led an uneventful existence beside them, under dynasties which have

MIDAS OF PHRYGIA.[1]

received merely passing notice at the hands of the Greek chroniclers. They credit it at the outset with the almost fabulous royal line of the Atyadæ, in one of whose reigns the Tyrseni are said to have migrated into Italy. Towards the twelfth century the Atyadæ were supplanted by a family of Heraclidæ, who traced their descent to a certain Agrôn, whose personality is only a degree less mythical than his ancestry; he was descended from Heracles through Alcæus, Belus, and Ninus. Whether

[1] Drawn by Faucher-Gudin, from a specimen in the *Cabinet des Médailles*. It is a bronze coin from Prymnessos in Phrygia, belonging to the imperial epoch.

these last two names point to intercourse with one or other of the courts on the banks of the Euphrates, it is difficult to say. Twenty-one Heraclidæ, each one the son of his predecessor, are said to have followed Agrôn on the throne, their combined reigns giving a total of five hundred years.[1] Most of these princes, whether Atyadæ or Heraclidæ, have for us not even a shadowy existence and what we know of the remainder is of a purely fabulous nature. For instance, Kambles is reported to have possessed such a monstrous appetite, that he devoured his own wife one night, while asleep.[2] The concubine of Meles, again, is said to have brought forth a lion, and the oracle of Telmessos predicted that the town of Sardes would be rendered impregnable if the animal were led round the city walls; this was done, except on the side of the citadel facing Mount Tmolus, which was considered unapproachable, but it was by that very path that the Persians subsequently entered the town. Alkimos, we are told, accumulated immense treasures, and under his rule his subjects enjoyed unequalled prosperity for fourteen

---

[1] The number is a purely conventional one, and Gutschmid has shown how it originated. The computation at first comprised the complete series of 22 Heraclidæ and 5 Mermnadæ, estimated reasonably at 4 kings to a century, *i.e.* $27 \times 25 = 675$ years, from the taking of Sardes to the supposed accession of Agrôn. As it was known from other sources that the 5 Mermnadæ had reigned 170 years, these were subtracted from the 675, to obtain the duration of the Heraclidæ alone, and by this means were obtained the 505 years mentioned by Herodotus.

[2] Another version, related by Nicolas of Damascus, refers the story to the time of Iardanos, a contemporary of Hercules; it shows that the Lydian chronographers considered Kambles or Kamblitas as being one of the last of the Atyad kings.

years. It is possible that the story of the expedition despatched into Palestine by a certain Akiamos, which ended in the foundation of Ascalon, is merely a feeble echo of the raids in Syrian and Egyptian waters made by the Tyrseni and Sardinians in the thirteenth century B.C. The spread of the Phrygians, and the subsequent progress of Greek colonisation, must have curtailed the possessions of the Heraclidæ from the eleventh to the ninth centuries, but the material condition of the people does not appear to have suffered by this diminution of territory. When they had once firmly planted themselves in the ports along the Asianic littoral—at Kymê, at Phocæa, at Smyrna, at Clazomenæ, at Colophon, at Ephesus, at Magnesia, at Miletus—the Æolians and the Ionians lost no time in reaping the advantages which this position, at the western extremities of the great high-road through Asia Minor, secured to them. They overran all the Lydian settlements in Phrygia—Sardes, Leontocephalos, Pessinus, Gordiæon, and Ancyra. The steep banks and the tortuous course of the Halys failed to arrest them; and they pushed forward beyond the mysterious regions peopled by the White Syrians, where the ancient civilisation of Asia Minor still held its sway. The search for precious metals mainly drew them on—the gold and silver, the copper, bronze, and above all iron, which the Chalybes found in their mountains, and which were conveyed by caravans from the regions of the Caucasus to the sacred towns of Teiria and Pteria.[1] The friendly relations into which they

---

[1] The site of Pteria has been fixed at Boghaz-keui by Texier, an identification which has been generally adopted; Euyuk is very probably Teiria, a

entered with the natives on these journeys resulted before long in barter and intermarriage, though their influence made itself felt in different ways, according to the character of the people on whom it was brought to bear. They gave as a legacy to Phrygia one of their alphabets, that of Kymê,

THE STEEP BANKS OF THE HALYS FAILED TO ARREST THEM.[1]

which soon banished the old Hittite syllabary from the monuments and they borrowed in exchange Phrygian customs musical instruments, traditions, and religious town of the Leucosyrians, mentioned by Hecatæus of Miletus in his work

[1] Drawn by Fauché-Gudin from a photograph by A Boissier. The road leading from Angora to Yuzgat crosses the river not far from the site shown here near the spot where the ancient road crossed

THE CONSTITUTION OF THE LYDIAN KINGDOM 105

orgies. A Midas sought in marriage Hermodikê, the daughter of Agamemnon the Kymæan, while another Midas, who had consulted the oracle of Delphi, presented to the god the chryselephantine throne on which he was wont to sit when he dispensed justice. This interchange

VIEW OVER THE PLAIN OF SARDES.[1]

of amenities and these alliances, however, had a merely superficial effect, and in no way modified the temperament and life of the people in inner Asia Minor. They remained a robust, hardworking race, attached to their fields and woods, loutish and slow of understanding, unskilled in war, and not apt in defending themselves in spite of their natural bravery. The Lydians, on the contrary, submitted readily to foreign influence, and the Greek leaven introduced

[1] Drawn by Boudier, from a photograph.

among them became the germ of a new civilisation, which occupied an intermediate place between that of the Greek and that of the Oriental world. About the first half of the eighth century B.C. the Lydians had become organised into a confederation of several tribes, governed by hereditary chiefs, who were again in their turn subject to the Heraclidæ occupying Sardes.¹ This town rose in terraces on the lower slopes of a detached spur of the Tmolus running in the direction of the Hermos, and was crowned by the citadel, within which were included the royal palace the treasury, and the arsenals. It was surrounded by an immense plain bounded on the south by a curve the Tmolus, and on the west by the distant mountains of Phrygia Katakekaumenê. The Mæonians still claimed primacy over the entire race, and the reigning family was chosen from among their nobles. The king, who was supposed to be descended from the gods, bore, as the insignia of his rank, a double-headed axe, the emblem his divine ancestors. The Greeks of later times said that the axe was that of their Heracles, which was wrested by him from the Amazon Hippolyta, and given to Omphalê.³

THE AXE BORNE BY ZEUS LABRAUNDOS.²

¹ Gelzer was the first, to my knowledge, to state that Lydia was a feudal state, and he defined its constitution. Radet refuses to recognise it as feudal in the true sense of the term, and he prefers to see in it a con federation of states under the authority of a single prince.

² Drawn by Faucher-Gudin, from a coin in the Cabinet des Médailles.

³ Gelzer sees in the legend about the axe related by Plutarch, a reminiscence of a primitive gynocracy. The axe is the emblem of the god

The king was the supreme head of the priesthood, as also of the vassal chiefs and of the army, but he had as a subordinate a " companion " who could replace him when occasion demanded, and he was assisted in the exercise of his functions by the counsel of " Friends," and further still in extraordinary circumstances by the citizens of the capital assembled in the public square. This intervention of the voice of the populace was a thing unknown in the East, and had probably been introduced in imitation of customs observed among the Greeks of Æolia or Ionia; it was an important political factor, and might possibly lead to an outbreak or a revolution. Outside the pale of Sardes and the province of Mæonia, the bulk of Lydian territory was distributed among a very numerous body of landowners, who were particularly proud of their noble descent. Many of these country magnates held extensive fiefs, and had in their pay small armies, which rendered them almost independent, and the only way for the sovereign to succeed in ruling them was to conciliate them at all hazards, and to keep them in perpetual enmity with their fellows. Two of these rival families vied with each other in their efforts to secure the royal favour; that of the Tylonidæ and that of the Mermnadæ, the principal domain of which latter lay at Teira, in the valley of the Cayster, though they had also other possessions at Dascylion, in Hellespontine Phrygia. The head sometimes of one and sometimes of the other family would fill that post of " companion " which placed all the resources of the kingdom at the disposal of the occupant.

**of war,** and, as such, belongs to the king : the coins **of** Mylasa exhibit it held by Zeus Labraundos.

The first of the Mermnadæ of whom we get a glimpse is Daskylos, son of Gyges, who about the year 740 was "companion" during the declining years of Ardys, over whom he exercised such influence that Adyattes, the heir to the throne, took umbrage at it, and caused him to be secretly assassinated, whereupon his widow, fearing for her own safety, hastily fled into Phrygia, of which district she was a native. On hearing of the crime, Ardys trembling with anger, convoked the Assembly, and as his advanced age rendered walking difficult, he caused himself to be carried to the public square in a litter Having reached the place, he laid the assassins under a curse, and gave permission to any who could find them to kill them; he then returned to his palace, where he died a few years later, about 730 B.C. Adyattes took the name of Meles on ascending the throne, and at first reigned happily, but his father's curse weighed upon him and before long began to take effect. Lydia having been laid waste by a famine, the oracle declared that, before appeasing the gods, the king must expiate the murder of the Mermnad noble, by making every atonement in his power, if need be by an exile of three years' duration Meles submitted to the divine decree. He sought out the widow of his victim, and learning that during her flight she had given birth to a son, called, like his father Daskylos, he sent to entreat the young man to repair immediately to Sardes, that he might make amends for the murder; the youth, however, alleged that he was as yet unborn at the hour of his father's death, and therefore not entitled to be a party to an arrangement which not personally affect him, and refused to return to his own country. Having failed in this attempt, Meles entrusted the regency of his kingdom to Sadyattes, son of Kadys, one of the Tylonidæ, who probably had already filled the post of companion to the king for some time past, and set out for Babylon. When the three years had elapsed, Sadyattes faithfully handed over to him the reins of government and resumed the second place. Myrsos succeeded Meles about 716,[1] and his accession immediately became the cause of uneasiness to the younger Daskylos, who felt that he was no longer safe from the intrigues of the Heraclidæ; he therefore quitted Phrygia and settled beyond the Halys among the White Syrians, one of whom he took in marriage, and had by her a son, whom he called Gyges, after his ancestor. The Lydian chronicles which have come down to us make no mention of him, after the birth of this child, for nearly a quarter of a century. We know, however, from other sources, that the country in which he took refuge had for some time past been ravaged by enemies coming from the Caucasus, known to us as the Cimmerians.[2] Previous to this period

---

[1] The lists of Eusebius give 36 years to Ardys, 14 years to Meles or Adyattes, 12 years to Myrsos, and 17 years to Candaules; that is to say, if we place the accession of Gyges in 687, the dates of the reign of Candaules are 704–687, of that of Mysros 716–704, of that of Meles 730–716, of that of Ardys I. 766–730. Gelzer thinks that the double names each represent a different king; Radet adheres to the four generations of Eusebius.

[2] I would gladly have treated at length the subject of the Cimmerians with its accompanying developments, but lack of space prevents me from doing more than summing up here the position I have taken. Most modern critics have rejected that part of the tradition preserved by Herodotus which refers to the itinerary of the Cimmerians, and have confused the Cimmerian

these had been an almost mythical race in the eyes of the civilised races of the Oriental world. They imagined them as living in a perpetual mist on the confines of the universe: "Never does bright Helios look upon them with his rays, neither when he rises towards the starry heaven, nor when he turns back from heaven towards the earth, but a baleful night spreads itself over these miserable mortals."[1] Fabulous animals, such as griffins with lions' bodies, having the neck and ears of a fox, and the wings and beak of an eagle, wandered over their plains and sometimes attacked them; the inhabitants were forced

A CONFLICT WITH TWO GRIFFINS.[2]

---

invasion with that of the Thracian tribes. I think that there is reason give weight to Herodotus' statement, and to distinguish carefully between two series of events: (1) a movement of peoples coming from Europe into Asia, by the routes that Herodotus indicates, about the latter half of the eighth century B.C., who would be more especially the Cimmerians; (2) a movement of peoples coming from Europe into Asia by the Thracian Bosphorus, and among whom there was perhaps, side by side with the Treres, a remnant of Cimmerian tribes who had been ousted by the Scythians. The two streams would have had their confluence in the heart of Asia Mino in the first half of the seventh century.

[1] *Odyssey*, xi. 14-19. It is this passage which Ephorus applies to the Cimmerians of his own time who were established in the Crimea, and which accounts for his saying that they were a race of miners, living perpetually underground.

[2] Drawn by Faucher-Gudin, from one of the reliefs on the crown of the Great Blinitza.

to defend themselves with axes, and did not always emerge victorious from these terrible conflicts. The few merchants who had ventured to penetrate into their country had returned from their travels with less fanciful notions concerning the nature of the regions frequented by them, but little continued to be known of them, until an un-

SCYTHIANS ARMED FOR WAR.[1]

foreseen occurrence obliged them to quit their remote steppes. The Scythians, driven from the plains of the Iaxartes by an influx of the Massagetæ, were urged forwards in a westerly direction beyond the Volga and the Don, and so great was the terror inspired by the mere report of their approach, that the Cimmerians decided to quit their own territory. A tradition current in Asia three centuries later, told how their kings had counselled them to make a stand against the invaders; the people, however, having refused to listen to their advice, their rulers and those who were loyal to them fell by each other's hands, and their burial-place was still shown near the banks of the Tyras. Some of their tribes took refuge

[1] Drawn by Faucher-Gudin, from the reliefs on the silver vase of Kul-Oba.

in the Chersonesus Taurica, but the greater number pushed forward beyond the Mæotic marshes; a body of Scythians followed in their track, and the united horde pressed onwards till they entered Asia Minor, keeping to the shores of the Black Sea.[1] This heterogeneous mass people came into conflict first with Urartu; then turning obliquely in a south-easterly direction, their advance guard fell upon the Mannai. But they were repulsed by Sargon's generals; the check thus administered forced them to fall back speedily upon other countries less vigorously defended. The Scythians, therefore, settled themselves in the eastern basin of the Araxes, on the frontiers of Urartu and the Mannai, where they formed themselves into a kind of marauding community, perpetually quarrelling with their neighbours.[2] The Cimmerians took their way westwards, and established themselves upon the upper waters of the Araxes, the Euphrates, the Halys, and the Thermodon,[3] greatly to

[1] The version of Aristæas of Proconnesus, as given by Herodotus and by Damastes of Sigæa, attributes a more complex origin to this migration, *i.e.* that the Arimaspes had driven the Issedonians before them, and that the latter had in turn driven the Scythians back on the Cimmerians.

[2] The Scythians of the tradition preserved by Herodotus must have been the Ashguzai or Ishkuzai of the cuneiform documents. The original name must have been Skuza, Shkuza, with a sound in the second syllable that the Greeks have rendered by *th*, and the Assyrians by *z:* the initial vowel has been added, according to a well-known rule, to facilitate the pronunciation of the combination SK, SHK. An oracle of the time of Esarhaddon shows that they occupied one of the districts really belonging to the Mannai: and it is probably they who are mentioned in a passage of *Jer.* li. 27, where the traditional reading *Ashchenaz* should be replaced by that of Ashkuz.

[3] It is doubtless to these events that the tradition preserved by Pompeius Trogus, which is known to us through his abbreviator Justin, or through

the vexation of the rulers of Urartu. They subsequently felt their way along the valleys of the Anti-Taurus, but finding them held by Assyrian troops, they turned their steps towards the country of the White Syrians, seized Sinôpê, where the Greeks had recently founded a colony, and bore down upon Phrygia. It would appear that they were joined in these regions by other hordes from Thrace which had crossed the Bosphorus a few years earlier, and among whom the ancient historians particularly make mention of the Treres;[1] the results of the Scythian invasion had probably been felt by all the tribes on the banks of the Dnieper, and had been the means of forcing them in the direction of the Danube and the Balkans, whence they drove before them, as they went, the inhabitants of the Thracian peninsula across into Asia Minor. It was about the year 750 B.C. that the Cimmerians had been forced to quit their first home, and towards 720 that they came into contact with the empires of the East; the Treres had crossed the Bosphorus about 710, and the meeting of the two streams of immigration may be placed in the opening years of the seventh century.[2] The

the compilers of a later period, refers, concerning the two Scythian princes Ylinus and Scolopitus : they seem to have settled along the coast, on the banks of the Thermodon and in the district of Themiscyra.

[1] Strabo says decisively that the Treres were both Cimmerians and Thracians ; elsewhere he makes the Treres synonymous with the Cimmerians. The Treres were probably the predominating tribe among the people which had come into Asia on that side.

[2] Gelzer thinks that the invasion by the Bosphorus took place about 705, and Radet about 708 ; and their reckoning seems to me to be so likely to be correct, that I do not hesitate to place the arrival of the Treres in Asia about the time they have both indicated—roughly speaking, about 710 B.C.

combined hordes did not at once attack Phrygia itself but spread themselves along the coast, from the mouths of the Rhyndakos to those of Halys, constituting a sort of maritime confederation of which Heraclea and Sinôpê were the chief towns. This confederation must not be regarded as a regularly constituted state, but rather as a vast encampment in which the warriors could leave their families and their spoil in safety; they issued from it nearly every year to spread themselves over the neighbouring provinces, sometimes in one direction, sometimes in another. The ancient sanctuaries of Pteria and the treasures they contained excited their cupidity, but they were not well enough equipped to undertake the siege of a strongly fortified place, and for want of anything better were content to hold it to ransom. The bulk the indigenous population lived even then in those subterranean dwellings so difficult of access, which are still used as habitations by the tribes on the banks of the Halys, and it is possible that they helped to swell the marauding troops of the new-comers. In the declining years of Sennacherib, it would appear that the Ninevite provinces possessed an irresistible attraction for these various peoples. The fame of the wealth accumulated in the regions beyond the Taurus and the Euphrates, in Syria and Mesopotamia, provoked their cupidity beyond all bounds, and the time was at hand when the fear alone of the Assyrian armies would no longer avail to hold them in check.

The last years of Sennacherib had been embittered by the intrigues which usually gathered around a monarc enfeebled by age and incapable of bearing the cares of government with his former vigour A fierce rivalry existed between those of his sons who aspired to the throne each of whom possessed his following of partisans both at court and among the people who were ready to

INHABITED CAVES ON THE BANKS OF THE HALYS.[1]

support him if need be even with the sword One of these princes probably the eldest of the king s remaining sons [2] named Assur-akhê-iddin, called by us Esarhaddon, had already been nominated his successor and had received the official investiture of the Babylonian kingdom under

Drawn by Boudier, from a photograph sent by Alfred Boissier.
[2] The eldest was perhaps that Assur-nadin shumu who reigned in Babylon and who was taken prisoner to Elam by King Khalludush.

the name of Assur-etilmukîn-pal.'¹ The catastrophe of 689 had not resulted in bringing about the ruin of Babylon as Sennacherib and his ministers had hoped. The temples it is true, had been desecrated and demolished, the palaces and public buildings razed to the ground, and the ramparts thrown down, but, in spite of the fact that the city had been set on fire by the conquerors, the quarters inhabited by the lower classes still remained standing, and those of the inhabitants who had escaped being carried away captive, together with such as had taken refuge in the surrounding country or had hidden themselves in neighbouring cities, had gradually returned to their desolated homes. They cleared the streets, repaired the damage inflicted during the siege, and before long the city, which was believed to be hopelessly destroyed, rose once more with the vigour, if not with the wealth, which it had enjoyed before its downfall. The mother of Esarhaddon was a Babylonian, by name Naki'a; and as soon as her son came into possession of his inheritance, an impulse of filial piety moved him to restore to his mother's city its former rank of capital. Animated by the strong religious feeling which formed the groundwork of his character Esarhaddon had begun his reign by restoring the sanctuaries which had been the cradle of the Assyrian religion, and his intentions, thus revealed at the very outset, had won for

¹ The idea of an enthronisation at Babylon in the lifetime of Sennacherib, put forward by the earlier Assyriologists, based on an inscription on a lion's head discovered at Babylon, has been adopted and confirmed by Winckler. It was doubtless on this occasion that Esarhaddon received as a present from his father the objects mentioned in the document which Sayce and Budge have called, without sufficient reason, *The Will of Sennacherib*.

him the sympathy of the Babylonians;[1] this, indeed, was excited sooner than he expected, and perhaps helped to secure to him his throne. During his absence from Nineveh, a widespread plot had been formed in that city, and on the 20th day of Tebeth, 681, at the hour when Sennacherib was praying before the image of his god, two of his sons, Sharezer and Adarmalik (Adrammelech), assassinated their father at the foot of the altar.[2] One half of the army proclaimed Sharezer king; the northern provinces espoused his cause; and Esarhaddon must for the moment have lost all hope of the succession. His father's tragic fate overwhelmed him with fear and grief; he rent his clothes, groaned and lamented like a lion roaring, and could be comforted only by the oracles pronounced by the priests of Babylon. An assurance that the gods favoured his cause reached him even from Assyria,

---

[1] A fragment seems to show clearly that the restoration of the temples was begun even in the lifetime of Sennacherib.

[2] We possess three different accounts of the murder of Sennacherib: 1. In the *Babylonian Chronicle of Pinches*. 2. In the Bible (2 **K**ings xix. 36, 37; cf. *Isa.* xxxvii. 37, 38; 2 *Chron.* xxxii. 21). 3. In Berosus. The biblical account alone mentions both murderers; the *Chronicle* and Berosus speak of only one, and their testimony seems to prevail with several historians. I believe that the silence of the *Chronicle* and of Berosus is explained by the fact that Sharezer was chief in the conspiracy, and the one among the sons who aspired to the kingdom: the second murderer merely acted for his brother, and consequently had no more right to be mentioned by name than those accomplices not of the blood-royal who shared in the murder. The name Sharezer is usually considered as an abbreviation of the Assyrian name Nergal-sharuzur, or Assur-sharuzur. Winckler thinks that he sees in it a corruption of Sharitir, abbreviated from Sharitir-assur, which he finds as a royal name on a fragment in the British Museum; he proposes to recognise in this Sharitir-assur, Sharezer enthroned after his father's death.

and Nineveh, after a few weeks of vacillation, acknow
ledged him as its sovereign, the rebellion being mercilessly
crushed on the 2nd of Adar.¹ Although this was a
considerable advantage to Esarhaddon's cause, it could
not be considered as decisive, since the provinces of the
Euphrates still declared for Sharezer; the gods, therefore
once more intervened. Ishtar of Arbela had long been
considered as the recognised patroness and oracle of the
dynasty. Whether it were a question of a foreign exped
tion or a rebellion at home, of a threatened plague
invasion, of a marriage or an alliance with some powerf l
neighbour, the ruling sovereign would invariably have
recourse to her, always with the same formula, to demand
counsel of her for the conduct of affairs in hand, and the
replies which she vouchsafed in various ways were taken
into consideration; her will, as expressed by the mouth
of her ministers, would hasten, suspend, or modify the
decisions of the king. Esarhaddon did not neglect to
consult the goddess, as well as Assur and Sin, Shamash
Bel, Nebo, and Nergal; and their words, transcribed upon
a tablet of clay, induced him to act without further delay
"Go, do not hesitate, for we march with thee and we will
cast down thine enemies!" Thus encouraged, he made
straight for the scene of danger without passing through

[1] The Bible alone tells us that Sharezer retired to Urartu (2 *Kings* xix
37). To explain the plan of this campaign, it is usually supposed that at
the time of his father's death Esarhaddon was either beyond Mount Tau us
or else on the Armenian frontier; the sequence of the dates in the *Babylonian
Chronicle of Pinches*, compels me to revert to the opinion that Esarhaddon
marched from Babylon against the rebels, and pursued them as far as Mount
Taurus, and beyond it to Khanigalbat.

Nineveh, so as to prevent Sharezer and his party having time to recover. His biographers depict Esarhaddon hurrying forward, often a day or more in advance of his battalions, without once turning to see who followed him, and without waiting to allow the horses of his baggage-waggons to be unharnessed or permitting his servants to pitch his tent; he rested merely for a few moments on the bare ground, indifferent to the cold and nocturnal frosts of the month of Sebat. It would appear as if Sharezer had placed his hopes on the Cimmerians, and had expected their chiefs to come to the rescue. This hypothesis seems borne out by the fact that the decisive battle took place beyond the Euphrates and the Taurus, in the country of Khanigalbat. Esarhaddon attributed his success to Ishtar, the goddess of bravery and of combat; she alone had broken the weapons of the rebels, she alone had brought confusion into their lines, and had inclined the hearts of the survivors to submit. They cried aloud, "This is our king!" and Sharezer thereupon fled into Armenia. The war had been brought to a close with such rapidity that even the most unsettled of the Assyrian subjects and vassals had not had time to take advantage of it for their own purposes; the Kaldâ on the Persian Gulf, and the Sidonians on the Mediterranean, were the only two peoples who had openly revolted, and were preparing to enter on a struggle to preserve their independence thus once more regained. Yet the events of the preceding months had shaken the power of Nineveh more seriously than we should at first suppose. For the first time since the accession of Tiglath-pileser III. the almost inevitable troubles which accompany the change of a sovereign had led to an open war. The vast army of Sargon and Sennacherib had been split up, and the two factions into which it was divided, commanded as they were by able generals and composed of troops accustomed to conquer, must have suffered more keenly in an engagement with each other than in the course of an ordinary campaign against a common enemy. One part at least of the military staff had become disorganised; regiments had been decimated, and considerable contingents were required to fill the vacancies in the ranks. The male population of Assyria, suddenly called on to furnish the necessary effective force, could not supply the demand without drawing too great a proportion of men from the country; and one of those crises of exhaustion was imminent which come upon a nation after an undue strain, often causing its downfall in the midst of its success, and yielding it an easy prey to the wiles of its adversaries.[1]

Esarhaddon was personally inclined for peace, and as soon as he was established on the throne he gave orders

---

[1] The information we possess concerning Esarhaddon is gathered from 1. *The Inscription of Cylinders A, B, C*, the second of the three better known as the *Broken Cylinder*. These texts contain a summary of the king's wars, in which the subject-matter is arranged geographically, not chronologically they cease with the *eponymy* of Akhazilu, *i.e.* the year 673. 2. Some mutilated fragments of the *Annals*. 3. *The Black Stone of Aberdeen*, on which the account of the rebuilding of Babylon is given. 4. *The Stele of Zindjirli*. 5. The consultations of the god Shamash by Esarhaddon in different circumstances of his reign. 6. A considerable number of small inscriptions and some tablets. The classification of the events of this reign presents serious difficulties, which have been partly overcome by passages in the *Babylonian Chronicle of Pinches*.

that the building works, which had been suspended during the late troubles, should be resumed and actively pushed forward; but the unfortunate disturbances of the times did not permit of his pursuing his favourite occupation without interruption, and, like those of his warlike predecessors, his life was passed almost entirely on the field of battle. Babylon, grateful for what he had done for her, tendered him an unbroken fidelity throughout the stormy episodes of his reign, and showed her devotion to him by an unwavering obedience. The Kaldâ received no support from that quarter, and were obliged to bear the whole burden of the war which they had provoked. Their chief, Nabu-zîru-kînish-lîshir, who had been placed over them by Sennacherib, now harassed the cities of Karduniash, and Ningal-shumiddin, the prefect of Uru, demanded immediate help from Assyria. Esarhaddon at once despatched such a considerable force that the Kaldu chief did not venture to meet it in the open field, and after a few unimportant skirmishes he gave up the struggle, and took refuge in Elam. Khumbân-khaldash, had died there in 680, a few months before the murder of Sennacherib, and his son, a second Khumbân-khaldash, had succeeded him; this prince appears either to have shared the peaceful tastes of his brother-king of Assyria, or more probably did not feel himself sufficiently secure of his throne to risk the chance of coming into collision with his neighbour. He caused Nabu-zîru-kînish-lîshir to be slain, and Nâîd-marduk, the other son of Merodach-baladan, who had shared his brother's flight, was so terrified at his murder that he at once sought refuge in Nineveh; he was reinstated in his paternal domain on condition of paying a tribute, and faithful to his oath of allegiance, he thenceforward came yearly in person to bring his dues and pay homage to his sovereign (679). The Kaldâ rising had, in short, been little more than a skirmish, and the chastisement of the Sidonians would have involved neither time nor trouble had not the desultory movements of the barbarians obliged the Assyrians to concentrate their troops on several points which were threatened on their northern frontier. The Cimmerians and the Scythians had not suffered themselves to be disconcerted by the rapidity with which the fate of Sharezer had been decided, and after a moment's hesitation they had again set out in various directions on their work of conquest, believing, no doubt, that they would meet with a less vigorous resistance after so serious an upheaval at Nineveh. The Cimmerians appear to have been the first to have provoked hostilities; their king Tiushpa, who ruled over their territory on the Black Sea, ejected the Assyrian garrisons placed on the Cappadocian frontier, and his presence in that quarter aroused all the insubordinate elements still remaining in the Cilician valleys. Esarhaddon brought him to a stand on the confines of the plain of Saros, defeated him in Khubushna,[1] and drove the remains

---

[1] Several Assyriologists have thought that Khubushna might be an e for Khubushkhia, and have sought the seat of war on the eastern frontie of Assyria: in reality the context shows that the place under discussion is a district in Asia Minor, identified with Kamisene by Gelzer, but left unidentified by most authorities. Jensen has shown that the name is met with as early as the inscriptions of Tiglath-pileser III., where we should ead Khubishna, and he places the country in Northern Syria, or perhaps further north in the western part of Taurus. The determinative proves that there

of the horde back across the Halys. Having thus averted the Cimmerian danger, he was able, without much difficulty, to bring the rebels of the western provinces into subjection.[1] His troops thrust back the Cilicians and Duha into the rugged fastnesses of the Taurus, and razed to the ground one and twenty of their strongholds, besides burning numberless villages and carrying the inhabitants away captive.[2] The people of Parnaki, in the bend of the Euphrates between Tel-Assur and the sources of the Balîkh, had taken up arms on hearing of the brief successes of Tiushpa, but were pitilessly crushed by Esarhaddon. The sheikh of Arzani, in the extreme south of Syria, close to the brook of Egypt, had made depredations on the Assyrian frontier, but he was seized by the nearest governor and sent in chains to Nineveh. A cage was built for him at the gate of the city, and he was exposed in it to the jeers of the populace, in company with the bears, dogs, and boars which the Ninevites were in the habit of keeping confined there. It would appear that Esarhaddon set himself to come to a final reckoning with Sidon and

was a town of this name as well as a district, and this consideration encourages me to recognise in Khubushna or Khubishna the town of Kabissos-Kabessos, the Sis of the kingdom of Lesser Armenia.

[1] These expeditions are not dated in any of the documents that deal with them: the fact that they are mentioned along with the war against Tiushpa and Sidon makes me inclined to consider them as being a result of the Cimmerian invasion. They were, strictly speaking, the quelling of revolts caused by the presence of the Cimmerians in that part of the empire.

[2] The Duua or Duha of this campaign, who are designated as neighbours of the Tabal, lived in the Anti-taurus: the name of the town, Tyana, *Tuana*, is possibly composed of their name and of the suffix -*na*, which is met with in Asianic languages.

Phœnicia, the revolt of which had irritated him all the more, in that it showed an inexcusable ingratitude towards his family. For it was Sennacherib who, in order to break the power of Elulai, had not only rescued Sidon from the dominion of Tyre, but had enriched it with the spoils taken from its former rulers, and had raised it to the first rank among the Phœnician cities. Ethbaal in his lifetime had never been wanting in gratitude, but his successor Abdimilkôt, forgetful of recent services, had chafed at the burden of a foreign yoke, and had recklessly thrown it off as soon as an occasion presented itself. He had thought to strengthen himself by securing the help of a certain Sanduarri, who possessed the two fortresses of Kundu and Sizu, in the Cilician mountains;[1] but neither this alliance nor the insular position of his capital was able to safeguard him, when once the necessity for stemming the tide of the Cimmerian influx was over, and the whole of the Assyrian force was free to be brought against him. Abdimilkôt attempted to escape by sea before the last attack, but he was certainly taken prisoner, though the circumstances are unrecorded, and Sanduarri fell into the enemy's hands a short time after. The suppression of the rebellion was as vindictive as the ingratitude which prompted it was heinous. Sidon was given up to the soldiery and then burnt, while opposite to the ruins of the island city the

[1] Some Assyriologists have proposed to locate these two towns in Cilicia others place them in the Lebanon, Kundi being identified with the modern village of Ain-Kundiya. The name of Kundu so nearly recalls that Kuinda, the ancient fort mentioned by Strabo, to the north of Anchialê, between Tarsus and Anazarbus, that I do not hesitate to identify them, and to place Kundu in Cilicia.

Assyrians built a fortress on the mainland, which they called Kar-Esarhaddon. The other princes of Phœnicia and Syria were hastily convoked, and were witnesses of the vengeance wreaked on the city, as well as of the installation of the governor to whom the new province was entrusted. They could thus see what fate awaited them in the event of their showing any disposition to rebel, and the majority of them were not slow to profit by the lesson. The spoil was carried back in triumph to Nineveh, and comprised, besides the two kings and their families, the remains of their court and people, and the countless riches which the commerce of the world had brought into the great ports of the Mediterranean—ebony, ivory, gold and silver, purple, precious woods, household furniture, and objects of value from all parts in such quantities that it was long before the treasury at Nineveh needed any replenishing.[1]

The reverses of the Cimmerians did not serve as a warning to the Scythians. Settled on the borders of Manna, partly, no doubt, on the territory formerly dependent on that state,[2] they secretly incited the

[1] The importance of the event and the amount of the spoil captured are apparent, if we notice that Esarhaddon does not usually record the booty taken after each campaign; he does so only when the number of objects and of prisoners taken from the enemy is extraordinary. The *Babylonian Chronicle of Pinches* places the capture of Sidon in the second, and the death of Abdimilkôt in the fifth year of his reign. Hence Winckler has concluded that Abdimilkôt held out for fully two years after the loss of Sidon. The general tenor of the account, as given by the inscriptions, seems to me to be that the capture of the king followed closely on the fall of the town: Abdimilkôt and Sanduarri probably spent the years between 679 and 676 in prison.

[2] One of the oracles of Shamash speaks of the captives as dwelling in a canton of the Mannai.

inhabitants to revolt, and to join in the raids which they made on the valley of the Upper Zab, and they would even have urged their horses up to the very walls Nineveh had the occasion presented itself. Esarhaddon warned of their intrigues by the spies which he sent among them, could not bring himself either to anticipate their attack or to assume the offensive, but anxiously consulted the gods with regard to them: "O Shamash he wrote to the Sun-god, " great lord, thou whom I question, answer me in sincerity! From this day forth the 22nd day of this month of Simanu, until the 21st day of the month of Duzu of this year, during these thirty days and thirty nights, a time has been foreordained favourable to the work of prophecy. In this time thus foreordained, the hordes of the Scythians who inhabit a district of the Mannai, and who have crossed the Mannian frontier,—will they succeed in their undertaking? Will they emerge from the passes of Khubushkia at the towns of Kharrânia and Anîsuskia; will they ravage the borders of Assyria and steal great booty, immense spoil? that doth thy high divinity know. Is it a decree, and in the mouth of thy high divinity, O Shamash, great lor ordained and promulgated? He who sees, shall he see it; he who hears, shall he hear it?"[1] The god comforted his faithful servant, but there was a brief delay before his answer threw light on the future, and the king's questions were constantly renewed as fresh couriers brought in

---

[1] The town of Anîsuskia is not mentioned elsewhere, but Kharrânia met with in the account of the thirty-first campaign of Shalmaneser III. with Kharrâna as its variant.

further information. In 678 B.C. the Scythians determined to try their fortune, and their king, Ishpakai,[1] took the field, followed by the Mannai. He was defeated and driven back to the north of Lake Urumiah, the Mannai were reduced to subjection, and Assyria once more breathed freely. The victory, however, was not a final one, and affairs soon assumed as threatening an aspect as before. The Scythian tribes came on the scene, one after another, and allied themselves to the various peoples subject either directly or indirectly to Nineveh.[2] On one occasion it was Kashtariti, the regent of Karkashshi,[3] who wrote to Mamitiarshu, one of the Median princes, to induce him to make common cause with himself in attacking the fortress of Kishshashshu on the eastern border of the empire. At another time we find the same chief plotting with the Mannai and the Saparda to raid the town of Kilmân, and Esarhaddon implores the god to show him how the place may be saved from their machinations.[4] He

[1] This king's name seems to be of Iranian origin. Justi has connected it with the name Aspakos, which is read in a Greek inscription of the Cimmerian Bosphorus; both forms have been connected with the Sanskrit Açvaka.

[2] This subdivision of the horde into several bodies seems to be indicated by the number of different royal names among the Scythians which are mentioned in the Assyrian documents.

[3] The site of Karkashshi is unknown, but the list of Median princes subdued by Sargon shows that it was situated in Media. Kishshashshu is very probably the same as Kishisim or Kishisu, the town which Sargon subdued, and which he called Kar-nergal or Kar-ninib, and which is mentioned in the neighbourhood of Parsuash, Karalla, Kharkhar, Media, and Ellipi. I think that it would be in the basin of the Gavê—Rud; Billerbeck places it at the ruins of Siama, in the upper valley of the Lesser Zab.

[4] The people of Saparda, called by the Persians Sparda, have been with good reason identified with the Sepharad of the prophet Obadiah (ver. 20):

opens negotiations in order to gain time, but the barbarity of his adversary is such that he fears for his envoy's safety, and speculates whether he may not have been put to death. The situation would indeed have become critical if Kashtariti had succeeded in bringing against Assyria a combined force of Medes, Scythians, Mannai, and Cimmerians, together with Urartu and its king, Rusas III.; but, fortunately, petty hatreds made the combination of these various elements an impossibility, and they were unable to arrive at even a temporary understanding. The Scythians themselves were not united as to the best course to be pursued, and while some endeavoured to show their hostility by every imaginable outrage and annoyance others, on the contrary, desired to enter into friendly relations with Assyria. Esarhaddon received on one occasion an embassy from Bartatua,[1] one of their kings who humbly begged the hand of a lady of the blood royal, swearing to make a lasting friendship with him if Esarhaddon would consent to the marriage. It was hard for a child brought up in the harem, amid the luxury and comfort of a civilised court, to be handed over to a semi barbarous spouse; but state policy even in those days was exacting, and more than one princess of the line of Sargon had thus sacrificed herself by an alliance which was to the interest of her own people.[2] What troubled Esarhaddon

the Assyrian texts show that this country should be placed in the neighbourhood of the Mannai of the Medes.

[1] Bartatua is, according to Winckler's ingenious observation, the Protothyes of Herodotus, the father of Madyes. [The name should more probably be read Masta-tua.—ED.]

[2] Sargon had in like manner given one of his daughters in marriage to

was not the thought of sacrificing a sister or a daughter, but a misgiving that the sacrifice would not produce the desired result, and in his difficulty he once more had recourse to Shamash. "If Esarhaddon, King of Assyria, grants a daughter of the blood (royal) to Bartatua, the King of the Iskuza, who has sent an embassy to him to ask a wife, will Bartatua, King of the Iskuza, act loyally towards Esarhaddon, King of Assyria? will he honestly and faithfully enter into friendly engagements with Esarhaddon, King of Assyria? will he observe the conditions (made by) Esarhaddon, King of Assyria? will he fulfil them punctually? that thy high divinity knoweth. His promises, in a decree and in the mouth of thy high divinity, O Shamash, great lord, are they decreed, promulgated?" It is not recorded what came of these negotiations, nor whether the god granted the hand of the princess to her barbarian suitor. All we know is, that the incursions and intrigues of the Scythians continued to be a perpetual source of trouble to the Medes, and roused them either to rebel against Assyria or to claim the protection of its sovereign. Esarhaddon, in the course of his reign, was more than once compelled to interfere in order to ensure peace and quietness to the provinces on the table-land of Iran, which Sargon had conquered and which Sennacherib had retained.[1] He had first to carry

Ambaris, King of Tabal, in order to attach him to the Assyrian cause, but without permanent success.

[1] Several recent historians allege that Sennacherib did not keep the territories that Sargon had conquered, and that the Assyrian frontier became contracted on that side; whereas the general testimony of the known texts seems to me to prove the contrary, namely, that he preserved nearly all the

his arms to the extreme edge of the desert, into the rugged country of Patusharra, lying at the foot of Demavend rich in lapis-lazuli, and as yet untrodden by any king Assyria.[1] Having reached his destination, he captured two petty kings, Eparna and Shîtirparna, and exiled them to Assyria, together with their people, their thoroughbred horses, and their two-humped camels,—in fine, all the possessions of their subjects. Shortly after this, three other Median chiefs, hitherto intractable—Uppis of Par takka, Zanasana of Partukka,[2] Ramatea of Urakazabarna— came to Nineveh to present the king with horses and lapis-lazuli, the best of everything they possessed, and piteously entreated him to forgive their misdeeds. They represented that the whole of Media was torn asunder by countless strifes, prince against prince, city against city and an iron will was needed to bring the more turbulent elements to order. Esarhaddon lent a favourable ear to their prayers; he undertook to protect them on condition

territory annexed by his father, and that Esarhaddon was far from diminishing this inheritance. If these two kings mention only insignificant deeds of arms in the western region, it is because the population, exhausted by the wars of the two preceding reigns, easily recognised the Ninevite supremacy and paid tribute to the Assyrian governors with sufficient regularity to prevent any important military expedition against them.

[1] The country of Patusharra has been identified with that of Patischorians mentioned by Strabo in Persia proper, who would have lived further north, not far from Demavend; Sachau calls attention to the existence of a mountain chain Patashwar-gar or Padishwar-gir, in front of Choarênê, and he places the country of Patusharra between Demavend and the desert.

[2] Partakka and Partukka seem to be two different adaptations of the name Paraituka, the Parætakênê of the Greek geographers; Tiele thinks Parthyênê. I think that these two names designate the northern districts of Parætakênê, the present Ashnakhor or the country near to it.

of their paying an annual tribute, and he put them under the protection of the Assyrian governors who were nearest to their territory. Kharkhar, securely entrenched behind its triple ramparts, assumed the position of capital to these Iranian marches.

It is difficult to determine the precise dates of these various events; we learn merely that they took place

THE TOWN OF KHARKHAR WITH ITS TRIPLE RAMPART.[1]

before 673, and we surmise that they must have occurred between the second and sixteenth year of the king's reign.[2] The outcome of them was a distinct gain to

---

[1] Drawn by Faucher-Gudin, from Flandin, in Botta.

[2] The facts relating to the submission of Patusharra and of Partukka are contained in Cylinder A, dated from the eponymous year of Akhazilu, in **673**. Moreover, the version which this document contains seems to have been made up of two pieces placed one at the end of the other: the first an account of events which occurred during an earlier period of the reign, and in which the exploits are classified in geographical order, from Sidon in the west the Arabs bordering on Chaldæa in the east; and the second consisting of

Assyria, in the acquisition of several new vassals. The recently founded kingdom of Ecbatana lacked as yet the prestige which would have enabled it to hold its against Nineveh; besides which, Deïokes, the contemporary ruler assigned to it by tradition, was of too complaisant a nature to seek occasions of quarrel. The Scythians, after having declared their warlike intentions, seem to have come to a more peaceable frame of mind, and to have curried favour with Nineveh; but the rulers of the capital kept a strict watch upon them, since their numbers, their intrepid character, and instinct for rapine made them formidable enemies—the most dangerous, indeed, that the empire had encountered on its north-eastern frontier for nearly a century.

This policy of armed *surveillance,* which proved so successful in these regions, was also carefully maintained by Esarhaddon on his south-eastern border against Assyria s traditional enemy, the King of Susa. Babylon, far from exhibiting any restlessness at her present position, showed

additional campaigns carried out after the completion of the former—which is proved by the place which these exploits occupy, out of their normal position in the geographical series—and making mention of Partusharra and Partukka, as well as of Belikisha. The editor of the *Broken Cylinder* has tried to combine these latter elements with the former in the order adopted by the original narrator. As far as can be seen in what is left of the columns, he has placed, after the Chaldæan events, the facts conce ning Partukka, then those concerning Patusharra, and finally the campaign against Bazu, the extreme limit of Esarhaddon's activity in the south Knowing that the campaign in the desert and the death of Abdimilkôt place in 676, and that we find them already alluded to in the first pa the narrative, as well as the events of 675 relating to the revolt of Dakkuri, we may conclude that the submission of Patusharra and that of Partukka occurred in 674, or at latest in the beginning of 673.

her gratitude for the favours which her suzerain had showered upon her by resigning herself to become the ally of Assyria. She regarded her late disaster as the punishment inflicted by Marduk for her revolts against Sargon and Sennacherib. The god had let loose the powers of evil against her, and the Arakhtu, overflowing among the ruins, had swept them utterly away; indeed, for the space of ten years, destruction and desolation seemed to have taken the place of her former wealth of temples and palaces. In the eleventh year, the divine wrath was suddenly appeased. No sooner had Esarhaddon mounted the throne, than he entreated Shamash, Rammân, and even Marduk himself, to reveal to him their will with regard to the city; whereupon the omens, interpreted by the seers, commanded him to rebuild Babylon and to raise again the temple of Ê-sagilla. For this purpose he brought together all the captives taken in war that he had at his disposal, and employed them in digging out clay and in brick-making; he then prepared the foundations, upon which he poured libations of oil, honey, palm-wine, and other wines of various kinds; he himself took the mason's hod, and with tools of ebony, cypress wood, and oak, moulded a brick for the new sanctuary. The work was, indeed, a gigantic undertaking, and demanded years of uninterrupted labour, but Esarhaddon pushed it forward, sparing neither gold, silver, costly stone, rare woods, or plates of enamel in its embellishment. He began to rebuild at the same time all the other temples and the two city walls—Imgurbel and Nimittibel; to clear and make good the canals which supplied the place with water, and

to replant the sacred groves and the gardens of the palace
The inhabitants were encouraged to come back to their
homes, and those who had been dispersed among distant
provinces were supplied with clothes and food for their
return journey, besides having their patrimony restored
to them. This rebuilding of the ancient city certainly
displeased and no doubt alarmed her two former rivals
the Kaldâ and Elam, who had hoped one day to wrest
her heritage from Assyria. Elam concealed its ill-feeling
but the Kaldâ of Bit-Dakkuri had invaded the almost
deserted territory, and appropriated the lands which
had belonged to the noble families of Babylon, Borsippa,
and Sippara. When the latter, therefore, returned from
exile, and, having been reinstituted in their rights
attempted to resume possession of their property the
usurpers peremptorily refused to relinquish it. Esarhaddon
was obliged to interfere to ensure its restoration, and as
their king, Shamash-ibni, was not inclined to comply w th
the order, Esarhaddon removed him from the throne and
substituted in his place a certain Nabushallim, son of
Belesys, who showed more deference to the suzerain s
wishes. It is possible that about this time the Kald
may have received some support from the Aramæans of
the desert and the Arab tribes encamped between the
banks of the Euphrates and Syria, or, on the other hand
the latter may have roused the wrath of Assyria by inroads
of a more than usually audacious character. However this
may be, in 676 Esarhaddon resolved to invade their desert
territory, and to inflict such reprisals as would force them
thenceforward to respect the neighbouring border provinces

His first relations with them had been of a courteous and friendly nature. Hazael of Adumu, one of the sheikhs of Kedar, defeated by Sennacherib towards the end of his reign, had taken the opportunity of the annual tribute to come to Nineveh with considerable presents, and to implore the restoration of the statues of his gods. Esarhaddon had caused these battered idols to be cleaned and repaired, had engraved upon them an inscription in praise of Assur, and had further married the suppliant sheikh to a woman of the royal harem, named Tabua. In consideration of this, he had imposed upon the Arab a supplementary tribute of sixty-five camels, and had restored to him his idols. All this took place, no doubt, soon after the king's accession. A few years later, on the death of Hazael, his son Yauta solicited investiture, but a competitor for the chieftaincy, a man of unknown origin, named Uahab, treacherously incited the Arabs to rebel, and threatened to overthrow him. Esarhaddon caused Uahab to be seized, and exposed him in chains at the gate of Nineveh; but, in consideration of this service to the Arabs, he augmented the tribute which already weighed upon the people by a further demand for ten gold *minas,* one thousand precious stones, fifty camels, and a thousand measures of spicery. The repression of these Arabs of Kedar thus confirmed Esarhaddon's supremacy over the extreme northern region of Arabia, between Damascus and Sippara or Babylon; but in a more southerly direction, in the wadys which unite Lower Chaldæa to the districts of the Jordan and the Dead Sea, there still remained several rich and warlike states—among others, Bazu,[1] whose rulers had never done homage to the sovereigns of either Assyria or Karduniash. To carry hostilities into the hear their country was a bold and even hazardous undertaking it could be reached only by traversing miles of arid and rocky plains, exposed to the rays of a burning sun, vast extents of swamps and boggy pasture land, desolate wastes infested with serpents and scorpions, and a mountain range of blackish lava known as Khâzu. It would have been folly to risk a march with the heavy Assyrian infantry in the face of such obstacles. Esarhaddon probably selected for the purpose a force composed of cavalry, chariots and lightly equipped foot-soldiers, and despatched them with orders to reach the Jauf by forced marches through the Wady Haurân. The Arabs, who were totally unprepared for such a movement, had not time to collect their forces eight of their chiefs were taken by surprise and killed after another—among them Kisu of Khaldili, Agbaru of Ilpiati, Mansaku of Magalani,—and also some reigning queens. Lâ, the King of Yadi, at first took refuge in the mountains, but afterwards gave himself up to the enemy, and journeyed as far as Nineveh to prostrate himself at Esarhaddon's feet, who restored to him his

---

[1] The Bazu of this text is certainly the Buz which the Hebrew books name among the children of Nahor (*Gen.* xxii. 21 ; *Jer.* xxv. 23). The ea ly Assyriologists identified Khazn with Uz, the son of Nahor ; Delitzsch compares the name with that of Hazo (Huz), the fifth son of Nahor (*Gen.* 22), and his opinion is admitted by most scholars. For the site of these countries I have followed the ideas of Delattre, who identifies them with the oases of Jauf and Meskakeh, in the centre of Northern Arabia. The Assyrians must have set out by the Wady Haurân or by one of the wadys near to Babylon, and have returned by a more southern wady.

gods and his crown, on the usual condition of paying tribute. A vassal occupying a country so remote and so difficult of access could not be supposed to preserve an unbroken fidelity towards his suzerain, but he no longer ventured to plunder the caravans which passed through his territory, and that in reality was all that was expected of him.

Esarhaddon thus pursued a prudent and unadventurous policy in the northern and eastern portions of his empire, maintaining a watchful attitude towards the Cimmerians and Scythians in the north, carrying on short defensive campaigns among the Medes in the east, preserving peace with Elam, and making occasional flying raids in the south,

SHABÎTOKU, KING OF EGYPT.[1]

rather from the necessity for repressing troublesome border tribes than with any idea of permanent conquest. This policy must have been due to a presentiment of danger from the side of Egypt, or to the inception of a great scheme for attacking the reigning Pharaoh. After the defeat of his generals at Altaku, Shabîtoku had made no further attempt to take the offensive; his authority over the feudal nobility of Egypt was so widely acknowledged that it causes us no surprise to meet with his cartouches on more than one ruin between Thebes and

[1] Drawn by Faucher-Gudin, from Lepsius.

Memphis,¹ but his closing years were marred by misfortune. There was then living at Napata a certain Taharqa, one of those scions of the solar race enjoyed the title of "Royal brothers," and from among whom Amon of the Holy Mountain was wont to choose his representative to reign over the land of Ethiopia whenever the throne became vacant. It does not appear that the father of Taharqa ever held the highest rank it was from his mother, Âkaluka, that he inherited his pretensions to the crown, and through her probably that he traced his descent from the family of the high priests. Tradition asserts that he did not gain the regal power without a struggle; having been proclaimed king in Ethiopia at the age of twenty, as the result of some revolution, he is said to have marched against Shabîtoku, and, coming up with him in the Delta, to have defeated him, taken him prisoner, and put him to death.² These events took place about 693 B.C.,³ and Taharqa employed the opening years of his reign in consolidating his authority over the double kingdom. He married the widow Sabaco, Queen Dikahîtamanu, and thus assumed the guardianship of Tanuatamanu, her son by her first husband and this marriage secured him supreme authority in

[1] His name or monuments of his erection have been discovered at Karnak.

[2] Eusebius, who cites the fact, had his information from a trustworthy Greek source, perhaps from Manetho himself. The inscription of Tanis seems to say that Taharqa was twenty years old at the time of his revolt.

[3] Most of the lists of kings taken from Manetho assign twelve yea s to the reign of Sébikhos; one alone, that of Africanus, assigns him fou teen years.

Ethiopia That he regarded Egypt as a conquered country can no longer be doubted seeing that he inserted its name on his monuments among those of the nations which he had vanquished He nevertheless felt obliged to treat it

TAHARQA AND HIS QUEEN DIKAHÎTAMANU.²

with consideration he respected the rights of the feudal princes and behaved himself in every way like a Pharaoh of the old royal line He summoned his mother from

The text of several documents only mentioned that Tanuata-manu was the son of his wife " which Oppert interpreted to mean son of Tabarqa himself, while others see in him a son of Kashto, a brother of Amenertas, or a son of Shabîtoku.

² Drawn by Faucher-Gudin, from the coloured plate in Lepsius

Napata, where he had left her, and after proclaiming her regent of the South and the North, he associated her with himself in the rejoicings at his coronation. This ceremony celebrated at Tanis with the usages customary in the Delta was repeated at Karnak in accordance with the Theban ritual, and a chapel erected shortly afterwards on the northern quay of the great sacred lake has preserved to us the memory of it. Âkaluka, installed with the rank and prerogatives of the "Divine Spouse" of Amon, presented her son to the deity, who bestowed upon him through his priests dominion over the whole world. She bent the bow and let fly the arrows towards the four cardinal points which she thereby symbolically delivered to him as wounded prisoners; the king, on his part, hurled against them bullets of stone, and by this attack figuratively accomplished their defeat. His wars in Africa were crowned with a certain meed of success,[1] and his achievements in this quarter won for him in after time so much popularity among the Egyptians, that they extolled him to the Greeks as one of their most illustrious conquering Pharaohs; they related that he had penetrated as far as the Pillars of Hercules in the west, and that he had invaded Europe in imitation of Sesostris. What we know to be a

---

[1] The list inscribed on the base of the statue discovered by Maiette contains a large number of names belonging to Africa. They are the same as those met with in the time of the XVIII[th] dynasty, and were probably copied from some monument of Ramses II., who had himself perhaps borrowed them from a document of the time of Thûtmosis III. A bas-relief at Medinet-Habu shows him to us in the act of smiting a group of tribes among which figure the Tepa, **Doshrît,** and "the humbled Kush;" this bas relief was appropriated later on by Nectanebo.

fact is, that he secured to the valley of the Nile nearly twenty years of prosperity, and recalled the glories of the great reigns of former days, if not by his victories, at least by the excellence of his administration and his activity. He planned the erection at Karnak of a hypostyle hall in front of the pylons of Ramses II., which should equal, if not surpass, that of Seti I.[1] The columns of the central aisle were disposed in two lines of six pillars each, but only one of these now remains standing in its original place; its height, which is the same as that of Seti's columns, is nearly sixty-nine feet. The columns of the side aisles, like those which should have flanked the immense colonnade at Luxor, were never even begun, and the hall of Taharqa, like that of Seti I., remains unfinished to this day. He bestowed his favour on Nubia and Ethiopia, as well as on Egypt proper; even Napata owed to his munificence the most beautiful portions of its temples. The temple of Amon, and subsequently that of Mût, were enlarged by him; and he decorated their ancient halls with bas-reliefs, representing himself, accompanied by his mother and his wife, in attitudes of adoration before the deity. The style of the carving is very good, and the hieroglyphics would not disgrace the walls of the Theban temples. The

---

[1] These columns have been looked upon as triumphal pillars, designed to support statues or divine emblems. Mariette thinks that they supported "an edifice in the architectural style of the kiosk at Philæ and the small hypæthral temple on the roof of Denderah." I am of opinion that the architect intended to make a hypostyle hall, but that when the columns were erected, he perceived that the great width of the aisle they formed would render the strength of the roof very doubtful, and so renounced the execution of his first design.

THE COLUMN OF TAHARQA, AT KARNAK.[1]

Ethiopian sculptors and painters scrupulously followed the traditions of the mother-country, and only a few insignificant

[1] Drawn by Faucher-Gudin, from a photograph by Beato.

details of ethnic type or costume enable us to detect a slight difference between their works and those of pure Egyptian art. At the other extremity of Napata, on the western side of the Holy Mountain, Taharqa excavated in

THE HEMISPEOS OF HÂTHOR AND BISÛ, AT GEBEL-BARKAL.[1]

the cliff a rock-hewn shrine, which he dedicated to Hâthor and Bisû (Bes), the patron of jollity and happiness, and the god of music and of war. Bisû, who was at first relegated to the lowest rank among the crowd of genii adored by the people, had gradually risen to the highest place in the

[1] Drawn by Faucher-Gudin, from a lithograph in Caillaud

hierarchy of the gods, and his images predominated in chapels destined to represent the cradle of the infant gods and the sacred spots where goddesses gave birth to their divine offspring. The portico erected in front of the pylon had a central avenue of pillars, against which stood

ENTRANCE TO THE HEMISPEOS OF BÎSÛ (BES), AT GEBEL-BARKAL.[1]

monstrous and grinning statues of Bîsû, his hands on his hips, and his head crowned with a large bunch of lotus flowers and plumes. Two rows of columns with Hathor headed capitals flanked the central aisle, which led to a hall supported by massive columns, also with Hathor capitals, and beyond it again lay the actual shrine similarly excavated in the rocky hill; two statues of Bîsû, standing

[1] Drawn by Faucher-Gudin, from a lithograph in **Caillaud.**

erect against their supporting columns, kept guard over the entrance, and their fantastic forms, dimly discernible in the gloom, must have appeared in ancient times to have prohibited the vulgar throng from approaching the innermost sanctuary. Half of the roof has fallen in since the building was deserted, and a broad beam of light falling through the aperture thus made reveals the hideous grotesqueness of the statues to all comers.

The portraits of Taharqa represent him with a strong, square-shaped head, with full cheeks, vigorous mouth, and determined chin, such as belong to a man well suited to deal with that troubled epoch, and the knowledge we as yet possess of his conflict with Assyria fully confirms the character exhibited by his portrait statues. We may surmise that,

TAHARQA.[1]

when once absolute master of Egypt, he must have cast his eyes beyond the isthmus, and considered how he might turn to his own advantage the secret grudge borne by the Syrians against their suzerain at Nineveh, but up to the present time we possess no indications as to the policy he pursued in Palestine. We may safely assume, however, that it gave umbrage to the Assyrians, and that Esarhaddon resolved to put an end once for all to the uneasiness it caused him. More than half a century had elapsed since the day when the kings of Syria, alarmed at the earliest victories of Tiglath-pileser III., had conceived

[1] Drawn by Faucher-Gudin, from a cast of the fragment preserved at Gizeh

the idea of pitting their former conquerors against those of the day, and had solicited help from the Pharaohs against Assyria.

None of the sovereigns to whom they turned had refused to listen to their appeals, or failed to promise subsidies and reinforcements; but these engagements however definite, had for the most part been left unfulfilled and when an occasion for their execution had occurred the Egyptian armies had merely appeared on the fields of battle to beat a hasty retreat: they had not prevented the subjugation of Damascus, Israel, Tyre, the Philistines, nor indeed, of any of the princes or people who trusted to their renown; yet, notwithstanding these numerous disappointments, the prestige of the Egyptians was still so great that insubordinate or rebel states invariably looked to them for support and entreated their help. The Assyrian generals had learnt by experience to meet them unmoved, being well aware that the Egyptian army was inferior to their own in organisation, and used antiquated weapons and methods of warfare; they were also well aware that the Egyptian and even the Ethiopian soldiery had never been able successfully to withstand a determined attack by the Assyrian battalions, and that when once the desert which protected Egypt had been crossed, she would, like Babylon fall an easy prey to their arms. It would merely be necessary to guard against the possible danger of opposition being offered to the passage of the invading host by the Idumæan and Arab tribes sparsely scattered over the country between the Nile and the Gulf of Akabah, as their hostility would be a cause of serious uneasiness. An expedition, sent against Milukhkha[1] in 675 B.C., had taught the inhabitants to respect the power of Assyria; but the campaign had not been brought to a satisfactory conclusion, for the King of Elam, Khumbân-khaldash II., seeing his rival occupied at the opposite extremity of his empire, fell unexpectedly upon Babylon, and pushing forward as far as Sippara, laid waste the surrounding country; and his hateful presence even prevented the god Shamash from making his annual progress outside the walls of the city. The people of Bît-Dakkuri seem to have plucked up courage at his approach, and invaded the neighbouring territory, probably that of Borsippa. Esarhaddon was absent on a distant expedition, and the garrisons scattered over the province were not sufficiently strong in numbers to risk a pitched battle: Khumbân-khaldash, therefore, marched back with his booty to Susa entirely unmolested. He died suddenly in his palace a few days after his return, and was succeeded by his brother, Urtaku, who was too intent upon seating himself securely on the throne to send his troops on a second raid in the following year.[2] Esarhaddon deferred his revenge to a more convenient season, and utilised the respite fate had accorded him on the Elamite border to hasten his attack on Egypt (673 B.C.). The expedition was a failure, and Taharqa was greatly elated at having issued with honour from this trial of strength. As most of the countries over which his enemy exercised his supremacy were those which had been ruled

---

[1] The name of Milukhkha, first applied to the countries in the neighbourhood of the Persian Gulf, had been transferred to the western coasts of Arabia, as well as that of Magan.

by his Theban ancestors in days gone by, Taharqa engraved on the base of his statue a list of nations and towns opied from one of the monuments of Ramses II. The Khâti, Carchemish, Mitanni, Arvad—in short, a dozen peoples already extinct or in their decline, and whose names were merely perpetuated in the stereotyped official lists,—were enumerated in the list of his vanquished foes side by side with Assyria. It was a mere piece of bravado for never, even when victorious, did he set foot on Syrian soil; but all the same the victory had caused the invading host to retire, and the fame of this exploit, spreading throughout Asia, was not without its effect on the minds of the inhabitants. The island of Tyre had never officially recognised the Assyrian suzerainty. The Tyrians had lived in peace since the defeat of Elulai, and had maintained constant commercial relations with the continent without interfering in active politics: they had, perhaps, even been permitted to establish some settlements on the coast of the mainland. Their king, Bâal, now deemed the moment a propitious one for coming forward and recovering his lost territory, and since the Greek princes of Cyprus had ranged themselves under the hegemony of Assyria, he thought he could best counterbalance their influence by seeking support from Egypt, whose ancient greatness was apparently reviving. He therefore concluded an alliance with Taharqa,[1]

[1] The alliance of Bâal with Taharqa is mentioned in the fragment of the *Annals*, under the date of year X., and the name Bâal is still decipherable amid the defaced lines which contained the account of events which took place before that year. I think we may reasonably assign the first understanding between the two sovereigns either to the actual year of the first campaign or to the following year.

and it would be no cause for astonishment if we should one day discover that Judah had followed his example. Hezekiah had devoted his declining years to religious reformation, and the organisation of his kingdom under the guidance of Isaiah or the group of prophets of which Isaiah was the leader. Judah had increased in population, and had quickly recovered its prosperity; when Hezekiah died, about 686 B.C., it had entirely regained its former vigour, but the memory of the disasters of 701 was still sufficiently fresh in the minds of the people to prevent the change of sovereign being followed by a change of policy. Manasseh, who succeeded his father, though he did not walk, as Hezekiah had done, in the ways of the Lord, at least remained loyal to his Assyrian masters. It is, however, asserted that he afterwards rebelled, though his reason for doing so is not explained, and that he was carried captive to Babylon as a punishment for this crime: he succeeded, nevertheless, in regaining favour, and was reinstated at Jerusalem on condition of not repeating his offence. If this statement is true, as I believe it to be, it was probably after the Egyptian campaign of 673 B.C.[1] that his conspiracy

[1] The fact of Manasseh's captivity is only known to us from the testimony of 2 *Chron.* xxxiii. 10–13, and most modern critics consider it apocryphal. The moral development which accompanies the narrative, and the conversion which follows it, are certainly later additions, but the story may have some foundation in fact; we shall see later on that Necho I., King of Sais, was taken prisoner, led into captivity, and received again into favour in the same way as Manasseh is said to have been. The exile to Babylon, which at one time appeared to demonstrate the unauthenticity of the passage, would be rather in favour of its authenticity. Esarhaddon was King of Babylon during the whole of his reign, and the great works which he executed in that city obliged him, we know, to transport

150    THE POWER OF ASSYRIA AT ITS ZENITH

with Bâal took place. The Assyrian governors of the neighbouring provinces easily crushed these attempts at independence, but, the islands of Tyre being secure from attack, they were obliged to be content with establishing a series of redoubts along the coast, and with prohibiting the Tyrians from having access to the mainland.

The promptitude of their action quenched the hopes of the Egyptian party and prevented the spread of the revolt Esarhaddon was, nevertheless, obliged to put off the fulfilment of his schemes longer than he desired: complica tions arose on his northern frontiers, near the sources the Tigris, which distracted his attention from the intrigues taking place on the banks of the Nile. Urartu hard pressed by the Cimmerians and Scythians, had lived for a quarter of a century in a condition of sullen peace with Assyria, and its kings avoided anything which could bring them into conflict with their hereditary rival Argistis II. had been succeeded by one of his sons, Rusas II., and both of them had been more intent upon strengthening their kingdom than on extending its area they had rebuilt their capital, Dhuspas, on a magnificent scale, and from the security of their rocky home they watched the course of events without taking any part in it unless forced to do so by circumstances. Andaria, chief of Lubdi, one of the remote mountain districts, so difficult of access that it always retained its independence in spite of frequent attacks, had seized Shupria, a province which had been from very early times subject to the sovereigns

thither a large proportion of the prisoners whom he brought back from his wars.

of Nineveh, and was the first to be colonised by them. The inhabitants, forgetful of their origin, had yielded voluntarily to Andaria; but this prince, after receiving their homage, was seized with alarm at his own audacity. He endeavoured to strengthen his position by an alliance with the Cimmerians,[1] and the spirit of insubordination which he aroused spread beyond the Euphrates; Mugallu of Milid, a king of the Tabal, resorted to such violent measures that Esarhaddon was alarmed lest the wild mountaineers of the Taurus should pour down upon the plain of Kuî and lay it waste. The danger would indeed have been serious had all these tribes risen simultaneously; but the Cimmerians were detained in Asia Minor by their own concerns,[2] and Mugallu, when he saw the Assyrian troops being concentrated to bring him to reason, remained quiet. The extension of Lubdi was not likely to meet with favour in the eyes of Rusas; he did not respond to the advances made to him, and Esarhaddon opened his campaign against the rebels without having to dread the intervention of Urartu. Andaria, besieged in his capital of Ubbumi, laid aside his royal robes, and, assuming the ragged garments of a slave, appeared upon the ramparts and pleaded for mercy in a voice choked with tears: " Shupria, the country which has sinned against thee, will yield to thee of her own accord; place thy oficers over her, she will vow obedience to thee; impose

[1] This seems, indeed, to be proved by a tablet in which Esarhaddon, addressing the god Shamash, asks him if the Cimmerians or Urartians will unite with a certain prince who can be no other than the King of Shupria.

[2] It was about this time they were dealing the death-blow to the kingdom of Phrygia.

on her a ransom and an annual tribute for ever. I am a robber, and for the crime I have committed I will make amends fifty-fold." Esarhaddon would listen to no terms before a breach had been effected in the city walls. This done, he pardoned the prince who had taken refuge in the citadel, but resumed possession of Shupria: its inhabitants were mercilessly punished, being condemned to slavery and their lands and goods divided among new colonists Many Urartians were numbered among the captives these Esarhaddon separated from the rest, and sent back to Rusas as a reward for his having remained neutral All this had barely occcupied the space of one month the month of Tebet. The firstfruits of the spoil reserved for Uruk had already reached that town by the month Kislev, and the year was not so far advanced as to render further undertakings impossible when the death of the queen, on the 5th Adar, suspended all warlike enterprises. The last months of the year were given up to mourning, and the whole of 671 B.C. passed without further action. The Ethiopian king was emboldened by this inactivity on the part of his foe renew his intrigues with Syria with redoubled energy at one moment, indeed, the Philistines of Ashkelon, secretly instigated, seemed on the point of revolt.[1] They held themselves, however, in check, and Esarhaddon, reassured as to their attitude, entered into negotiations with the

---

[1] Ashkelon is mentioned in two of the prayers in which Esarhaddon consults Shamash on the subject of his intended campaign in Egypt he seems to fear lest that city and the Bedâwin of the Idumæan desert should espouse the cause of the King of Ethiopia.

sheikhs of the Arab tribes, and purchased their assistance to cross the desert of Sinai. He bade them assemble at Raphia, at the western extremity of Palestine, each chief bringing all the camels he could command, and as many skins of water as their beasts could carry: this precaution, a wise one at any time, might secure the safety of the army in case Taharqa should have filled up the wells which marked the stages in the caravan route.[1] When all was ready, Esarhaddon consulted the oracle of Shamash, and, on receiving a favourable reply from the god, left Nineveh in the beginning of the month Nisân, 670 B.C., to join the invading army in Syria.[2] He made a detour in order to inspect the lines of forts which his generals had established along the coast opposite Tyre, and strengthened their garrisons to prevent Bâal from creating a diversion in the rear of his base of operations; he then proceeded southwards to the neighbourhood of Aphek, in the territory of the tribe of Simeon. The news which there met him must doubtless have informed him that the Bedâwin had been won over in the interval by the emissaries of Taharqa, and that he would run great risk by proceeding with his campaign before bringing them back to a sense of their

[1] This information is furnished by the fragment of the *Annals*. The Assyrian text introduces this into the narrative in such a manner that it would appear as if these negotiations were carried on at the very commencement of the campaign; it is, however, more probable that they were concluded beforehand, as occurred later on, in the time of Cambyses, when the Persians invaded Egypt.

[2] The published texts refer to the second Egyptian campaign of Esarhaddon. The reply of the god is not easy to interpret, but it was certainly favourable, since the expedition took place.

duty. On leaving Aphek[1] he consequently turned south
wards, and plunged into the heart of the desert, as if he
had renounced all designs upon Egypt for that season
and was bent only on restoring order in Milukhkha
Magân before advancing further. For six weeks he
marched in short stages, without other water than the
supply borne, in accordance with his commands, by the
Arab camels, passing through tracts of desert infested by
strange birds and double-headed serpents; when he had at
length dispersed the bands which had endeavoured to
oppose his advance, he suddenly turned in a north-wester y
direction, and, following the dry bed of the torrent of
Muzur, at length reached Raphia. From thence he did
not select the usual route, which follows the coast-line and
leads to Pelusium, a place which he may have feared was
too well defended, but he again pressed forward across the
sands of the desert, and in the first days of Tammuz
reached the cultivated land of the Delta by way of
Wady Tumilât. The frontier garrisons, defeated on the
of Tammuz near Ishkhupri,[2] retreated in good order

[1] The defaced name of the country in which this Aphek was situated was read as Samirina and translated "Samaria" by the first editor. This interpretation has been adopted by most historians, who have seen in Aphek the town of this name belonging to the western portion of Manasseh. Budge read it Samina, and this reading, verified by Craig, gave Winckler the idea of identifying Samina or Simina with the tribe of Simeon, and Aphek with the Aphekah (*Josh.* xv. 53) in the mountains of Judah.

[2] The text on the stele at Zinjirli gives a total of fifteen days' march from Ishkhupri to Memphis, while *Pinches' Babyl. Chron.* indicates three battles as having been fought on the 3rd, 16th, and 18th of Tammuz, and the taking of Memphis as occurring on the 22nd of the same month. If fifteen days is precisely accurate for the length of march, Esarhaddon would have reached Ishkhupri about the 27th of Sivan.

Taharqa, hastening to their succour, disputed the ground inch by inch, and engaged the invaders in several conflicts, two at least of which, fought on the 16th and 18th of Tammuz, were regular pitched battles, but in every case the Assyrian tactics triumphed in spite of the dashing onslaught of the Egyptians; Memphis succumbed on the 22nd, after an assault lasting merely a few hours, and was mercilessly sacked. The Ethiopian king, with his army decimated and exhausted, gave up the struggle, and beat a hasty retreat southwards. The attack had been made with such rapidity that he had had no time to remove his court from the "palace of the White Wall" to the Saîd; the queen, therefore, together with other women of less exalted rank, fell into the hands of the conqueror, besides the crown-prince, Ushana-horu, several younger sons and daughters, and such of the children of Sabaco and Shabîtoku as resided at court. But the victory had cost the Assyrians dearly, and the enemy still appeared to them so formidable that Esarhaddon prudently abstained from pursuing him up the Nile Valley. He favourably received those feudal lords and petty kings who presented themselves to pay him homage, and confirmed them in possession of their fiefs, but he placed over them Assyrian governors and imposed new official names on their cities; thus Athribis was officially called Limir-pateshî-assur, and other cities received the names Assur-makan-tishkul, Bît-marduk-sha-assur-taru, Shaîmuk-assur. He further imposed on them a heavy annual tribute of more than six talents of gold and six hundred talents of silver, besides robes and woven stuffs, wine, skins, horses, sheep, and asses; and having accomplished this, he retraced his steps towards the north east with immense booty and innumerable convoys of prisoners. The complete defeat of the Ethiopian power filled not only Esarhaddon himself but all Asia with

SOUTHERN PROMONTORY AT THE MOUTH OF THE NAHR-EL-KELB.[1]

astonishment. His return to Nineveh was a triumphal progress; travelling through Syria by short stages, he paraded his captives and trophies before the peoples and princes who had so long relied on the invincible power of the Pharaoh. Esarhaddon's predecessors had more than once inscribed the record of their campaigns on rocks of the Nahr-el-Kelb, beside the bas-relief engraved

[1] Drawn by Boudier, from a photograph recently brought back by Lortet.

there by Ramses II, and it had been no small gratification to their pride thus to place themselves on a footing of equality with one of the most illustrious heroes of the ancient Egyptian empire. The footpath which skirts the southern bank of the river, and turning to the south is continued along the seashore, was bordered by the great stelæ in which, one after another, they had thought to immortalise their glory; following their example, Esarhaddon was in like manner pleased to celebrate his prowess, and exhibit the ancient lords of the world subjugated to his will. He erected numerous triumphal monuments along his route, and the stele which was discovered at one of the gates of

STELE OF ESARHADDON AT THE NAHR-EL-KELB.[1]

[1] Drawn by Faucher-Gudin, from a photograph brought back by Lortet.

Zinjirli is, doubtless, but an example of those which he erected in other important cities. He is represented on the Zinjirli stele standing erect, while at his feet are two kneeling prisoners, whom he is holding by a bridle of cord fastened to metal rings passed through their lips; these figures represent Bâal of Tyre and Taharqa of Napata, the latter with the uræus on his forehead As a matter of fact, these kings were safe beyond his reach one surrounded by the sea, the other above the cataracts, and the people were well aware that they did not form part of the band of prisoners which defiled before their eyes; but they were accustomed to the vain and extravagant boastings of their conquerors, and these very exaggerations enabled them to understand more fully the extent of the victory. Esarhaddon thenceforward styled himself King of Egypt, King of the Kings of Egypt, of the Saïd and of Kush, so great was his pride at having trampled underfoot the land of the Delta. And, in fact, Egypt had

STELE OF ZINJIRLI.[1]

[1] Drawn by Faucher-Gudin, from a photograph of the original in Berlin Museum.

for a century, been the only one of the ancient Eastern states which had always eluded the grasp of Assyria. The Elamites had endured disastrous defeats, which had cost them some of their provinces; the Urartians had been driven back into their mountains, and no longer attempted to emerge from them; Babylon had nearly been annihilated in her struggles for independence; while the Khâti, the Phœnicians, Damascus, and Israel had been absorbed one after another in the gradual extension of Ninevite supremacy. Egypt, although she had had a hand in all their wars and revolutions, had never herself paid the penalty of her intrigues, and even when she had sometimes risked her troops on the battle-fields of Palestine, her disasters had not cost her more than the loss of a certain number of men: having once retired to the banks of the Nile, no one had dared to follow, and the idea had gained credence among her enemies as well as among her friends that Egypt was effectually protected by the desert from every attack. The victory of Esarhaddon proved that she was no more invulnerable than the other kingdoms of the world, and that before a bold advance the obstacles, placed by nature in the path of an invader, disappeared; the protecting desert had been crossed, the archers and chariots of Egypt had fled before the Assyrian cavalry and pikemen, her cities had endured the ignominy and misery of being taken by storm, and the wives and daughters of her Pharaohs had been carried off into servitude in common with the numerous princesses of Elam and Syria of that day. Esarhaddon filled his palaces with furniture and woven stuffs, with vases of precious metal and sculptured ivories, with glass ornaments and statuettes looted from Memphis: his workers in marble took inspiration from the sphinxes of Egypt to modify the winged, human-headed lions upon which the columns of their palaces rested, and the plans of his architects became more comprehensive at the mere announcement of such a vast amount of spoil. The palace they had begun to build at Nineveh, on the ruins of an ancient edifice, already surpassed all previous architectural efforts The alabaster quarries of the Assyrian mountains and the forests of Phœnicia had alike been put under contribution to face the walls of its state apartments; twenty-two chiefs of the country of the Khâti, of Phœnicia, and of the Mediterranean littoral—among them the Greek kings of Cyprus—had vied with one another in supplying Esarhaddon with great beams of pine, cedar, and cypress for its construction. The ceilings were of cedar supported by pillars of cypress-wood encircled by silver and iron; stone lions and bulls stood on either side of the gates, and the doors were made of cedar and cypress incrusted or overlaid with iron, silver and ivory. The treasures of Egypt enabled Esarhaddon to complete this palace and begin a new one at Calah, where the build ings erected somewhat hurriedly by Tiglath-pileser III had already fallen into ruin. Some of the slabs on which the latter conqueror had engraved his Annals, and counted the principal episodes of his campaigns, were removed and transferred to the site selected by Esar haddon, and one of the surfaces of each was pared down in order to receive new pictures and fresh inscriptions

They had, however, hardly been placed in the stonemason's hands when the work was interrupted.[1] It may have been that Esarhaddon had to suspend all his operations while putting down some conspiracy. At any rate, we know that in 669 B.C. many high personages of his court were seized and executed. The question of the succession to the throne was still undecided; Sinidinabal, the son whom Esarhaddon had previously designated as his heir presumptive, was dead, and the people feared lest he should choose from among his other sons some prince who had not their interests at heart. The king's affection for Babylon had certainly aroused jealousy and anxiety among his Assyrian subjects,

ASSYRIAN SPHINX IN EGYPTIAN STYLE SUPPORTING THE BASE OF A COLUMN.[2]

---

[1] The date of the building of the palace at Calah is furnished by the inscriptions, in which Esarhaddon assumes the title of King of Egypt.

[2] Drawn by Boudier, from the alabaster sculpture reproduced by Layard.

and perhaps some further tokens of preference made them uneasy lest he should select Shamash-shumukîn, one of his children who manifested the same tendencies, and who was, moreover, the son of a Babylonian wife. Most of the nobles who had been led to join the conspiracy paid for their indiscretion with their heads, but their opposition gave the sovereign cause for reflection, and decided him to modify his schemes. Convinced that it was impossible to unite Babylon and Nineveh permanently under the same ruler, he reluctantly decided to divide his kingdom into two parts—Assyria, the strongest portion falling naturally to his eldest son, Assur-bani-pal, while Babylonia was assigned to Shamash-shumukîn, on condition of his paying homage to his brother as suzerain [1] The best method to ensure his wishes being carried into effect was to prepare their way for the fulfilment while he was still alive; and rebellions which broke out about t is time beyond the isthmus afforded a good opportunity for so doing.

Egypt was at this period divided into twenty states of various dimensions, very nearly the same as had existed a century before, when Piônkhi had, for the first time brought the whole country under Ethiopian rule.[2] In the south, the extensive Theban province occupied both sides of the river from Assuan to Thinis and Khemmis. It was nominally governed by Amenertas or her daughter

[1] Winckler considers that Assur-bani-pal was the leader of the conspiracy, and that he obliged his father to recognise him as heir to the crown of Assyria, and to associate him on the throne.

[2] The list of the principalities in the time of Esarhaddon and Assu bani-pal is found on the cylinders of Assur-bani-pal.

Shapenuapît, but the administration was, as usual, entrusted to a member of the priestly college, at that time to Montumihâît, Count of Thebes, and fourth prophet of Amon.[1] The four principalities of Thinis, Siut, Hermopolis, and Heracleopolis separated it from the small kingdom of Memphis and Sais, and each of the regions of the Delta was divided into one or two fiefs, according to the number and importance of the towns it contained. In the south, Thebes was too directly under the influence of Ethiopia to be able to exercise an independent policy with regard to the rest of the country. In the north, two families contested the supremacy more or less openly. One of them, whose hereditary domains included the Arabian, and parts of the surrounding nomes, was then represented by a certain Pakruru. He had united under his banner the numerous petty chiefs of the eastern side of the Delta, the heirs of the ancient dynasties of Tanis and Bubastis, and his energy or ability must have made a good impression on the minds of his contemporaries, for they handed down his memory to their successors, who soon metamorphosed him into a popular legendary hero, famed both for his valour and wisdom. The nobles of the western nomes acknowledged as their overlords the regents of Sais, the descendants of that Bocchoris who had for a short while brought the whole valley of the Nile under his sway. Sabaco, having put his rival to death, had installed in his hereditary domains an Ethiopian named Ammeris, but this

[1] The Assyrian name of this personage, spelt first Mantimiankhi, has been more accurately transcribed Mantimikhi. The identification with the Montumihâît of the Theban documents, is now generally adopted.

Ammeris had disappeared from the scene about the same time as his patron, in 704 B.C., and after him three princes at least had succeeded to the throne, namely, Stephinates, Nekhepsos, and Necho.[1] Stephinates had died about 680 B.C., without accomplishing anything which was worth recording. Nekhepsos had had no greater opportunities distinguishing himself than had fallen to the lot of his father, and yet legends grew up round his name as round that of Pakruru: he was reputed to have been a great soothsayer, astrologer, and magician, and medical treatises were ascribed to him, and almanacs much esteemed by the superstitious in the Roman period.[2] Necho had already occupied the throne for three or four years when the invasion of 670 B.C. delivered him from the Ethiopian supremacy. He is represented as being brave, energetic and enterprising, ready to hazard everything in order to attain the object towards which the ambition of his ancestors had been tending for a century past, namely, to restore unity to the ancient kingdom under the rule of the house of Sais. The extent of his realm, and, above all, the

[1] The lists of Eusebius give the series Ammeres, Stephinates, Nekhepsos, Necho I., but Lepsius displaced Ammeres and identified him with the queen Amenertas; others have thought to recognise in him Miamun Piônkhi, or Tanuatamanu, the successor of Taharqa. He must, however, be left in this place in the list, and we may perhaps consider him as the founder of the XXVI[th] dynasty. If the number of *seven* years for the reign of Stephinates is adopted, we must suppose either that Manetho passed over the name of a prince at the beginning of the XXVI[th] dynasty, or that Ammeris was on y enthroned at Memphis after the death of Sabaco; but the lists of the Syncellus and of Sothis assign 27 years to the reign of Stephinates.

[2] The astrological works of Nekhepsos are cited, among others, by Pliny and it is probably he whom a Greek papyrus of the Salt Collection mentions under the name of Nekheus.

possession of Memphis, gave him a real superiority, and Esarhaddon did not hesitate to esteem him above his competitors; the Ninevite scribes placed him in the first rank, and he heads the list of the Egyptian vassals. He soon had an opportunity of proving his devotion to his foreign suzerain. Taharqa did not quietly accept his defeat, and Egypt looked to him to be revenged on the Assyrian as soon as he should have reorganised his army. He once more, accordingly, took the field in the middle of 669 B.C.; the barons of the Saîd rallied to his standard without hesitation, and he soon re-entered the "White Wall," but there his advance was arrested. Necho and the neighbouring chiefs of the Delta, held in check by the presence of Semitic garrisons, did not venture to proclaim themselves on his side, and awaited under arms the arrival of Assyrian reinforcements.[1] Esarhaddon, in spite of failing health, assumed command of the troops, and before leaving home carried out the project to which the conspiracy of the preceding year had given rise; he assigned the government of Babylon to Shamash-shumukîn, and solemnly designated Assur-bani-pal as the heir to Assyria proper, and to the suzerainty over the whole empire.[2] On the 12th of Iyyar,

[1] The first Egyptian campaign of Assur-bani-pal is also the last campaign of Esarhaddon, and Assur-bani-pal appropriated all the earlier incidents of it, some of which belong to the sole reign of his father, and some to the few weeks in which he shared the throne with him.

[2] The association of Assur-bani-pal with his father on the throne was pointed out by G. Smith, who thought he could fix the date about 673 B.C., three or four years before the death of Esarhaddon. Tiele showed that Assur-bani-pal was then only made viceroy, and assigned his association in the sovereignty to the year 671 or 670 B.C., about the time of the second Egyptian campaign, while Hommel brought it down to 669. Winckler has,

668 B.C., on the day of the feast of Gula, he presented their new lord to all the inhabitants of Assyria, both small and great, who had assembled to be present at the ceremony, which ended in the installation of the prince in the palace of Bîtriduti, reserved for the heirs-apparent. A few weeks later Esarhaddon set out for Egypt, but his malady became more serious on the journey, and he died on the 10th of Arakhsamna, in the twelfth year of his reign.[1] When we endeavour to conjure up his image before us, we fancy we are right in surmising that he was not cast in the ordinary mould of Assyrian monarchs. The history of his campaigns shows that he was as active and resolute as Assur-nazir-pal and Shalmaneser III., but he did not add to these good qualities their inflexible harshness towards their subjects, nor their brutal treatment of conquered foes. Circumstances in which they would have shown themselves merciless, he seized upon as occasions for clemency, and if massacres and executions are recorded among the events of his reign, at least he does not class them among the most important : the records of his wars do not continually speak of rebels flayed alive, kings impaled before the gates of their cities, and whole populations decimated by fire and sword. Of all the Assyrian conquerors, he is almost the

with much reason, placed the date in 668 B.C. The Assyrian documents do not mention the coronation of Shamash-shumukîn, for Assur-bani-pal afterwards affected to consider his brother a mere viceroy, appointed by himself after the death of his father Esarhaddon ; but an examination of all the circumstances has shown that the enthronement of Shamash-shumukîn at Babylon was on a par with that of Assur-bani-pal at Nineveh, and that both owed their elevation to their father.

[1] Arakhsamna corresponds to the Jewish Marcheswân, and to our month of May.

only one for whom the historian can feel any regard, or from the study of whose reign he passes on with regret to pursue that of others in due course.

As soon as Esarhaddon had passed away, the separation of the two parts of the empire which he had planned was effected almost automatically: Assur-bani-pal proclaimed himself King of Assyria, and Shamash-shumukîn, in like manner, King of Babylon. One fact, which seems insignificant enough to us when we read it in the Annals, but was decisive in the eyes of their contemporaries, sanctioned the transformation thus accomplished: Bel and the gods of Accad quitted Assur in the month of Iyyâr and returned to their resting-place in Babylon. The restoration of the images to their own country became necessary as soon as it was decided to have a king in Karduniash, even though he were an Assyrian. To enable him to exercise legitimate authority, he must have celebrated the rites and "taken the hands of Bel," but it was a question whether this obligation could be fulfilled if Bel remained a prisoner in the neighbouring capital. Assur-bani-pal believed for a moment that this difficulty could be obviated, and consulted Shamash on this delicate question: "Shamash-shumukîn, the son of Esarhaddon, the King of Assyria, can he in this year take the hands of Bel, the mighty lord Marduk, in this very city, and then go to Babylon with the favour of Bel! If that would be pleasing to thy great divinity and to the mighty lord Marduk, thy great divinity must know it." The reply was not favourable, and Shamash gave it as his opinion that Bel could not act as a sovereign lord while still languishing in prison in a city which was not his own. Assur-bani-pal had to resign himself to the release his captive, and he did it with a good grace. He proceeded in pomp to the temple of Assur, where Marduk was shut up, and humbly entreated the exiled deity to vouchsafe to return to his own country. "Think on Babylon, which thou didst bring to nought in the rage of thy heart, and turn thy face towards the temple of Ê-sagilla, the lofty seat of thy divinity! Revisit thy city which thou hast forsaken to inhabit a place which is not worthy of thee, and do thou thyself, O Marduk, lord of the gods, give the command to return to Babylon." The statue set out on its journey, and was escorted by a solemn procession headed by the two kings. The gods, by one accord, came forth from their cities and saluted the traveller as he passed by—Beltis of Agadê, Nebo of Borsippa, Shamash of Sippara, and Nirgal. At length he reached his beloved city, and entered Ê-sagilla in the midst of an immense throng of people. The kings headed

ASSUR-BANI-PAL AS A BEARER OF OFFERINGS.[1]

[1] Drawn by Boudier, from a photograph in Lehmann.

the *cortège*, and the delighted multitude joined their two names with that of the god in their acclamations: it was a day never to be forgotten. Assur-bani-pal, in his capacity of suzerain, opened the sacred edifice, and then presented his brother, who thereupon "took the hands of Bel." A quarter of a century had not passed since the victorious Sennacherib had, as he thought, inflicted a mortal blow on the one power which stood in the way of Assyria's supremacy in Western Asia; already, in spite of his efforts, the city had sprung up from its ruins as vigorous as ever, and his sons and grandsons had felt themselves irresistibly drawn to resuscitate that which their ancestors had desired to annihilate irrevocably. Babylon had rebuilt her palaces, her walls, and her temples; she had received back her gods without a war, and almost without any agitation, by the mere force of the prestige she exercised over all around her, and even over her conquerors. As a matter of fact, she had not regained her former position, and was still depressed and enfeebled by the blow which had laid her low; in addition to this, her king was an Assyrian, and a vassal of Assyria, but

SHAMASH-SHUMUKÎN AS A BEARER OF OFFERINGS.[1]

[1] Drawn by Boudier, from a photograph in Lehmann.

nevertheless he was her own king, and hers alone. Her dependence was already half regained. Shamash-shumukîn established his court at Babylon, and applied himself from the outset to restore, as far as he was able, the material and moral forces of his kingdom. Assur-bani-pal, on his side, met with no opposition from his subjects, but prudence cautioned him not to estrange them; the troubles of the preceding year were perhaps not so completely suppressed as to prevent the chiefs who had escaped punishment from being encouraged by the change of sovereign to renew their intrigues. The king, therefore, remained in Nineveh to inaugurate his rule, and confided to his generals the charge of conducting the expeditions which had been undertaken during his father's lifetime.[1] One of these undertakings was unimportant. Tandaî of Kirbit, a petty chief, was continually engaged in harassing the inhabitants of Yamutbal; he bore down upon them every year, and after dealing a blow, retreated to his hiding-place in the mountains. He was attacked in his stronghold, and carried away captive with all his people into Egypt, at the furthest extremity of the empire, to serve in Assyrian garrisons in the midst of the fellahîn.[2]

[1] In the numerous documents relating to the reign of Assur-bani-pal the facts are arranged in geographical order, not by the dates of the successive expeditions, and the chronological order of the campaigns is all the mo e difficult to determine accurately, as *Pinches' Babylonian Chronicle* fails us after the beginning of this reign, immediately after the mention of above-mentioned war with Kirbit. Even the *Eponym Canon* is only accu ate down to 666 B.C.; in that year there is a break, and although we possess the succeeding period more than forty names of eponyms, their classification is not at present absolutely certain.

[2] The expedition against Kirbit is omitted in certain documents; it is

Meanwhile, the army which Esarhaddon had been leading against Taharqa pursued its course under command of the Tartan.[1] Syria received it submissively, and the twenty-two kings who still possessed a shadow of autonomy in the country sent assurances of their devotion to the new monarch: even Yakînlu, King of Arvad, who had aroused suspicion by frequent acts of insubordination,[2] thought twice before rebelling against his terrible suzerain, and joined the rest in paying both homage and tribute. Cyprus and also Phœnicia remained faithful to their allegiance, and, what was of still more consequence, the states which lay nearest to Egypt—Philistia, Judah, Moab, and Ammon; the Assyrians were thus able to push forward to the Delta without losing time in repressing rebellions along their route. The Ethiopians had entrenched themselves at Karbanîti;[3] they were, however, once more defeated, and

inserted in the others in the fourth place, between the wars in Asia Minor and the campaign against the Mannai. The place assigned to it in the *Bab. Chron.* quite in the beginning of the reign, is confirmed by a fragment of a tablet quoted by Winckler. Perhaps it was carried out by a Babylonian army: although Assur-bani-pal claimed the glory of it, by reason of his suzerainty over Karduniash.

[1] The text of *Tablet K 2675–K 228 of the Brit. Mus.*, states distinctly that the Tartan commanded the first army.

[2] Assur-bani-pal, acting in the name of his father, Esarhaddon, King of Assyria, had consulted Shamash on the desirability of sending troops against Arvad: the prince of this city is called Ikkalu, which is a variant of Yakînlu. Winckler concluded that the campaign against Arvad took place before 668 B.C., in the reign of Esarhaddon. It seems to me more natural to place it on the return from Egypt, when the people of Arvad were demoralised by the defeat of the Pharaoh whose alliance they had hoped for.

[3] I had compared Karbanîti with the Qarbîna mentioned in the *Great Harris Papyrus*, and this identification was accepted by most Egyptologists, even after Brugsch recognised in Qarbîna the name of Canopus or a town

left so many of their soldiers dead upon the field, that Taharqa had not sufficient troops left to defend Memphis He retreated upon Thebes, where he strongly fortified himself; but the Tartan had not suffered less than his adversary, and he would have been unable to pursue him had not reinforcements promptly reached him. The Rab shakeh, who had been despatched from Nineveh with some Assyrian troops, had summoned to his aid the principal Syrian feudal chiefs, who, stimulated by the news of the victories achieved on the banks of the Nile, placed themselves unreservedly at his disposal. He ordered thei vessels to proceed along the coast as far as the Delta where he purposed to collect a fleet to ascend the river while their troops augmented the force already under his command. The two Assyrian generals, the Tartan and the Rabshakeh, quitted Memphis, probably in the early par of 667 B.C., and, cautiously advancing southwards, covered the distance separating the two Egyptian capitals in a steady march of forty days. When the Assyrians had advanced well up the valley, the princes of the Delta thought the opportunity had arrived to cut them off by a single bold stroke. They therefore opened cautious negotiations with the Ethiopian king, and proposed an arrangement which should secure their independence "We will divide the country between us, and neither us shall exercise authority over the other." However

---

near Canopus. It has been contested by Steindorff, and, in fact, Karbanîti could not be identified with Canopus, any more than the Qarbîna of Harris Papyrus; its site must be looked for in the eastern or central pa t of the Delta.

secretly these negotiations were conducted, they were certain to come to the knowledge of the Assyrian generals: the couriers were intercepted; and discovering from the despatches the extent of the danger, the Assyrians seized as many of the leaders of the league as they could. As a warning they sacked Sais, Mendes, and Tanis, demolishing the fortifications, and flaying or impaling the principal citizens before their city gates; they then sent two of the intriguing chiefs, Necho and Sharludari of Pelusium, bound hand and foot with chains, to Nineveh. Pakruru, of the Arabian nome, managed, however, to escape them. Taharqa, thus bereft of his allies, was no longer in a condition to repel the invader: he fled to Ethiopia, abandoning Thebes to its fate. The city was ransomed by despoiling the temple of Amon of half its treasures: Montumihâît transferred his allegiance unhesitatingly to Assur-bani-pal, and the whole of Egypt from the Mediterranean to the first cataract once more became Assyrian territory. The victory was so complete that Assur-bani-pal thought he might without risk show clemency to his prisoners. He summoned them to his presence, and there, instead of putting out their eyes or subjecting them to some horrible form of torture, he received them back into favour, and confirmed Necho in the possession of all the honours which Esarhaddon had conceded to him. He clothed him in a mantle of honour, and bestowed on him a straight-bladed sword with an iron scabbard ornamented with gold, engraved with his names and titles, besides rings, gold bracelets, chariots, horses, and mules; in short, all the appurtenances of royalty. Not content with restoring to him the cities of Sais and

Memphis, he granted him the fief of Athrîbis for his eldest son, Psammetichus. Moreover, he neglected no measure likely to show his supremacy. Athrîbis received the new name of Limir-patesi-assur, *may the high priest of Assur be*

MONTUMIHÂÎT, PRINCE OF THEBES.[1]

*glorious*, and Sais that of Kar-bel-matâti, *the fortress of the lord of the countries*. Psammetichus was called Nebo shezib-anni, *Nebo, deliver me*, and residents were installed at his court and that of his father, who were entrusted wit the *surveillance* of their conduct, and the task of keeping

[1] Drawn by Boudier, from the photograph by Miss Benson. It is not quite certain that this statue represents Montumihâît, as the inscription is wanting: the circumstances of the discovery, however, render it very probable.

them to the path of duty Necho thus well guarded thenceforward never faltered in his allegiance

The subjection of Egypt reacted on Syria and Asia Minor Of the only two states still existing along the Phœnician seaboard, one, namely Tyre had been in revolt for many years and the other Arvad showed symptoms of disaffection. Esarhaddon from lack of a sufficient fleet had never been able to subdue the former but he had interrupted the communications of the island with the mainland and the blockade which was constantly increasing in strictness had already lasted for four years On receipt of the news from Egypt Bâal realised that further resistance was hopeless he therefore delivered up to the victor his heir apparent Yahî-melek and one of his daughters together with other hostages besides silver gold and wood and intreated for pardon Assur bani pal left him in possession of his kingdom on condition of paying the regular tribute but Yakînlu, the King of Arvad met with harsher treatment In vain did he give up his sons his daughters and all his treasures his intractability had worn out the patience of his suzerain he was carried away captive to Nineveh and replaced by Azîbaal, his eldest

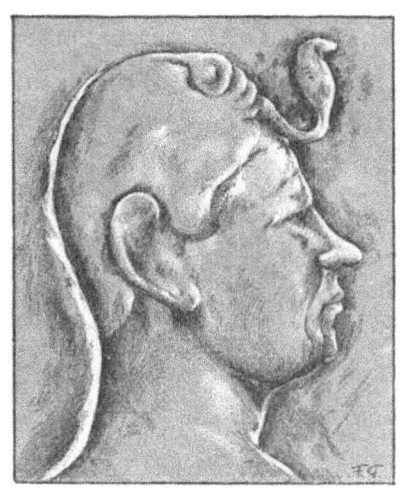

PSAMMETICHUS.[1]

Drawn by Faucher-Gudin, from a bas-relief in the British Museum son. Two chiefs of the Taurus—Mugallu of Tabal, who had given trouble to Esarhaddon in the last years of his life, and Sanda-sarmê of Cilicia—purchased immunity from the punishment due for various acts of brigandage, by gifts of horses, and by handing over each of them a daughter richly dowered, to the harem of the king at Nineveh. But these were incidents of slight moment, and their very insignificance proves how completely resigned to foreign domination the nations of the Mediterranean coast had now become. Vassal kings, princes, cities, peasants of the plain or shepherds of the mountains, all who were subject directly or indirectly to Assyria, had almost ceased to imagine that a change of sovereign afforded them any chance of regaining their independence. They no longer considered themselves the subjects of a conqueror whose death might free them from allegiance; they realised that they were the subjects of an empire whose power did not depend on the genius or incapacity of one man, but was maintained from age to age in virtue of the prestige it had attained, whatever might be the qualities of the reigning sovereign. The other independent states had at length come to the same conclusion, and the news of the accession of a fresh Assyrian king no longer awakened among them hopes of conquest or, at all events, of booty; such an occasion was regarded as a suitable opportunity for strengthening the bonds of neighbourly feeling or conciliatory friendship which united them to Assyria, by sending an embassy to congratulate the new sovereign. One of these embassies, which arrived about 667 B.C., caused much excitement at the court of Nineveh, and greatly flattered the vanity of the king. Reports brought back by sailors or the chiefs of caravans had revealed the existence of a kingdom of Lydia in the extreme west of Asia Minor, at the place of embarcation for crossing the sea.[1] It was known to be celebrated for its gold and its horses, but no direct relations between the two courts had ever been established, and the Lydian kings had hitherto affected to ignore the existence of Assyria. A revolution had broken out in this province a quarter of a century previously, which had placed on the throne of the Heraclidæ that family of the Mermnadæ whose previous history had been so tragic. Dascylus, who had made his home for a long time among the White Syrians, had no intention of abandoning his adopted country, when one day, about the year 698 B.C., a messenger arrived bidding him repair to Sardes without delay. His uncle Ardys, prince of Tyrrha, having no children, had applied to Sadyattes, beseeching him to revoke the sentence of banishment passed on his nephew. "My house is desolate," said he, "and all my kinsfolk are dead; and furthermore, Dascylus and his house have already been pardoned by thine ancestors." Sadyattes consented, but Dascylus, preferring not to return, sent his son Gyges, then about eighteen years of age, in his stead. Gyges was a tall and very beautiful youth, and showed unusual skill as a charioteer and in the use of weapons, so that his renown soon spread throughout the country. Sadyattes desired to see him, and being captivated by his bold demeanour,

[1] It is called *nagu sha nibirti tâmtim*, "the country of the crossing of the sea," or more concisely, "the country this side the sea."

enrolled him in his bodyguard, loaded him with presents and took him into his entire confidence. Gyges was clever enough to utilise the king's favour in order to enlarge his domains and increase his riches, and thus win partisans among the people and the body of "Friends." Carian mercenaries at that time formed one of the most vigorous and best disciplined contingents in the armies of the period.[1] The Carians were, above all, a military race, and are said to have brought the shield and helmet to their highest perfection; at Sardes they formed the garrison the citadel, and their captains were in high favour with the king. Gyges formed a fast friendship with Arselis of Mylasa, one of the chief of these officers, and thus made sure of the support of the garrison, and of the possibility recruiting a corps among the Carian clans who remained in their own country.[2] He thus incurred the bitter jealousy of the Tylonidæ, whose chief, Lixos, was ready to adopt any measures which might damage his rival, eve going so far as to simulate madness and run through streets of Sardes crying out that Gyges, the son Dascylus, was about to assassinate the king; but this stratagem did not succeed any better than his other treacherous devices. Meanwhile Sadyattes had sought the hand of Toudô,[3] daughter of Arnossos of Mysia, and sent his favourite to receive his affianced bride at the hand of

[1] Archilochus of Paros, a contemporary of Gyges, mentions the Carian mercenaries, and later on Ephorus said of them, that they had been the first to sell their services to strangers.

[2] The connection between Arselis and Gyges is mentioned by Plutarch.

[3] It is not certain whether the name is **Toudô or Trydô**.

her father. Gyges fell in love with her on the journey, and tried in vain to win her favour. She repulsed his advances with indignation, and on the very night of her marriage complained to her husband of the insult which had been offered her. Sadyattes swore that he would avenge her on the morrow; but Gyges, warned by a servant, slew the king before daybreak. Immediately after thus assassinating his sovereign, Gyges called together the "Friends," and ridding himself of those who were hostile to him, induced the others by bribes to further his designs; then descending to the place of public assembly, he summoned the people to a conclave. After a long and stormy debate, it was decided to consult the oracle at Delphi, which, corrupted by the gold from the Pactolus, enjoined on the Lydians to recognise Gyges as their king. He married Toudô, and by thus espousing the widow of the Heraclid sovereign, obtained some show of right to the crown; but the decision of the oracle was not universally acceptable, and war broke out, in which Gyges was victorious, thanks to the bravery of his Carian mercenaries.

His career soon served as the fabric on which the popular imagination was continually working fresh embroideries. He was reported at the outset to have been of base extraction, a mere soldier of fortune, who had raised himself by degrees to the highest posts and had finally supplanted his patron. Herodotus, following the poet Archilochus of Paros, relates how the last of the Heraclidæ, whom he calls by his private name of Kandaules, and not his official name of Sadyattes,[1] forcibly

[1] Schubert considers that the names Sadyattes and Kandaules belong to

insisted on exposing to the admiration of Gyges the naked beauty of his wife; the queen, thus outraged called upon the favourite to avenge the insult to her modesty by the blood of her husband, and then bestowed on him her hand, together with the crown. Plato made this story the groundwork of a most fantastic tale. Gyges according to him, was originally a shepherd, who, after a terrible storm, noticed a fissure in the ground, into which he crept; there he discovered an enormous bronze horse, half broken, and in its side the corpse of a giant with a gold ring on his finger. Chance revealed to that this ring rendered its wearer invisible: he set for the court in quest of adventures, seduced the queen murdered the king and seized his crown, accomplishing all this by virtue of his talisman.[1] According to a third legend, his crime and exaltation had been presaged by a wondrous prodigy. Two eagles of supernatural size had alighted on the roof of Tondô's room while she was still dwelling in her father's house, and the soothsayers who were consulted prognosticated that the princess would be the wife of two kings in a single night; and, in fact Gyges, having stabbed Sadyattes when his marriage but just consummated, forced Tondô to become his wife

two distinct persons. Kandaules, according to him, was probably a second son of Myrsos, who, after the murder of Sadyattes, disputed the possession of the crown with Gyges; in this case he was killed in battle by the Carian commander, Arselis, as related by Plutarch, and Gyges was not really king till after the death of Kandaules.

[1] This version is curious, because it has preserved for us one of earliest examples of a ring which renders its wearer invisible; it is well known how frequently such a talisman appears in Oriental tales of a late period.

on the spot without waiting for the morrow. Other stories were current in which the events were related with less of the miraculous element and which attributed the success of Gyges to the unbounded fidelity shown him by the Carian Arselis. In whatever manner it was brought about his accession marked the opening of a new era for Lydia. The country had always been noted for its valiant

LYDIAN HORSEMEN

and warlike inhabitants but the Heraclidæ had not expended its abundant resources on foreign conquest and none of the surrounding peoples suspected that it could again become the seat of a brilliant empire as in fabulous times

Gyges endeavoured to awaken the military instincts of his subjects. If he were not actually the first to organise that admirable cavalry corps which for nearly a century proved itself invincible on the field of battle at least

Drawn by Faucher-Gudin from a Lydian bas-relief now in the British Museum

he enlarged and disciplined it, giving it cohesion and daring; and it was well he did so, for a formidable danger already menaced his newly acquired kingdom. The Cim merians and Treres, so long as they did not act in concert had been unable to overcome the resistance offered by the Phrygians; their raids, annually renewed, had never resulted in more than the destruction of a city pillaging of an ill-defended district. But from 690 680 B.C. the Cimmerians, held in check by the bold front displayed by Sennacherib and Esarhaddon, had at last broken away from the seductions of the east, and poured down in force on the centre of the peninsula. King Midas after an heroic defence, at length gave way before their overwhelming numbers, and, rather than fall alive into the hands of the barbarians, poisoned himself by drinking the blood of a bull (676 B.C.).[1] The flower of his nobility perished with him, and the people of lower rank who survived were so terrified by the invasion, that they seemed in one day to lose entirely the brave and energetic character which had hitherto been their safeguard. The Cimmerians seized town after town;[2] they descended from the basin of the Sangarios into that of the Rhyndakos; they laid waste the Troad, and, about 670 B.C.,

---

[1] The date of 676 B.C. has been borrowed from Julius Africanus by the Christian chronologists of the Byzantine period; these latter made the fal of the Phrygian kingdom coincide with the reign of Amon in Judæa, this date is accepted by most modern historians.

[2] One fact alone, probably taken from the *Lydiaca* of Xanthus, is known to us concerning their operations in Phrygia, namely, the taking of and the capture of enormous stores of corn which were laid up in the silos in that city.

established themselves securely in the stronghold of Antandros, opposite the magnificent Æolian island of Lesbos, and ere long their advanced posts were face to face on all sides with the outposts of Lydia. Gyges resolutely held his own, and successfully repulsed them; but the struggle was too unequal between their vast hordes, recruited incessantly from their reserves in Thrace or the Caucasus, and his scanty battalions of Lydians, Carians, and Greeks. Unaided, he had no chance of re-opening the great royal highway, which the fall of the Phrygian monarchy had laid at the mercy of the barbarians along the whole of its middle course, and yet he was aware that a cessation of the traffic which passed between the Euphrates and the Hermos was likely to lead in a short time to the decay of his kingdom. If the numerous merchants who were wont to follow this ancient traditional route were once allowed to desert it and turn aside to one of the coast-roads which might replace it—either that of the Pontus in the north or of the Mediterranean in the south—they might not be willing to return to it even when again opened to traffic, and Lydia would lose for ever one of her richest sources of revenue.[1] We may well conceive that Gyges, whose fortune and very existence was thus in jeopardy, would seek assistance against these barbarians from the sovereign whose interests appeared

[1] Radet deserves credit for being the first to point out the economic reasons which necessarily led Gyges to make his attempt at forming an alliance with Assur-bani-pal. He has thus definitely dismissed the objections which some recent critics had raised against the authenticity of this episode in order to defend classic tradition and diminish the authority of the Assyrian texts.

identical with his own. The renown of the Assyrian
empire had penetrated far into the west; the Achæans
of Cyprus who were its subjects, the Greek colonists
Cilicia, and the soldiers whom the exigencies of the coast
trade brought to Syrian ports, must all have testified to
its splendour; and the fame of its conquests over the
Tabal and the peoples on the Halys had spread abroad
more than once during the previous century, and had
reached as far as the western extremity of the peninsula
of Asia Minor, by means of the merchants of Sardes or
Ionia. The Cimmerians had harassed Assyria, and still
continued to be a source of anxiety to her rulers; Gyges
judged that participation in a common hatred or danger
would predispose the king in his favour, and a dream
furnished him with a pretext for notifying to the court
of Nineveh his desire to enter into friendly relations with
it. He dreamed that a god, undoubtedly Assur, had
appeared to him in the night, and commanded him to
prostrate himself at the feet of Assur-bani-pal: "In his
name thou shalt overcome thine enemies." The next
morning he despatched horsemen to the great king, but
when the leader of the embassy reached the frontier and
met the Assyrians for the first time, they asked him
"Who, then, art thou, brother, thou from whose land
no courier has as yet visited our country?" The language
he spoke was unknown to them; they only gathered that
he desired to be conducted into the presence of the king
and consequently sent him on to Nineveh under good
escort. There the same obstacle presented itself, for none
of the official interpreters at the court knew the Lydian

tongue; however, an interpreter was at length discovered, who translated the story of the dream as best he could. Assur-bani-pal joyfully accepted the homage offered to him from such a far-off land, and from thenceforward some sort of alliance existed between Assyria and Lydia—an alliance of a very Platonic order, from which Gyges at least derived no sensible advantage. Some troops sent into the country of the White Syrians may have disquieted the Cimmerians, and, by causing a diversion in their rear, procured a respite for Lydia; but the caravan route across Asia Minor was only of secondary importance to the prosperity of Nineveh and the Syrian provinces, since the Phœnician navy provided sufficient outlets for their trade in the west. Assur-bani-pal lavished friendly speeches on the Lydians, but left them to bear the brunt of the attack alone, and devoutly thanked Assur for the security which their determined courage procured for the western frontier of his empire.

The Cimmerian peril being, for the present at least, averted, there no longer remained any foe to trouble the peace of the empire on the northern or eastern frontier, Urartu, the Mannai, and the Medes having now ceased to be formidable. Urartu, incessantly exposed to the ravages of the barbarians, had drawn closer and closer to Assyria; and though not actually descending to the point of owning its rival's superiority in order to obtain succour against these terrible foes, it yet carefully avoided all pretexts for war, and persistently maintained friendly relations with its powerful neighbour. Its kings, Rusas II. and his successor Erimenas, no longer meditated feats of arms and successful raids, but devoted themselves to building their city walls erecting palaces and temples, and planning pleasant retreats in the mountain fastnesses, where they lived surrounded by gardens planted at great cost, watered by streams brought thither from distant springs. The Mannai submitted without a murmur to their Assyrian governors and the Medes, kept in check by the garrisons of Parsua and Kharkhar, seemed to have laid aside much of their fierce and turbulent disposition. Esarhaddon had endeavoured to conciliate the good will of Elam by a signal service. He had supplied its inhabitants with corn, wine and provisions of all sorts during a famine which had afflicted the country about 670 B.C.; nor had his good will ended there. He refused to bring into servitude those Elamite subjects who had taken refuge with their families on Assyrian territory to escape the scourge, although the rights of nations authorised him so to do, but havi g nourished them as long as the dearth lasted, he then sent them back to their fellow-citizens. Urtaku of Elam had thenceforward maintained a kind of sullen neutrality entering only into secret conspiracies against Babylonian prefects on the Tigris. The Aramæans in valleys of the Ulaî, indeed, were restless, and several their chiefs, Bel-ikîsha of the Gambulâ, and Nabo shumirîsh, plotted in secret with Marduk-shumibni, the Elamite general in command on the frontier. But no hint of this had yet transpired, and peace apparently reigned there as elsewhere. Never had the empire been so respected; never had it united so many diverse nations under one sceptre—Egyptians, Syrians, tribes of the

Taurus, and the mountain districts round the Tigris and Euphrates, Manuai, Medes, Babylonians, and Arabs; never, moreover, had it possessed greater resources wherewith to compel obedience from the provinces or defend them against foreign attack. Doubtless the population of Assyria proper, and the ancient districts whose contingents formed the nucleus of the army, were still suffering from the results of the civil war which had broken out more than fifteen years before, after the assassination of Sennacherib; but under the easy rule of Esarhaddon the natural increase of population, unchecked by any extraordinary call for recruits, must have almost repaired their losses. The Egyptian campaigns, partially carried out by Syrian auxiliaries, had not sensibly retarded this progress, and, provided that peace were maintained for some years longer, the time seemed at hand when the king, having repaired his losses, could call upon the nation to make fresh efforts in offensive or defensive warfare, without the risk of seeing his people melt and disappear before his eyes. It seems, indeed, as if Assur-bani-pal, either by policy or natural disposition, was inclined for peace. But this did not preclude, when occasion demanded, his directing his forces and fighting in person like any other Assyrian monarch;

ASSUR-BANI-PAL.[1]

[1] Drawn by Faucher-Gudin, from one of the bas-reliefs from Kouyunjik in the British Museum.

he, however, preferred repose, and when circumstances forced war upon him, he willingly delegated the conduct of the army to his generals. He would probably have renounced possession of Egypt if he could have done so with safety and such a course would not have been without wisdom, the retention of this newly acquired province being difficult and costly. Not to speak of differences in language, religion, and manners, which would prevent it from ever becoming assimilated to Assyria as Damascus, Hamath, and Samaria, and most of the Asiatic states had been, it was merely connected with the rest of the empire by the thin chain of rocks, desert, and marshes stretching between the Red Sea and the Mediterranean. A revolt of the cities of the Philistines, or of one of the Idumæan sheikhs, would have sufficed to isolate it, and, communications once interrupted, the safety of the numerous Assyrian officers and garrisons would be seriously jeopardised, all of whom must be maintained there if the country was to be permanently retained. The inclination to meddle in the affairs of Syria always displayed by the Pharaohs, and their obsolete claims to rule the whole country as far as the Euphrates, did not allow of their autonomy being restored to them at the risk of the immediate renewal of their intrigues with Tyre or Judah, and the fomenting of serious rebellions among the vassal princes of Palestine. On the other hand, Egypt was by its natural position so detached from the rest of the empire that it was certain to escape from the influence of Nineveh as soon as the pressure of circumstances obliged the suzerain to relax his efforts to keep it in subjection. Besides this, Ethiopia lay behind

Egypt, almost inaccessible in the fabled realms of the south, always ready to provoke conspiracies or renew hostilities when the occasion offered. Montumihâit had already returned to Thebes on the retreat of the Assyrian battalions, and though Tabarqa, rendered inactive, as it was said, by a dream which bade him remain at Napata,[1] had not reappeared north of the cataract, he had sent Tanuatamanu, the son of his wife by Sabaco, to administer the province in his name.[2] Taharqa died shortly after (666 B.C.), and his stepson was preparing to leave Thebes in order to be solemnly crowned at Gebel Barkal, when he saw one night in a dream two serpents, one on his right hand, the other on his left. The soothsayers whom he consulted on the matter prognosticated for him a successful career: "Thou holdest the south countries; seize thou those of the north, and let the crowns of the two regions gleam upon thy brow!" He proceeded at once to present himself before his divine father Amon of Napata, and encountering no opposition from the Ethiopian priests nobles, he was able to fulfil the prediction almost immediately after his coronation.[3] The Saîd hailed his

---

[1] The legend quoted by Herodotus relates that Sabaco, having slain Necho I., the father of Psammetichus, evacuated Egypt which he had conquered, and retired to Ethiopia in obedience to a dream. The name Sabaco was very probably substituted for that of Tabarqa in the tradition preserved in Sais and Memphis, echoes of which reached the Greek historian in the middle of the fifth century B.C.

[2] It appears, from the *Stele of the Dream*, that Tanuatamanu was in the Thebaid at the time of his accession to the throne.

[3] Steindorff thinks that Tanuatamanu had been officially associated with himself on the throne by Tabarqa, and Schæfer supposes that the dream dates from the first year of their joint reign. The presence of Tanuatamanu

return with joy, and the inhabitants, massed upon either bank of the river, acclaimed him as he glided past them on his boat: "Go in peace! mayest thou have peace Restore life to Egypt! Rebuild the ruined temples, set up once more the statues and emblems of the deities! Reestablish the endowments raised to the gods and goddesses even the offerings to the dead! Restore the priest to place, that he may minister at all the rites!"

The Assyrian officials and the princes of the north, with Necho at their head, were drawn up beneath the walls of Memphis to defy him. He overcame them, however captured the city, and pushed on into the Delta in pursuit of the retreating foe. Necho either fell in a skirmish was taken prisoner and put to death: his son Psammetichus escaped to Syria, but the remaining princes shut themselves up, each in his own stronghold, to await reinforcements from Asia, and a series of tedious and interminable sieges began. Impatient at this dilatory method of warfare Tanuatamanu at length fell back on Memphis, and there opened negotiations in the hope of securing at least a nominal submission, which might enable him to withdraw from the affair with honour. The princes of the east received his overtures favourably, and consented to prostrate themselves before him at the White Wall under the auspices of Pakruru. "Grant us the breath of life for he who acknowledges thee not cannot live, and we

---

beside Tabarqa, in the small Theban temple, the bas-reliefs of which were published by Mariette, does not necessarily prove that the two kings reigned conjointly: it may equally well indicate that the one accomplished the work commenced by the other.

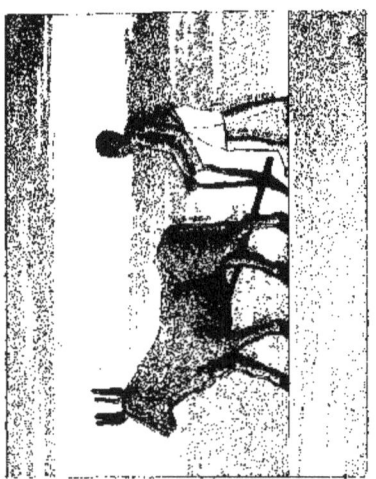
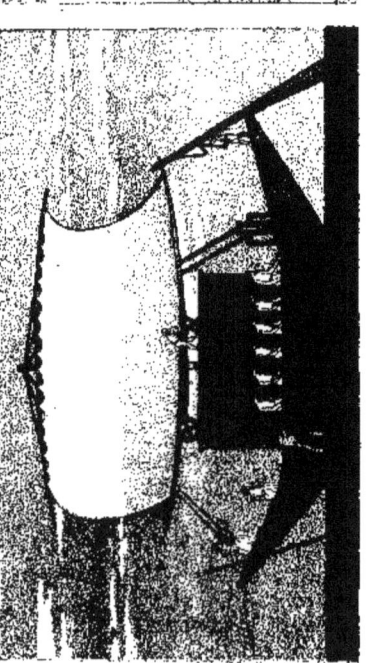

MURAL DECORATIONS FROM THE GROTTOS.

will be thy vassals as thou didst declare at the beginning on the day in which thou becames king" The heart of

KING TANUATAMANU INDAR TION BEFORE THE GODS OF THEBES [1]

his Majesty was filled with joy when he heard this discourse he bestowed upon them in abundance bread beer

Drawn by Boudier from a photograph by Legrain, taken in the small temple at Thebes

and all manner of good things. After sojourning some days at the court of Pharaoh their lord, they said to him, " Why stay we here, O prince our master ? " His Majesty replied " Wherefore ? " They answered then, " Graciously permi us to return to our own cities, that we may give commands to our subjects, and may bring thee our tribute offerings ! " They returned ere long, bringing the promised gifts, and the king withdrew to Napata loaded with spoil.[1] The Delta proper at once ceased to obey him, but Memphis as well as Thebes, still acknowledged his sway for some two or three years longer.[2] It was neither indolence nor fear which had kept Assur-bani-pal from marching to the succour of his subjects as soon as the movement under Tanuatamanu became manifest, but serious complications had arisen in the south-east which had for the moment obliged him to leave Egypt to itself. Elam had at last laid aside the mask, and Urtaku, yielding to the entreaties of the Aramæan sheikhs, who were urged on by Marduk shumibni, had crossed the Tigris. Shamash-shumukîn, thus taken unawares, could only shut himself up in Babylon and in all haste send information of his plight to his brother and suzerain. Assur-bani-pal, preoccupied with the

[1] Tanuatamanu was at first identified by Haigh with the person whose name Assyriologists read as Urdamani, but the impossibility of recognising the name *Tanuatamanu* in *Urdamani* decided E. de Rougé, and subsequently others, to admit an Urdamani different from Tanuatamanu. The discovery of the right reading of the name *Tandamanu* by Steindorff has banished all doubts, and it is now universally admitted that the person mentioned in the Assyrian documents is identical with the king who erected the *Stele of the Dream* at Gebel Barkal.

[2] A monument still exists which was dedicated at Thebes in the third year of Tanuatamanu.

events taking place on the Nile, was for a moment in doubt whether this incursion was merely a passing raid or the opening of a serious war, but the reports of his scouts soon left no doubt as to the gravity of the danger: "The Elamite, like a swarm of grasshoppers, covers the fields, he covers Accad; against Babylon he has pitched his camp and drawn out his lines." The city was too strong to be taken by storm. The Assyrians hastened to relieve it, and threatened to cut off the retreat of the aggressors; the latter, therefore, gave up the siege, and returned to their own country, but their demeanour was still so undaunted that Assur-bani-pal did not cross the frontier in pursuit of them (665 B.C.). He doubtless fully expected that they would soon return in larger numbers, and perhaps his fear would not have proved unfounded had not fate suddenly deprived them of all their leaders. Bel-ikîsha was killed in hunting by a wild boar, Nabu-shumirîsh was struck down by dropsy, and Marduk-shumibni perished in a mysterious manner. Finally Urtaku succumbed to an attack of apoplexy, and the year which had been so fatal to his allies proved not less so to himself (664 B.C.). It now seemed as if Assur-bani-pal might breathe freely, and inflict his long-deferred vengeance on Tanuatamanu, but the death of Urtaku did not remove all causes of uneasiness. Peace was not yet concluded, and it depended on the new King of Elam whether hostilities would be renewed. Fortunately for the Assyrians, the transmission of power had rarely taken place at Susa for a century past without a disturbance, and Urtaku himself had gained the throne by usurpation, possibly accompanied by murder. As he had treated his elder brother Khumbân-khaldash and the children of the latter, so did his younger brother Tammaritu now treat his sons. Tammaritu was "a devil" incarnate, whose whole thoughts were of murder and rapine; at least, this was the idea formed of him by his Assyrian contemporaries, who declared that he desired to put to death the sons of his two predecessors out of sheer cruelty. But we do not need a very vivid imagination to believe that these princes were anxious to dethrone him, and that in endeavouring to rid himself of them he was merely forestalling their secret plots. They escaped his murderous designs, however, and fled to Assyria,—Khumbân-igash, Khumbân-appa, and Tammaritu, sons of Urtaku, and Kuduru and Parru, sons of Khumbân-khaldash, followed by sixty other princes of royal blood, together with archers and servants—forming, in fact, a small army of Elamites. Assur-bani-pal received them with honour, for their defection furnished him with a powerful weapon against the usurper: by succouring them he could rouse half Elam and involve it in civil war, in which the pretenders would soon exhaust their resources. It was now a favourable moment to renew hostilities in Egypt, while Tammaritu, still insecure on his throne, would not venture to provoke a conflict.[1] As a matter of fact, Tanuatamanu did not

[1] The time of the war against Urtaku and the expedition against Tanuatamanu is indicated by a passage in a cylinder as yet unedited. There we read that the invasion of Urtaku took place at the moment when Tanuatamanu ascended the throne. These preliminary difficulties with Elam would thus have coincided with the two years which elapsed between the accession of Tanuatamanu and his conquest of Memphis, up to the third year mentioned in the Berlin inscription; the testimony of the Egyptian

## DESPOILING THE TEMPLES AND PALACES 195

risk the defence of Memphis, but concentrated his forces at Thebes. Once more the Assyrian generals ascended the Nile, and, after a voyage lasting six weeks, at length reached the suburbs of the great city. Tanuatamanu had fled towards Kipkip, leaving Thebes at the mercy of the invaders. It was given up to pillage, its population was carried off into slavery, and its temples and palaces were despoiled of their treasures—gold, silver, metals, and precious stones, broidered and richly dyed stuffs, and horses of the royal stud. Two of the obelisks which adorned the temple of Amon were taken down from their pedestals and placed on rafts to be transported to Nineveh, and we shall perhaps unearth them some day from its ruins. This work of reprisal accomplished, the conquerors made their way northwards, and the bulk of the army recrossed the isthmus: Ethiopian rule had ceased north of the cataract, and Egypt settled down once more under the Assyrian yoke (663–662 B.C.).[2]

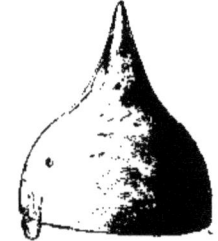

ASSYRIAN HELMET FOUND AT THEBES.[1]

Impoverished and decayed as Thebes had now long since become, the nations whom she had afflicted so sorely in the days of her glory had retained for her feelings of

monuments would thus be in almost complete accord with the Assyrian documents on this point.

[1] Drawn by Faucher-Gudin, from the photograph by Petrie.

[2] The dates which I have adopted follow from the date of 666 B.C. given for the death of Taharqa and the accession of Psammetichus I. The expedition against Thebes must have taken place at the end of the third or beginning of the fourth year of the reign of Tanuatamanu, shortly after the inscription of the third year, and was engraved either in 663 or 662 B.C. at the latest.

respect and almost of awe: the rumour of her fall, spread through the Eastern world, filled them with astonishment and pity. The Hebrews saw in it the chastisement flicted by their God on the tyrant who had oppressed their ancestors, and their prophets used it to impress upon the minds of their contemporaries the vanity of human prosperity. Half a century later, when Nineveh, menaced in her turn, was desperately arming herself to repel the barbarians, Nahum the Elkoshite demanded of her, amid his fierce denunciations, whether she vaunted herself to be better than " No-amon (city of Amon), that was situate among the rivers, that had the waters round about her whose rampart was the sea, and her wall was of the sea Ethiopia and Egypt were her strength, and it was infinite Put and Lubim (Libya and the Nubians) came to her succour. Yet was she carried away, she went into captivity: her young children also were dashed in pieces at the top of all the streets: and they cast lots for her honourable men, and all her great men were bound in chains."[1] Assur-bani-pal, lord of Egypt and conqueror of Ethiopia, might reasonably consider himself invincible it would have been well for the princes who trembled at the name of Assur-bani-pal, if they had taken this lesson to heart, and had learned from the downfall of Tanuatamanu what fate awaited them in the event of their daring to arouse the wrath of Assyria by any kind of intrigue Unfortunately, many of them either failed to see the warning or refused to profit by it. The Manuai had quickly recovered from the defeat inflicted on them by

[1] *Nahum* iii. **8–10.**

Esarhaddon, and their king, Akhsheri, in spite of his advancing years, believed that his own energy and resources were sufficient to warrant him in anticipating a speedy revenge. Perhaps a further insight into the real character of Assur-bani-pal may have induced him to venture on hostilities. For the king's contemporaries had begun to realise that, beneath his apparent bravery and ostentation, he was by nature indolent, impatient of restraint, and fond of ease and luxury. When not absorbed in the routine of the court and the pleasures of the harem, he spent his leisure in hunting on the Mesopotamian plains, or in the extensive parks which had been laid out by himself or his predecessors in the vicinity of their summer palaces. Urus-stalking had become merely a memory of the past: these animals had been so persistently hunted for centuries that the species had almost become extinct; solitary specimens only were occasionally met with in remote parts of the forest or in out-of-the-way marshes. The wild ass was still to be found in large numbers, as well as the goat, the ostrich, and small game, but the lion was now rarely met with, and the beaters were no longer sure of finding him in his ancient haunts. Specimens had to be sought by the royal gamekeepers in the provinces, and when successfully trapped were forthwith despatched to one or other of the king's country seats. The beast was often kept for several days in a cage while preparations were made for a fête, at which he was destined to form one of the chief attractions, and when the time came he was taken to the appointed place and let loose; the sovereign pursued him either in a chariot or on horseback and did not desist from the chase till he had pierced his quarry with arrows or lance Frequently the beast would be turned loose in the park and left there till accustomed to his surroundings so that later on he might be run down under conditions somewhat resembling his native freedom Assur bani pal did not shun a personal

A LION ISSUING FROM ITS CAGE.[1]

encounter with an infuriated lion he displayed in this hazardous sport a bravery and skill which rivalled that of his ancestors and he never relegated to another the task of leading the attack or dealing the final death blow This however was not the case when it was a question of starting on some warlike expedition he would then leave to his Tar ans or to the Rabshakeh, or to some

Drawn by Faucher-Gudin, from a photograph taken from the o iginal in the British Museum other chosen officer, the entire conduct of all operations.¹ This did not preclude the king from taking an interest in what was passing beyond the frontier, nor did he fail in his performance of the various religious duties which custom imposed on an Assyrian sovereign: he consulted the oracles of Shamash or Ishtar, he offered sacrifices, he fasted and humbled himself in the temples to obtain the success of his troops, and when they returned laden with spoil from the campaign, he attributed their victories no less to his prayers than to their courage or to the skill of their leaders. His generals, thoroughly equipped for their task, and well supported by their troops, had no need of the royal presence to ensure their triumph over any foe they might encounter; indeed, in the absence of the king they experienced a liberty of action and boldness in pressing their victories to the uttermost which they would not have enjoyed had he been in command. Foreigners, accustomed to see the sovereigns of Nineveh conduct their armies in person, as long as they were not incapacitated by age, thought that the indolence of Assur-bani-pal was the unconscious expression of weariness or of his feeble control of the empire, and Akhsheri determined to be one of the first to take advantage of it. Events proved that he was mistaken in his calculations. No sooner had his intentions become known, than a division of Assyrian troops appeared on his frontier, and prepared to attack him. Resolving to take the initiative, he fell

---

¹ We have seen, for example, that after the death of Esarhaddon, the Egyptian campaign was conducted by one of the Tartans and the Rabshakeh.

one night unexpectedly upon the Assyrian camp, but fortune declared against him : he was driven back, and his broken ranks were closely pursued for a distance twenty-three miles. Eight of his strongholds fell after the other, and he was at length forced to abandon his capital of Izirtu, and flee precipitately to his fortress of Adrana in the heart of the mountains. Even there he did not find the security he desired, for the conqueror pursued him thither, methodically devastating by the way the districts through which he passed : he carried everything—men, slaves, and herds of cattle—and he never retired from a city or village without previously setting it on fire. Paddir, Arsiyanîsh, and Eristiana were thus laid waste, after which the Assyrians returned to their camp, having re-established the authority of their master over several districts which had been lost to them for some generations previously. Akhsheri had shown no sign of yielding, but his people, weary of a hopeless resistance, put him to death, and hurling his corpse over the wall of Adrana, proclaimed his son Ualli as king. The new sovereign hastened to conclude a treaty with the Assyrians on reasonable terms: he gave up his eldest son, Erisinni, and one of his daughters as hostages, and promised to pay the former tribute augmented by an annual present of thirty horses; peace was not again disturbed on this side except by some unimportant skirmishes. In one of these, a Median chieftain named Biriz-khadri, made an alliance with two princes the people of the Sakhi, Sarâti, and Parikhia, sons of Gâgu,

[1] The name of Biriz-khadri has an Iranian appearance. The first element

to ravage the marches of the Greater Zab; but their territory was raided in return, and they themselves taken prisoners. A little later, Andaria, prince of Lubdi, forgetful of his oath of allegiance to the aged Esarhaddon, made a night attack on the towns of Kullimir and Ubbumî: the inhabitants armed in haste, and he was not only defeated, but was taken captive, and his head cut off to be sent to Nineveh. The garrisons and military colonies along the north-east frontier were constantly required to be on the alert; but they usually had sufficient available resources to meet any emergency, and the enemies who molested them were rarely dangerous enough to necessitate the mobilisation of a regular army.

This was not the case, however, in the south-west, where Tiummân, counting on the military strength of Elam, made continual hostile demonstrations. He was scarcely settled on his throne before he hastened to form alliances with those Aramæan states which had so often invoked the aid of his predecessors against the ancestors of Assur-bani-pal. The Kaldâ rejected his proposals, as did

*Biriz* recalls the Zend *bereza, berez,* "tall, large;" the second, which appears in the names Bisi-khadir and Khali-khadri, is of uncertain derivation, and has been connected with *atar,* "fire," or with *khwathra,* "brilliance." Gâgu, which is found as the name of a people (Gagâti) in the Tel-el-Amarna tablets, has been identified from the first with the name of Gog, prince of Rosh, Meshech, and Tubal *(Ezek.* xxxviii. 2, 3; xxxix. 1. The name of the country of Sakhi, which has not been met with elsewhere, has been compared with that of the Sacæ, which seems to have existed not only in the name of the province of Sakasenê mentioned by the classical geographers, but in that of Shakê known to the old Armenian geographers; the country itself, however, as it seems to me, cannot be sought in the direction of Sakasenê, and consequently the proposed identification cannot hold good.

most of the tribes of the littoral; but the Gambulâ yielded to his solicitations, and their king, Dunânu, son of Bel ikîsha, entered into an offensive and defensive alliance with Elam. Their defection left the eastern frontier Karduniash unprotected, and, by opening to the Elamite the fords of the Tigris, permitted him to advance Babylon unhindered by any serious obstacle. As soon as the compact was sealed, Tiummân massed his battalions the middle course of the Uknu, and, before crossing the frontier, sent two of his generals, the Susian Khumba-dar and the Chaldæan Nabu-damîq, as the bearers of insolent ultimatum to the court of Nineveh : he offered the king the choice between immediate hostilities, or the extradition of the sons of Urtaku and Khumbân-khaldash, as well as of their partisans who had taken refuge in Assyria. To surrender the exiles would have been an open confession of inferiority, and such a humiliating acknow ledgment of weakness promptly reported throughout the Eastern world might shortly have excited a general revolt hence Assur-bani-pal disdainfully rejected the proposal of the Elamite sovereign, which had been made rather as a matter of form than with any hope of its acceptance, but the issue of a serious war with Susa was so uncertain that his refusal was accompanied with serious misgivings. It needed many favourable omens from the gods to encourage him to believe in his future success. The moon-god Sin was the first to utter his prediction : he suffered eclipse in the month of Tammuz, and for three successive days, at nightfall, showed himself in the sky surrounded by strange appearances which heralded the death of a king in Elam and foretold calamity to that country. Then Assur and Ishtar struck Tiummân with violent convulsions; they caused his lips and eyes to be horribly distorted, but he despised their warning, and as soon as his seizure had passed, set out to assume command of his army. The news of his action reached Nineveh in the month of Ab, on the morning of the solemn festival of Ishtar. Assur-bani-pal was at Arbela, celebrating the rites in honour of the goddess, when the messenger appeared before him and repeated, together with the terms of the declaration of war, the scornful words which Tiummân had uttered against him and his patroness: "This prince whose wits have been crazed by Ishtar—I will let him escape no more, when once I have gone forth and measured my strength against him!" This blasphemy filled the Assyrian king with horror. That very evening he betook himself to the sanctuary, and there, prostrate before the image of the goddess, he poured forth prayers mingled with tears: "Lady of Arbela, I am Assur-bani-pal, King of Assyria, the creature of thy hands, the offspring of a father whom thou didst create! Behold now, this Tiummân, the King of Elam, who despises the gods of Assyria, hath sent forth his host and prepared himself for the conflict; he hath called for his arms to rush to attack Assyria. Do thou, O archer of the gods, like a bolt falling in the midst of the battle, overthrow him, and let loose upon him a tempest, and an evil wind!" Ishtar heard his prayer, and her voice sounded through the gloom: "Fear not," said she, comforting him: "since thou hast raised thy hands to me in supplication, and thine eyes are bedewed with tears I grant thee a boon!" Towards the end of that night, a seer slept in the temple and was visited by a dream. Ishtar of Arbela appeared to him, with a quiver on either side, a bow in one hand and a drawn sword in the other. She advanced towards the king, and spoke to him as if she had been his mother: "Make war boldly! whichever way thou turnest thy countenance, there will I go!" And the king replied to her, "Where thou goest, will I go with thee sovereign lady!" But she answered, "Stay thou here Dwell in this home of Nebo, eat thy food and drink thy wine, listen to joyful songs and honour my divinity, until I have gone and accomplished this work. Let not thy countenance grow pale, nor thy feet fail under thee, and expose not thyself to the danger of battle." "And then O king," added the seer, "she hid thee in her bosom as a mother, and protected thy image. A flame shall spring forth before her, and shall spread abroad to destroy thine enemies: against Tiummân, King of Elam, who has angered her, has she set her face!" Like Mînephtah of old, in the days of the Libyan invasions of Egypt, Assur bani-pal allowed himself to be readily convinced by the decision of the gods; he did not quit Arbela, but gave orders to his troops to proceed to the front. His generals opened the campaign in the month of Elul, and directed the main body of their forces against the fortress of Durîlu, at the point on the frontier nearest to Susa. Tiummân was not expecting such a prompt and direct attack: he had reckoned doubtless on uniting his forces with those of Dunânu with a view to invading Karduniash, and suddenly realised that his adversary had forestalled him and was advancing on the heart of his empire. He slowly withdrew his advanced guard, and concentrated his forces round the town of Tullîz, a few leagues on this side of Susa, and there awaited the enemy's attack.[1]

His position was a strong one, flanked on the right by a wood and on the left by the Ulaî, while the flower of the Elamite nobility was ranged around him. The equipment of his soldiers was simpler than that of the enemy: consisting of a low helmet, devoid of any crest, but furnished with a large pendant tress of horsehair to shade the neck; a shield of moderate dimensions; a small bow, which, however, was quite as deadly a weapon as that of the Assyrians, when wielded by skilful hands; a lance, a mace, and a dagger. He had only a small body of cavalry, but the chariotry formed an important force, and presented several original features. The chariot did not follow the classic model, rounded in front and open at the back; it was a kind of light car, consisting of a square footboard placed flat on the axle of the wheels, and furnished with triangular side-pieces on two sides only, the vehicle being drawn by a pair of horses. Such chariots were easier to manage, better adapted for rapid motion, and must have been more convenient for a reconnaissance or for skirmishes with infantry; but when thrown in a mass against the heavy chariotry of the peoples of the Euphrates, they were far too slightly built to overthrow the latter, and at close

---

[1] The site of Tullîz is unknown. Billerbeck considers, and with reason, I think, that the battle took place to the south of Susa, on the river Shavur, which would correspond to the Ulai, on the lowest spurs of the ridge of hills bordering the alluvial plain of Susiana.

quarters were of necessity crushed by the superior weight of the adversary. Tiummân had not succeeded in collecting all his forces before the first columns of the Assyrian army advanced to engage his front line, but as he was

ITUNI BREAKS HIS BOW WITH A BLOW OF HIS SWORD, AND GIVES HIMSELF UP TO THE EXECUTIONER.[1]

expecting reinforcements, he endeavoured to gain time by despatching Ituni, one of his generals, with orders to negotiate a truce. The Assyrian commander, suspecting a ruse, would not listen to any proposals, but ordered the envoy to be decapitated on the spot: Ituni broke his bow with a blow of his sword, and stoically yielded his neck to the

[1] Drawn by Boudier, from a photograph taken from the original in the British Museum.

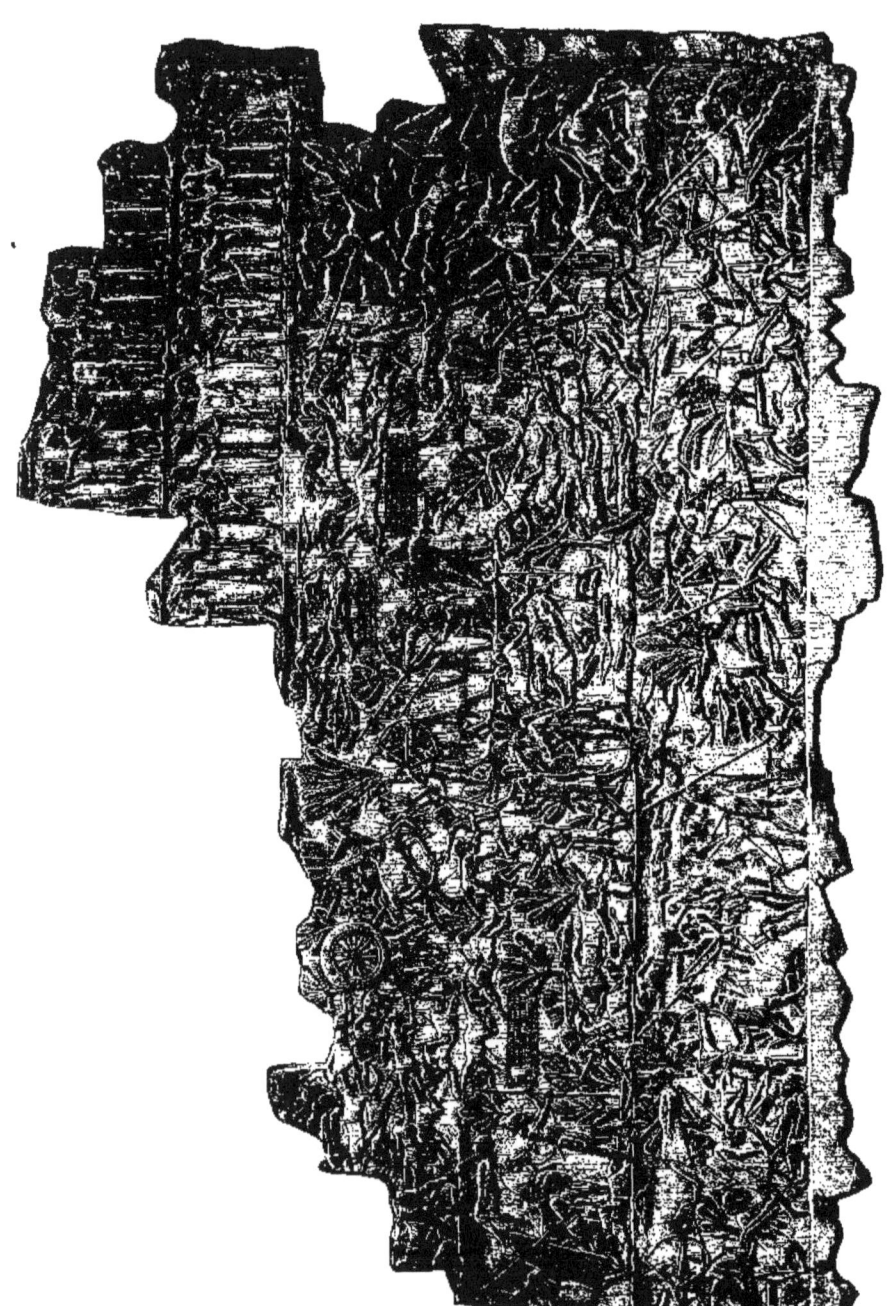

THE BATTLE OF TULLIZ.

Drawn by Boudier, from a photograph of the original in the British Museum.

THE BATTLE OF TULLÎZ 209

executioner. The issue of the battle was for a long time undecided, but the victory finally remained with the heavy regiments of Assyria. The left wing of the Susians, driven into the Ulaî, perished by drowning, and the river was choked with the corpses of men and horses, and the *débris* of arms and broken chariots. The right wing took to flight under cover of a wood, and the survivors tried to reach the

URTAKU, COUSIN OF TIUMMÂN, SURRENDERING TO AN ASSYRIAN.[1]

mountains. Urtaku, the cousin of Tiummân, was wounded by an arrow; perceiving an Assyrian soldier coming up to him, he told him who he was, and recommended him to carry his head to the general: " He will pay you handsomely for it," he added. Tiummân had led in person several charges of his body-guard; and on being wounded, his son Tammaritu had succeeded in rescuing him from the thick of the fight: both seated together in a chariot, were

[1] Drawn by Boudier, from a photograph of the original in the British Museum.

in full flight, when one of the wheels caught against a tree and was shattered, the shock flinging the occupants to the ground. A large body of Assyrians were in close pursuit, led by one of the exiled Susian princes, a second Tammaritu, son of Urtaku. At the first discharge an arrow wounded Tiummân in the right side, and brought him to

THE LAST ARROW OF TIUMMÂN AND HIS SON.[1]

his knee. He felt that all was over, and desiring at all events to be revenged, he pointed out the deserter prince to his companion, crying indignantly, " Let fly at him The arrow missed its mark, and a flight of hostile darts stretched the young man on the ground: the traitor Tammaritu dealt the son his death-blow with his mace while an Assyrian decapitated the father. The corpses were left on the field, but the head of the king, after being

[1] Drawn by Boudier, from a photograph taken in the British Museum

taken to the general in command was carried through the camp on one of the chariots captured during the action and was eventually sent to the palace of Arbela by the hand of a well mounted courier The day concluded with

DEATH OF TIUMMÂN AND HIS SON.[1]

the making of an inventory of the spoil and by an enumeration of the heads of the slain prisoners from the rank and file were beaten to death according to custom and several of the principal officers had their tongues torn out or were flayed alive The news of the disaster was brought to Susa towards evening by the fugitives and produced a revolution in the city The partisans of the exiled princes seizing

Drawn by Boudier, from a photograph taken in the British Museum

the adherents of Tiummân, put them in chains, and
delivered them up to the conqueror. The shattered
remnants of the army rallied round them, and a throng of
men and women in festal garb issued forth along the banks
of the Ulaî to meet the Assyrians. The priests and sac ed
singers marched to the sound of music, marking the
rhythm with their feet, and filling the air with the noise
their harps and double flutes, while behind them came a
choir of children, chanting a hymn under the direction
the consecrated eunuchs. The Tartan met them, and,
acting in accordance with the orders of Assur-bani-pal,
presented to the multitude Khumbân-igash, the eldest son
of Urtaku, as their king. The people joyfully hailed the
new sovereign, and the Assyrians, after exacting tribute
from him and conferring the fief of Khaîdalu on his brother
Tammaritu, withdrew, leaving to the new princes the task
of establishing their authority outside the walls of Susa and
Madaktu. As they returned, they attacked the Gambul
speedily reducing them to submission. Dunânu, besieged
in his stronghold of Shapîbel, surrendered at discretion
and was carried away captive with all his family. Thus
Assur-bani-pal had scrupulously obeyed the orders of Ishtar
While his generals were winning his victories he had been
eating and drinking, hunting, dallying with his wives, and
living in the open air. He was taking his pleasure with
the queen in the palace garden when the head of Tiummân
was brought to him: he caused it to be suspended from the
branch of a pine tree in full view of the whole court, and
continued his banquet to the sound of harps and singing
Rusas III., King of Urartu, died about this time, and his

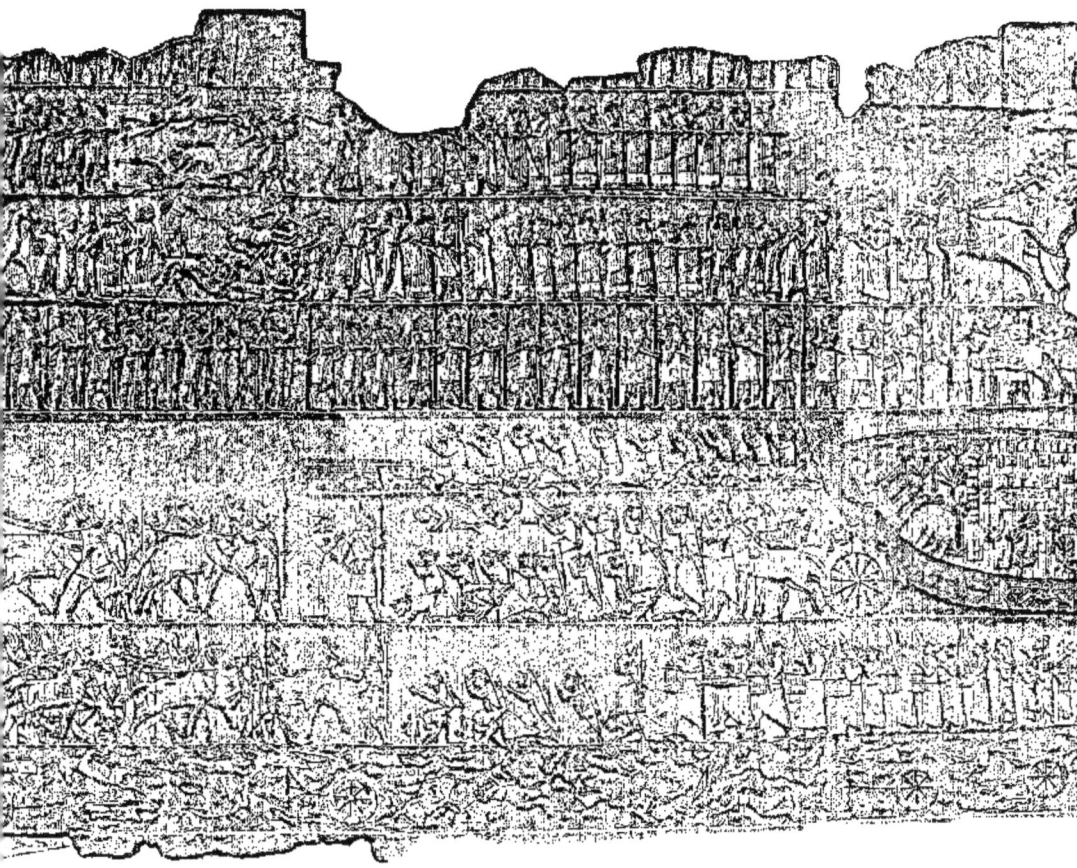

KHUMBAN-IGASH ACCLAIMED AS KING AFTER THE BATTLE OF TULLÎZ.
Drawn by Boudier, from a photograph of the original in the British Museum.

successor, Sharduris III., thought it incumbent on him to announce his accession at Nineveh Assur bani pal received the embassy at Arbela with the graciousness befitting a suzerain whom a faithful vassal honours by his dutiful homage, and in order to impress the Urartians still further with an idea of his power, he showed them the two

THE HEAD OF TIUMMÂN SENT TO NINEVEH.[1]

Elamite delegates Khumba-darâ and Nabu-damîq, in chains at his feet [2] These wretched men had a more cruel ordeal

    Drawn by Boudier, from a photograph taken in the British Museum. The chariot speeding along at a gallop in the topmost series of pictures carries a soldier bearing the head of Tiummân in his hand behind him under a tent scribes are registering the heads which are brought in In the two lower bas-reliefs are displayed the closing scenes of the battle
    [2] Belck and Lehmann have very ingeniously connected the embassy

yet in store for them : when the Assyrian army re-entered Nineveh, Assur-bani-pal placed them on the route along which the cortège had to pass, and made them realise to the full the humiliation of their country. Dunânu walked at the head of the band of captive chiefs, with the head of Tiummân, taken from its tree, suspended round his neck. When the delegates perceived it, they gave way to despair:

ASSUR BANI-PAL BANQUETING WITH HIS QUEEN.[1]

Khumba-darâ tore out his beard by handfuls, and Nabu damîq, unsheathing the dagger which hung from his belt plunged it into his own breast. The triumphal entry was followed by the usual tortures. The head of Tiummân was fixed over the gate of Nineveh, to rot before the eyes of the multitude. Dunânu was slowly flayed alive, and then bled like a lamb; his brother Shamgunu had his throat cut, and his body was divided into pieces, which were distributed

mentioned in the Assyrian documents, with the fact of the accession of the king who sent it.

[1] Drawn by Boudier, from a photograph of the original in the British Museum. The head of Tiummân hangs on the second tree on the left hand side.

over the country as a warning Even the dead were not spared the bones of Nabu-shumirîsh were disinterred and transported to Assyria where his sons were forced to bray t em in a mortar We may estimate the extent of the alarm which had been felt at Nineveh by the outburst of brutal joy with which the victory was hailed The experience of the past showed what a terrible enemy Assyria had in Elam,

TWO ELAMITE CHIEFS FLAYED ALIVE AFTER THE BATTLE OF TULLÎZ.[2]

and how slight was the chance of a successful issue in a war against her Her kings had often invaded Chaldæa and had more than once brought it directly under their sway they had ravaged its cities and pillaged its temples and the sanctuary of Susa were filled with statues of the

---

[1] The fullest text of all those which narrate the campaign against **Tiummân** and Dunânu is that on *Cylinder B of the British Museum*. It **pre**tends as usual that the king led the army **in** person but the words which the seer places in the mouth of Ishtar prove that the king remained at Arbela by divine command, and the inscription on one **of** the bas-reliefs as well as *Tablet* K *2674,* mentions without giving his **name** the general who was sent against Susa

[2] Drawn by **Boudier,** from a photograph taken in the **British** Museum

gods or with bas-reliefs which they had dedicated after their campaigns on the Euphrates. Although they had not been successful against Assyria to the same extent, they had at least always victoriously repelled her attacks: they had held their own against Sargon, given much trouble to Sennacherib, and defied the power of Esarhaddon with impunity. Never till now had an Assyrian army gained such an important victory over Elam, and though it was by no means decisive, we can easily believe that Assur-bani-pal was filled with pride and delight, since it was the first time that a king of Nineveh had imposed on Elam a sovereign of his own choice.

Since homage was voluntarily rendered him by the rulers of foreign nations, Assur-bani-pal doubtless believed that he might exact it without hesitation from the vassal princes dependent on the empire; and not from the weaker only like those who were still to be found in Syria, but also from the more powerful, not excepting the lord of Karduniash. Shamash-shumukîn had fully risen to his position as King of Babylon, and the unbroken peace which he had enjoyed since the death of Urtaku had enabled him almost to complete the restoration of the kingdom begun under Esarhaddon. He had finished the rebuilding of the walls of Babylon, and had fortified the approaches to the city, thus rendering it capable of withstanding a long siege; he had repaired the temple of Sippara, which had never recovered from the Elamite invasion; and while unstintingly lavishing his treasures in honour of the gods and for the safety of his capital he watched with jealous care over the interests of his subjects. He obtained for them the privilege of being treated on the same footing as the Assyrians throughout his father's ancestral domains; they consequently enjoyed the right of trading without restriction throughout the empire, and met with the same degree of protection from the officials of Nineveh as from the magistrates of their own country. Assur-bani-pal had at the outset furthered the wishes of his brother to the utmost of his power: he had granted the privileges demanded, and whenever a Chaldæan of noble birth arrived at his court, he received him with special marks of favour. The two states enjoyed a nearly absolute equality during the opening years of his reign, and though the will of Esarhaddon had made Babylon dependent on Assyria, the yoke of vassalage was far from heavy. The suzerain reserved to himself the honour of dedicating the mighty works begun by his father, the restoration of the temple of Bel-Marduk and of the double wall of fortification; he claimed, in his inscriptions, the whole merit of the work, but he none the less respected his brother's rights, and in no way interfered in the affairs of the city except in state ceremonies in which the assertion of his superior rank was indispensable. But with success his moderation gradually gave place to arrogance. In proportion as his military renown increased, he accentuated his supremacy, and accustomed himself to treat Babylon more and more as a vassal state. After the conquest of Elam his infatuated pride knew no bounds, and the little consideration he still retained for Shamash-shumukîn vanished completely. He thenceforward refused to regard him as being more than a prefect bearing a somewhat higher title than his fellows, a viceroy owing his crown, not to the will their common father, but to the friendship of his brother and liable to be deprived of it at any moment through the caprice of the sovereign. He affected to consider all that took place at Babylon as his own doing, and brother as being merely his docile instrument, not serving mention any more than the ordinary agents who carried out his designs; and if, indeed, he condescended to mention him, it was with an assumption of disdainful superiority. It is a question whether Shamash-Shumukîn at this juncture believed that his brother was meditating a design to snatch the reins of government from his hand or whether he merely yielded to the impulse of wounded vanity in resolving to shake off a yoke which had become intolerable. Knowing that his power was not equal to that of Assur-bani-pal, he sought to enter into relations with foreign allies who shared the same fears, or nursed a similar feeling of bitterness. The nobles and priests of the ancient Sumerian and Accadian cities were already on his side, but the Aramæans had shown themselves hostile at his accession, and had brought down on him the forces of Elam. He found means, however, to conciliate them, together with the tribes which dwelt the Tigris and the Uknu, as well as those of the lower Euphrates and the Arabian desert. He won over to his projects Nabu-bêlzikri, the chief of the Kaldâ—grandson of that Merodach-baladan who had cherished invincible hatred against Sargon and Sennacherib—besides the lor s of the Bît-Dakkuri and Bît-Amukkâni, and the sheikh of the Pukudu. Khumbân-igash ought to have remained loyal to the friend to whom he owed his kingdom, but he chafed at the patronage of Assyria, and Assur-banipal had just formulated a demand to which he, not unreasonably, hesitated to accede. The archaic statue of Nanâ, stolen from Uruk by Kutur-nakhunta sixteen centuries before, and placed by that prince in one of the temples of Susa, had become so naturalised in its new abode that the kings of Elam, not content with rendering it an official cult, were wont to send presents to Babylonia, to the image which had replaced it in its original sanctuary. Assur-bani-pal now required Khumbân-igash to give back the original statue, but the Elamite could not obey this mandate without imperilling both his throne and his person: he would thereby have risked incurring the displeasure both of the nobles, whose pride would have suffered at the loss of so precious a trophy, and of the common people, who would have thus been deprived of one of their most venerable objects of devotion. The messengers of Shamash-shumukîn, arriving at the moment when this question was agitating the court of Susa, found the way already prepared for a mutual understanding. Besides, they held in their hands an irresistible argument, the treasures of Bel-Marduk of Babylon, of Nebo of Borsippa, and of Nergal of Kuta, which had been confided to them by the priests with a view to purchasing, if necessary, the support of Elam. Khumbân-igash thereupon promised to send a detachment of troops to Karduniash, and to invade the provinces of Assyria the moment war should be declared. The tribes of Guti were easily won over, and were followed by the kings of Phœnicia and the Bedâwin of Melukhkha, and perhaps Egypt itself was implicated in the plot. The Prince of Kedar, Amuladdin, undertook to effect a diversion on the frontiers of Syria, and Uatê, son of Layali, one of the Arab kings who had paid homage to Esarhaddon, was not behindhand in furnishing his contingent of horsemen and wild native infantry. The coalition already extended from the shores of the Mediterranean and the Red Sea to the Persian Gulf before Assur-bani-pal became aware of its existence.

An unforeseen occurrence suddenly broke in upon his peace and revealed the extent of the peril which threatened him.[1] Kudur, the Assyrian prefect of Uruk, learnt from Sin-tabnî-uzur, the governor of Uru, that certain emissaries of Shamash-shumukîn had surreptitiously entered that city and were secretly fomenting rebellion among the people. Sin-tabnî-uzur himself had been solicited to join the movement, but had absolutely refused to do so, and considering himself powerless to repress the disaffection with the few soldiers at his disposal, he had demanded reinforcements. Kudur first furnished him with five hundred men of his own troops, and subsequently sent some battalions which

---

[1] The chronology of this war has been determined by G. Smith from the dates attached to the documents in the British Museum, which give the names of three *limmi*, Assur-duruzur, Zagabbu, and Bel-kharrân-shadua: these he assigned respectively to the years 650, 649, and 648 B.C. Tiele has shown that these three *limmi* must be assigned to the years 652–650 B.C. Though these dates seem in the highest degree probable, we must wait before we can consider them as absolutely certain till chance restores to us the missing parts of the Canon.

were under the command of the governors of Arrapkha and Amidi, but which were, for some unknown reason, encamped in the neighbourhood. It would appear that Shamash-shumukîn, finding his projects interfered with by this premature exposure, tried to counteract its effects by protestations of friendship: a special embassy was despatched to his brother to renew the assurances of his devotion, and he thus gained the time necessary to complete his armaments. As soon as he felt himself fully prepared, he gave up further dissimulation, and, throwing away the mask, proclaimed himself independent of Assyria, while at the same moment Khumbân-igash despatched his army to the frontier and declared war on his former protector. Assur-bani-pal was touched to the quick by what he truly considered the ingratitude of the Babylonians. "As for the children of Babylon, I had set them upon seats of honour, I had clothed them in robes of many colours, I had placed rings of gold upon their fingers; the children of Babylon had been established in Assyria, and were admitted into my presence. But Shamash-shumukîn, the false brother, he has not observed my ordinances, but has raised against me the peoples of Akkad, the Kaldâ, the Aramæans, the peoples of the country of the sea, from Akabah to Bab-salimêti!" Nineveh was at first in a state of trepidation at this unexpected blow; the sacred oracles gave obscure replies, and presaged evil four times out of five. At last, one day, a seer slept and dreamed a dream, in which he saw this sentence written on the ground in the temple of Sin: "All those who are meditating evil against Assur-bani-pal, King of Assyria, and who are preparing themselves to fight with him, I will inflict on them a terrible death: by the swift sword, by flinging them into fire, by famine and by pestilence, will I destroy their lives!" The courage of the people being revived by this prophecy, Assur-bani-pal issued a proclamation to the Babylonians, in which he denounced his brother's treason and commanded them to remain quiet as they valued their lives, and, having done this, he boldly assumed the offensive (652 B.C.).[1] The only real danger came from the side of Elam; this state alone was in a condition to oppose him with as numerous and determined an army as that which he himself could put into the field; if Elam were disabled, it would be impossible for Babylon to be victorious, and its fall would be a mere question of time The opening of the campaign was a difficult matter Khumbân-igash, having sold his support dearly, had at all events spared no pains to satisfy his employer, and had furnished him with the flower of his nobility, comprising Undashi, one of the sons of Tiummân; Zazaz, prefect of Billatê; Parru, chief of Khilmu; Attamîtu, commanding the archers; and Nesu, commander-in-chief of his forces In order to induce Undashi to serve under him, he had not hesitated to recall to his memory the sad fate of Tiummân: "Go, and avenge upon Assyria the murder of the father who begat thee!" The two opposing forces continued to watch one another's movements without any serious engagement taking place during the greater part of the

---

[1] The proclamation is dated in the eponymous year of Assur-duruzur, corresponding to 652 B.C.; the events which immediately preceded the proclamation ought, very probably, to be assigned to the same year.

year 651 B.C.; though the Assyrians won some slight advantages, killing Attamîtu in a skirmish and sending his head to Nineveh, some serious reverses soon counterbalanced these preliminary successes. Nabo-bel-shumi had arrived on the scene with his Aramæan forces, and had compelled the troops engaged in the defence of Uruk and Uru to lay down their arms: their leaders, including Sin-tabnî-uzur himself, had been forced to renounce the supremacy of Assyria, and had been enrolled in the rebel ranks.[1] Operations seemed likely to be indefinitely prolonged, and Assur-bani-pal, anxious as to the issue, importunately besought the gods to intervene on his behalf, when discords breaking out in the royal family of Elam caused the scales of fortune once more to turn in his favour. The energy with which Khumbân-igash had entered on the present struggle had not succeeded in effacing the disagreeable impression left on the minds of the majority of his subjects, by the fact that he had returned to his country in the chariots of the stranger and had been enthroned by the decree of an Assyrian general. Tammaritu, of Khaîdalu, who had then fought at his side

[1] The official accounts say nothing of the intervention of Nabo-bel-shumi at this juncture, but the information furnished by *Tablet* K *159* in the British Museum makes up for their silence. The objection raised by Tiele to the interpretation given by G. Smith that this passage cannot refer to Assyrian deserters, falls to the ground if one admits that the Assyrian troops led into Elam at a subsequent period by Nabo-bel-shumi, were none other than the garrisons of the Lower Euphrates which were obliged to side with the insurgents in 651 B.C. The two despatches, K *4696* and K *28* in the British Museum, which refer to the defection of Sin-tabnî-uzur, are dated the 8th and 11th Abu in the eponymous year of Zagabbu, corresponding to the year 651 B.C., as indicated by Tiele with very good reason.

in the ranks of the invaders, was now one of those who reproached him most bitterly for his conduct. He frankly confessed that his hand had cut off the head of Tiummân, but denied that he did so in obedience to the hereditary enemies of his country; he had but avenged his personal injuries, whereas Khumbân-igash, following the promptings of ambition, had kissed the ground at the feet of a slave of Assur-bani-pal and had received the crown as a recompense for his baseness. Putting his rival to death, Tammaritu seized the throne, and in order to prove that he was neither consciously nor unconsciously an instrument of Ninevite policy, he at once sent reinforcements to the help of Babylon without exacting in return any fresh subsidy The Assyrians, taking advantage of the isolated position of Shamash-shumukîn, had pressed forward one of their divisions as far as the districts on the sea coast, which they had recovered from the power of Nabo-bel-shumi, and had placed under the administration of Belibni, a person of high rank. The arrival of the Elamite force was on the point of further compromising the situation, and rekindling the flames of war more fiercely than ever, when a second revolution broke out, which shattered for ever the hopes Shamash-shumukîn. Assur-bani-pal naturally looked upon this event as the result of his supplications and sacrifices Assur and Ishtar, in answer to his entreaties, raised up Indabigash, one of the most powerful feudal lords of the kingdom of Susa, and incited him to revolt. Tammaritu fled to the marshes which bordered the Nâr-marratum, and seizing a vessel, put out to sea with his brothers, his cousins, seventeen princes of royal blood, and eighty-four faithful followers: the ship, driven by the wind on to the Assyrian shore, foundered, and the dethroned monarch, demoralised by sea-sickness, would have perished in the confusion had not one of his followers taken him on his back and carried him safely to land across the mud. Belibni sent him prisoner to Nineveh with all his suite, and Assur-bani-pal, after allowing him to humble himself before him, raised him from the ground, embraced him, and assigned to him apartments in the palace and a train of attendants befitting the dignity which he had enjoyed for a short time at Susa. Indabigash was too fully occupied with his own affairs to interfere again in the quarrel between the two brothers: his country, disorganised by the successive shocks it had sustained, had need of repose, for some years at least, before re-entering the lists, except at a disadvantage. He concluded no direct treaty with the Assyrian king, but he at once withdrew the troops which had entered Karduniash, and abstained from all hostile demonstrations against the garrisons of the border provinces: for the moment, indeed, this was all that was required of him (650 B.C.).

Deprived of the support of Elam, Babylon was doomed to fall. The Aramæans deserted her cause, and Nabu-bel-shumi, grandson of Merodach-baladan, despairing of ever recovering the heritage of his family, withdrew to his haunts among the reed beds of the Ukuu, taking back with him as hostages the Assyrians whom he had forced to join his army at the beginning of the campaign. Shamash-shumukîn, however, was not disconcerted: he probably hoped that his distant allies might yet effect a diversion in his favour, and thus oblige his brother to withdraw half of the forces employed against him. Indeed after the blockade had already begun, a band of Arabs under the two sheikhs Abiyatê and Aamu forced a way through the besieging lines and entered the city. Th s was the last succour which reached Babylon from without: for many long months all communication between her citizens and the outer world was completely cut off. The Assyrians laid waste the surrounding country with ruthless and systematic cruelty, burning the villages, razing to the ground isolated houses, destroying the trees, breaking down the dykes, and filling up the canals. The year B.C. was spent in useless skirmishes; the city offered an energetic and obstinate resistance, and as the walls were thick and the garrison determined, it would not have succumbed had not the supply of provisions finally failed Famine raged in the city, and the inhabitants devoured even their own children, while pestilence spreading among them mowed them down by thousands. The Arab auxiliaries at this juncture deserted the cause of the defenders, and their sheikhs surrendered to Assur-bani-pal, who received and pardoned them; but the Babylonians themselves knowing that they could expect no mercy, held out some time longer: at length, their courage and their strength exhausted, they rose against their chiefs, whose ambition or patriotic pride had brought them to such a pass, and determined to capitulate on any terms. Shamash-shumukîu, not wishing to fall alive into the hands of his brother, shut himself up in his palace, and there immolated himself a funeral pyre with his wives his children, his slaves

and his treasures at the moment when his conquerors were breaking down the gates and penetrating into the palace precincts.[1] The city presented a terrible spectacle, and shocked even the Assyrians, accustomed as they were to horrors of this sort. Most of the numerous victims to pestilence or famine lay about the streets or in the public squares, a prey to the dogs and swine; such of the inhabitants and of the soldiery as were comparatively strong had endeavoured to escape into the country, and only those remained who had not sufficient strength left to drag themselves beyond the walls. Assur-bani-pal pursued the fugitives, and, having captured nearly all of them, vented on them the full fury of his vengeance. He caused the tongues of the soldiers to be torn out, and then had them clubbed to death. He massacred the common folk in front of the great winged bulls which had already witnessed a similar butchery half a century before, under his grandfather Sennacherib; the corpses of his victims remained long unburied, a prey to all unclean beasts and birds. When the executioners and the king himself were weary of the slaughter, the survivors were pardoned; the remains of the victims were collected and piled up in specified places, the streets were cleansed, and the temples, purified by solemn lustrations, were reopened

[1] G. Smith thought that the Babylonians, rendered furious by their sufferings, had seized Shamash-shumukîn and burnt him to death. It is, however, certain that Shamash-shumukîn killed himself, according to the Eastern custom, to escape the tortures which awaited him if he fell alive nto the hands of his enemies. The memory of this event, transferred by the popular imagination to Assur-bani-pal, appears in the concluding portion the legendary history of Sardanapalus.

for worship.¹ Assur-bani-pal proclaimed himself king in his brother's room: he took the hands of Bel, and, according to custom, his Babylonian subjects gave him a new name, that of Kandalanu, by which he was henceforth known among them.² Had he been wise, he would have completed the work begun by famine, pestilence, and the sword, and, far from creating a new Babylon, he would have completed the destruction of the ancient city. The same religious veneration which had disarmed so many of his predecessors probably withheld him from giving free rein to his resentment, and not daring to follow the example of Sennacherib, he fell back on the expedient adopted by Tiglath-pileser III. and Sargon, adhering to their idea of two capitals for two distinct states, but endeavouring to unite in his own person the two irreconcilable

---

¹ The date of 648–647 B.C. for the taking of Babylon and the death of Shamash-shumukîn is corroborated by the Canon of Ptolemy and the fragments of Berosus, both of which attribute twenty or twenty-one years to the reign of Saosdukhîn (Sammughes). Lehmann points out a document dated in the XX[th] year of Shamash-shumukîn, which confirms the exactitude of the information furnished by the Greek chronologists.

² The Canon of Ptolemy gives as the successor of Saosdukhîn a certain Kinêladan, who corresponds to Kandalanu, whose date has been fixed by contemporary documents. The identity of Kinêladan with Assur-bani-pal was known from the Greek chronologists, for whereas Ptolemy puts Kinêladan after Saosdukhîn, the fragments of Berosus state that the successor of Sammughes was his *brother;* that is to say, Sardanapalus or Assur-bani-pal. This identification had been proposed by G. Smith, who tried to find the origin of the form Kinêladan in the name of Sinidinabal, which seems to be borne by Assur-bani-pal in *Tablet* K *195 of the British Museum,* and which is really the name of his elder brother; it found numerous supporters as soon as Pinches had discovered the tablets dated in the reign of Kandalanu, and the majority of Assyriologists and historians hold that Kandalanu and Assur-bani-pal are one and the same person.

sovereignties of Marduk and Assur. He delegated the administration of Babylonian affairs to Shamash-danâni, one of his high officers of State,[1] and re-entered Nineveh with an amount of spoil almost equalling that taken from Egypt after the sack of Thebes. Kuta, Sippara, and Borsippa, the vassal states of Babylon, which had shared the misfortune of their mistress, were, like her, cleared of their ruins, rebuilt and repeopled, and were placed under the authority of Shamash-danâni : such was their inherent vitality that in the short space of ten or a dozen years they had repaired their losses and reattained their wonted prosperity. Soon no effect of their disaster remained except an additional incentive for hating Nineveh, and a determination more relentless than ever not to spare her when the day of her overthrow should come and they should have her in their power.

It was impossible for so violent and so prolonged a crisis to take place without in some degree injuring the prestige of the empire. Subjects and allies of long standing remained loyal, but those only recently subjugated by conquest, as well as the neighbouring independent kingdoms, without hesitation threw off the yoke of suzerainty or of obligatory friendship under which they had chafed. Egypt freed herself from foreign domination as soon as the possibilities of war with Elam had shown themselves, and it was Psammetichus of Sais, son of Necho, one of the princes most favoured by the court of Nineveh, who set

[1] This Shamash-danâni, who was *limmu* in **644 B.C.**, was called at that date prefect of Akkad, that is to say, of Babylon. He probably entered on this office immediately after the taking of the city.

on foot this campaign against his former patron. He expelled the Assyrian garrisons, reduced the petty native princes to submission, and once more set up the kingdom of the Pharaohs from Elephantinê to the Syrian desert, without Assur-bani-pal having been able to spare a single soldier to prevent him, or to bring him back to a sense of his duty. The details of his proceedings are unknown to us: we learn only that he owed his success to mercenaries imported from Asia Minor, and the Assyrian chroniclers, unaccustomed to discriminate between the different peoples dwelling on the shores of the Ægean, believed that these auxiliaries were supplied to the Pharaoh by the only sovereign with whom they had had any dealings, namely, Gyges, King of Lydia. That Gyges had had negotiations with Psammetichus and procured assistance for him has not yet been proved, but to assert that he was incapable of conceiving and executing such a design is quite a different matter. On the contrary, all the information we possess concerning his reign shows that he was daring in his political undertakings, and anxious to court alliances with the most distant countries. The man who tried to draw Assur-bani-pal into a joint enterprise against the Cimmerians would not have hesitated to ally himself with Psammetichus if he hoped to gain the least profit from so doing. Constant intercourse by sea took place between Ionia or Caria and Egypt, and no event of any importance could occur in the Delta without being promptly reported in Ephesus or Miletus. Before this time the Heraclid rulers of Sardes had lived on excellent terms with most of the Æolian or Ionian colonies: during the anxious years which followed his accession Gyges went still further, and entered into direct relations with the nations of Greece itself. It was no longer to the gods of Asia, to Zeus of Telmissos, that he addressed himself in order to legitimatise his new sovereignty, but, like Midas of Phrygia, he applied to the prophetic god of Hellas, to the Delphian Apollo and his priests. He recompensed them lavishly for pronouncing judgment in his favour: beside the silver offerings with which he endowed the temple at Delphi, he presented to it a number of golden vases, and, among others, six *craters* weighing thirty talents each, which, placed by the side of the throne of Midas, were still objects of admiration in the treasury of the Corinthians in the time of Herodotus. To these he added at various times such valuable gifts that the Pythian priestess, who had hitherto been poor, was in later times accounted to have owed to him her wealth. Having made sure of the good will of the immortals, Gyges endeavoured to extend his influence among the Greek colonies along

PSAMMETICHUS I.[1]

[1] Drawn by **Boudier**, from a photograph.

the coast, and if he did not in every case gain a footing amongst them, his failure seems to have been due, not to his incapacity, but to the force of circumstances or to the ambiguous position which he happened to occupy with regard to these colonies. Ambition naturally incited him to annex them and make them into Lydian cities, but the bold disposition of their inhabitants and their impatience of constraint never allowed any foreign rule to be established over them: conquest, to be permanent, would have to be preceded by a long period of alliance on equal terms, and of discreet patronage which might insensibly accustom them to recognise in their former friend, first a protector, and then a suzerain imbued with respect for their laws and constitution. Gyges endeavoured to conciliate them severally, and to attach them to himself by treaties favourable to their interests or flattering to their vanity, and by timely and generous assistance in their internecine quarrels; and thus, secretly fostering their mutual jealousies, he was able to reduce some by force of arms without causing too much offence to the rest. He took Colophon, and also, after several fruitless campaigns, the Magnesia which lay near Sardes, Magnesia of Sipylos, tradition subsequently adorning this fortunate episode in his history with various amusing anecdotes. According to one account he had a favourite in a youth of marvellous beauty called Magnes, whom the Magnesians, as an act of defiance to Gyges, had mutilated till he was past recognition; and it was related that the king appealed to the fortune of war to avenge the affront. By a bold stroke he seized the lower quarters of Smyrna, but was unable to take the citadel,[1] and while engaged in the struggle with this city, he entered into a friendly understanding with Ephesus and Miletus. Ephesus, situated at the mouth of the river Cayster, was the natural port of Sardes, the market in which the gold of Lydia, and the commodities imported from the East by the caravans which traversed the royal route, might be exchanged for the products of Hellas and of the countries of the West visited by the Greek mariners. The city was at this time under the control of a family of rich shipowners, of whom the head was called Melas: Gyges gave him his daughter in marriage, and by this union gained free access to the seaboard for himself and his successors. The reason for his not pushing his advantages further in this direction is not hard to discover; since the fall of the kingdom of Phrygia had left his eastern frontier unprotected, the attacks of the Cimmerians had obliged him to concentrate his forces in the interior, and though he had always successfully repulsed them, the obstinacy with which these inroads were renewed year after year prevented him from further occupying himself with the Greek cities. He had carefully fortified his vast domains in the basin of the Rhyndakos, he had reconquered the Troad, and though he had been unable to expel the barbarians from Adramyttium, he prevented them from having any inland communications. Miletus rendered vigorous assistance in this work of

[1] Herodotus mentions this war without entering into any details. We know from Pausanias that the people of Smyrna defended themselves bravely, and that the poet Mimnermus composed an elegy on this episode in their history.

consolidating his power, for she was interested in maintaining a buffer state between herself and the marauders who had already robbed her of Sinope; and it was for this reason that Gyges, after mercilessly harassing her at the beginning of his reign, now preferred to enter into an alliance with her. He had given the Milesians permission to establish colonies along the Hellespont and the Propontid at the principal points where communication took place between Europe and Asia; Abydos, Lampsacus, Parium, and Cyzicus, founded successively by Milesian admirals, prevented the tribes which remained in Thrace from crossing over to reinforce their kinsfolk who were devastating Phrygia.

Gyges had hoped that his act of deference would have obtained for him the active support of Assur-banipal, and during the following years he perseveringly continued at intervals to send envoys to Nineveh: on one occasion he despatched with the embassy two Cimmerian chiefs taken in battle, and whom he offered in token of homage to the gods of Assyria. Experience however, soon convinced him that his expectations were vain; the Assyrians, far from creating a diversion in his favour, were careful to avoid every undertaking which might draw the attention of the barbarians on themselves. As soon as Gyges fully understood their policy he broke off all connection with them, and thenceforth relied on himself alone for the protection of his interests The disappointment he thus experienced probably stirred up his anger against Assyria, and if he actually came to the aid of Psammetichus, the desire of giving expression to a secret feeling of rancour no doubt contributed to his decision. Assur-bani-pal deeply resented this conduct, but Lydia was too far off for him to wreak his vengeance on it in a direct manner, and he could only beseech the gods to revenge what he was pleased to consider as base ingratitude: he therefore prayed Assur and Ishtar that "his corpse might lie outstretched before his enemies, and his bones be scattered far and wide." A certain Tugdami was at that time reigning over the Cimmerians, and seems to have given to their hitherto undisciplined hordes some degree of cohesion and guidance.[1] He gathered under his standard not only the Trêres, the Thracian kinsfolk of the Cimmerians, but some of the Asianic tribes, such as the Lycians,[2] who were beginning to feel uneasy at the growing prosperity of Gyges, and let them loose upon their Lydian quarry. Their heavy cavalry, with metal helmets and long steel swords, overran the peninsula from end to end, treading down everything under their horses' hoofs. Gyges did his best to stand up against the storm, but his lancers quailed beneath the shock and fled in confusion: he himself perished in the flight, and his corpse remained in the

[1] The name Tugdami, mentioned in the hymn published by Strong, has been identified by Sayce with the Cimmerian chief mentioned by Strabo under the name of Lygdamis. The opinion of Sayce has been adopted by other Assyriologists. The inscription makes Tugdami a king of the Manda, and thus overthrows the hypothesis that Lygdamis or Dygdamis was a Lycian chief who managed to discipline the barbarian hordes.

[2] The alliance of the Lycians with the Cimmerians and Trêres is known from the evidence of Callisthenes preserved for us by Strabo. It is probable that many of the marauding tribes of the Taurus—Isaurians, Lycaonians, and Pamphylians—similarly joined the Cimmerians.

enemy's hands (652 B.C.). The whole of Lydia was mercilessly ravaged, and the lower town of Sardes was taken by storm.¹ Ardys, who had succeeded his father on the throne, was able, however, to save the citadel: he rallied around him the remnants of his army and once more took the field. The cities of Ionia made common cause with him; their hoplites issued victorious

BATTLE OF THE CIMMERIANS AGAINST THE GREEKS ACCOMPANIED BY THEIR DOGS.²

from more than one engagement, and their dogs, trained to harry fearlessly the horses of the enemy, often took an active part in the battle. City after city was attacked by the barbarians, and the suburbs plundered. Ephesus, on account of the wealth it contained, formed their chief attraction, but their forces dashed themselves fruitlessly against its walls; they avenged themselves for their failure by setting on fire the temple of Artemis which stood

¹ Strabo states definitely that it was Lygdamis who took the city. The account given by the same author of a double destruction of Sardes in 652 and 682 B.C. is due to an unfortunate borrowing from the work of Callisthenes.

² Drawn by Faucher-Gudin, from the sarcophagus of Clazomenæ.

in the outskirts. This act of sacrilege profoundly stirred the whole Hellenic world, and when the first fury of pillage was exhausted, the barbarians themselves seemed to have been struck with superstitious horror at their crime: deadly fevers contracted in the marshes near the city thinned their ranks, and in the scourge which struck down their forces they recognised the chastisement of the goddess.[1] The survivors abandoned the siege and withdrew in disorder towards the mountains of the interior. On their way they surprised Magnesia on the Mæander and entirely destroyed it, but this constituted their sole military success: elsewhere, they contented themselves with devastating the fields without venturing to attack the fortified towns. Scarcely had Ardys freed himself from their unwelcome presence, than, like his father before him, he tried to win the support of Assyria. He sent an envoy to Nineveh with a letter couched in very humble terms: "The king whom the gods acknowledge, art thou; for as soon as thou hadst pronounced imprecations against my father, misfortune overtook him. I am thy trembling servant; receive my homage graciously, and I will bear thy yoke!" Assur-bani-pal did not harden his heart to this suppliant who confessed his fault so piteously, and circumstances shortly constrained him to give a more efficacious proof of his favour to Ardys than he had done in the days of Gyges. On quitting Lydia,

[1] The invasion of Ionia by the Cimmerians is indicated in general terms by Herodotus; the details of the attack on Ephesus and the destruction of the temple of Artemis are preserved in a passage of Callimachus, and in the fragments quoted by Hesychius.

Tugdami, with his hordes, had turned eastwards, bent upon renewing in the provinces of the Taurus and the Euphrates the same destructive raids which he had made among the peoples of the Ægean seaboard; but in the gorges of Cilicia he came into contact with forces much superior to his own, and fell fighting against them about the year 645 B.C. His son Sanda-khshatru led the survivors this disaster back towards the centre of the peninsula but the conflict had been so sanguinary that the Cimmerian power never fully recovered from it. Assur-banipal celebrated the victory won by his generals with a solemn thanksgiving to Marduk, accompanied by substantial offerings of gold and objects of great value.[1] The tranquillity of the north-west frontier was thus for a time secured, and this success most opportunely afforded the king leisure to turn his attention to those of his vassals who, having thrown off their allegiance during the war against Shamash-shumukîn, had not yet returned to their obedience. Among these were the Arabs and the petty princes of Egypt. The contingents furnished by Yauta son of Hazael, had behaved valiantly during the siege of Babylon, and when they thought the end was approaching, their leaders, Abiyatê and Aamu, had tried to cut a way through the Assyrian lines: being repulsed, they had laid down their arms on condition of their lives being

[1] Strabo was aware, perhaps from Xanthus of Lydia, that Lygdamis fallen in battle in Cilicia. The hymn to Marduk published by Strong informs us that the Cimmerian chief fell upon the Assyrians and that his son Sandakhshatru carried on hostilities some time longer. Sanda-khshatru is an Iranian name of the same type as that of the Median king Uvakhshatra or Cyaxares.

spared. There now remained the bulk of the Arab tribes to be reduced to submission, and the recent experiences of Esarhaddon had shown the difficulties attending this task. Assur-bani-pal entrusted its accomplishment to his subjects in Edom, Moab, Ammon, the Haurân, and Damascus, since, dwelling on the very borders of the desert, they were familiar with the routes and the methods of warfare best suited to the country. They proved victorious all along the line. Yauta, betrayed by his own subjects, took refuge with the Nabatæans; but their king, Nadanu, although he did not actually deliver him up to the Assyrians, refused to grant him an asylum, and the unhappy man was finally obliged to surrender to his pursuers. His cousin Uatê, son of Birdadda, was made chief in his place by the Assyrians, and Yauta was sent to Nineveh, where he was exposed at one of the city gates, chained in a niche beside the watch-dogs. Amuladdin, the leading prince of Kedar, met with no better fate: he was overcome, in spite of the assistance rendered him by Adîya, the queen of a neighbouring tribe, and was also carried away into captivity. His defeat completed the discouragement of the tribes who still remained unsubdued. They implored mercy, which Assur-bani-pal granted to them, although he deposed most of their sheikhs, and appointed as their ruler that Abiyatê who had dwelt at his court since the capitulation of Babylon. Abiyatê took the oath of fidelity, and was sent back to Kedar, where he was proclaimed king of all the Arab tribes under the suzerainty of Assyria.[1]

[1] The *Cylinder B of the Brit. Mus.* attributes to the reign of Assur-bani-pal

Of all the countries which had thrown off their allegiance during the late troubles, Egypt alone remained unpunished, and it now seemed as if its turn had come to suffer chastisement for its rebellion. It was, indeed, not to be tolerated that so rich and so recently acquired a province should slip from the grasp of the very sovereign who had completed its conquest, without his making an effort on the first opportunity to reduce it once more to submission. Such inaction on his part would be a confession of impotence, of which the other vassals of the empire would quickly take advantage: Tyre, Judah, Moab the petty kings of the Taurus, and the chiefs of Media would follow the example of Pharaoh, and the whole work of the last three centuries would have to be done over again. There can be no doubt that Assur-bani-pal cherished the secret hope of recovering Egypt in a short campaign, and that he hoped to attach it to the empire by more permanent bonds than before, but as a preliminary to executing this purpose it was necessary to close and settle if possible the account still open against Elam Recent events had left the two rival powers in such a position that neither peace nor even a truce of long duration could possibly exist between them. Elam injured, humiliated, and banished from the plains of the Lower Euphrates, over which she had claimed at times an almost exclusive right of pillage, was yet not

a whole series of events, comprising the first submission of Yauta and the restitution of the statues of Atarsamaîn, which had taken place under Esarhaddon. The Assyrian annalists do not seem to have always clealy distinguished between Yauta, son of Hazael, and Uatê, son of Birdadda.

sufficiently enfeebled by her disasters to be convinced of her decided inferiority to Assyria. Only one portion of her forces, and that perhaps the smallest, had taken the field and sustained serious reverses: she had still at her disposal, besides the peoples of the plain and the marshes who had suffered the most, those almost inexhaustible reserves of warlike and hardy mountaineers, whose tribes were ranged on the heights which bounded the horizon, occupying the elevated valleys of the Uknu, the Ulai, and their nameless affluents, on the western or southern slopes or in the enclosed basins of the Iranian table-land. Here Elam had at her command at least as many men as her adversaries could muster against her, and though these barbarian contingents lacked discipline and systematic training, their bravery compensated for the imperfection of their military education. Elam not only refused to admit herself conquered, but she believed herself sure of final victory, and, as a matter of fact, it is not at all certain that Assur-bani-pal's generals would ever have completely triumphed over her, if internal discords and treason had not too often paralysed her powers. The partisans of Khumbân-igash were largely responsible for bringing about the catastrophe in which Tiummân had perished, and those who sided with Tammaritu had not feared to provoke a revolt at the moment when Khumbân-igash was occupied in Chaldæa; Indabigash in his turn had risen in rebellion in the rear of Tammaritu, and his intervention had enabled the Assyrians to deal their final blow at Shamash-shumukîn. The one idea of the non-reigning members of the royal house was to depose the reigning sovereign, and they considered all means to this end as justifiable, whether assassination, revolt desertion to the enemy, or defection on the very field of battle. As soon as one of them had dethroned another hatred of the foreigner again reigned supreme in his breast and he donned his armour with a firm determination to bring the struggle to an end, but the course he had pursued towards his predecessor was now adopted by one of his relatives towards himself; the enemy meanwhile was still under arms, and each of these revolutions brought him a step nearer to the goal of his endeavours, the complete overthrow of the Elamite kingdom and its annexation to the empire of Nineveh. Even before the struggle with Babylon was concluded, Assur-bani-pal had demanded of Indabigash the release of the Assyrians whom Nabo-bel-shumu had carried off in his train, besides the extradition of that personage himself. Indabigash had no desire for war at this juncture, but hesitated to surrender the Kaldâ, who had always served him faithfully: he entered into negotiations which were interminably prolonged, neither of the two parties being anxious to bring them to a close. After the fall of Babylon, Assur-bani-pal, who was tenacious in his hatred, summoned the Elamite ambassadors, and sent them back to their master with a message conceived in the following menacing terms: "If thou dost not surrender those men, I will go and destroy thy cities, and lead into captivity the inhabitants of Susa, Madaktu, and Khaîdalu. I will hurl thee from thy throne, and will set up another thereon: as aforetime I destroyed Tiummân, so will I destroy thee." A detachment of troops was sent to enforce the message of defiance, but when the messengers had reached the frontier town of Dêri, Indabigash was no longer there: his nobles had assassinated him and had elected Khumbân-khaldash, the son of Attamêtush, king in his stead. The opportunity was a favourable one to sow the seeds of division in the Elamite camp, before the usurper should have time to consolidate his power Assur-bani-pal therefore threw himself into the cause of Tammaritu, supporting him with an army to which many malcontents speedily rallied. The Aramæans and the cities of the marsh-lands on the littoral, Khilmu, Billatê, Dummuku, Sulâa, Lakhiru, and Dibirîna, submitted without a struggle, and the invaders met with no resistance till they reached Bît-Imbi. This town had formerly been conquered by Sennacherib, but it had afterwards returned to the rule of its ancient masters, who had strongly fortified it It now offered a determined resistance, but without success its population was decimated, and the survivors mutilated and sent as captives into Assyria—among them the commander of the garrison, Imbappi, son-in-law of Khumbân-khaldash, together with the harem of Tiummân, with his sons and daughters, and all the members of his family whom his successors had left under guard in the citadel. The siege had been pushed forward so rapidly that the king had not been able to make any attempt to relieve the defenders : besides this, a pretender had risen up against him, one Umbakhabua, who had been accepted as king by the important district of Bubîlu. The fall of Bît-Imbi filled the two competitors with fear : they abandoned their homes and fled, the one to the mountains, the other to the lowlands on the shores of the Nar-Marratum. Tammaritu entered Susa in triumph and was enthroned afresh; but the insolence and rapacity of his auxiliaries was so ruthlessly manifested, that at the end of some days resolved to rid himself of them by the sword. A traitor having revealed the design, Tammaritu was seized, stripped of his royal apparel, and cast into prison. The generals Assur-bani-pal had no one whom they could proclaim king in his stead, and furthermore, the season being well advanced, the Elamites, who had recovered from their first alarm, were returning in a body, and threatened to cut off the Assyrian retreat: they therefore evacuated Susa, and regained Assyria with their booty. They burnt all the towns along the route whose walls were insufficient to protect them against a sudden escalade or an attack of a few hours' duration, and the country between the capital and the frontier soon contained nothing but heaps of smoking ruins (647 B.C.).[1]

The campaign, which had been so successful at the outset, had not produced all the results expected from it. The Assyrians had hoped henceforth to maintain control of Elam through Tammaritu, but in a short time they had been obliged to throw aside the instrument with which they counted on effecting the complete humiliation of the nation: Khumbânkhaldash had reoccupied Susa, following on the heels of the last Assyrian detachment, and he reigned as king once more without surrendering Nabo-bel

---

[1] The difficulty we experience in locating on the map most of the names of Elamite towns is the reason why we cannot determine with any certainty the whole itinerary followed by the Assyrian army.

shumi, or restoring the statue of Nana, or fulfilling any of the conditions which had been the price of a title to the throne. Assur-bani-pal was not inclined to bear patiently this partial reverse; as soon as spring returned he again demanded the surrender of the Chaldæan and the goddess, under pain of immediate invasion. Khumbân-khaldash offered to expel Nabo-bel-shumi from Lakhiru where he had entrenched himself, and to thrust him towards the Assyrian frontier, where the king's troops would be able to capture him. His offer was not accepted, and a second embassy, headed by Tammaritu, who was once more in favour, arrived to propose more trenchant terms. The Elamite might have gone so far as to grant the extradition of Nabo-bel-shumi, but if he had yielded the point concerning Nana, a rebellion would have broken out in the streets of Susa: he preferred war, and prepared in desperation to carry it on to the bitter end. The conflict was long and sanguinary, and the result disastrous for Elam. Bit-Imbi opened its gates, the district of Rashi surrendered at discretion, followed by the city of Khamanu and its environs, and the Assyrians approached Madaktu: Khumbân-khaldash evacuated the place before they reached it, and withdrew beneath the walls of Dur-Undasi, on the western bank of the Ididi. His enemies pursued him thither, but the stream was swift and swollen by rain, so that for two days they encamped on its bank without daring to cross, and were perhaps growing discouraged, when Ishtar of Arbela once more came to the rescue. Appearing in a dream to one of her seers, she said, "I myself go before Assur-bani-pal, the king whom my hands have created;" the army, emboldened by this revelation overcame the obstacle by a vigorous effort, and dashed impetuously over regions as yet unvisited by any conqueror The Assyrians burnt down fourteen royal cities, numberless small towns, and destroyed the cornfields, the vines, and the orchards; Khumbân-khaldash, utterly exhausted, fled to the mountains "like a young dog." Banunu and the districts of Tasarra, twenty cities in the country of Khumir, Khaîdalu, and Bashimu, succumbed one after another, and when the invaders at length decided to retrace their steps to the frontier, Susa, deserted by her soldiers and deprived of her leaders, lay before them an easy prey. It was not the first time in the last quarter of a century that the Assyrians had had the city at their mercy. They had made some stay in it after the battle of Tullîz, and also after the taking of Bît-Imbi in the preceding year; but on those occasions they had visited it as allies, to enthrone a king owing allegiance to their own sovereign, and political exigencies had obliged them to repress their pillaging instincts and their long-standing hatred. Now that they had come as enemies, they were restrained by no considerations of diplomacy: the city was systematically pillaged and the booty found in it was so immense that the sack lasted an entire month. The royal treasury was emptied of its gold and silver, its metals and the valuable objects which had been brought to it from Sumir, Accad, and Karduniash at successive periods from the most remote ages down to that day, in the course of the successful invasions conducted by the princes of Susa beyond the Tigris; among them, the riches of the Babylonian temples,

DESECRATION OF THE PROPHETIC STATUES 251

which Shamash-shumukîn had lavished on Tiummân to purchase his support, being easily distinguishable The furniture of the palace was sent to Nineveh in a long procession it comprised beds and chairs of ivory and chariots encr sted with enamel and precious stones the horses of which were caparisoned with gold The soldiers made their way into the ziggurât, tore down the plates of

STATUES OF THE GODS CARRIED OFF BY ASSYRIAN SOLDIERY.[1]

ruddy copper violated the sanctuary and desecrated the prophetic statues of the gods who dwelt within it shrouded in the sacred gloom and whose names were only uttered by their devotees with trembling lips Shumudu, Lagamar Partikira, Ammankasibar, Udurân, Sapak, Aîpaksina, Bilala Panintimri, and Kindakarpu, were now brought forth to the light and made ready to be carried into exile together with their belongings and their priests Thirty two statues of the kings both ancient and modern in silver gold

Drawn by Faucher-Gudin, from LAYARD, *The Monuments of Nineveh.*

bronze, and marble, escorted the gods on their exodus among their number being those of Khumbânigash, son Umbadarâ, Shutruk-nakhunta, and Tammaritu II., the sovereigns who had treated Assyria with the greatest indignity. The effigy of Khalludush was subjected to humiliating outrage: "his mouth, with its menacing smile was mutilated; his lips, which breathed forth defiance were slit; his hands, which had brandished the bow against Assur, were cut off," to avenge, though tardily, the ill success of Sennacherib. The sacred groves shared the fate of the temples, and all the riches collected in them by generations of victors were carried off in cartloads. They contained, amongst other edifices, the tombs of the ancient heroes of Elam, who had feared neither Assur nor Ishtar and who had often brought trouble on the ancestors Assur-bani-pal. Their sepulchres were violated, their coffins broken open, their bones collected and despatched to Nineveh, to crumble finally into dust in the land exile: their souls, chained to their mortal bodies, shared their captivity, and if they were provided with the necessary sustenance and libations to keep them from annihilation, it was not from any motives of compassion or pity, but from a refinement of vengeance, in order that they might the longer taste the humiliation of captivity. The image of Nana was found among those of the native gods: it was now separated from them, and after having been cleansed from pollution by the prescribed ceremonies, it was conducted to Uruk, which it entered in triumph on the 1st of the month Kislev. It was reinstated in the temple it had inhabited of old: sixteen hundred and thirty-five years

THE GREAT TUMULUS OF SUSA.
Drawn by Boudier, from a photographic panorama by Dieulafoy.

had passed since it had been carried off, in the reign of Kutur-nakhunta, to dwell as a prisoner in Susa.

Assur-bani-pal had no intention of preserving the city of Susa from destruction, or of making it the capital of a province which should comprise the plain of Elam. Possibly it appeared to him too difficult to defend as long as the mountain tribes remained unsubdued, or perhaps the Elamites themselves were not so completely demoralised as he was pleased to describe them in his inscriptions, and the attacks of their irregular troops would have rendered the prolonged sojourn of the Assyrian garrison difficult, if not impossible. Whatever the reason, as soon as the work of pillage was fully accomplished, the army continued its march towards the frontier, carrying with it the customary spoil of the captured towns, and their whole population, or all, at least, who had not fled at the approach of the enemy. The king reserved for himself the archers and pikemen, whom he incorporated into his own bodyguard, as well as the artisans, smelters, sculptors, and stonemasons, whose talents he turned to account in the construction and decoration of his palaces; the remainder of the inhabitants he apportioned, like so many sheep, to the cities and the temples, governors of provinces, officers of state, military chiefs, and private soldiers. Khumbân-khaldash reoccupied Susa after the Assyrians had quitted it, but the misery there was so great that he could not endure it: he therefore transferred his court to Madaktu, one of the royal cities which had suffered least from the invasion, and he there tried to establish a regular government. Rival claimants to the throne had sprung up, but he overcame them without much difficulty: one of them, named Paê, took refuge in Assyria, joining Tammaritu and that little band of dethroned kings or pretenders to the throne of Susa, of whom Assur-bani-pal had so adroitly made use to divide the forces of his adversary. Khumbân-khaldash might well believe that the transportation of the statue of Nana and the sack of Susa had satisfied the vengeance of the Assyrians, at least for a time, and that they would afford him a respite, however short; but he had reckoned without taking into consideration the hatred which had pursued Nabo-bel-shumi during so many years: an envoy followed him as far as Madaktu, and offered Khumbân-khaldash once more the choice between the extradition of the Chaldæan or the immediate reopening of hostilities. He seems to have had a moment's hesitation, but when Nabo-bel-shumi was informed of the terms offered by the envoy, "life had no more value in his eyes: he desired death." He ordered his shield-bearer to slay him, and when the man refused to do so, declaring that he could not live without his master, they stabbed each other simultaneously, and perished, as they had lived, together. Khumbân-khaldash, delivered by this suicide from his embarrassments, had the corpse of the master and the head of the faithful shield-bearer duly embalmed, and sent them to Nineveh. Assur-bani-pal mutilated the wretched body in order to render the conditions of life in the other world harder for the soul: he cut off its head, and forbade the burial of the remains, or the rendering to the dead of the most simple offerings. About this time the inhabitants of Bît-Imbi, of Til-Khumba, and a dozen other small towns, who had fled for refuge to the woods of Mount Saladri, came forth from their hiding-places and cast themselves on the mercy of the conqueror: he deigned to receive them graciously, and enrolled them in his guard, together with the prisoners taken in the last campaign. He was contented to leave Elam to itself for the moment, as he was disquieted at the turn affairs were taking in Arabia. Abiyatê, scarcely seated on the throne, had refused to pay tribute, and had persuaded Uatê and Nadanu to join him in his contumacy; several cities along the Phœnician seaboard, led away by his example, shut their gates and declared themselves independent. Assur-bani-pal had borne all this patiently, while the mass of his troops were engaged against Khumbân-khaldash; but after the destruction of Susa, he determined to revenge himself. His forces left Nineveh in the spring of 642 B.C., crossed the Euphrates, and the line of wooded hills which bordered the course of the river towards the west, provisioned themselves with water at the halting-place of Laribda, and plunged into the desert in search of the rebels. The Assyrians overran the country of Mash, from the town of Iarki to Azalla, where "there dwell no beasts of the field, where no bird of the sky builds its nest," and then, after filling their water-skins at the cisterns of Azalia, they advanced boldly into the thirsty lands which extend towards Qurazite; they next crossed the territory of Kedar, cutting down the trees, filling up the wells, burning the tents, and reached Damascus from the north-east side, bringing in their train innumerable flocks of asses, sheep, camels, and slaves The Bedâwin of the north had remained passive, but the Nabatheans, encouraged by the remoteness of their country and the difficulty of access to it, persisted in their rebellion. The Assyrian generals did not waste much time in celebrating their victory in the Syrian capital: on the 3rd of Ab, forty days after leaving the Chaldæan frontier, they started from Damascus towards the south and seized the stronghold of Khalkhuliti, at the foot of the basaltic plateau overlooked by the mountains the Haurân; they then destroyed all the fortresses the country one after another, driving the inhabitants to take shelter in the rugged range of volcanic rocks, where they were blockaded, and finally reduced by famine: Abiyatê capitulated, Nadanu ransomed himself by a promise of tribute, and the whole desert between Syria and the Euphrates fell once more into the condition of an Assyrian province. Before returning to Nineveh, Assur-bani-pal's generals inflicted chastisement on Akko and Ushu, the two chief Tyrian cities which had revolted, and this vigorous action confirmed the fidelity of the Assyrian vassals in Palestine. Uatê's life was spared, but his lip and cheek were pierced by the hand of the king himself, and he was led by a cord passed through the wounds, as if he had been a wild beast intended for domestication; a dog's collar was riveted round his neck, and he was exposed in a cage at one of the gates of Nineveh. Aam the brother of Abiyatê, was less fortunate, for he was flayed alive before the eyes of the mob. Assyria was glutted with the spoil: the king, as was customary reserved for his own service the able-bodied men for the purpose of recruiting his battalions, distributing the remainder among his officers and soldiers. The camels captured were so numerous that their market-value was for a long time much reduced; they were offered in the open market, like sheep, for a half-shekel of silver apiece, and the vendor thought himself fortunate to find a purchaser even at this price.

The final ruin of Elam followed swiftly on the subjugation of Arabia. While one division of the army was scouring the desert, the remainder were searching the upland valleys of the Ulaî and the Uknu, and relentlessly pursuing Khumbân-khaldash. The wretched monarch was now in command of merely a few bands of tattered followers, and could no longer take the field; the approach of the enemy obliged him to flee from Madaktu, and entrench himself on the heights. Famine, misery, and probably also the treachery of his last adherents, soon drove him from his position, and, despairing of his cause, he surrendered himself to the officers who were in pursuit of him. He was the third king of Elam whom fate had cast alive into the hands of the conqueror: his arrival at Nineveh afforded the haughty Assur-bani-pal an occasion for celebrating one of those triumphal processions in which his proud soul delighted, and of going in solemn state to thank the gods for the overthrow of his most formidable enemy. On the day when he went to prostrate himself before Assur and Ishtar, he sent for Tammaritu, Paê, and Khumbân-khaldash, and adding to them Uatê, who was taken out of his cage for the occasion, he harnessed all four to his chariot of state, and caused himself to be drawn through Nineveh by this team of fallen sovereigns to the gate of the temple of Ê-mashmash. And, indeed at that moment, he might reasonably consider himself as having reached the zenith of his power. Egypt, it is true, still remained unpunished, and its renewed vitality under the influence of the Saïte Pharaohs allowed no hope of its being speedily brought back into subjection but its intrigues no longer exerted any influence over Syria, and Tyre itself appeared to be resigned to the loss of its possessions on the mainland. Lydia under the rule of Ardys continued to maintain intermittent intercourse with its distant protector. The provinces the Taurus, delivered from the terror inspired by the Cimmerians, desired peace above all things, and the Mannai had remained quiet since the defeat of Akhsheri. Babylon was rapidly recovering from the ills she had endured. She consoled herself for her actual servitude by her habitual simulation of independence; she called Assur-bani-pal Kandalanu, and this new name allowed her to fancy she had a separate king, distinct from the King of Assyria. Elam no longer existed. Its plains and marsh lands were doubtless occupied by Assyrian garrisons, and formed an illdefined annexation to Nineveh the mountain tribes retained their autonomy, and although still a source of annoyance to their neighbours by their raids or sudden incursions, they no longer constituted a real danger to the state: if there still remained some independent Elamite states, Elam itself, the most ancient except Babylon of all the Asiatic kingdoms, was erased from the map of the world. The memories of her actual history were soon effaced, or were relegated to the region of legend, where the fabulous Memnon supplanted in the memory of men those lines of hardy conquerors who had levied tribute from Syria in the day when Nineveh was still an obscure provincial town. Assyria alone remained, enthroned on the ruins of the past, and her dominion seemed established for all time; yet, on closer investigation, indications were not wanting of the cruel sufferings that she also had endured. Once again, as after the wars of Tiglath-pileser I. and those of Assur-nazir-pal and Shalmaneser III., her chiefs had overtaxed her powers by a long series of unremitting wars against vigorous foes. Doubtless the countries comprised within her wide empire furnished her with a more ample revenue and less restricted resources than had been at the command of the little province of ancient days, which had been bounded by the Khabur and the Zab, and lay on the two banks of the middle course of the Tigris; but, on the other hand, the adversaries against whom she had measured her forces, and whom she had overthrown, were more important and of far greater strength than her former rivals. She had paid dearly for humiliating Egypt and laying Babylon in the dust. As soon as Babylon was overthrown, she had, without pausing to take breath, joined issue with Elam, and had only succeeded in triumphing over it by drawing upon her resources to the utmost during many years: when the struggle was over, she realised to what an extent she had been weakened by so lavish an outpouring of the blood of her citizens. The Babylonian and Elamite recruits whom she incorporated into her army after eac of her military expeditions, more or less compensated for the void which victory itself had caused in her population and her troops; but the fidelity of these vanquished foes of yesterday, still smarting from their defeat, could not be relied on, and the entire assimilation of their children to their conquerors was the work of at least one or two generations. Assyria, therefore, was on the eve of one of those periods of exhaustion which had so often enfeebled her national vitality and imperilled her very existence On each previous occasion she had, it is true, recovered after a more or less protracted crisis, and the brilliancy of her prospects, though obscured for a moment, appeared to be increased by their temporary eclipse. There was therefore, good reason to hope that she would recover from her latest phase of depression; and the only danger to be apprehended was that some foreign power, profiting by her momentary weakness, might rise up and force her while still suffering from the effects of her heroic labours to take the field once more.

# THE MEDES AND THE SECOND CHALDÆAN EMPIRE

THE FALL OF NINEVEH AND THE RISE OF THE CHALDÆAN AND MEDIAN EMPIRES—THE XXVI[th] EGYPTIAN DYNASTY: CYAXARES, ALYATTES, AND NEBUCHADREZZAR.

*The legendary history of the kings of Media and the first contact of the Medes with the Assyrians: the alleged Iranian migrations of the Avesta—Media proper, its fauna and flora; Phraortes and the beginning of the Median empire—Persia proper and the Persians; conquest of Persia by the Medes—The last monuments of Assur-bani-pal: the library of Kouyunjik—Phraortes defeated and slain by the Assyrians.*

*Cyaxares and his first attack on Nineveh—The Assyrian triangle and the defence of Nineveh: Assur-bani-pal summons the Scythians to his aid—The Scythian invasion—Judah under Manasseh and Amon: development in the conceptions of the prophets—The Scythians in Syria and on the borders of Egypt: they are defeated and driven back by Cyaxares—The last kings of Nineveh and*

*Nabopolassar—Taking and destruction of Nineveh: division of the Assyrian empire between the Chaldæans and the Medes* (608 B.C.).

*The XXVI*ᵗʰ *Egyptian dynasty—Psammetichus I. and the Ionian and Carian mercenaries; final retreat of the Ethiopians and the annexation of the Theban principality; the end of Egypt as a great power—First Greek settlements in the Delta; flight of the Mashauasha and the reorganisation of the army—Resumption of important works and the renaissance of art in Egypt—The occupation of Ashdod, and the Syrian policy of Psammetichus I.*

*Josiah, King of Judah: the discovery and public reading of the Book of the Covenant; the religious reform—Necho II. invades Syria: Josiah slain at Megiddo, the battle of Carchemish—Nebuchadrezzar II.: his policy with regard to Media—The conquests of Cyaxares and the struggles of the Mermnadæ against the Greek colonies—The war between Alyattes and Cyaxares: the battle of the Halys and the peace of 585 B.C.—Necho reorganises his army and his fleet: the circumnavigation of Africa—Jeremiah and the Egyptian party in Jerusalem: the revolt of Jehoiakim and the captivity of Jehoiachin.*

*Psammetichus I. and Zedekiah—Apries and the revolt of Tyre and of Judah: the siege and destruction of Jerusalem—The last convulsions of Judah and the submission of Tyre; the successes of Apries in Phœnicia—The Greeks in Libya and the founding of Cyrene: the defeat of Irasa and the fall of Apries—Amasis and the campaign of Nebuchadrezzar against Egypt—Relations between Nebuchadrezzar and Astyages—The fortifications of Babylon and the rebuilding of the Great Ziggurât—The successors of Nebuchadrezzar: Nabonidus.*

SCYTHIANS LASSOING HORSES.[1]

# CHAPTER III

## THE MEDES AND THE SECOND CHALDÆAN EMPIRE

The fall of Nineveh and the rise of the Chaldæan and Median empires—The XXVI[th] Egyptian dynasty: Cyaxares, Alyattes, and Nebuchadrezzar.

THE East was ever a land of kaleidoscopic changes and startling dramatic incidents. An Oriental empire, even when built up by strong hands and watched over with constant vigilance, scarcely ever falls to pieces in the slow and gradual process of decay arising from the ties that bind it together becoming relaxed or its constituent elements growing antiquated. It perishes, as a rule, in a cataclysm; its ruin comes like a bolt

[1] Drawn by Faucher-Gudin, from the silver vase of Tchertomlitsk, now in the museum of the Hermitage. The vignette is also drawn by Faucher-Gudin, and represents an Egyptian torso in the Turin museum; the cartouche which is seen upon the arm is that of Psammetichus I.

from the blue, and is consummated before the commencement of it is realised. One day it stands proud and stately in the splendour of its glory; there is no report abroad but that which tells of its riches, its industry, its valour, the good government of its princes and the irresistible might of its gods, and the world, filled with envy or with fear, deeming its good fortune immutable, never once applies to it, even in thought, the usual commonplaces on the instability of human things. Suddenly an ill wind, blowing up from the distant horizon, bursts upon it in destructive squalls, and it is overthrown in the twinkling of an eye, amid the glare of lightning, the resounding crash of thunder, whirlwinds of dust and rain: when the storm has passed away as quickly as it came, its mutterings heralding the desolation which it bears to other climes, the brightening sky no longer reveals the old contours and familiar outlines, but the sun of history rises on a new empire, emerging, as if by the touch of a magic wand, from the ruins which the tempest has wrought. There is nothing apparently lacking of all that, in the eyes of the many, invested its predecessor with glory; it seems in no wise inferior in national vigour, in the number of its soldiers, in the military renown of its chiefs, in the proud prosperity of its people, or in the majesty of its gods; the present fabric is as spacious and magnificent, it would seem, as that which has but just vanished into the limbo of the past. No kingdom ever shone with brighter splendour, or gave a greater impression of prosperity, than the kingdom of Assyria in the days succeeding its triumphs over Elam and Arabia: precisely at this point the monuments and other witnesses of its activity fail us, just as if one of the acts of the piece in which it had played a chief part having come to an end, the drop curtain must be lowered, amid a flourish of trumpets and the illuminations of an apotheosis, to allow the actors a little breathing space. Half a century rolls by, during which we have a dim perception of the subdued crash of falling empires, and of the trampling of armies in fierce fight; then the curtain rises on an utterly different drama, of which the plot has been woven behind the scenes, and the exciting *motif* has just come into play. We no longer hear of Assyria and its kings; their palaces are in ruins; their last faithful warriors sleep in unhonoured graves beneath the ashes of their cities, their prowess is credited to the account of half a dozen fabulous heroes such as Ninus, Sardanapalus, and Semiramis—heroes whose names call up in the memory of succeeding generations only vague but terrible images, such as the phantasies of a dream, which, although but dimly remembered in the morning, makes the hair to stand on end with terror. The nations which erewhile disputed the supremacy with Assyria have either suffered a like eclipse— such as the Khâti, Urartu, the Cossæans, and Elam—or have fallen like Egypt and Southern Syria into the rank of second rate powers It is Chaldæa which is now in the van of the nations in company with Lydia and with Media, whose advent to imperial power no one would have ventured to predict forty or fifty years before.

The principality founded by Deïokes about the beginning of the seventh century B.C., seemed at first destined to play but a modest part; it shared the fortune of the semi-barbarous states with which the Ninevite conquerors came in contact on the western boundary of the Iranian plateau, and from which the governors of Arrapkha or of Kharkhar had extorted tribute to the utmost as often as occasion offered. According to one tradition, it had only three kings in an entire century: Deïokes up till 655 B.C., Phraortes from 655 to 633, and after the latter year Cyaxares, the hero of his race.[1] Another tradition claimed an earlier foundation for the monarchy, and doubled both the number of the kings and the age of the kingdom.[2] This

[1] This is the tradition gleaned by Herodotus, probably at Sardes, from the mouths of Persians residing in that city.

[2] This is the tradition derived from the court of Artaxerxes by Ctesias of Cnidus. Volney discovered the principle upon which the chronology of his Median dynasty was based by Ctesias. If we place his list side by side with that of Herodotus—

| HERODOTUS. | | CTESIAS. | |
|---|---|---|---|
| *Interregnum* | x | Arbakes | 28 |
| Deïokes | 53 | Mandaukas | 50 |
| | | Sosarmos | 30 |
| | | Artykas | 50 |
| Phraortes | 22 | Arbianes | 22 |
| | | Artaios | 40 |
| | | Artynes | 22 |
| Cyaxares | 40 | Astibaras | 40 |

we see that, while rejecting the names given by Herodotus, Ctesias repeats twice over the number of years assigned by the latter to the reigns of his kings, at least for the four last generations—

Phraortes . 22 $\begin{cases} \text{Arbianes} & . \quad 22 \\ \text{Artynes} & . \quad 22 \end{cases}$ $\begin{rcases} \text{Artaios} & . \quad . \quad 40 \\ \text{Astibaras} & . \quad 40 \end{rcases}$ Cyaxares . . 40

At the beginning Herodotus gives before Deïokes an interregnum of uncertain duration. Ctesias substituted the round number of fifty years for the fifty-three assigned to Deïokes, and replaced the interregnum by a

tradition ignored the monarchs who had rendered the second Assyrian empire illustrious, and substituted for them a line of inactive sovereigns, reputed to be the descendants of Ninus and Semiramis. The last of them, Sardanapalus, had, according to this account, lived a life of self-indulgence in his harem, surrounded by women, dressing himself in their garb, and adopting feminine occupations and amusements. The satrap of Media, Arbakes, saw him at his toilet, and his heart turned against yielding obedience to such a painted doll: he rebelled in concert with Belesys the Babylonian. The imminence of the danger thus occasioned roused Sardanapalus from his torpor, and revived in him the warlike qualities of his ancestors; he placed himself at the head of his troops, overcame the rebels, and was about to exterminate them, when his hand was stayed by the defection of some Bactrian auxiliaries. He shut himself up in Nineveh, and for two whole years heroically repulsed all assaults; in the third year, the Tigris, swollen by the rains, overflowed its banks and broke down the city walls for a distance of twenty stadia. The king thereupon called to mind an oracle which had promised him victory until the day when

reign which he estimated at the mean duration of a human generation, thirty years; he then applied to this new pair of numbers the process of doubling he had employed for the couple mentioned above—

| | | | | |
|---|---|---|---|---|
| Deïokes . . 53 | Mandaukas 50 | Arbakes . . 28 | *Interregnum* . *x* |
| | | Sosarmos . 30 | |
| | Artykas . 50 | | |

The number twenty-eight has been attributed to the reign of Arbakes, instead of the number thirty, to give an air of truthfulness to the whole catalogue.

the river should betray him. Judging that the prediction was about to be accomplished, he resolved not to yield himself alive to the besieger, and setting fire to his palace, perished therein, together with his children and his treasures, about 788 B.C. Arbakes, thus rendered an independent sovereign, handed down the monarchy to his son Mandaukas, and he in his turn was followed succesively by Sosarmos, Artykas, Arbianes, Artaios, Artynes, and Astibaras.[1] These names are not the work of pure invention; they are met with in more than one Assyrian text: among the petty kings who paid tribute to Sargon are enumerated some which bear such names as Mashdaku,[2] Ashpanda,[3] Arbaku, and Khartukka,[4] and many others, of whom traces ought to be found some day among the archives of princely families of later times. There were in these archives, at the disposal of scribes and strangers inclined to reconstruct the history of Asia, a supply of materials of varying value—authentic documents inscribed on brick tablets, legends of fabulous exploits, epic poems and records of real victories and conquests, exaggerated in

[1] Oppert thought that the names given by Herodotus represented "Aryanised forms of Turanian names, of which Ctesias has given the Persian translation."

[2] Mashdaku is identified by Rost with the Mandaukas or Maydaukas of Ctesias, which would then be a copyist's error for Masdaukas. The identification with Vashd[t]aku, Vashtak, the name of a fabulous king of Armenia is rejected by Rost; Mashdaku would be the Iranian Mazdaka, preserved in the Mazakes of Arrian.

[3] Ashpanda is the Aspandas or Aspadas which Ctesias gives instead of the Astyages of Herodotus.

[4] The name of Artykas is also found in the secondary form Kardikeas, which is nearer the Khartukka of the Assyrian texts.

accordance with the vanity or the interest of the composer: from these elements it was easy to compile lists of Median kings which had no real connection with each other as far as their names, order of succession, or duration of reign were concerned. The Assyrian chronicles have handed down to us in place of these dynasties which were alleged to have exercised authority over the whole territory, a considerable number of noble houses scattered over the country, each of them autonomous, and a rival of its neighbour, and only brought into agreement with one another at rare intervals by their common hatred of the invader. Some of them were representatives of ancient races akin to the Susians, and perhaps to the first inhabitants of Chaldæa; others belonged to tribes of a fresh stock, that of the Aryans, and more particularly to the Iranian branch of the Aryan family. We catch glimpses of them in the reign of Shalmaneser III., who calls them the Amadaî; then, after this first brush with Assyria, intercourse and conflict between the two nations became more and more frequent every year, until the "distant Medes" soon began to figure among the regular adversaries of the Ninevite armies, and even the haughtiest monarchs refer with pride to victories gained over them. Rammân-nirâri waged ceaseless war against them, Tiglath-pileser III. twice drove them before him from the south-west to the north-east as far as the foot of Demavend, while Sargon, Sennacherib, and Esarhaddon, during their respective reigns, kept anxious watch upon them, and endeavoured to maintain some sort of authority over the tribes which lay nearest to them. Both in the personal names and names of objects which have come down to us in the records of these campaigns, we detect Iranian characteristics, in spite of the Semitic garb with which the inscriptions have invested them: among the names of countries we find Partukka, Diristânu, Patusharra, Nishaîa, Urivzân, Abîruz, and Ariarma, while the men bear such names as Ishpabarra, Eparna, Shîtirparna, Uarzân, and Dayaukku. As we read through the lists, faint resemblances in sound awaken dormant classical memories, and the ear detects familiar echoes in the names of those Persians whose destinies were for a time linked with those of Athens and Sparta in the days of Darius and of Xerxes it is like the first breath of Greek influence, faint and almost imperceptible as yet, wafted to us across the denser atmosphere of the East.

The Iranians had a vague remembrance of a bygone epoch, during which they had wandered, in company with other nations of the same origin as themselves, in that cradle of the Aryan peoples, Aryanem-Vaêjô. Modern historians at first placed their mythical birthplace in the wilder regions of Central Asia, near the Oxus and the Jaxartes, and not far from the so-called table-land of Pamir, which they regarded as the original point of departure of the Indo-European races. They believed that a large body of these primitive Aryans must have descended southwards into the basin of the Indus and its affluents, and that other detachments had installed themselves in the oases of Margiana and Khorasmia, while the Iranians would have made their way up to the plateau which separates the Caspian Sea from the Persian Gulf, where they sought to win for themselves a territory sufficient for their wants. The compilers of the sacred books of the Iranians claimed to be able to trace each stage of their peregrinations, and to describe the various accidents which befell them during this heroic period of their history. According to these records, it was no mere chance or love of adventure which had led them to wander for years from clime to clime, but rather a divine decree. While Ahurômazdaô, the beneficent deity whom they worshipped, had provided them with agreeable resting-places, a perverse spirit, named Angrômaînyus, had on every occasion rendered their sojourn there impossible, by the plagues which he inflicted on them. Bitter cold, for instance, had compelled them to forsake Aryanem-Vaêjô and seek shelter in Sughdhâ and Mûru.[1] Locusts had driven them from Sughdhâ; the incursions of the nomad tribes, coupled with their immorality, had forced them to retire from Mûru to Bâkhdhî, "the country of lofty banners,"[2] and subsequently to Nisaya, which lies to the south-east, between Mûru and Bâkhdhî. From thence they made their way into the narrow valleys of the Harôyu, and overran Vaêkereta, the land of noxious shadows.[3] From this point forwards, the countries

[1] Sughdhâ is Sogdiana; Mûru, in ancient Persian Margush, is the modern Merv, the Margiana of classical geographers.

[2] Bâkhdhî is identical with Bactriana, but, as Spiegel points out, this Avestic form is comparatively recent, and readily suggests the modern Balkh, in which the consonants have become weakened.

[3] The Avesta places Nisaya between Mûru and Bâkhdhî to distinguish it from other districts of the same name to be found in this part of Asia: Eugène Burnouf is probably correct in identifying it with the Nêsæa of Strabo and of Ptolemy, which lay to the south of Margiana, at the junction of the roads leading to Hyrcania in one direction and Bactriana in the other.

mentioned by their chroniclers are divided into two groups, lying in opposite directions: Arahvaiti, Haêtumant,

and Haptahindu[1] on the east; and on the west, Urvâ,[2]

Harôyu or Haraêva is the Greek Aria, the modern province of Herat. The Pehlevi commentators identify Vaêkereta with Kabulistan, and also volunteer the following interpretation of the title which accompanies the name: "The shadow of the trees there is injurious to the body, or as some say, the shadow of the mountains," and it produces fever there. Arguing from passages of similar construction, Lassen was led to recognise in the epithet *duzhako-shayanem* a place-name, " inhabitant of Duzhakô," which he identified with a ruined city in this neighbourhood called Dushak ; Haug believed he had found a confirmation of this hypothesis in the fact that the Pairika Khnâthaiti created there by Angrô-maînyus recalls in sound, at any rate the name of the people Parikani mentioned by classical writers, as inhabiting these regions.

[1] Arahvaiti, the Harauvatish of the Achæmenian inscriptions, is the Greek Arachosia, and Haêtumant the basin of their Etymander, the modern Helmend; in other words, the present province of Seistan. Hapta-Hindu is the western part of the Indian continent, *i.e.* the Punjaub.

[2] The Pehlevi commentators identify Urvâ with Mesênê, mentioned by classical writers, at the confluence of the Tigris and Euphrates, or perhaps the plain around Ispahan which bore the name of Masân in the Sassanid period. Fr. Lenormant had connected it with the name Urivzân, which is applied in the Assyrian inscriptions to a district of Media in the time of Tiglath-pileser III.

Khnenta-Vehrkâna,[1] Rhagâ,[2] and Chakhra,[3] as far as the districts of Varena[4] and the basin of the Upper Tigris.[5] This legend was composed long after the event, in order to explain in the first place the relationship between the two great families into which the Oriental Aryans were divided, viz. the Indian and Iranian, and in the second to account for the peopling by the Iranians of a certain number of provinces between the Indus and the Euphrates. As a matter of fact, it is more likely that the Iranians came originally from Europe, and that they migrated from the steppes of Southern Russia into the plains of the Kur and the Araxes by way of Mount Caucasus.[6] It is possible that some of their hordes may have endeavoured

---

[1] The name Khnenta seems to have been Hellenised into that of Kharindas, borne by a river which formed the frontier between Hyrcania and Media; according to the Pehlevi version it was really a river of Hyrcania, the Djordjân. The epithet Vehrkâna, which qualifies the name Khnenta, has been identified by Burnouf with the Hyrcania of classical geographers.

[2] Raghâ is identified with Azerbaijân in the Pehlevi version of the Vendidâd, but is, more probably, the Rhagæ of classical geographers, the capital of Eastern Media.

[3] Chakhra seems to be identical with the country of Karkh, at the north-western extremity of Khorassan.

[4] Varena is identified by the Pehlevi commentators with Patishkhvargâr, *i.e.* probably the Patusharra of the Assyrian inscriptions.

[5] Haug proposed to identify this last station with the regions situated on the shores of the Caspian, near the south-western corner of that sea. But, as Garrez points out, the Pehlevi commentators prove that it must be the countries on the Upper Tigris.

[6] Spiegel has argued that Aryanem-Vaêjô is probably Arrân, the modern Kazabadagh, the mountainous district between the Kur and the Aras, and his opinion is now gaining acceptance. The settlement of the Iranians in Russia, and their entrance into Asia by way of the Caucasus, have been admitted by Rost. Classical writers reversed this order of things, and derived the Sauromatæ and other Scythian tribes from Media.

to wedge themselves in between the Halys and the Euphrates as far as the centre of Asia Minor. Their presence in this quarter would explain why we encounter Iranian personal names in the Sargonide epoch on the two spurs of Mount Taurus, such as that of the Kushtashpi, King of Kummukh, in the time of Tiglath-pileser III., and of the Kundashpi mentioned in the *Annals* of Shalmaneser III. in the ninth century B.C.[1] The main body, finding its expansion southwards checked by Urartu, diverged in a south-easterly direction, and sweeping before it all the non-Aryan or Turanian tribes who were too weak to stem its progress, gradually occupied the western edge of the great plateau, where it soon became mainly represented by the two compact groups, the Persians to the south the farthest confines of Elam, and the Medes between the Greater Zab, the Turnât, and the Caspian. It is probable that the kingdom founded by Deïokes originally included what was afterwards termed *Media Magna* the Græco-Roman geographers. This sovereignty was formed by the amalgamation under a single monarch of six important tribes—the Buzæ, Parætakeni, Struchatæ, Arizanti, Budii, and Magi. It extended north-westwards as far as the Kiziluzên, which formed the frontier between

---

[1] The name Kushtashpi has been compared with that of Vistâspa or Gushtâsp by Fr. Lenormant, the name Kundashpi with that of Vindâspa Gutschmid, and, later on, Ball has added to these a long list of names Egyptian and Assyrian inscriptions which he looks upon as Iranian. Kundashpi recalls at first sight Gundobunas, a name of the Sassanid epoch, if this latter form be authentic. Tiele adopts the identification of Kushtashpi with Vistâspa, and Justi has nothing to say against it, nor against the identification of Kundashpi with Vindâspa.

the Persians and the Mannai on this side. Northwards, it reached as far as Demavend; the salt desert that rendered Central Iran a barren region, furnished a natural boundary on the east; on both the south and west, the Assyrian border-lands of Ellipi, Kharkhar, and Arrapkha prevented it from extending to the chief ranges of the Zagros and Gordiæan mountains. The soil, though less fertile than that of Chaldæa or of Egypt, was by no means deficient in resources. The mountains contained copper, iron, lead, some gold and silver,[1] several kinds of white or coloured marble,[2] and precious stones, such as topaz, garnets, emeralds, sapphires, cornelian, and lapis-lazuli, the latter being a substance held in the highest esteem by Eastern jewellers from time immemorial; Mount Bikni was specially celebrated for the fine specimens of this stone which were obtained there.[3] Its mountains were in those days clothed with dense forests, in which the pine, the oak, and the poplar grew side by side with the eastern plane tree, the cedar, lime, elm, ash, hazel, and terebinth.[4] The intermediate valleys were veritable

[1] Rawlinson has collected traditions in reference to gold and silver mining among the mountains in the neighbourhood of Takht-i-Suleimân; one of these is still called *Zerreh-Sharân*, the mount of the *gold-washers*.

[2] The best known was the so-called Tauris marble quarried from the hills in the neighbourhood of Lake Urumiyah.

[3] The list of precious stones which Pliny tells us were found in Media, contains several kinds which we are unable to identify. *e.g.* the Zathênê, the gassinades and narcissitis. Pliny calls lapis-lazuli *sapphirus*, and declares that the bright specks of pyrites it contained rendered it unsuitable for engraving. In the Assyrian inscriptions Mount Bikni, the modern Demavend, is described as a mountain of Uknu, or lapis-lazuli.

[4] A large part of the mountains and plains is now treeless, but it is manifest, both from the evidence of the inscriptions and from the

orchards, in which the vegetation of the temperate zones mingled with tropical growths. The ancients believed that the lemon tree came originally from Persia.[1] To this day the peach, pear, apple, quince, cherry, apricot, almond filbert, chestnut, fig, pistachio-nut, and pomegranate still flourish there: the olive is easily acclimatised, and the vine produces grapes equally suitable for the table or the wine press.[2] The plateau presents a poorer and less promising appearance—not that the soil is less genial, but the rivers become lost further inland, and the barrenness of the country increases as they come to an end one after another. Where artificial irrigation has been introduced the fertility of the country is quite as great as in the neighbourhood of the mountains;[3] outside this irrigated region no trees are to be seen, except a few on the banks of rivers or ponds, but wheat, barley, rye, oats, and an abundance of excellent vegetables grow readily in places where water is present. The fauna include, besides wild beasts of the more formidable kinds, such as lions, tigers, leopards, and bears, many domestic animals, or animals capable of being turned to domestic use, such as the ass, buffalo, sheep goat, dog, and dromedary, and the camel with two humps whose gait caused so much merriment among the Ninevite

observations of travellers, that the whole of Media was formerly well wooded.

[1] The apple obtained from Media was known as the *Medicum malum*, and was credited with the property of being a powerful antidote to poison: it was supposed that it would not grow anywhere outside Media.

[2] In some places, as, for instance, at Kirmânshahân, the vine-stocks have to be buried during the winter to protect them from the frost.

[3] Irrigation was effected formerly, as now, by means of subterranean canals with openings at intervals, known as *kanât*.

idlers when they beheld it in the triumphal processions of their kings there were moreover several breeds of horses amongst which the Nisæan steed was greatly prized on account of its size strength and agility In short Media was large enough and rich enough to maintain a numerous

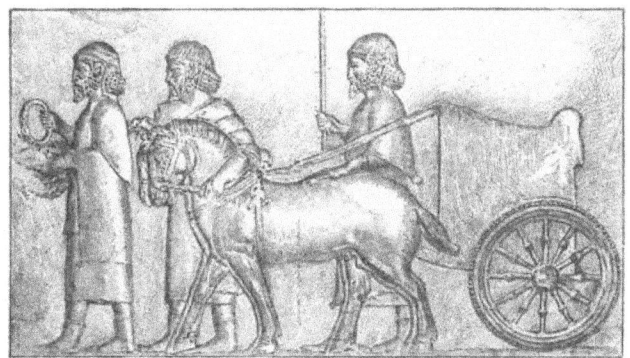

NISÆAN HORSES HARNESSED TO A ROYAL CHARIOT

population and offered a stable foundation to a monarch ambitious of building up a new empire [3]

In the time of the Seleucides, Media supplied nearly the whole of Asia with these animals and the grazing-lands of Bagistana, the modern Behistun are said to have supported 160,000 of them Under the Parthian kings Media paid a yearly tribute of 3000 horses and the Nisæan breed was still celebrated at the beginning of the Byzantine era. Horses are mentioned among the tribute paid by the Medic chiefs to the kings of Assyria

[2] Drawn by Boudier, from a photograph of the bas-relief from Persepolis now in the British Museum

[3] The history of the Medes remains shrouded in greater obscurity than that of any other Asiatic race We possess no original documents which owe their existence to this nation and the whole of our information concerning its history is borrowed from Assyrian and Babylonian inscriptions and from the various legends collected by the Greeks especially by Herodotus and Ctesias from Persian magnates in Asia Minor or at the court of the Achæmenian kings, or from fragments of vanished works such as the writings of Berosus And yet modern archæologists and philologists have during

The first person to conceive the idea of establishing one was, perhaps, a certain Fravartish, the Phraortes of the Greeks, whom Herodotus declares to have been the son and successor of Deïokes.[1] He came to the throne about 655 B.C., at a time when the star of Assur-bani-pal was still in the ascendant, and at first does not seem to have thought of trying to shake off the incubus of Assyrian rule. He began

THE PERSIAN REALM
Scale.

the last thirty years, allowed their critical faculties, and often thei imagination as well, to run riot when dealing with this very period. After carefully examining, one after another, most of the theories put forward, I have adopted those hypotheses which, while most nearly approximating to the classical legends, harmonise best with the chronological framework—far too imperfect as yet—furnished by the inscriptions dealing with the closing years of Nineveh; I do not consider them all to be equally probable, but though they may be mere stop-gap solutions, they have at least the merit of reproducing in many cases the ideas current among those races of antiquity who had been in direct communication with the Medes and with the last of their sovereigns.

[1] The ancient form of the name, Fravartish or Frawarti, has been handed down to us by a passage in the great inscription of Behistun; it means the man who proclaims faith in Ahura-mazda, the believer.

very wisely by annexing such of the petty neighbouring states as had hitherto remained independent, and then set himself to attack the one other nation of Iranian blood which, by virtue of the number and warlike qualities of its clans, was in a position to enter into rivalry with his own people. The Persians, originally concentrated in the interior, among the steep valleys which divide the plateau on the south, had probably taken advantage of the misfortunes of Elam to extend their own influence at its expense. Their kings were chosen from among the descendants of a certain Akhâmanish, the Achæmenes of the Greeks, who at the time of the Iranian invasion had been chief of the Pasargadæ, one of the Persian clans. Achæmenes is a mythical hero rather than a real person; he was, we are told, fed during infancy by an eagle—that mighty eagle whose shadow, according to a Persian belief in mediæval times, assured the sovereignty to him on whom it chanced to fall. Achæmenes would seem to have been followed by a certain Chaispi—or Teispes—a less fabulous personage, described in the legends as his son. It was, doubtless, during his reign that Assur-bani-pal, in hot pursuit of Tiummân and Khumbân-khaldash, completed the downfall of Susa; Chaispi claimed the eastern half of Elam as his share of the spoil, and on the strength of his victory styled himself King of Anshân —a title on which his descendants still prided themselves a hundred years after his death.[1] Persia, as then

---

[1] The fact that Teispes was the immediate successor of Achæmenes, indicated by Herodotus, is affirmed by Darius himself in the Behistun inscription. According to Billerbeck, the Anzân (Anshân) of the early

constituted, extended from the mouths of the Oroatis—the modern Tab—as far as the entrance to the Straits of Ormuzd.[1] The coast-line, which has in several places been greatly modified since ancient times by the formation of alluvial deposits, consists of banks of clay and sand, which lie parallel with the shore, and extend a considerable distance inland; in some places the country is marshy in others parched and rocky, and almost everywhere barren and unhealthy. The central region is intersected through out its whole length by several chains of hills, which rise terrace-like, one behind the other, from the sea to the plateau; some regions are sterile, more especially in the north and east, but for the most part the country is well wooded, and produces excellent crops of cereals. Only a few rivers, such as the Oroatis, which forms the boundary between Persia and Susiana,[2] the Araxes, and the Bagradas succeed in breaking through the barriers that beset their course, and reach the Persian Gulf;[3] most of the others find no outlet, and their waters accumulate at the bottom of the valleys, in lakes whose areas vary at the different

Achæmenides was merely a very small part of the ancient Anzân (Anshân), viz. the district on the east and south-east of Kuh-i-Dena, which includes the modern towns of Yezdeshast, Abadeh, Yeklîd, and Kushkiserd.

[1] Herodotus imagined Carmania and Persia Proper to be one and the same province; from the Alexandrine period onwards historians and geo graphers drew a distinction between the two.

[2] The form of the name varies in different writers. Strabo calls it the Oroatis, Nearchus the Arosis; in Pliny it appears as Oratis and Zarotis, and in Ammianus Marcellinus as Oroates.

[3] The Araxes is the modern Bendamîr. The Kyros, which flowed past Persepolis, is now the Pulwar, an affluent of the Bendamîr. The Bagradas of Ptolemy, called the Hyperis by Juba, is the modern Nabend.

SCENE IN THE MOUNTAINS OF PERSIA.
Drawn by Boudier, from COSTE and FLANDIN, *Voyage en Perse*, vol. i. pl. xcvi.

seasons. The mountainous district is furrowed in all directions by deep ravines, with almost vertical sides, at the bottom of which streams and torrents follow a headlong course. The landscape wears a certain air of savage grandeur; giant peaks rise in needle-like points perpendicularly to the sky; mountain paths wind upward, cut into the sides of the steep precipices; the chasms are spanned by single-arched bridges, so frail and narrow that they seem likely to be swept away in the first gale that blows. No country could present greater difficulties to the movements of a regular army or lend itself more readily to a system of guerrilla warfare. It was unequally divided between some ten or twelve tribes:[2] chief among these were the Pasargadæ, from which the royal family took its origin; after them came the Maraphii and Maspii. The chiefs of these two tribes were elected from among the members of seven families, who, at first taking equal rank with that of the Pasargadæ, had afterwards been reduced to

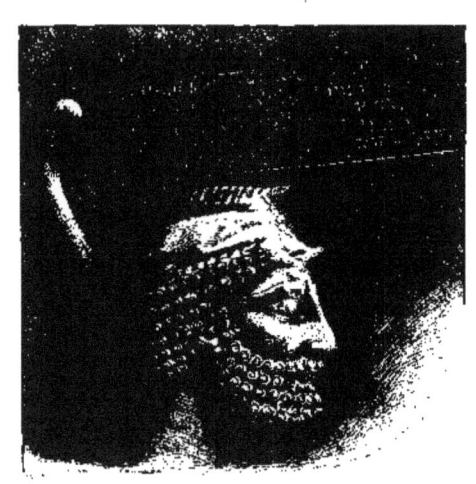

HEAD OF A PERSIAN ARCHER.[1]

---

[1] Drawn by Boudier, from a photograph of the Naksh-i-Rustem bas-relief taken by Dieulafoy.

[2] Herodotus only mentions ten Persian tribes; Xenophon speaks of twelve.

subjection by the Achæmenides, forming a privileged class at the court of the latter, the members of which shared the royal prerogatives and took a part in the work of government. Of the remaining tribes, the Panthialæi, Derusiæi, and Carmenians lived a sedentary life, while the Dai, Mardians, Dropici, and Sagartians were nomadic in their habits. Each one of these tribes occupied its own allotted territory, the limits of which were always accurately defined; we know that Sagartia, Paræta kênê, and Mardia lay towards the north, on the confines of Media and the salt desert,[1] Taokênê extended along the seaboard, and Carmania lay to the east. The tribes had constructed large villages, such as Armuza, Sisidôna, Apostana, Gogana, and Taôkê, on the sea-coast (the last named possessing a palace which was one of the three chief residences of the Achæmenian kings),[2] and Carmana Persepolis, Pasargadæ, and Gabæ in the interior.[3] The

[1] Parætakênê, which has already been identified with the Partukkanu (or Partakkanu) of the Assyrian inscriptions, is placed by Ptolemy in Persia; Mardia corresponds to the mountainous district of Bebaban and Kazrun.

[2] The position of most of these towns is still somewhat doubtful Armuza is probably Ormuz (or Hormuz) on the mainland, the forerunne the insular Hormuz of the Portuguese, as the French scholar d'Anville pointed out; Sisidôna has been identified with the modern village of Mogu near Ras-Jerd, Apostana with the town of Shewâr, the name seeming to be perpetuated in that of the Jebel Asban which rises not far from there Gogana is probably Bender Kongûn, and Taokê, at the mouth of the Granis is either Khor Gasseîr or Rohilla at the mouth of the Bishawer.
palace, which was one of the three principal residences of the Achæmenian kings, is probably mentioned by Strabo, and possibly in Dionysius Periegetes.

[3] Carmana is the modern Kermân; the exact position of Gabæ, which also possesses a palace, is not known.

Persians were a keen-witted and observant race, inured to all kinds of hardships in their occupation as mountain shepherds, and they were born warriors. The type preserved on the monuments differs but little from that which still exists at the present day in the more remote districts. It was marked by a tall and slender figure, with sturdy shoulders and loins, a small head, with a thick shock of hair and curling beard, a straight nose, a determined mouth, and an eye steady and alert. Yet, in spite of their valour, Phraortes overpowered them, and was henceforward able to reckon the princes of Anshân among his vassals; strengthened by the addition of their forces to his own, he directed his efforts to the subjection of the other races of the plateau. If we may believe the tradition of the Hellenic epoch, he reduced them to submission, and, intoxicated by his success, ventured at last to take

A PERSIAN[1]

up arms against the Assyrians, who for centuries past had held rule over Upper Asia.

This was about 635 B.C., or less than ten years after the downfall of Elam, and it does not seem likely that the vital

[1] Drawn by Boudier, from a photograph of one of the bas-reliefs at Persepolis in Dieulafoy.

forces of Assyria can have suffered any serious diminution within so short a space of time.[1] Assur-bani-pal, weary of fighting, even though he no longer directed operations in person, had apparently determined to remain entirely on the defensive, and not to take the field, unless absolutely compelled to do so by rebellion at home or an attack from outside. In view of the growing need of rest for the Assyrian nation, he could not have arrived at a wiser decision, provided always that circumstances allowed of its being carried into effect, and that the tributary races and frontier nations were willing to fall in with his intentions. They did so at first, for the fate of Elam had filled even the most unruly among them with consternation, and peace reigned supreme from the Persian Gulf to the Mediterranean. Assur-bani-pal took advantage of this unexpected lull to push forward the construction of public works in the valleys of the Tigris and Euphrates. The palace of Sennacherib, though it had been built scarcely fifty years before, was already beginning to totter on its foundations; Assur-bani-pal entirely remoddled and restored it—a proceeding which gave universal satisfaction. The common people had, as usual, to make the bricks with their own hands and convey them to the spot, but as the chariots employed for this purpose formed part of the booty recently brought back from Elam, the privilege of using these

[1] The date is indicated by the figures given by Herodotus in regard to the Medic kings, based on the calculations of himself or his authorities. Phraortes died in 634 B.C., after a reign of twenty-two years, and as the last year of his reign coincides with the war against Assyria, the preparations for it cannot have been much earlier than 635 or 636 B.C., a year or two before the catastrophe.

trophies did something to lighten the burden of the tasks imposed on them. Moreover, they had the satisfaction of seeing at work among the squads of labourers several real kings, the Arabian chiefs who had been pursued and captured in the heart of the desert by Assur-bani-pal's generals; they plodded along under their heavy baskets, stimulated by the crack of the whip, amid insults and jeers. This palace was one of the largest and most ornate ever built by the rulers of Assyria. True, the decoration does not reveal any novel process or theme; we find therein merely the usual scenes of battle or of the chase, but they are designed and executed with a skill to which the sculptor of Nineveh had never before attained. The animals, in particular, are portrayed with a light and delicate touch—the wild asses pursued by hounds, or checked while galloping at full speed by a cast of the lasso; the herds of goats and gazelles hurrying across the desert; the wounded lioness, which raises herself with a last dying effort to roar at the beaters. We are conscious of Egyptian influence underlying the Asiatic work, and the skilful arrangement of the scenes from the Elamite campaigns also reminds us of Egypt. The picture of the battle of Tullîz recalls, in the variety of its episodes and the arrangement of the perspective, the famous engagement at Qodshu, of which Ramses II. has left such numerous presentments on the Theban pylons. The Assyrians, led by the vicissitudes of invasion to Luxor and the Ramesseum, had, doubtless, seen these masterpieces of Egyptian art in a less mutilated state than that in which we now possess them, and profited by the remembrance when called upon to depict the private life of their king and the victories gained by his armies. It was in this magnificent residence that Assur-bani-pal led an existence of indolent splendour, such as the chroniclers of a later age were wont to ascribe to all the Assyrian monarchs from the

A HERD OF WILD GOATS—A BAS-RELIEF OF THE TIME OF ASSUR-BANI-PAL.[1]

time of Semiramis onwards.[2] We would gladly believe that he varied the monotony of his hunting expeditions his banquets, and entertainments in the gardens in company with the women of the harem, by pleasures of a more refined nature, and that he took an unusual interes in the history and literature of the races who had become

[1] Drawn by Faucher-Gudin, from the sketch by Place.
[2] Stories of the effeminacy of Sardanapalus had been collected by Ctesias of Cnidus; they soon grew under the hands of historians in the time of Alexander, and were passed on by them to writers of the Roman and Byzantine epochs.

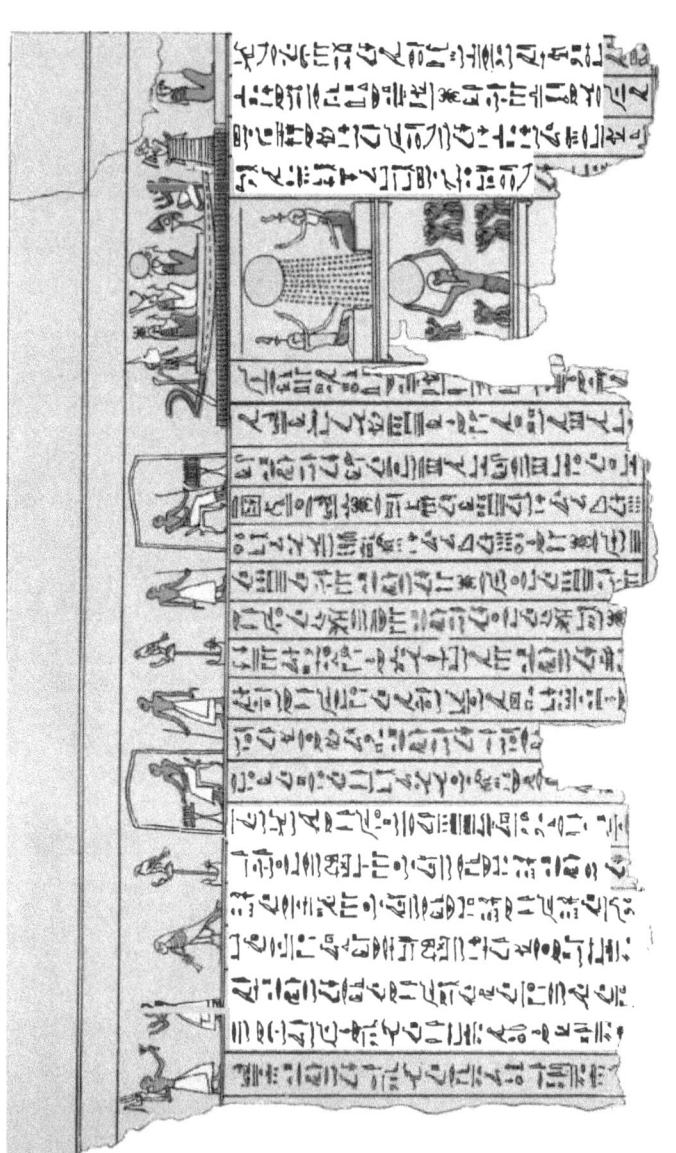

ILLUSTRATED MANUSCRIPT ON PAPYRUS

# THE LIBRARY OF ASSUR-BANI-PAL AT KOUYUNJIK 291

subject to his rule. As a matter of fact, there have been discovered in several of the ruined chambers of his palaces the remains of a regular library, which must originally have contained thousands of clay tablets, all methodically arranged and catalogued for his use. A portion of them furnish us at first-hand with the records of his reign, and include letters exchanged with provincial governors, augural predictions, consultation of oracles, observations made by the royal astrologers, standing orders, accounts of income and expenditure, even the reports of physicians in regard to the health of members of the royal family or of the royal household: these documents reveal to us the whole machinery of government in actual operation, and we almost seem to witness the secret mechanism by which the kingdom was maintained in activity. Other tablets contain authentic copies of works which were looked upon as classics in the sanctuaries of the Euphrates. Probably, when Babylon was sacked, Sennacherib had ordered the books which lay piled up in Ê-Sagilla and the other buildings of the city to be collected and carried away to Nineveh along with the statues and property of the gods. They had been placed in the treasury, and there they remained until Esarhaddon re-established the kingdom of Karduniash, and Assur-bani-pal was forced to deliver up the statue of Marduk and restore to the sanctuaries, now rebuilt, all the wealth of which his grandfather had robbed them: but before sending back the tablets, he ordered copies to be made of them, and his secretaries set to work to transcribe for his use such of these works as they considered worthy of reproduction. The majority of them were treatises compiled by the most celebrated adepts in the sciences for which Chaldæa had been famous from time immemorial; they included collections of omens, celestial and terrestrial, in which the mystical meaning of each phenomenon and its influence on the destinies of the world was explained by examples borrowed from the Annals of world-renowned conquerors, such as Naramsin and Sargon of Agadê; then there were formulæ for exorcising evil spirits from the bodies of the possessed, and against phantoms, vampires, and ghosts, the recognised causes of all disease; prayers and psalms, which had to be repeated before the gods in order to obtain pardon for sin; and histories of divinities and kings from the time of the creation down to the latest date. Among these latter were several versions of the epic of Gilgames, the story of Etana, of Adapa, and many others; and we may hope to possess all that the Assyrians knew of the old Chaldæan literature in the seventh century B.C., as soon as the excavators have unearthed from the mound at Kouyunjik all the tablets, complete or fragmentary, which still lie hidden there. Even from the shreds of information which they have already yielded to us, we are able to piece together so varied a picture that we can readily magine Assur-bani-pal to have been a learned and studious monarch, a patron of literature and antiquarian knowledge. Very possibly he either read himself, or had read to him, many of the authors whose works found a place in his ibrary: the kings of Nineveh, like the Pharaohs, desired now and then to be amused by tales of the marvellous, and they were doubtless keenly alive to the delightful rhythm and beautiful language employed by the poets of the past in singing the praises of their divine or heroic ancestors. But the mere fact that his palace contained the most important literary collection which the ancient East has so far bequeathed to us, in no way proves that Assur-bani-pal displayed a more pronounced taste for literature than his predecessors; it indicates merely the zeal and activity of his librarians, their intelligence, and their respect and admiration for the great works of the past. Once he had issued his edict ordering new editions of the old masters to be prepared, Assur-bani-pal may have dismissed the matter from his mind, and the work would go on automatically without need for any further interference on his part. The scribes enriched his library for him, in much the same way as the generals won his battles, or the architects built his monuments: they were nothing more than nameless agents, whose individuality was eclipsed by that of their master, their skill and talent being all placed to his credit. Babylonia shared equally with Assyria in the benefits of his government. He associated himself with his brother Shamash-shumukîn in the task of completing the temple of Ê-Sagilla; afterwards, when sole monarch, he continued the work of restoration, not only in Babylon, but in the lesser cities as well, especially those which had suffered most during the war, such as Uru, Uruk, Borsippa, and Cutha.[1] He remodelled the temple of Bel at Nippur, the walls built there by him being even now distinguishable

---

[1] He refers to the works at Borsippa and Kuta towards the end of the account of his campaign against Shamash-shumukîn, and to those at Uruk in describing the war against Khumbân-khaldash.

from the rest by the size of the bricks and the careful dressing of the masonry. From the shores of the Persian Gulf to the mountains of Armenia, Assyria and Karduniash

REMAINS OF ASSUR-BANI-PAL'S WALL AT NIPPUR.[1]

were covered with building-yards just as they had been in the most peaceful days of the monarchy.

It was at this unique juncture of apparent grandeur and prosperity that Phraortes resolved to attack Assur-bani-pal. There is nothing to indicate that his action took place simultaneously with some movement on the part of other peoples, or with a serious insurrection in any of the

[1] Drawn by Faucher-Gudin, from the photograph published by Peters.

Assyrian provinces. For my part, I prefer to set it down to one of those sudden impulses, those irresistible outbursts of self-confidence, which from time to time actuated the princes tributary to Nineveh or the kings on its frontier. The period of inactivity to which some previous defeat inflicted on them or on their predecessors had condemned them, allowed them to regain their strength, and one or two victories over less powerful neighbours served to obliterate the memory of former humiliation and disaster; they flew to arms full of hope in the result, and once more drew down defeat upon their heads, being lucky indeed if their abortive rising led to nothing worse than the slaughter of their armies, the execution of their generals, and an increase in the amount of their former tribute. This was the fate that overtook Phraortes; the conqueror of the Persians, when confronted by the veteran troops of Assyria, failed before their superior discipline, and was left dead upon the field of battle with the greater part of his army. So far the affair presented no unusual features; it was merely one more commonplace repetition of a score of similar episodes which had already taken place in the same region, under Tiglath-pileser III. or the early Sargonides; but Huvakshatara, the son of Phraortes, known to the Greeks as Cyaxares,[1] instead of pleading for mercy, continued to offer a stubborn resistance. Cyaxares belongs to history, and there can be no doubt that he exercised a decisive

---

[1] The original form of the name is furnished by passages in the Behistun inscription, where Chitrantakhma of Sagartia and Fravartish of Media, two of the claimants for the throne who rose against Darius, are represented as tracing their descent from Huvakshatara.

influence over the destinies of the Oriental world, but precise details of his exploits are wanting, and his personality is involved in such obscuring mists that we can scarcely seize it; the little we have so far been able to glean concerning him shows us, not so much the man himself, as a vague shadow of him seen dimly through the haze. His achievements prove him to have been one of those perfect rulers of men, such as Asia produces every now and then, who knew how to govern as well as how to win battles—a born general and lawgiver, who could carry his people with him, and shone no less in peace than in war.[1] The armies at the disposal of his predecessors had been little more than heterogeneous assemblies of feudal militia; each clan furnished its own contingent of cavalry archers, and pikemen, but instead of all these being combined into a common whole, with kindred elements contributed by the other tribes, each one acted separately thus forming a number of small independent armies within the larger one. Cyaxares saw that defeat was certain so long as he had nothing but these ill-assorted masses to match against the regular forces of Assyria: he therefore broke up the tribal contingents and rearranged the units of which they were composed according to their natural

[1] G. Rawlinson takes a somewhat different view of Cyaxares' character; he admits that Cyaxares knew how to win victories, but refuses to credit him with the capacity for organisation required in order to reap the full benefits of conquest, giving as his reason for this view the brief duration of the Medic empire. The test applied by him does not seem to me a con elusive one, for the existence of the second Chaldæan empire was almost as short, and yet it would be decidedly unfair to draw similar inferences touching the character of Nabopolassar or Nebuchadrezzar from this fact.

affinities, grouping horsemen with horsemen, archers with archers, and pikemen with pikemen, taking the Assyrian

MEDIC AND PERSIAN FOOT-SOLDIERS.[1]

cavalry and infantry as his models.[2] The foot-soldiers wore a high felt cap known as a tiara; they had long tunics

[1] Drawn by Faucher-Gudin, after Coste and Flandin. The first and third figures are Medes, the second and fourth Persians.

[2] Herodotus tells us that Cyaxares was " the first to divide the Asiatics into different regiments, separating the pikemen from the archers and horsemen; before his time, these troops were all mixed up haphazard together." I have interpreted his evidence in the sense which seems most in harmony with what we know of Assyrian military tactics. It seems incredible that the Medic armies can have fought pell-mell, as Herodotus declares, seeing that for two hundred years past the Medes had been frequently engaged against such well-drilled troops as those of Assyria: if the statement be authentic, it merely means that Cyaxares converted all the small feudal armies which had hitherto fought side by side on behalf of the king into a single royal army in which the different kinds of troops were kept separate.

with wide sleeves tied in at the waist by a belt and sometimes reinforced by iron plates or scales as well as gaiters buskins of soft leather and large wickerwork shields covered with ox-hide which they bore in front of them like a movable bulwark their weapons consisted of a short sword which depended from the belt and lay along the thigh one or two light javelins a bow with a strongly pronounced curve and a quiver full of arrows made from reeds Their horsemen like those of other warlike nations of the East used neither saddle nor stirrups and though they could make skilful use of lance and sword their favourite weapon was the bow[3] Accustomed from their earliest childhood to all kinds of equestrian exercises they seemed to sit their horses as though they actually formed part of the animal. They seldom fought in line

A MEDIC HORSEMAN.[2]

Herodotus describes the equipment of the Persians in much the same terms as I have used above and then adds in the following chapter that "the Medes had the same equipment, for it is the equipment of the Medes and not that of the Persians"

Drawn by Faucher-Gudin, from a cast of the Medic intaglio in the Cabinet des Médailles

[3] Herodotus says that the Medic horsemen were armed in the same manner as the infantry.

but, from the very beginning of an action, hung like a dense cloud on the front and flanks of the enemy, and riddled them with missiles, without, however, coming to close quarters. Like the Parthians of a later epoch, they waited until they had bewildered and reduced the foe by their ceaseless evolutions before giving the final charge which was to rout them completely. No greater danger could threaten the Assyrians than the establishment of a systematically organised military power within the borders of Media. An invader starting from Egypt or Asia Minor, even if he succeeded in overthrowing the forces sent out to meet him, had still a long way to go before he could penetrate to the heart of the empire. Even if Cilicia and Syria should be conquered, nothing was easier than to oppose a further advance at the barrier of the Euphrates; and should the Euphrates be crossed, the Khabur still remained, and behind it the desert of Singar, which offered the last obstacle between Nineveh and the invaders. The distances were less considerable in the case of an army setting out from Urartu and proceeding along the basin of the Tigris or its affluents; but here, too, the difficulties of transit were so serious that the invader ran a great risk of gradually losing the best part of his forces on the road. On the north-east and east, however, the ancient heritage of Assur lay open to direct and swift attack. An enemy who succeeded in destroying or driving back the garrisons stationed as outposts on the rim of the plateau, from Kharkhar to Parsua, if he ventured to pursue his advantage and descended into the plain of the Tigris, had no less than three routes to choose from— the Kirind road on the south,

300 THE MEDES AND THE SECOND CHALDÆAN EMPIRE

the Baneh road on the north, and the Suleimanyeh road between the two. The last was the easiest of all, and led almost straight to the fords of Altun-Keupri and the banks of the Lesser Zab, on the confines of Assyria proper, close under the walls of Arbela, the holy city of Ishtar. He needed but to win two victories, one upon leaving the mountains, the other at the passage of the Zab, and two or three weeks' steady marching would bring him from Hamadân right up to the ramparts of Nineveh.

Cyaxares won a victory over Assur-bani-pal's generals, and for the first time in over a hundred years Assyria proper suffered the ignominy of foreign invasion The various works constructed by twenty generations kings had gradually transformed the triangle enclosed between the Upper Zab, the Tigris, and the Jebel-Makhlub into a regular fortified camp. The southern point of this triangle was defended by Calah from the attacks of Chaldæa or from foes coming down from Media by Holwân and Suleimanyeh, while Nineveh guarded it on the northeast, and several lines of walled cities—among which Dur-Sharrukîn and Imgur-Bel can still be identified—protected it on the north and east, extending from the Tigris as far as the Ghazîr and Zab. It was necessary for an enemy to break through this complex defensive zone, and even after this had been successfully accomplished and the walls of the capital had been reached, the sight which would meet the eye was well calculated to dismay even the most resolute invader.

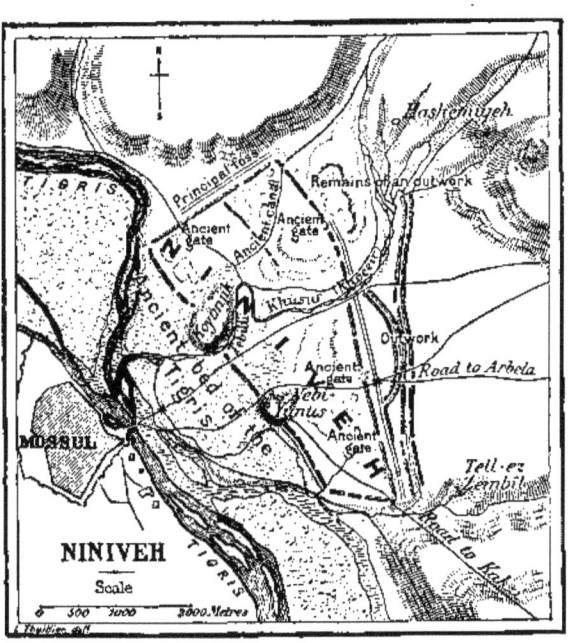

Viewed as a whole, Nineveh appeared as an irregular quadrilateral figure, no two sides of which were parallel, lying on the left bank of the Tigris. The river came right up to the walls on the west, and the two mounds of Kouyunjik and Nebi-Yunus, on which stood the palaces of the Sargonides, were so skilfully fortified that a single wall connecting the two sufficed to ward off all danger of attack on this side. The south wall, which was the shortest of the four, being only about 870 yards in length, was rendered inaccessible by a muddy stream, while the north wall, some 2150 yards long, was protected by a wide moat which could be filled from the waters of the Khuzur. The eastern front had for a long time depended for its safety on a single wall reinforced by a moat, but Sennacherib,

PART OF THE FOSSE AT NINEVEH.[1]

deeming it insufficiently protected against a sudden attack, had piled up obstacles in front of it, so that it now presented a truly formidable appearance. It was skirted throughout its whole length by a main rampart, 5400 yards long, which described a gentle curve from north to south, and rose to a height of about 50 feet, being protected by two small forts placed close to the main gates. The fosse did not run along the foot of the wall, but at a distance of about fifty yards in front of it, and

[1] Drawn by **Boudier,** from a sketch in Layard.

was at least some 20 feet deep and over 150 feet in width. It was divided into two unequal segments by the Khuzur: three large sluice-gates built on a level with the wall and the two escarpments allowed the river to be dammed back, so that its waters could be diverted into the fosse and thus keep it full in case of siege. In front of each segment was a kind of demi-lune, and—as though this was not precaution enough—two walls, each over 4300 yards long, were built in front of the demi-lunes, the ditch which separated them being connected at one end with the Khuzur, and allowed to empty itself into a stream on the south. The number of inhabitants sheltered behind these defences was perhaps 300,000 souls;[1] each separate quarter of the city was enclosed by ramparts, thus forming, as it were, a small independent town, which had to be besieged and captured after a passage had been cut through the outer lines of defence. Cyaxares might well have lost heart in the face of so many difficulties, but his cupidity, inflamed by reports of the almost fabulous wealth of the city, impelled him to attack it with extraordinary determination: the spoils of Susa, Babylon, and Thebes, in fact, of the whole of Western Asia and Ethiopia, were, he felt, almost within his reach, and would inevitably fall into his hands provided his courage and perseverance did not fail him. After shutting up the remnant of the Assyrian army inside Nineveh he laid patient siege to the city, and the fame of his victories being noised abroad on all sides, it awoke among the subject races that longing

[1] Jones and G. Rawlinson credit Nineveh with a population of not more than 175,000.

for revenge which at one time appeared to have been sent to sleep for ever. It almost seemed as though the moment was approaching when the city of blood should bleed in its turn, when its kings should at length undergo the fate which they had so long imposed on other monarchs. Nahum the Elkoshite,[1] a Hebrew born in the Assyrian province of Samaria, but at that time an exile in Judah, lifted up his voice, and the echo of his words still resounds in our ears, telling us of the joy and hope felt by Judah, and with Judah, by the whole of Asia, at the prospect. Speaking as the prophet of Jahveh, it was to Jahveh that he attributed the impending downfall of the oppressor: "Jahveh is a jealous God and avengeth; Jahveh avengeth and is full of wrath; Jahveh taketh vengeance on His adversaries, and He reserveth wrath for His enemies. Jahveh is slow to anger and great in power, and will by no means clear the guilty; Jahveh hath His way in the whirlwind and in the storm, and the clouds are the dust of His feet. He rebuketh the sea and maketh it dry, and drieth up all the rivers Bashan languisheth, and Carmel, and the flower of Lebanon languisheth."[2] And, "Behold upon the mountains the feet of him that bringeth good tidings."[3] Then he goes on to unfold before the eyes of his hearers a picture of

---

[1] Elkosh is identified by Eusebius with Elkese, which St. Jerome declares to have been in Galilee, the modern el-Kauzeh, two and a half hours' walk south of Tibnin. The prophecy of Nahum has been taken by some as referring to the campaign of Phraortes against Assyria, but more frequently to the destruction of Nineveh by the Medes and Chaldæans. It undoubtedly refers to the siege interrupted by the Scythian invasion.

[2] *Nahum* i. 2–4.        [3] *Nahum* i. 15.

Nineveh, humiliated and in the last extremity. There she lies, behind her bastions of brick, anxiously listening for the approach of the victorious Medes. "The noise of the whip, and the noise of the rattling of wheels; and prancing horses and jumping chariots; the horsemen mounting, and the flashing sword, and the glittering spear; and a multitude of slain and a great heap of carcases: and there is no end of the corpses; they stumble upon their corpses: because of the multitude of the whoredoms of the well-favoured harlot, the mistress of witchcrafts, that selleth nations through her whoredoms, and families through her witchcrafts. Behold, I am against thee, saith Jahveh of hosts, and I will discover thy skirts upon they face; and I will show the nations thy nakedness, and the kingdoms thy shame. And I will cast abominable filth upon thee, and make thee vile, and will set thee as a gazing-stock. And it shall come to pass that all they that look upon thee shall flee from thee, and say, Nineveh is laid waste: who will bemoan her? Whence shall I seek comforters for thee?"[1] Thebes, the city of Amon, did not escape captivity; why then should Nineveh prove more fortunate? "All thy fortresses shall be like fig trees with the **firstripe** figs: if they be shaken they fall into the mouth of the eater. Behold, thy people in the midst of thee are women; the gates of thy land are set wide open unto thine enemies: the fire hath devoured thy bars. Draw thee water for the siege, strengthen thy fortresses: go into the clay and tread the mortar, make strong the brick-kiln. There shall

[1] *Nahum* iii 2–7.

the fire devour thee; the sword shall cut thee off, . . . make thyself many as the cankerworm, make thyself many as the locusts. Thou hast multiplied thy merchants as the stars of heaven: the cankerworm spoileth and flieth away. Thy crowned are as the locusts and thy marshals as the swarms of grasshoppers, which camp in the hedges in the cold day, but when the sun ariseth they flee away, and their place is not known where they are. Thy shepherds slumber, O King of Assyria: thy worthies are at rest: thy people are scattered upon the mountains, and there is none to gather them. There is no assuaging of thy hurt; thy wound is grievous: all that hear the bruit of thee clap the hands over thee; for upon whom hath not thy wickedness passed continually?"[1]

On this occasion Nineveh escaped the fate with which the prophet had threatened it, but its safety was dearly bought. According to the tradition accepted in Asia Minor two hundred years later, a horde of Scythians under King Madyes, son of Protothyes, setting out from the Russian steppes in pursuit of the Cimmerians, made their appearance on the scene in the nick of time. We are told that they flung themselves through the Caspian Gates into the basin of the Kur, and came into contact with the Medes at the foot of Mount Caucasus. The defeat of the Medes here would necessarily compel them to raise the siege of Nineveh. This crisis in the history of Asia was certainly not determined by chance. For eighty years Assyria had been in contact with the Scythians, and the Assyrian kings had never ceased to

[1] *Nahum* iii. 12–19.

keep an eye upon their movements, or lose sight of the
advantage to which their bellicose temper might be turned
in circumstances like the present. They had pitted them
against the Cimmerians, then against the Medes, and
probably against the kings of Urartu as well, and the
intimacy between the two peoples came to be so close
that the Scythian king Bartatua did not hesitate to
demand one of the daughters of Esarhaddon in marriage.
From the very beginning of his reign Assur-bani-pal had
shown them the utmost consideration, and when King
Madyes, son of his ally Bartatua, intervened thus opportunely in the struggle, he did so, not by mere chance,
as tradition would have us believe, but at the urgent
request of Assyria. He attacked Media in the rear, and
Cyaxares, compelled to raise the siege of Nineveh,
hastened to join battle with him. The engagement
probably took place on the banks of the Lower Araxes
or to the north of Lake Urumiah, in the region formerly
inhabited by the Mannai; but after defeating his foe
and dictating to him the terms of submission, Madyes,
carried away by the lust of conquest, did not hesitate
to turn his arms against his ally. Exhausted by her
recent struggle, Assyria lay at his mercy, her fortresses
alone being able to offer any serious resistance: he
overran the country from end to end, and though the
walled cities withstood the fury of his attack, the rural
districts were plundered right and left, and laid desolate
for many a year to come. The Scythians of this epoch
probably resembled those whom we find represented on
the monuments of Greek art two centuries later. Tall,

fierce-looking men, with unkempt beards, their long and straggling locks surmounted by the *kyrbasis*, or pointed national cap of felt; they wore breeches and a blouse of embroidered leather, and were armed with lances, bows, and battle-axes. They rode bareback on untrained horses, herds of which followed their tribes about on their wanderings; each man caught the animal he required with the help of a lasso, put bit and bridle on him, and vaulting on to his back at a single bound, reduced

SCYTHIANS TENDING THEIR WOUNDED.[1]

him to a state of semi-obedience. No troops could stand their ground before the frantic charge of these wild horsemen; like the Huns of Roman times, the Scythians made a clean sweep of everything they found in their path. They ruined the crops, carried off or slaughtered the herds, and set fire to the villages from sheer love of destruction, or in order to inspire terror; every one who failed to fly to the mountains or take refuge in some fortress, was either massacred on the spot or led away into slavery. Too ignorant of the arts of war to undertake a siege in the regular way, they usually contented themselves with levying ransoms on fortified towns; occasionally, however, when the wealth accumulated behind the walls held out a prospect of ample

[1] Drawn by Faucher-Gudin, from the reliefs on a silver vase from Kul-Oba.

booty, they blockaded the place until famine compelled it to surrender. More than one ancient city which, thanks to the good government of its rulers and the industry of its citizens, had amassed treasure of inestimable value, was put to fire and sword, and more than one fertile and populous region left untilled and deserted.[1] Most of the states which for the last three centuries had fought so stubbornly against the Assyrians for independence, went down before the storm, including the kingdoms of Urartu, of the Mushku, and of the Tabal,[2] their miserable end furnishing the Hebrew prophets full fifty years later with a theme of sombre rejoicing. "There is Meshech, Tubal, and all her multitude; her graves are round about her: all of them uncircumcised, slain by the sword; for they caused their terror in the land of the living. And they shall not lie with the mighty that are fallen of the uncircumcised, which are gone down to hell with their weapons of war, and have laid their swords under their heads,[3] and their iniquities are upon their bones; for they were the terror of the

---

[1] This may be deduced from the passage in Herodotus, where he says that "the Scythians were masters of Asia for twenty-eight years, and overturned everything by their brutality and stupidity: for, in addition to tribute, they exacted from every one whatever they chose, and, moreover, they prowled here and there, plundering as they thought good."

[2] Strabo refers in general terms to the presence of Scythians (or, as he calls them, *Sacæ*) in Armenia, Cappadocia, and on the shores of the Black Sea.

[3] This, doubtless, means that the **Mushku** and Tabal had been so utterly defeated that they could not procure honourable burial for their dead, *i.e.* with their swords beneath their heads and their weapons on their bodies.

mighty in the land of the living."[1] The Cimmerians, who, since their reverses in Lydia and on Mount Taurus, had concentrated practically the whole of their tribes in Cappadocia and in the regions watered by the Halys and Thermodon, shared the good fortune of their former adversaries. At that time they lived under the rule of a certain Kôbos, who seems to have left a terrible reputation behind him; tradition gives him a place beside Sesostris among the conquerors of the heroic age, and no doubt, like his predecessor Dugdamis, he owed this distinction to some expedition or other against the peoples who dwelt on the shores of the Ægean Sea, but our knowledge of his career is confined to the final catastrophe which overtook him. After some partial successes, such as that near Zela, for instance, he was defeated and made prisoner by Madyes. His subjects, as vassals of the Scythians, joined them in their acts of brigandage,[2] and together they marched from province to province, plundering as they went; they overran the western regions of the Assyrian kingdom from Melitene and Mesopotamia to Northern Syria, from Northern Syria to Phœnicia, Damascus, and Palestine,[3] and at length made their appearance on the Judæan frontier. Since the day when Sennacherib had been compelled to return to Assyria without having succeeded in destroying Jerusalem, or

[1] *Ezek.* xxxii. 26, 27.

[2] It seems probable that this was so, when we consider the confusion between the Scythians or Sakæ, and the Cimmerians in the Babylonian and Persian inscriptions of the Achæmenian epoch.

[3] Their migration from Media into Syria and Palestine is expressly mentioned by Herodotus.

even carrying it by storm, Judah had taken little or no part in external politics. Divided at first by a conflict between the party of prudence, who advised submission to Nineveh, and the more warlike spirits who advocated an alliance with Egypt, it had ended by accepting its secondary position, and had on the whole remained fairly loyal to the dynasty of Sargon. On the death of Hezekiah, his successor, Manasseh, had, as we know, been tempted to intervene in the revolutions of the hour, but the prompt punishment which followed his first attempt put an end for ever to his desire for independence. His successor, Amon, during his brief reign of two years,[2] had no time to desert the ways of his father, and Josiah,[3] who came to the throne in 638 B.C., at the age of eight, had so far

IRANIAN SOLDIERS FIGHTING AGAINST THE SCYTHIANS.[1]

---

[1] Drawn by Faucher-Gudin, from the cast of a cylinder given by Cunningham. The cylinder is usually described as Persian, but the dress is that of the Medes as well as of the Persians.

[2] 2 *Kings* xxi. 18–26; cf. 2 *Chron.* xxxiii. 20–25. The reign of fifty-five years attributed to Manasseh by the Jewish annalists cannot be fitted into the chronology of the period; we must either take off ten years, thus reducing the duration of the reign to forty-five years, or else we must assume the first ten of Manasseh to be synchronous with the last ten of Hezekiah.

[3] 2 *Kings* xxii. 1; cf. 2 *Chron.* xxxiv. 1.

manifested no hostility towards Assyria. Thus, for more than fifty years, Judah enjoyed almost unbroken peace, and led as happy and prosperous an existence as the barrenness of its soil and the unruly spirit of its inhabitants would permit.

But though its political activity had been almost nothing during this interval, its spiritual life had seldom been developed with a greater intensity. The reverse sustained by Sennacherib had undoubtedly been a triumph for Isaiah, and for the religious party of which we are accustomed to regard him as the sole representative. It had served to demonstrate the power of Jahveh, and His aversion for all idolatrous worship and for all foreign alliances. In vain did the partisans of Egypt talk loudly of Pharaoh and of all those principalities of this world which were drawn round in Pharaoh's orbit; Egypt had shown herself incapable of safeguarding her friends, and things had gone steadily from bad to worse so long as these latter held the reins of government; their removal from office had been, as it were, the signal for a welcome change in the fortunes of the Jews. Jahveh had delivered His city the moment when, ceasing to rely upon itself, it had surrendered its guidance into His hands, and the means of avoiding disaster in the future was clearly pointed out to it. Judah must be content to follow the counsels which Isaiah had urged upon it in the name of the Most High, and submissively obey the voice of its prophets. "Thine eyes shall see thy teachers: and thine ears shall hear a word behind thee, saying, This is the way, walk ye in it, when ye turn to the right hand, and when ye turn to the left. And ye shall defile the over-laying of thy graven images of silver, and the plating of thy molten images of gold : thou shalt cast them away as an unclean thing ; thou shalt say unto it, Get thee hence."[1] Isaiah seems to disappear after his triumph, and none of his later prophecies have come down to us : yet the influence of his teaching lasted throughout the reign of Hezekiah, and the court, supported by the more religious section of the people, not only abjured the worship of false gods, but forsook the high places and discontinued the practices which he had so strenuously denounced. The great bulk of the nation, however, soon returned to their idolatrous practices, if, indeed, they had ever given them up, and many of the royal advisers grew weary of the rigid observances which it was sought to impose upon them ; rites abhorrent to Jahveh found favour even among members of the king's own family, and on Hezekiah's death, about 686 B.C., a reaction promptly set in against both his religious views and the material reforms he had introduced.[2] Manasseh was only thirteen years old when he came to the throne, and his youth naturally inclined him towards the less austere forms of divine worship : from the very first he tolerated much that his father had forbidden, and the spirit of eclecticism which prevailed among his associates rendered him, later on, an object of special detestation to the orthodox historians of Jerusalem. Worshippers again began openly to frequent

[1] *Isa.* xxx. 20-22.
[2] 2 *Kings* xxi. 2-7 (cf. 2 *Chron.* xxxiii 2-7), where, in spite of manifest recensions of the text, the facts themselves seem to have been correctly set forth.

the high places; they set up again the prostrate idols replanted the sacred groves, and even "built altars for all the host of heaven in the two courts of the house of Jahveh." The chariots and horses of the sun reappeared within the precincts of the temple, together with the sacred courtesans. Baal and the Phœnician Astarte were worshipped on Mount Sion. The valley of Hinnom, where Ahaz had already burnt one of his children during a desperate crisis in the Syrian wars, was again lighted up by the flames of the sacred pyre. We are told that Manasseh himself set the example by passing his son through the flames; he also had recourse to astrologers soothsayers, fortune-tellers, and sorcerers of the lowest type. The example of Assyria in matters of this kind exercised a preponderant influence on Jewish customs, and certainly it would have been a miracle if Jerusalem had succeeded in escaping it; did not Nineveh owe the lofty place it occupied to these occult sciences and to the mysterious powers of its gods? In thus imitating its conqueror, Judah was merely borrowing the weapons which had helped him to subdue the world. The partisans of the ancient religions who were responsible for these innovations must have regarded them as perfectly legitimate reforms and their action was received with favour in the provinces before long the latter contained as many sanctuaries as there were towns,[2] and by thus multiplying the centres of

---

[1] *Jer.* ii. 26–30. For the quotation see also *Jer.* xi. 13: "For according to the number of thy cities are thy gods, O Judah; and according to the number of the streets of Jerusalem have ye set up altars to the shameful thing, even altars to burn incense unto Baal."

worship, they hoped that, in accordance with ancient belief, the ties which existed between Jahveh and His chosen people would also be increased. The fact that the provinces had been ravaged from end to end in the days of Sennacherib, while Jerusalem had been spared, was attributed to the circumstance that Hezekiah had destroyed the provincial sanctuaries, leaving the temple on Mount Sion alone standing. Wherever Jahveh possessed altars, He kept guard over His people, but His protection was not extended to those places where sacrifices were no longer offered to Him. The reaction was not allowed to take place without opposition on the part of the prophets and their followers. We are told that Manasseh "shed innocent blood very much till he had filled Jerusalem from one end to another;" there is even a Rabbinic tradition to the effect that, weary of the admonitions of the aged Isaiah, he put him to death by shutting him up in the hollow trunk of a tree, and causing him to be sawn in two.[1] For a long time after this no instance can be found of a prophet administering public affairs or directing the actions of the king himself; the priests and reformers, finding no outlet for their energy in this direction, fell back on private preaching and literary propaganda. And, above all, they applied themselves to the task of rewriting the history of Israel, which, as told by the chroniclers of the previous century, presented the national Deity in too material a light, and one which failed to harmonise with the ideals

---

[1] 2 *Kings* xxi. 16. The tradition in regard to the fate of Isaiah took its foundation in this text, and it is perhaps indirectly referred to in *Heb.* xi. 37.

then obtaining. So long as there were two separate Hebrew kingdoms, the existence of the two parallel versions of the Elohist and Jahvist gave rise to but little difficulty: each version had its own supporters and readers, whose consciences were readily satisfied by the interpolation of a few new facts into the text as occasion arose. But now that Samaria had fallen, and the whole political and religious life of the Hebrew race was centred in Judah alone, the necessity for a double and often contradictory narrative had ceased to exist, and the idea occurred of combining the two in a single work. This task, which was begun in the reign of Hezekiah and continued under Manasseh, resulted in the production of a literature of which fragments have been incorporated into the historical books of our Bible.[1]

The reign of Amon witnessed no alteration in the policy initiated by his predecessor Manasseh; but when, after less than two years' rule, he was suddenly struck down by the knife of an assassin, the party of reform carried the day, and the views of Hezekiah and Isaiah regained their ascendency. Josiah had been king, in name at any rate, for twelve years,[2] and was learning to act on

[1] The scheme of the present work prevents me from doing more than allude in passing to these preliminary stages in the composition of the Priestly Code. I shall have occasion to return briefly to the subject at the close of Volume IX.

[2] The date is supplied by the opening passage of the prophecy of Jeremiah, "to whom the word of Jehovah came in the days of Josiah, the son of Amon, King of Judah, in the thirteenth year of his reign" (i. 2). Volney recognised that chaps. i., iv., v., and vi. of Jeremiah refer to the Scythian invasion, and since his time it has been admitted that, with the exception of certain interpolations in chaps. i. and iii., the whole of the first

## SIGNS OF THE DIVINE WRATH

his own responsibility, when the Scythian danger appeared on the horizon. This barbarian invasion, which burst upon the peace of Assyria like a thunderbolt from a cloudless sky, restored to the faithful that confidence in the omnipotence of their God which had seemed about to fail them; when they beheld the downfall of states, the sack of provinces innumerable, whole provinces in flames and whole peoples irresistibly swept away to death or slavery, they began to ask themselves whether these were not signs of the divine wrath, indicating that the day of Jahveh was at hand. Prophets arose to announce the approaching judgment, among the rest a certain Zephaniah, a great-grandson of Hezekiah:[1] "I will utterly consume all things from off the face of the ground, saith Jahveh. I will consume man and beast; I will consume the fowls of the heaven, and the fishes of the sea, and the stumbling-blocks with the wicked; and I will cut off man from the face of the earth, saith Jahveh. And I will stretch out My hand upon Judah, and upon all the inhabitants of Jerusalem; and I will cut off the remnant of Baal from this place, and the name of the Chemarim with the priests; and them that worship the host of heaven upon the housetops;

six chapters date from this period, but that they underwent slight modifications in the recension which was made in the fourth year of Jehoiachin in order to make them applicable to the threatened Chaldæan invasion. The date is important, since by using it as a basis we can approximately restore the chronology of the whole period. If we assume the thirteenth year of Josiah to have been 627–626 B.C., we are compelled to place all the early Medic wars in the reign of Assur-bani-pal, as I have done.

[1] Zephaniah gives his own genealogy at the beginning of his prophecy (i. 1), though, it is true, he does not add the title "King of Judah" after the name of his ancestor Hezekiah.

and them that worship, which swear to Jahveh and swear by Malcham; and them that are turned back from following Jahveh; and those that have not sought Jahveh nor inquired after Him. Hold thy peace at the presence of the Lord Jahveh; for the day of Jahveh is at hand; for Jahveh hath prepared a sacrifice, He hath sanctified His guests."[1] "That day is a day of wrath, a day of trouble and distress, a day of wasteness and desolation, a day of darkness and gloominess, a day of clouds and thick darkness, a day of the trumpet and alarm, against the fenced cities, and against the high battlements. And I will bring distress upon men, that they shall walk like blind men because they have sinned against Jahveh: and their blood shall be poured out as dust, and their flesh as dung Neither their silver nor their gold shall be able to deliver them in the day of Jahveh's wrath; but the whole land shall be devoured by the fire of His jealousy; for He shall make an end, yea, a terrible end, of all them that dwell in the land."[2] During this same period of stress and terror, there came forward another prophet, one of the greatest among the prophets of Israel—Jeremiah, son of Hilkiah. He was born in the village of Anathoth, near Jerusalem, being descended from one of those priestly families in which the faith had been handed down from generation to generation in all its original purity.[3] When

---

[1] *Zeph.* i. 2–7. [2] *Zeph.* i. 15–18.

[3] The descent and birthplace of Jeremiah are given at the beginning of his prophecies (i. 1). He must have been quite young in the thirteenth year of Josiah, as is evident from the statement in i. 6. We are told in chap. xxxvi. that in the fourth year of Jehoiakim he dictated a summary of all the prophecies delivered by him from the thirteenth year of

Jahveh called him, he cried out in amazement, "Ah, Lord God! behold, I cannot speak: for I am a child." But Jahveh reassured him, and touching his lips, said unto him, "Behold, I have put My words in thy mouth: see, I have this day set thee over the nations and over the kingdoms, to pluck up and to break down, and to destroy and to overthrow, to build and to plant." Then the prophet perceived a seething cauldron, the face of which appeared from the north, for the Eternal declared to him that "Out of the north evil shall break out upon all the inhabitants of the land."[1] Already the enemy is hastening: "Behold, he shall come up as clouds, and his chariots shall be as the whirlwind: his horses are swifter than eagles. Woe unto us! for we are spoiled. O Jerusalem, wash thine heart from wickedness, that thou mayest be saved. How long shall thine evil thoughts lodge within thee? For a voice declareth from Dan, and publisheth evil from the hills of Ephraim: make ye mention to the nations; behold, publish against Jerusalem!" The Scythians had hardly been mentioned before they were already beneath the walls, and the prophet almost swoons with horror at the sound of their approach. "My bowels, my bowels! I am pained at my very heart: my heart is disquieted in me; I cannot hold my peace; because thou hast heard, O my soul, the sound of the trumpet, the alarm of war. Destruction upon destruction is cried; for the whole land is spoiled, and my curtains in a moment. How long shall

Josiah up to the date indicated to his servant Baruch, and that later on he added a number of others of the same kind.

[1] *Jer.* i. 4-14.

I see the standard and hear the sound of the trumpet?"[1] It would seem that the torrent of invasion turned aside from the mountains of Judah; it flowed over Galilee Samaria, and the Philistine Shephelah, its last eddies dying away on the frontiers of Egypt. Psammetichus is said to have bribed the barbarians to retire. As they fell back they plundered the temple of Derketô, near Ashkelon we are told that in order to punish them for this act of sacrilege, the goddess visited them with a disease which caused serious ravages amongst them, and which the survivors carried back with them to their own country[2] There was, however, no need to introduce a supernatural agency in order to account for their rapid disappearance The main body of invaders had never quitted Media or the northern part of the Assyrian empire, and only the southern regions of Syria were in all probability exposed to the attacks of isolated bands. These stragglers, who year after year embarked in one desperate adventure after another must have found great difficulty in filling up the gaps which even victories made in their ranks; enervated by the relaxing nature of the climate, they could offer little resistance to disease, and excess completed what the climate had begun, the result being that most of them

[1] *Jer.* iv. 13–16, 19–21.

[2] Herodotus calls the goddess Aphroditê Urania, by which we must understand Derketô or Atargatis, who is mentioned by several other classical authors, *e.g.* Xanthus of Lydia, Diodorus Siculus, Strabo, Pliny. According to Justin, the Scythians were stopped only by the marshes of the Delta The disease by which the Scythians were attacked is described by Hippo crates; but in spite of what he tells us about it, its precise nature has not yet been determined.

died on the way, and only a few survived to rejoin the main body with their booty. For several months the tide of invasion continued to rise, then it ebbed as quickly as it had risen, till soon nothing was left to mark where it had passed save a pathway of ruins, not easily made good, and a feeling of terror which it took many a year to efface. It was long before Judah forgot the "mighty nation, the ancient nation, the nation whose language thou knowest not, neither understandest thou what they say."[1] Men could still picture in imagination their squadrons marauding over the plains, robbing the fellah of his crops, his bread, his daughters, his sheep and oxen, his vines and fig trees, for "they lay hold on bow and spear; they are cruel and have no mercy; their voice roareth like the sea, and they ride upon horses; every one set in array as a man to the battle,[2] against thee, O daughter of Sion. We have heard the fame thereof; our hands wax feeble; anguish hath taken hold of us, and pangs as of a woman in travail."[3]

The supremacy of the Scythians was of short duration. It was said in after-times that they had kept the whole of Asia in a state of terror for twenty-eight years, dating from their defeat of Cyaxares; but the length of this period is exaggerated.[4] The Medes soon recovered from their

---

[1] *Jer.* v. 15; it seems curious that the Hebrew prophet should use the epithet "ancient," when we remember that the Scythians claimed to be the oldest nation in the world, older than even the Egyptians themselves.

[2] An obvious allusion to the regular formation adopted by the Scythian squadrons.

[3] *Jer.* v. 17; vi. 23, 24.

[4] The authenticity of the number of years given in Herodotus has been energetically defended by some modern historians, and not less forcibly

disaster, but before engaging their foes in open conflict they desired to rid themselves of the prince who had conquered them, and on whom the fortunes of the whole Scythian nation depended. Cyaxares, therefore, invited Madyes and his officers to a banquet, and after plying them to excess with meat and drink, he caused them all to be slain.[1] The barbarians made a brave resistance, in spite the treason which had deprived them of their leaders : they yielded only after a long and bloody campaign, the details of which are unknown to us. Iranian legends wove into the theme of their expulsion all kinds of fantastic romantic incidents. They related, for instance, how, in combination with the Parthians, the Scythians, under the leadership of their queen Zarinæa, several times defeated the Medes: she consented at last to conclude a treaty on equal terms, and peace having been signed, she retired to her capital of Roxanakê, there to end her days. One body

denied by others, who reduce it, for example, in accordance with a doubtful passage of Justin, to eight years. By assigning all the events relating to the Scythian invaders to the mean period of twenty years, we should obtain the length of time which best corresponds to what is actually known of the general history of this epoch.

[1] This episode is regarded as legendary by many modern historians Winckler even goes so far as to deny the defeat of the Scythians : according to his view, they held possession of Media till their chief, Astyages, was overthrown by Cyrus; Rost has gone even further, deeming even Cyaxares himself to have been a Scythian. For my part, I see no reason to reject the tradition of the fatal banquet. Without referring to more ancient illust tions, Nöldeke recalls the fact that in a period of only ten years, from 1030 to 1040 A.D., the princes reigning over the Iranian lands rid themselves by similar methods of the Turcoman bands which harassed them. Such a proceeding has never been repugnant to Oriental morality, and it is of a kind to fix itself in the popular mind : far from wishing to suppress it I should be inclined to see in it the nucleus of the whole tradition.

of the survivors re-entered Europe through the Caspian Gates, another wandered for some time between the Araxes and the Halys, seeking a country adapted to their native instincts and customs.[1] Cyaxares, relieved from the pressure put upon him by the Scythians, immediately resumed his efforts against Assyria, and was henceforward able to carry his plans to completion without encountering any serious obstacle. It would be incorrect to say that the Scythian invasion had overthrown the empire of the Sargonids: it had swept over it like a whirlwind, but had not torn from it one province, nor, indeed, even a single city. The nations, already exhausted by their struggles for independence, were incapable of displaying any energy when the barbarians had withdrawn, and continued to bow beneath the Ninevite yoke as much from familiarity with habitual servitude as from inability to shake themselves free. Assur-bani-pal had died about the year 625 B.C., after a reign of forty-two years, and his son Assur-etililâni had assumed the double crown of Assyria and Babylon without opposition.[2] Nineveh had been saved from pillage by the

---

[1] Herodotus speaks of these Scythians as having lived at first on good terms with Cyaxares.

[2] The date of Assur-bani-pal's death is not furnished by any Assyrian monument, but is inferred from the Canon of Ptolemy, where Saosduchîn or Shamash-shumukîn and Chinaladan or Assur-bani-pal each reigns forty-two years, from 668 or 667 to 626 or 625 B.C. The order of succession of the last Assyrian kings was for a long time doubtful, and Sin-shar-ishkun was placed before Assur-etililâni; the inverse order seems to be now conclusively proved. The documents which seemed at one time to prove the existence of a last king of Assyria named Esarhaddon, identical with the Saracos of classical writers, really belong to Esarhaddon, the father of Assur-bani-pal. [Another king, Sin-sum-lisir, is mentioned in a contract dated at Nippur in his

strength of her ramparts, but the other fortresses, Assur, Calah, and Dur-Sharrukîn, had been destroyed during the late troubles; the enemy, whether Medes or Scythians had taken them by storm or reduced them by famine, and they were now mere heaps of ruin, deserted save for a few wretched remnants of their population. Assur-etililâni made some feeble attempts to restore to them a semblance of their ancient splendour. He erected at Calah, on the site of the palaces which had been destroyed by fire, a kind of castle rudely built, and still more rudely decorated, the rooms of which were small and low, and the walls of sun-dried brick were panelled only to the height of about a yard with slabs of limestone roughly squared, and without sculpture or inscription: the upper part of the walls was covered with a coating of uneven plaster. We do not know how long the inglorious reign of Assur-etililâni lasted nor whether he was assassinated or died a natural death His brother, Sin-shar-ishkun,[1] who succeeded him about 620 B.C., at first exercised authority, as he had done, over Babylon as well as Nineveh,[2] and laboured, like his

accession year. He may have been the immediate predecessor of Sarakos.— ED.]

[1] The name of this king was discovered by G. Smith on the fragments of a cylinder brought from Kouyunjik, where he read it as Bel-zakir-iskun. The real reading is Sin-shar-ishkun, and the similarity of this name with that of Saracos, the last king of Assyria according to Greek tradition, strikes one immediately. The relationship of this king to Assur-etililâni was pointed out by Father Seheil from the fragment of a tablet on which Sin-shar-ishkun is declared to be the son of Assur-bani-pal, king of Assyria.

[2] This may be deduced from a passage of Abydenus, where Saracos or Sin-shar-ishkun sends Bussalossoros (that is, Nabopolassar) to defend Chaldæa against the invasion of the peoples of the sea; so according to

predecessor, to repair the edifices which had suffered by the invasion, making war on his neighbours, perhaps even on the Medes, without incurring serious losses. The Chaldæans, however, merely yielded him obedience from force of habit, and the moment was not far distant when they would endeavour to throw off his yoke. Babylon was at that time under the rule of a certain Nabu-bal-uzur, known to us as Nabopolassar, a Kaldu of ancient lineage, raised possibly by Assur-bani-pal to the dignity of governor, but who, in any case, had assumed the title of king on the accession of Assur-etililâni.[1] His was but a local sovereignty, restricted probably to the city and its environs; and for twelve or thirteen years he had rested content with this secondary position, when an unforeseen incident presented him with the opportunity of rising to the first rank. Tradition asserted that an immense army suddenly landed at the mouths of the Euphrates and the Tigris; probably under this story is concealed the memory of one of those revolts of the Bît-Yakîn and the tribes dwelling on the shores of the Nar-Marratum, such as had often produced consternation in the minds of the Sargonid

Abydenus, or rather Berosus, from whom Abydenus indirectly obtained his information, Saracos was King of Babylon as well as of Nineveh at the beginning of his reign.

[1] The Canon of Ptolemy makes Nabopolassar the direct successor of Chinaladan, and his testimony is justified by the series of Babylonian contracts which exist in fairly regular succession from the second to the twenty-first years of Nabopolassar. The account given by Berosus makes him a general of Saracos, but the contradiction which this offers to the testimony of the Canon can be explained if he is considered as a vassal-king; the kings of Egypt and of Media were likewise only satraps, according to Babylonian tradition.

kings.¹ Sin-shar-ishkun, distracted doubtless by other anxieties, acted as his ancestors had done in similar circumstances, and enjoined on his vassal to march against the aggressors and drive them into the sea; but Nabopolassar, instead of obeying his suzerain, joined forces with the rebels, and declared his independence. Assur-etililâni and his younger brother had possibly neglected to take the hands of Bel, and were therefore looked upon as illegitimate sovereigns. The annalists of later times erased their names from the Royal Canon, and placed Nabopolassar immediately after Assur-bani-pal, whom they called Kandalanu. But however feeble Assyria had become, the cities on the Lower Euphrates feared her still, and refused to ally themselves with the pretender. Nabopolassar might perhaps have succumbed, as so many before him had done, had he been forced to rely entirely on his own resources, and he might have shared the sad fate of Merodach-baladan or Shamash-shumukîn; but Marduk, who never failed to show favour to his faithful devotees, "raised up help for him and secured him an ally." The eyes of all who were oppressed by the cruel yoke of Nineveh were now turned on Cyaxares, and from the time that he had dispersed the Scythian hordes it was to him that they looked for salvation. Nabopolassar besought his assistance, which the Median king graciously promised;² it is even affirmed

¹ Formerly these barbarians were identified with the remains of the Scythian hordes, and this hypothesis has been recently revived by Prashek. G. Rawlinson long ago recognised that the reference must be to the Chaldæans, who were perhaps joined by the Susians.

² The *Cylinder of Nabonidos*, the only original document in which allusion is made to the destruction of Nineveh, speaks of the Ummân-Manda and

that a marriage concluded between one of his daughters, Amytis, and Nebuchadrezzar, the heir to the throne of Babylon, cemented the alliance.[1] The western provinces of the empire did not permit themselves to be drawn into the movement, and Judah, for example, remained faithful

their king, whom it does not name, and it has been agreed to recognise Cyaxares in this sovereign. On the other hand, the name of Ummân-Manda certainly designates in the Assyrian texts the wandering Iranian tribes to whom the Greeks gave the name of Sakæ or Scythians; the result, in the opinions of several Assyriologists of the present day, is that neither Astyages nor Cyaxares were Medes in the sense in which we have hitherto accepted them as such on the evidence of Herodotus, but that they were Scythians, the Scythians of the great invasion. This conclusion does not seem to me at present justified. The Babylonians, who up till then had not had any direct intercourse either with the Madai or the Ummân-Manda, did as the Egyptians had done whether in Saite or Ptolemaic times, continuing to designate as Khari, Kafîti, Lotanu, and Khâti the nations subject to the Persians or Macedonians; they applied a traditional name of olden days to present circumstances, and I see, at present, no decisive reason to change, on the mere authority of this one word, all that the classical writers have handed down concerning the history of the epoch according to the tradition current in their days.

[1] The name of the princess is written Amuhia, Amyitis. The classical sources, the only ones which mention her, make her the daughter of Astyages, and this has given rise to various hypotheses. According to some, the notice of this princess has no historical value. According to others, the Astyages mentioned as her father is not Cyaxares the Mede, but a Scythian prince who came to the succour of Nabopolassar, perhaps a predecessor of Cyaxares on the Median throne, and in this case Phraortes himself under another name. The most prudent course is still to admit that Abydenus, or one of the compilers of extracts to whom we owe the information, has substituted the name of the last king of Media for that of his predecessor, either by mistake, or by reason of some chronological combinations. Amyitis, transported into the harem of the Chaldæan monarch, served, like all princesses married out of their own countries, as a pledge for the faithful observance by her relatives of the treaty which had been concluded.

to its suzerain till the last moment,[1] but Sin-shar-ishkun received no help from them, and was obliged to fight his last battles single-handed. He shut himself up in Nineveh, and held out as long as he could; but when all his resources were exhausted—ammunitions of war, men and food supplies—he met his fate as a king, and burnt himself alive in his palace with his children and his wives, rather than fall alive into the hands of his conquerors (608 B.C.). The Babylonians would take no part in pillaging the temples out of respect for the gods, who were practically identical with their own, but the Medes felt no such scruples "Their king, the intrepid one, entirely destroyed the sanctuaries of the gods of Assur, and the cities of Accad which had shown themselves hostile to the lord of Accad and had not rendered him assistance. He destroyed their holy places, and left not one remaining; he devastated their cities, and laid them waste as it were with a hurricane." Nineveh laid low, Assyria no longer existed After the lapse of a few years, she was named only among the legends of mythical days: two centuries later, her very site was forgotten, and a Greek army passed almost under the shadow of her dismantled towers, without a suspicion that there lay before it all that remained of the city where Semiramis had reigned in her glory.[2] It is true that Egypt, Chaldæa, and the other military nations of the East

[1] It was to oppose the march of Necho *against the King of Assyria* that Josiah fought the battle of Megiddo (2 Kings xxiii. 29, 30; cf. 2 *Chron.* xxxv. 20-24, where the mention of the King of Assyria is suppressed).

[2] This is what the *Ten Thousand* did when they passed before Larissa and Mespila. The name remained famous, and later on the town which bore it attained a relative importance.

had never, in their hours of prosperity, shown the slightest consideration for their vanquished foes; the Theban Pharaohs had mercilessly crushed Africa and Asia beneath their feet, and had led into slavery the entire population of the countries they had subdued. But the Egyptians and Chaldæans had, at least, accomplished a work of civilization whose splendour redeemed the brutalities of their acts of reprisal. It was from Egypt and Chaldæa that the knowledge and the arts of antiquity—astronomy, medicine, geometry, physical and natural sciences—spread to the ancestors of the classic races; and though Chaldæa yields up to us unwillingly, with niggard hand, the monuments of her most ancient kings, the temples and tombs of Egypt still exist to prove what signal advances the earliest civilised races made in the arts of the sculptor and the architect. But on turning to Assyria, if, after patiently studying the successive centuries during which she held supreme sway over the Eastern world, we look for other results besides her conquests, we shall find she possessed nothing that was not borrowed from extraneous sources. She received all her inspirations from Chaldæa—her civilisation, her manners, the implements of her industries and of agriculture, besides her scientific and religious literature: one thing alone is of native growth, the military tactics of her generals and the excellence of her soldiery. From the day when Assyria first realised her own strength, she lived only for war and rapine; and as soon as the exhaustion of her population rendered success on the field of battle an impossibility, the reason for her very existence vanished, and she passed away.

Two great kingdoms rose simultaneously from her ruins Cyaxares claimed Assyria proper and its dependencies on the Upper Tigris, but he specially reserved for himself the yet unconquered lands on the northern and eastern frontiers whose inhabitants had only recently taken part in the political life of the times. Nabopolassar retained the suzerainty over the lowlands of Elam, the districts of Mesopotamia lying along the Euphrates, Syria, Palestine and most of the countries which had hitherto played a part in history;[1] he claimed to exert his supremacy beyond the Isthmus, and the Chaldæan government looked upon the Egyptian kings as its feudatories because for some few years they had owned the suzerainty of Nineveh.[2] The Pharaoh, however, did not long tolerate this pretension, and far from looking forward to bend the knee before a Chaldæan monarch, he believed himself strong enough to reassert his ancestral claims to the possession of Asia. Egypt had experienced many changes since the day when Tanuatamanu, returning to Ethiopia had abandoned her to the ambition of the petty dynasties

[1] There was no actual division of the empire, as has been often asserted but each of the allies kept the portion which fell into his power at the moment of their joint effort. The two new states gradually increased in power by successive conquests, each annexing by degrees the ancient provinces of Assyria nearest to its own frontier.

[2] This seems to be implied by the terms in which Berosus speaks Necho: he considers him as a rebel satrap over the provinces of Egypt Cœle-Syria, and Phœnicia, and enumerates Egypt in conjunction with Syria, Phœnicia, and Arabia among the dependencies of Nabopolassar and Nebuchadrezzar. Just as the Egyptian state documents never mentioned the Lotanu or the Kharu without entitling them *Children of Rebellion*, so the Chaldæan government, the heir of Assyria, could only look upon the kings of Syria, Arabia, and Egypt as rebellious vassals.

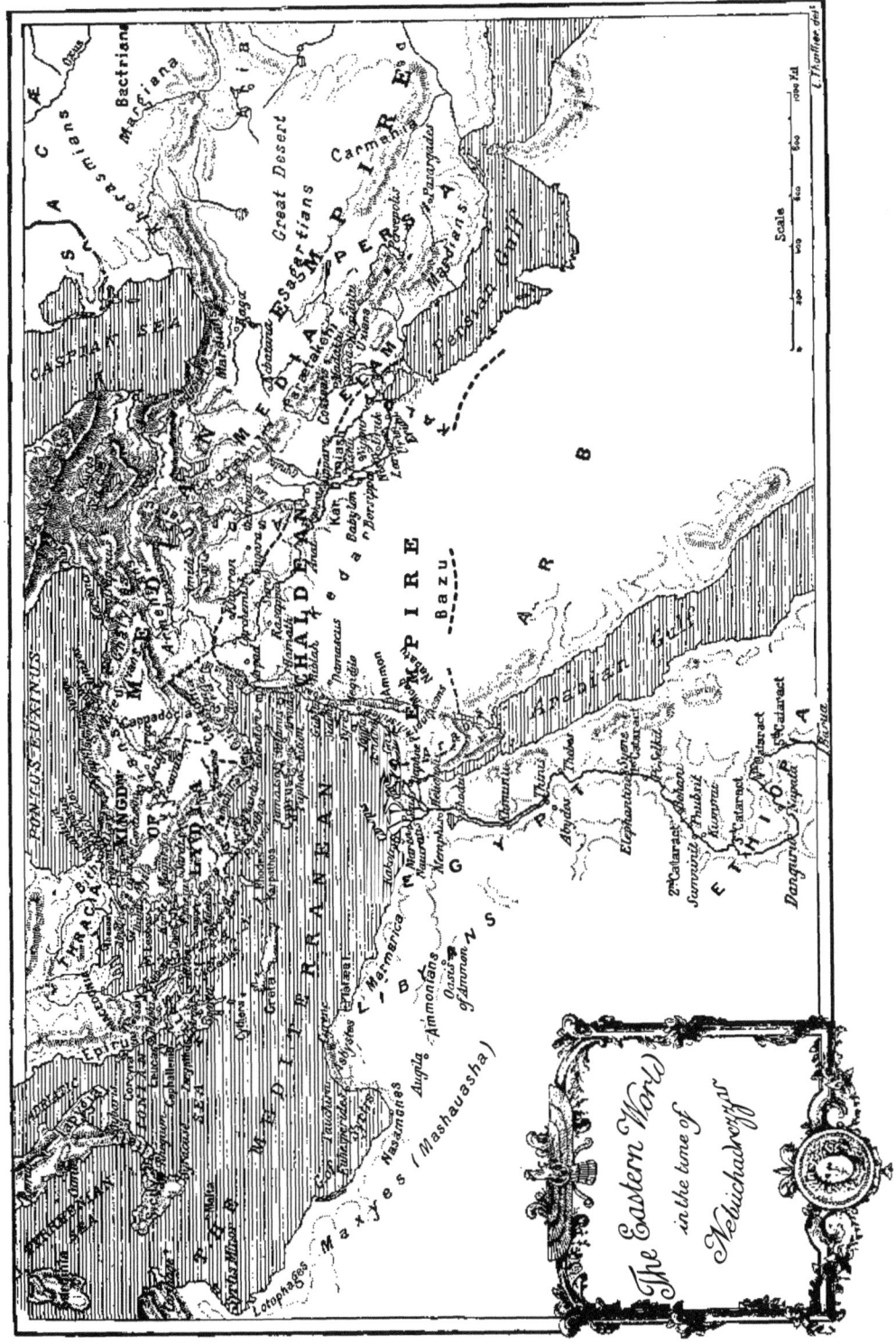

of the Delta. One of the romances current among the people of Sais in the fifth century B.C. related that at that time the whole land was divided between twelve princes. They lived peaceably side by side in friendly relations with each other, until an oracle predicted that the whole valley would finally belong to that prince among them who should pour a libation to Phtah into a brazen cup, and thenceforward they jealously watched each other each time they assembled to officiate in the temple of Memphis. One day, when they had met together in state, and the high priest presented to them the golden cups they were wont to use, he found he had mistaken their number, and had only prepared eleven. Psammetichus was therefore left without one, and in order not to disarrange the ceremonial he took off his brazen helmet and used it to make his libation; when the rest perceived this, the words of the oracle came to their remembrance, and they exiled the imprudent prince to the marshes along the sea-coast, and forbade him ever to quit them. He secretly consulted the oracle of Isis of Buto to know what he might expect from the gods, and she replied that the means of revenge would reach him from the sea, on the day when brazen soldiers should issue from its waters. He thought at first that the priests were mocking him, but shortly afterwards Ionian and Carian pirates, clad in their coats of mail, landed not far from his abode. The messenger who brought tidings of their advent had never before seen a soldier fully armed, and reported that brazen men had issued from the waves and were pillaging the country. Psammetichus, realising at once that the prediction was

being fulfilled, ran to meet the strangers, enrolled the
in his service, and with their aid overthrew successively
his eleven rivals.[1] A brazen helmet and an oracle had
dethroned him; another oracle and brazen men had replaced him on his throne. A shorter version of these
events made no mention of the twelve kings, but related
instead that a certain Pharaoh named Tementhes had been
warned by the oracle of Amon to beware of cocks. Now
Psammetichus had as a companion in exile a Carian
named Pigres, and in conversing with him one day, he
learned by chance that the Carians had been the first
people to wear crested helmets; he recalled at once the
words of the oracle, and hired from Asia a number
these "cocks," with whose assistance he revolted and
overthrew his suzerain in battle under the walls
Memphis, close to the temple of Isis. Such is the

[1] The account given by Diodorus of these events is in general derived
from that of Herodotus, with additional details borrowed directly or
indirectly from some historian of the same epoch, perhaps Hellanicus
of Mitylene: the reason of the persecution endured by Psammetichus
is, according to him, not the fear of seeing the prediction fulfilled, but
jealousy of the wealth the Saite prince had acquired by his comme ce
with the Greeks. I have separated the narrative of Herodotus f om
his account of the Labyrinth which did not originally belong to it, but
was connected with a different cycle of legends. The original romance
was part of the cycle which grew up around the oracle of Buto, so celebrated
in Egypt at the Persian epoch, several other fragments of which
preserved in Herodotus; it had been mixed up with one of the versions
of the stories relating to the Labyrinth, probably by some dragoman
the Fayyûm. The number twelve does not correspond with the information
furnished by the Assyrian texts, which enumerate more than twenty
Egyptian princes; it is perhaps of Greek origin, like the *twelve* great
gods which the informants of Herodotus tried to make out in Egypt
and was introduced into the Egyptian version by a Greek interpreter.

legendary account of the Saite renaissance its true history is not yet clearly and precisely known Egypt was in a state of complete disintegration when Psammetichus at length revived the ambitious projects of his family, but the dissolution of the various component parts had not everywhere taken place in the same manner In the north the Delta and the Nile valley as far as Siut were in the power of a military aristocracy supported by

THREE HOPLITES IN ACTION.[1]

irregular native troops and bands of mercenaries, for the most part of Libyan extraction who were always designated by the generic name of Mashauasha. Most of these nobles were in possession of not more than two or three cities apiece they had barely a sufficient number of supporters to maintain their precarious existence in their restricted domains and would soon have succumbed to the attacks of their stronger neighbours had they not found a powerful protector to assist them They had finally separated themselves into two groups divided roughly by the central arm of the Nile One group comprised the districts that

Drawn by Faucher-Gudin, from an archaic vase painting in the collection of Salzmann.

might be designated as the Asiatic zone of the country—Heliopolis, Bubastis, Mendes, Tanis, Busiris, and Sebennytos—and it recognised as chief the lord of one or other of those wealthy cities, now the ruler of Bubastis, now of Tanis, and lastly Pakruru of Pisaptit. The second group centred in the lords of Sais, to whom the possession of Memphis had secured a proponderating voice in the counsels of the state for more than a century.[1] The fiefs and kingdoms of Middle Egypt wavered between the two groups, playing, however, a merely passive part in affairs: abandoning themselves to the stream of events rather than attempting to direct it, they owed allegiance to Sais and Tanis alternately as each prevailed over its rival. On passing thence into the Thebaid a different world appeared to be entered. There Amon reigned, ever increasingly supreme, and the steady advance of his influence had transformed his whole domain into a regular theocracy, where the women occupied the highest position and could alone transmit authority. At first, as we have seen, it was passed on to their husbands and their children, but latterly the rapidity with which the valley had changed masters had modified this law of succession in a remarkable way. Each time the principality shifted its allegiance from one king to another, the new sovereign naturally hastened to install beside the *divine female worshipper* a

[1] This grouping, which might already have been suspected from the manner in which the Assyrian and Egyptian monuments of the period show us the feudal princes rallying round Necho I. and Pakruru, is indicated by the details in the demotic romance published by Krall, where the foundation of the story is the state of Egypt in the time of the " twelve kings."

man devoted to his interests, who should administer the fief to the best advantage of the suzerain. It is impossible to say whether he actually imposed this minister on her as a husband, or whether the time came when she was obliged to submit to as many espousals as there occurred revolutions in the destinies of Egypt.[1] However this may be, we know that from the first half of the seventh century B.C. the custom arose of placing beside "the divine worshipper" a princess of the dominant family, whom she adopted, and who thus became her heiress-designate. Tabarqa had in this way associated one of his sisters, Shapenuapît II., with the queen Amenertas when the latter had lost her husband, Piônkhi; and Shapenuapît, succeeding her adopted mother, had reigned over Thebes in the Ethiopian interest during many years. There is nothing to show that she was married, and perhaps she was compensated for her official celibacy by being authorised to live the free life of an ordinary Pallacide;[2] her minister Montumihâît directed her affairs for her so completely that the Assyrian conquerors looked upon him as petty king of Thebes. Tanuatamanu confirmed him in his office when the Assyrians evacuated the Saîd, and the

[1] They would have been, in fact, in the same condition as the Hova queens of our century, who married the ministers who reigned in their names.

[2] It is perhaps these last female descendants of the high priests that are intended in a passage where Strabo speaks of the Pallacides who were chosen from among the most noble families of the city. Diodorus mentions their tombs, quoting from Hecatæus of Abdera, but he does not appear to know the nature of their life; but the name of Pallacides which he applies to them proves that their manner of life was really that which Strabo describes.

338 THE MEDES AND THE SECOND CHALDÆAN EMPIRE

few years which had elapsed since that event had in no way modified the *régime* established immediately on their departure.

It is uncertain how long Assur-bani-pal in the north and Tanuatamanu in the south, respectively maintained a precarious sovereignty over the portions of Egypt nearest to their own capitals. The opening of the reign of Psammetichus seems to have been fraught with difficulties, and the tradition which represents him as proscribed by his peers, and confined to the marshes of the sea-coast, has probably a certain basis of truth. Pakruru, who had brought all the western part of the Delta under his own influence, and who, incessantly oscillating between Assyria and Ethiopia, had yet been able to preserve his power and his life, had certainly not of his own free will renounced the hope of some day wearing the double crown. It was against him or his successor that Psammetichus must have undertaken his first wars, and it was perhaps with the help of Assyrian governors that the federal coalition drove him back to the

STATUE OF A THEBAN QUEEN.[1]

[1] Drawn by Boudier, from a photograph by M. de Bissing. The statue, whose feet are missing, represents either Amenertas I. or Mutertas; it was never completely finished, and several of the parts have never received their final polish.

coast. He extricated himself from this untoward situation by the help of Greek and Asiatic mercenaries, his Ionians and Carians. Some historians stated that the decisive battle was fought near Memphis, in sight of the temple of Isis; others affirmed that it took place at Momemphis, that several of the princes perished in the conflict, and that the rest escaped into Libya, whence they never returned; others, again, spoke of an encounter on the Nile, when the fleet of the Saite king dispersed that of his rivals. It is, in fact, probable that a single campaign sufficed for Psammetichus, as formerly for the Ethiopian pretenders, to get the upper hand, and that the Egyptian feudal lords submitted after one or two defeats at most, hoping that, as in days gone by, when the first dash made by the new Pharaoh was over, his authority would decline, and their own would regain the ascendency. Events showed that they were deceived. Psammetichus, better served by his Hellenes than Tafnakhti or Bocchoris had been by their Libyans, or Piônkhi and Tanuatamanu by their Ethiopians, soon consolidated his rule over the country he had conquered. From 660 or 659 B.C. he so effectively governed Egypt that foreigners, and even the Assyrians themselves commonly accorded him the title of king. The fall of the Ninevite rule had been involved in that of the feudal lords, but it was generally believed that Assur-banipal would leave no means untried to recall the countries of the Nile to their obedience : Psammetichus knew this, and knew also that, as soon as they were no longer detained by wars or rebellions elsewhere, the Assyrian armies would reappear in Egypt. He therefore entered into an alliance with Gyges,[1] and subsequently, perhaps, with Shamash-shumukîn also; then, while his former suzerain was waging war in Elam and Chaldæa, he turned southwards, in 658 B.C., and took possession of the Thebaid without encountering any opposition from the Ethiopians, as his ancestor Tafnakhti had from Piônkhi-Miamun. Montumihâit negotiated this capitulation of Thebes, as he had already negotiated so many others; in recompense for this service, he was confirmed in his office, and his queen retained her high rank.[2] A century or two earlier Psammetichus would have married one of the princesses of sacerdotal lineage, and this union would have sufficed to legalise his position; perhaps he actually associated Shapenuapît with himself by a show of marriage, but in any case he provided her with an adopted daughter according to the custom instituted by the Ethiopian Pharaohs. She already had one daughter by adoption, whom she had received at the hands of Taharqa, and who, in changing her family, had assumed the name of Amenertas in honour of the queen who had preceded Shapenuapît:

[1] The annexation of the Thebaid and the consequent pacification of Egypt was an accomplished fact in the year IX. of Psammetichus I. The analogy of similar documents, e.g. the stele of the high priest Menkhopirrî, shows that the ceremony of adoption which consecrated the reunion of Upper and Lower Egypt cannot have been separated by a long interval from the completion of the reunion itself: in placing this at the end of the year VIII., we should have for the two events the respective dates of 658–657 and 657–656 B.C.

[2] The part played by Montumihâit in this affair is easily deduced (1) from our knowledge of his conduct some years previously under Taharqa and Tanuatamanu; (2) from the position he occupied at Thebes, in the year IX., with regard to Shapenuapît, according to the stele of Legrain.

Psammetichus forced her to replace the Ethiopian princess by one of his own daughters, who was henceforth called Shapenuapît, after her new mother. A deputation of the nobles and priests of Thebes came to escort the princess from Memphis, in the month of Tybi, in the ninth year of the reign: Psammetichus formally presented her to them, and the ambassadors, having listened to his address, expatiated in the customary eulogies on his splendour and generosity. "They shall endure as long as the world lasteth; all that thou ordainest shall endure. How beautiful is that which God hath done for thee, how glorious that which thy divine father hath done for thee? He is pleased that thy double should be commemorated, he rejoices in the pronouncing of thy name, for our lord Psammetichus has made a gift to his father Amon, he has given him his eldest daughter, his beloved Nitauqrît Shapenuapît, to be his divine spouse, that she may shake the sistrum before him!" On the 28th of Tybi the princess left the harem, clothed in fine linen and adorned with ornaments of malachite, and descended to the quay, accompanied by an immense throng, to set out for her new home. Relays stationed along the river at intervals made the voyage so expeditious that at the end of sixteen days the princess came in sight of Thebes. She disembarked on the 14th of Khoiak, amid the acclamations of the people: "She comes, the daughter of the King of the South, Nitauqrît, to the dwelling of Amon, that he may possess her and unite her to himself; she comes, the daughter of the King of the North, Shapenuapît, to the temple of Karnak, that the gods may there chant her praises." As soon as the aged Shapenuapît had seen her coadjutor, "she loved her more than all things," and assigned her a dowry, the same as that which she had received from her own parents, and which she had granted to her first adopted daughter Amenertas. The magnates of Thebes—the aged Montumihâît, his son Nsiphtah, and the prophets of Amon—vied with each other in their gifts of welcome: Psammetichus, on his side, had acted most generously, and the temples of Egypt assigned to the princess an annual income out of their revenues, or bestowed upon her grants of houses and lands, in all constituting a considerable inheritance, which somewhat consoled the Thebans for their subjection to a dynasty emanating from the cities of the north. The rest of the principality imitated the example of Thebes and the whole of Egypt, from the shores of the Mediterranean to the rocks of the first cataract, once more found itself reunited under the sceptre of an Egyptian king. A small part of Nubia, the portion nearest to Elephantinê, followed this movement, but the greater part refused to cut itself off from the Ethiopians. These latter were henceforth confined to the regions along the middle course of the Nile, isolated from the rest of the world by the deserts, the Red Sea, and Egypt. It is probable that they did not give up without a struggle the hope of regaining the ground they had lost, and that their armies made more than one expedition in a northerly direction. The inhabitants of the Thebaid could hardly fail to remain faithful to them at heart, and to recognise in them the ligitimate representatives of the posterity of Amon;

it is possible that now and again they succeeded in penetrating as far as the ancient capital, but if so, their success was always ephemeral, and their sojourn left no permanent traces. The same causes, however, which had broken up the constituent elements, and destroyed the unity of Greater Egypt at the end of the Theban period, were still at work in Saite times to prevent the building up again of the empire. The preservation of the balance of power in this long and narrow strip of country depended on the centre of attraction and on the seat of government being nearly equidistant from the two extremities. This condition had been fulfilled as long as the court resided at Thebes; but as the removal of the seat of government to the Delta caused the loss and separation of the southern provinces, so its sudden return to the extreme south, with a temporary sojourn at Napata, necessarily produced a similar effect, and led to the speedy secession of the northern provinces. In either case, the dynasty placed at one extremity of the empire was unable to sustain for any length of time the weight depending on it at the other; when once the balance became even slightly disturbed, it could not regain its equilibrium, and there was consequently a sudden dislocation of the machinery of government.

The triumph of the Saite dynasty accomplished the final ruin of the work begun under the Papis and brought to completion by the Amenemhâîts and the Usirtasens. Greater Egypt ceased to exist, after more than twenty centuries of glorious life, and was replaced by the Little Egypt of the first ages of history. The defeat of the military chiefs of the north, the annexation of the principality of Amon, and the final expulsion of the Ethiopians and the Asiatics had occupied scarcely nine years, but these feats constituted only the smaller part of the work Psammetichus had to accomplish: his subsequent task lay in restoring prosperity to his kingdom, or, at all events, in raising it from the state of misery into which two centuries of civil wars and invasions had plunged it. The important cities had suffered grievously: Memphis had been besieged and taken by assault by both Piônkhi and Esarhaddon, Thebes had been twice sacked by the veterans of Assur-bani-pal, and from Syenê to Pelusium there was not a township but had suffered at the hands of foreigners or of the Egyptians themselves. The country had enjoyed a moment's breathing-space under Sabaco, but the little good which this prince had been able to accomplish was effaced immediately after his death: the canals and dykes had been neglected, the supervision of the police relaxed, and the population, periodically decimated or driven to take refuge in the strongholds, had often allowed the lands to lie waste, so that famine had been superadded to the other evils under which the land already groaned. Psammetichus, having forced the feudal lords to submit to his supremacy, deprived them of the royal titles they had unduly assumed; he no longer tolerated their habits of private warfare, but restricted them to the functions of hereditary governors, which their ancestors had exercised under the conquering dynasties of former times,[1] and this

[1] During the last few years records of a certain number of persons have been discovered whose names and condition prove that they were the

enforced peace soon allowed the rural population to devote themselves joyfully to their regular occupations. With so fertile a soil, two or three years of security, during which the fellahin were able to sow and reap their crops free from the fear of marauding bands, sufficed to restore abundance, if not wealth, to the country, and Psammetichus succeeded in securing both these and other benefits to Egypt, thanks to the vigilant severity of his administration. He would have been unable to accomplish these reforms had he relied only on the forces which had been at the disposal of his ancestors—the native troops demoralised by poverty, and the undisciplined bands of Libyan mercenaries, which constituted the sole normal force of the Tanite and Bubastite Pharaohs and the barons of the Delta and Middle Egypt. His experience of these two classes of soldiery had decided him to look elsewhere for a less precarious support, and ever since chance had brought him in contact with the Ionians and Carians, he had surrounded himself with a regular army of Hellenic and Asiatic mercenaries. It is impossible to exaggerate the terror that the apparition of these men produced in the minds of the African peoples, or the revolution they effected, alike in peace or war, in Oriental states: the charge of the Spanish soldiery among the lightly clad foot-soldiers of Mexico and Peru could not have caused more dismay than did that of the hoplites from beyond the sea among the

descendants of semi-independent princes of the Ethiopian and Bubastite periods: *e.g.* a certain Akaneshu, who was prince of Sebennytos under Psammetichus I., and who very probably was the grandson of Akaneshu, prince of the same town under Piônkhi; and a Sheshonq of Busiris, who was perhaps a descendant of Sheshonq, prince of Busiris under Piônkhi.

half-naked archers and pikemen of Egypt and Libya With their bulging corselets, the two plates of which protected back and chest, their greaves made of a single piece of bronze reaching from the ankle to the knee, their square or oval bucklers covered with metal, their heavy rounded helmets fitting closely to the head and neck, and surmounted by crests of waving plumes, they were, in truth, men of brass, invulnerable to any Oriental weapon. Drawn up in close array beneath their "tortoise," they received almost unhurt the hail of arrows and stones hurled against them by the lightly armed infantry, and then when their own trumpet sounded the signal for attack, and they let themselves fall with their whole weight upon the masses of the enemy, brandishing their spears above the upper edge of their bucklers, there was no force of native troops or company of Mashauasha that did not waver beneath the shock and finally give way before their attack. The Egyptians felt themselves incapable of overcoming them except by superior numbers or by stratagem, and it was the knowledge of their own hopeless inferiority which prevented the feudal lords from attempting to revenge themselves on Psammetichus. To make themselves his equals, they would have been obliged either to take a sufficient number of similar warriors into their own pay—and this they were not able to afford—or they must have won over those already in the employ of their suzerain; but the liberality with which Psammetichus treated his mercenaries gave them good cause to be faithful, even if military honour had not sufficed to keep them loyal to their employer. Psammetichus granted to them and their compatriots, who were attracted by the fame of Egypt, a concession of the fertile lands of the Delta stretching along the Pelusiac branch of the Nile, and he was careful to separate the Ionians from the Carians by the whole breadth of the river: this was a wise precaution, for their union beneath a common flag had not extinguished their inherited hatred of one another, and the authority of the general did not always suffice to prevent fatal quarrels breaking out between contingents of different nationalities. They occupied, moreover, regularly entrenched camps, enclosed within massive walls, containing

THE SAITE FORTRESS OF DAPHNÆ.[1]

a collection of mud huts or houses of brick, the whole enclosure commanded by a fortress which formed the headquarters of the general and staff of officers. Some merchants from Miletus, emboldened by the presence of their fellow-countrymen, sailed with thirty vessels into the mouth of the Bolbitine branch of the Nile, and there founded a settlement which they named the Fort of the Milesians, and, following in their wake, successive relays of emigrants arrived to reinforce the infant colony. The king entrusted a certain number of Egyptian children to the care of these Greek settlers, to be instructed in their

[1] Drawn by Faucher-Gudin, from a restoration by Fl. Petrie.

language,[1] and the interpreters thus educated in their schools increased in proportion as the bonds of commercial and friendly intercourse between Greece and Egypt became strengthened, so that ere long, in the towns of the Delta they constituted a regular class, whose function was to act as intermediaries between the two races. By thus bringing his subjects in contact with an active, industrious, and enterprising nation, full of youthful vigour, Psammetichus no doubt hoped to inspire them with some of the qualities which he discerned in the colonists, but Egypt during the last two centuries had suffered too much at the hands of foreigners of all kinds to be favourably disposed to these new-comers It would have been different had they presented themselves in humble guise like the Asiatics and Africans to whom

EGYPTIAN GREEK.[2]

EGYPTIAN GREEK.[3]

---

[1] Diodorus, or rather the historian whom he follows, assures us that Psammetichus went still further, and gave his own children a Greek education; what is possible and even probable, is, that he had them taught Greek. A bronze Apis in the Gizeh Museum was dedicated by an interpreter who inscribed on it a bilingual inscription in hieroglyphics and Carian

[2] Drawn by Faucher-Gudin, from Fl. Petrie. The original statuette in alabaster is now in the Gizeh Museum; the Cyprian style of the figure is easily recognised.

[3] Drawn by Faucher-Gudin, from Fl. Petrie. The original limestone statuette is in the Gizeh Museum.

Egypt had opened her doors so freely after the XVIII$^{th}$ dynasty, and if they had adopted the obsequious manners of the Phœnician and Hebrew merchants; but they landed from their ships fully equipped for war, and, proud of their own courage and ability, they vied with the natives of the ancient race, whether of plebeian or noble birth, for the favour of the sovereign. Their language, their rude military customs, their cunning devices in trade, even the astonishment they manifested at the civilisation of the country, rendered them objects of disdain, as well as of jealous hatred to the Egyptian. The food of which they partook made them unclean in native estimation, and the horrified fellah shunned contact with them from fear of defiling himself, refusing to eat with them, or to use the same knife or cooking-vessel: the scribes and members of the higher classes, astonished at their ignorance, treated them like children with no past history, whose ancestors a few generations back had been mere savages.

Although unexpressed at first, this hostility towards the Hellenes was not long in manifesting itself openly. The Saite tradition attributed it to a movement of wounded vanity. Psammetichus, to recompense the prowess of his Ionian and Carian soldiers, had attached them to his own person, and assigned to them the post of honour on the right wing when the army was drawn up for review or in battle array[1] They reaped thus the double advantage

---

[1] Diodorus Siculus states that it was during the Syrian war that the king thus honoured his mercenary troops Wiedemann thinks this is an erroneous inference drawn from the passage of Herodotus in which he explains the meaning of the word Asmakh.

of the glory, which they greatly prized, and of the higher pay attached to the title of body-guard, but the troops who had hitherto enjoyed these advantages were naturally indignant at losing them, and began to murmur. One particularly galling circumstance at last caused their discontent to break out. The eastern and southern frontiers of Egypt were conterminous with those of two conquering empires, Assyria and Ethiopia, and on the west the Libyan tribes along the shores of the Mediterranean were powerful enough to demand constant vigilance on the part of the border garrisons. Psammetichus, among other reforms, had reorganised the ancient system of defence. While placing outposts at the entrance to the passes leading from the desert into the Nile valley, he had concentrated considerable masses of troops at the three most vulnerable points—the outlets of the road to Syria, the country surrounding Lake Mareotis, and the first cataract; he had fortified Daphnæ, near the old town of Zalu, as a defence against the Assyrians, Marea against the Libyan Bedâwin, and Elephantinê against the Ethiopians. These advanced posts had been garrisoned with native troops who were quartered there for a year at a time. To be condemned to such an exile for so long a period raised in them a sense of profound indignation, but when the king apparently forgot them and left them there three years without sending other troops to relieve them, their anger knew no bounds. They resolved to put an end to such treatment, and as the hope of a successful rebellion seemed but small, they decided to leave the country. Two hundred and forty thousand of them assembled on a given day with their arms and baggage, and marched in good order towards Ethiopia. Psammetichus, warned of their intentions when it was too late, hastened after them with a handful of followers, and coming up with them, besought them not to desert their national gods, their wives, and their children. He had nearly prevailed on them to return, when one soldier, with a significant gesture, intimated that while manhood lasted they had power to create new families wherever they might chance to dwell. The details of this story betray the popular legend, but nevertheless have a basis of truth. The inscriptions from the time of Psammetichus onwards never mention the Mashauasha, while their name and their exploits constantly recur in the history of the preceding dynasties: henceforth they and their chiefs vanish from sight, and discord and brigandage simultaneously cease in the Egyptian nomes. It was very probably the most turbulent among these auxiliaries who left the country in the circumstances above narrated: since they could not contest the superiority of their Greek rivals, they concluded that their own part was played out, and rather than be relegated to the second rank, they preferred to quit the land in a body. Psammetichus, thus deprived of their support at the moment when Egypt had more than ever need of all her forces to regain her rightful position in the world, reorganised the military system as best he could. He does not seem to have relied much upon the contingents from Upper Egypt, to whom was doubtless entrusted the defence of the Nubian frontier, and who could not be withdrawn from their posts without danger of invasion or revolt. But the source of imminent peril did not lie in this direction, where Ethiopia, exhansted by the wars of Taharqa and Tanuatamanu, perhaps needed repose even more than Egypt itself, but rather on the Asiatic side, where Assur-bani-pal, in spite of the complications constantly arising in Karduniash and Elam, had by no means renounced his claims to the suzerainty of Egypt. The Pharaoh divided the feudatory militia of the Delta into two classes, which resided apart in different sets of nomes. The first group, who were popularly called Hermotybies, were stationed at Busiris Sais, and Khemmis, in the island of Prosopitis, and in one half of Natho—in fact, in the district which for the last century had formed the centre of the principality of the Saite dynasty: perhaps they were mostly of Libyan origin, and represented the bands of Mashauasha who from father to son, had served under Tafnakhti and his descendants. Popular report numbered them at 160,000 men, all told, and the total number of the other class known as the Calasiries, at 250,000; these latter belonged in my opinion, to the pure Egyptian race, and were met with at Thebes, while the troops of the north, who were more generally called out, were scattered over the territory which formerly supported the Tanite and Bubastite kings, and latterly Pakruru, and which comprised the towns of Bubastis, Aphthis, Tanis, Mendes, Sebennytos, Athribis Pharbæthos, Thmuis, Onuphis, Anysis, and Myecphoris. Each year one thousand Hermotybies and one thousand Calasiries were chosen to form the royal body-guard, and these received daily five minæ of bread apiece, two minæ of beef, and four bowls of wine; the jealousy which had been excited by the Greek troops was thus lessened, as well as the discontent provoked by the emigration.[1] The King of Napata gladly welcomed the timely reinforcements which arrived to fill up the vacancies in his army and among his people, weakened by a century of rapid changes, and generously gave them permission to conquer for themselves some territory in the possession of his enemies! Having driven out the barbarians, they established themselves in the peninsula formed by the White and Blue Niles, and their numbers increased so greatly that in course of time they became a considerable nation. They called themselves Asmakh, the men who stand on the king's left hand, in memory of the affront put upon them, and which they had avenged by their self-exile: Greek travellers and geographers called them sometimes Automoli, sometimes Sembrites, names which clung to them till almost the beginning of our present era.

This departure of the Mashauasha was as the last blast of wind after a storm: the swell subsided by degrees, and peace reigned in the interior. Thebes accommodated

---

[1] *Calasiris*, the exact transcription of K*hal*a-*shiri*, K*hal*a-*shere*, signifying *young man*. The meaning and original of the word transcribed Hermotybies by Herodotus, and Hermotymbies according to a variant given by Stephen of Byzantium, is as yet unknown, but it seems to me to conceal a title analogous to that of *Hir-mazaîu*, and to designate what remained of Libyan soldiers in Egypt. This organisation of the army is described by Herodotus as existing in his own days, and there were Calasiries and Hermotybies in the Egyptian contingent which accompanied the army of Mardonius to Greece; it is nowhere stated that it was the work of Psammetichus, but everything points to the conclusion that it was so, at all events in the form in which it was known to the Greeks.

itself as best it could to the new order of things under the nominal administration of the Divine Spouses, the two Shapenuapîts. Building works were recommenced at all points where it appeared necessary, and the need of restoration was indeed pressing after the disorders occasioned by the Assyrian invasion and the Ethiopian suzerainty At Karnak, and in the great temples on both banks of the Nile, Psammetichus, respecting the fiction which assigned the chief authority to the Pallacides, effaced himself in favour of them, allowing them to claim all the merit of the work; in the cities they erected small chapels, in which they are portrayed as queens fulfilling their sacerdotal functions, humbly escorted by the viceroy who in other respects exercised the real power. The king's zeal for restoration is manifest all along the Nile, at Coptos, Abydos,[1] and in the plains of the Delta, which are crowded with memorials of him. His two favourite capitals were Memphis and Sais, on both of which he impartially lavished his favours. At Memphis he built the propylons on the south side of the temple of Phtah, and the court in which the living Apis took his exercise and was fed: this court was surrounded by a colonnade, against the pillars of which were erected statues twelve cubits high, probably representing Osiris as in the Ramesseum and at Medinet-Habu. Apis even when dead also received his share of attention. Since the days when Ramses II. had excavated the subterranean Serapeum as

[1] The first Egyptologists attributed the prenominal cartouche of Psammetichus I. to Psammetichus II., and *vice versâ*: this error must always be kept in mind in referring to their works.

a burial-place of the sacred bulls, no subsequent Pharaoh who had reigned at Memphis had failed to embellish their common tomb, and to celebrate with magnificence their rites of sepulture. The body of the Apis, carefully

CHAMBER AND SARCOPHAGUS OF AN APIS.[1]

embalmed, was sealed up in a coffin or sarcophagus of hard stone, the mouth of the vault was then walled up, and against the fresh masonry, at the foot of the neighbouring rocks, on the very floor of the passage, or

[1] Drawn by Faucher-Gudin, from an engraving published in Mariette.

wherever there was a clear space available, the high dignitaries, the workmen or the priests who had taken any part in the ceremonial, set up a votive stele calling down upon themselves and their families divine benedictions. The gallery was transformed by degrees into a

THE GREAT GALLERY OF THE SERAPEUM.[1]

kind of record-office, where each dynasty in turn recorded its name, whenever a fresh apotheosis afforded them the opportunity: these records were discovered in our own time by Mariette, almost perfect in spite of the destroying hand of men, and comprised inscriptions by the Bubastites by Bocchoris, and even by the Ethiopians. Taharqa when menaced by the Assyrians, had stayed at Memphis

[1] Drawn by Faucher-Gudin, from an engraving of Devéria.

only a year before his death, in the interval between two campaigns, in order to bury an Apis, and Psammetichus likewise took care not to neglect this part of his regal duties. He at first was content to imitate his predecessors, but a subsidence having occurred in that part of the Serapeum where the Apis who had died in the twentieth year of his reign reposed, he ordered his engineers to bore another gallery in a harder vein of limestone, and he performed the opening ceremony in his fifty-second year. It was the commencement of a thorough restoration. The vaults in which the sacred bulls were entombed were severally inspected, the wrappings were repaired together with the mummy cases, the masonry of the chapel was strengthened, and the building endowed with woods, stuffs, perfumes, and the necessary oils. No less activity apparently was displayed at Sais, the native home and favourite residence of the Pharaoh; but all the monuments which adorned the place, including the temple of Nît, and the royal palace, have been entirely destroyed; the enclosing wall of unbaked bricks alone remains, and here and there, amid the *débris* of the houses, may be seen some heaps of shattered stone where the public buildings once stood. On several blocks the name and titles of Psammetichus may yet be deciphered, and there are few cities in the Delta which cannot make a similar show. From one end of the Nile valley to the other the quarries were reopened, and the arts, stimulated by the orders which flowed in, soon flourished anew. The engraving of hieroglyphics and the art of painting both attained a remarkable degree of elegance; fine statues and bas-reliefs were executed in large numbers, and a widely spread school of art was developed. The local artists had scrupulously observed and handed down the traditions which obtained in the time of the Pyramids, and more especially those of the first Theban period; even the few fragments that have come down to us of the works of these artists in the age of the Ramessides recall rather the style of the VI$^{th}$ and XII$^{th}$ dynasties than that of their Theban contemporaries. Their style, brought to perfection by evident imitation of the old Memphite masters, pleases us by its somewhat severe elegance, the taste shown in the choice of detail, and the extraordinary skill displayed in the working of the stone. The Memphites had by preference used limestone for their sculpture, the Thebans red and grey granite or sandstone; but the artists of the age of Psammetichus unhesitatingly attacked basalt, breccia, or serpentine, and obtained marvellous effects from these finely grained materials of regular and even texture. The artistic renaissance which they brought to its height had been already inaugurated under the Ethiopians and many of the statues we possess of the reign of Taharqa are examples of excellent workmanship That of Amenertas was over praised at the time of its discovery; the face half buried by the wig which we usually associate with the statues of the goddesses has a dull and vacant expression in spite of its set smile, and the modelling of the figure is rather weak; but nevertheless there is something easy and refined in the gracefulness of the statue as a whole A statuette of another " Divine Spouse" though mutilated and unfinished is pleasing from its greater breadth of style although such breadth is rarely found in the works of this school which toned down elongated, and attenuated the figure till it often lost in vigour what it gained in distinction The one point in which the Saite artists made a real advance was in the treatment of the heads of their models The expression is often refined and idealised as in the case of older works, but occasionally the portraiture is exact even to coarseness It was not

MEMPHITE BAS-RELIEF OF THE SAITE EPOCH.[1]

the idealised likeness of Montumihâît which the artist wished to portray but Montumihâît himself with his low forehead his small close set eyes his thin cheeks and the deep lines about his nose and mouth And besides this the wrinkles the crows feet the cranial projections the shape of ear and neck are brought out w th minute fidelity A statue was no longer as in earlier days merely a piece of sacred stone the support of the divine or human double in which artistic value

[1] Drawn by Boudier, from a heliogravure in Mariette The bas-relief was worked into the masonry of a house in Memphis in the Byzantine period and it was in order to fit it to the course below that the masons bevelled the lower part of it

was an accessory of no importance and was esteemed only as a guarantee of resemblance: without losing aught of its religious significance, a statue henceforward became a work of art, admired and prized for the manner in which the sculptor faithfully represented his model, as well as for its mystic utility.

The reign of Psammetichus lasted till nearly the end of the century, and was marked by peace both at home and abroad. No doubt skirmishes of some kind took place in Lydia and Nubia, but we know nothing of them, nor have we any account of engagements with the Asiatics which from time to time must have taken place during this reign. Psammetichus followed with a vigilant eye the revolutionary changes beyond the isthmus, actuated at first by the fear of an offensive movement on the part of Syria, and when that ceased to be a danger, by the hope of one day recovering, in Southern Syria, at all events, that leading position which his predecessors had held so long. Tradition asserts that he wisely confined his ambition to the conquest of the Philistine Pentapolis; it is even reported that he besieged Ashdod for twenty-nine years before gaining possession of it. If we disregard the cipher, which is evidently borrowed from some popular romance, the fact in itself is in no way improbable. Ashdod was a particularly active community, and had played a far more important part in earlier campaigns than any other member of the Pentapolis. It possessed outside the town proper, which was situated some little distance from the coast, a seaport similar to that of Gaza, and of sufficient size to shelter a whole fleet.

Whoever held this harbour could exercise effective control over the main routes leading from Syria into Egypt. Psammetichus probably undertook this expedition towards the end of his life, when the victories gained by the Medes

THE RUINS OF SAIS.[1]

had demonstrated the incapacity of Assyria to maintain the defence of her distant provinces.[2] The attack of the

[1] Drawn by Boudier, from a photograph by Golénischeff.
[2] At one time I was inclined to explain this period of twenty-nine years by assuming that the fall of Ashdod took place in the twenty-ninth year of the king's reign, and that Herodotus had mistaken the date of its surrender for the duration of the siege: such an hypothesis is, however, unnecessary,

Scythians, which might have proved dangerous to Egypt, had it been pushed far enough, had left her unharmed, and was in the end even advantageous to her. It was subsequent to the retreat of the barbarians, no doubt, that Psammetichus sent his troops into Philistia and succeeded in annexing the whole or part of it. After this success he was content to wait and watch the course of events. The surprising revival of Egypt must have had the effect of infusing fresh life into the Egyptian factions existing in all the autonomous states, and in the prefectures of Syria. The appearance of the Pharaoh's troops, and the toleration of their presence within the territory of the Assyrian empire, aroused on all sides the hope of deliverance, and incited the malcontents to take some immediate action.

We do not know what may have happened at Tyre and Sidon, or among the peoples of Edom and Arabia, but Judah, at any rate, under the rule of Josiah, carefully abstained from any action inconsistent with the pledge of fidelity which it had given to Assyria. Indeed, the whole kingdom was completely absorbed in questions of a theological nature, and the agitations which affected the religious life of the nation reacted on its political

since it is very probable that we have here one of those exaggerated estimates of time so dear to the hearts of popular historians. If we are to believe the account given by Diodorus, it was in Syria that Psammetichus granted the honour of a place in the right wing of his army to the Greek mercenaries: the capture of Ashdod must, in this case, have occurred before the emigration of the native troops. In *Jer.* xxv. 20, reference is made to "the remnant of Ashdod," in the fourth year of Jehoiakim, *i.e.* about 603 B.C., and the decadence of the city is generally attributed to the war with Egypt; it might with equal probability be ascribed to the Scythian invasion.

life as well. Josiah, as he grew older, began to identify himself more and more with the doctrines taught by the prophets, and, thanks to his support, the party which sought to complete the reforms outlined by Hezekiah gained fresh recruits every day. The opposition which they had formerly aroused among the priests of the temple had gradually died out, partly as the result of genuine conviction, and partly because the priests had come to realise that the establishment of a single exclusive sanctuary would work for their own interest and advantage. The high priest Hilkiah took up the line followed by Jeremiah, and was supported by a number of influential personages such as Shaphan the scribe, son of Azaliah, Ahikam, Achbor son of Micaiah, and a prophetess named Huldah, who had married the keeper of the royal wardrobe. The terrors of the Scythian invasion had oppressed the hearts and quickened the zeal of the orthodox. Judah, they declared, had no refuge save Jahveh alone; all hope was lost if it persisted in the doctrines which had aroused against the faithless the implacable wrath of Jahveh; it must renounce at once those idols and superstitious rites with which His worship had been disfigured, and overthrow the altars which were to be found in every part of the country in order to concentrate all its devotion on the temple of Solomon. In a word, Judah must return to an observance of the strict letter of the law, as it had been followed by their forefathers. But as this venerable code was not to be found either in the "Book of the Covenant" or in any of the other writings held sacred by Israel, the question naturally arose as to where it was now hidden. In the eighteenth year of his reign, Josiah sent Shaphan the scribe to the temple in order to audit the accounts of the sums collected at the gates for the maintenance of the building. After the accounts had been checked, Hilkiah suddenly declared that he had "found the Book of the Law" in the temple, and thereupon handed the document to Shaphan, who perused it forthwith. On his return to the palace, the scribe made his report: "Thy servants have emptied out the money that was found in the house, and have delivered it into the hand of the workmen;" then he added "Hilkiah the priest hath delivered me a book, and proceeded to read it to the king. When the latter had heard the words contained in this Book of the Law, he was seized with anguish, and rent his garments; then, unable to arrive at any decision by himself, he sent Hilkiah, Shaphan, Ahikam, Achbor, and Asaiah to inquire of Jahveh for him and for his people, "for great is the wrath of the Lord that is kindled against us, because our fathers have not hearkened unto the words of this book, to do according unto all that which is written concerning us." The envoys betook themselves not to the official oracle or the recognised prophets, but to a woman, the prophetess Huldah, who was attached to the court in virtue of her husband's office; and she bade them, in the name of the Most High, to summon a meeting of the faithful, and, after reading the new code to them, to call upon all present to promise that they would henceforth observe its ordinances: thus Jahveh would be appeased, and since the

# THE BOOK OF THE LAW 365

king had "rent his garments and wept before Me, I also have heard thee, saith Jahveh. Therefore, behold, I will gather thee to thy fathers, and thou shalt be gathered to thy grave in peace." Josiah thereupon having summoned the elders of Judah and Jerusalem, went up into the temple, and there, standing on the platform, he read the Book of the Law in the presence of the whole people.[1]

It dealt with questions which had been frequent subjects of debate in prophetic circles since the days of Hezekiah, and the anonymous writer who had compiled it was so strongly imbued with the ideas of Jeremiah, and had so closely followed his style, that some have been inclined to ascribe the work to Jeremiah himself. It has always been a custom among Orientals to affirm that any work for which they profess particular esteem was discovered in the temple of a god; the Egyptian priests, for instance, invented an origin of this nature for the more important chapters of their Book of the Dead, and for the leading treatises in the scientific literature of Egypt. The author of the Book of the Law had ransacked the distant past for the name of the leader who had delivered Israel from captivity in Egypt. He told how Moses, when he

---

[1] 2 K*ings* xxii. 3-20; xxiii. 1, 2. The narrative has undergone slight interpolation in places, *e.g.* verses 4*b*, 5*a*, 6, and 7, where the compiler has made it harmonise with events previously recorded in connection with the reign of Joash (2 K*ings* xii. 6-16). The beginning of Huldah's prophecy was suppressed, when the capture of Jerusalem proved that the reform of divine worship had not succeeded in averting the wrath of Jahveh. It probably contained directions to read the *Book of the Coven*ant to the people, and to persuade them to adopt its precepts, followed by a promise to save Judah provided it remained faithful to its engagements.

began to feel the hand of death upon him, determined to declare in Gilead the decrees which Jahveh had delivered to him for the guidance of His people.[1] In these ordinances the indivisible nature of God, and His jealousy of any participation of other deities in the worship of His people, are strongly emphasised. "Ye shall surely destroy all the places wherein the nations which ye shall possess served their gods, upon the high mountains and upon the hills, and under every green tree: and ye shall break down their altars, and dash in pieces their pillars, and burn their Asherim with fire; and ye shall hew down the graven images of their gods; and ye shall destroy their name out of that place."[2] Even were a prophet or dreamer of dreams to arise in the midst of the faithful and direct them by a sign or a miracle to turn aside after those accursed gods, they must not follow the teaching of these false guides, not even if the sign or miracle actually came to pass, but must seize and slay them. Even "if thy brother, the son of thy mother, or thy son, or thy daughter, or the wife of thy bosom, or thy friend which is as thine own soul, entice thee secretly, saying, Let us go and serve other gods, . . . thou shalt not consent unto him nor hearken unto him: neither shall thine eye pity him, neither shalt thou spare, neither shalt thou conceal him: but thou shalt surely kill him; thine hand shall be first upon him to put him to

---

[1] Even St. Jerome and St. John Chrysostom admitted that Deuteronomy was the book discovered by Hilkiah in the temple during the reign of Josiah, and this view is accepted at present, though it is applied, not to the book of Deuteronomy as it appears in the Pentateuch, but rather to the nucleus of this book, and especially chaps. xii.–xxvi.

[2] *Deut.* xii. 2, 3.

death, and afterwards the hand of all the people. And thou shalt stone him with stones that he die; because he hath sought to draw thee away from Jahveh!"[1] And this Jahveh was not the Jahveh of any special place. He was not the Jahveh of Bethel, or of Dan, or of Mizpah, or of Geba, or of Beersheba; He is simply Jahveh.[2] Yet the seat of His worship was not a matter of indifference to Him. "Unto the place which Jahveh shall choose out of all your tribes to put His name there, even unto His habitation shall ye seek, and thither shalt thou come : and thither shall ye bring your ... sacrifices and your tithes."[3] Jerusalem is not mentioned by name, but the reference to it was clear, since every one knew that the suppression of the provincial sanctuaries must necessarily benefit it. One part of the new code dealt with the relations between different members of the community. The king was to approximate as closely as possible to the ideal priest; he was not to lift up his heart above his brethren, nor set his mind on the possession of many chariots, horses, or wives, but must continually read the law of God and ponder over His ordinances, and observe them word for word all the days of his life.[4] Even in time of war he was not to put his trust in his soldiers or in his own personal valour; here

---

[1] *Deut.* xiii. **1–10.**

[2] *Deut.* vi. 4. The expression found in *Zech.* xiv. 9 was borrowed from the second of the introductions added to *Deuteronomy* at a later date; the phrase harmonises so closely with the main purpose of the book itself, that there can be no objection to employing it here.

[3] *Deut.* xii. 5, 6.

[4] *Deut.* xvii. 14–20 ; cf. xx. 1–9 for the regulations in regard to the levying of troops.

again he must allow himself to be guided by Jahveh, and must undertake nothing without first consulting Him through the medium of His priests. The poor,[1] the widow and the orphan,[2] the bondservant,[3] and even the stranger within the gates—in remembrance of the bondage in Egypt[4]—were all specially placed under the divine protection; every Jew who had become enslaved to a fellow-countryman was to be set at liberty at the end of six years, and was to receive a small allowance from his master which would ensure him for a time against starvation.[5] The regulations in regard to divine worship had not as yet been drawn up in that spirit of hair-splitting minuteness which, later on, became a characteristic of Hebrew legislation. Only three great festivals are mentioned in the Book of the Law. The Passover was celebrated in the month of Abîb, when the grain is in the ear, and had already come to be regarded as commemorative of the Exodus; but the other two, the Feast of Weeks and the

---

[1] As to the poor, and the charitable obligations towards them imposed by their common religion, cf. *Deut.* xv. 7–11; as to the rights of the hired servant, cf. xxiv. 14, 15.

[2] *Deut.* xxiv. 17–22 forbids the taking of a widow's clothing in pledge and lays down regulations in regard to gleaning permitted to widows and orphans (cf. *Lev.* xix. 9, 10); reference is also made to their share in triennial tithe (*Deut.* xiv. 28, 29; xxvi. 12, 13) and in the solemn festivals (*Deut.* xvi. 11–14).

[3] Slaves were allowed to share in the rejoicings during the great festivals (*Deut.* xvi. 11, 14), and certain rights were accorded to women taken prisoners in war who had become their captors' concubines (*Deut.* xxi 10–14).

[4] Participation of the stranger in the triennial tithe (*Deut.* xiv. 28, 29; xxvi. 12, 13).

[5] *Deut.* xv. 12–18.

Feast of Tabernacles, were merely associated with the agricultural seasons, and took place, the former seven weeks after the beginning of the harvest, the latter after the last of the crops had been housed.[1] The claim of the priest to a share in the victim and in the offerings made on various occasions is maintained, and the lawgiver allows him to draw a similar benefit from the annual and triennial tithes which he imposes on corn and wine and on the first-born of cattle, the produce of this tithe being devoted to a sort of family festival celebrated in the Holy Place.[2] The priest was thus placed on the same footing as the poor, the widow, the orphan, and the stranger, and his influence was but little greater than it had been in the early days of the monarchy. It was to the prophet and not to the priest that the duty belonged of directing the public conscience in all those cases for which the law had made no provision. "I will put My words into his mouth (said Jahveh), and he shall speak unto them all that I shall command him. And it shall come to pass that whosoever will not hearken unto My words which he shall speak in My name, I will require it of him. But the prophet which shall speak a word presumptuously in My name, which I have not commanded him to speak, or that shall speak in the name of other gods, that same prophet shall die. And if thou say in thine heart, How shall we know the word which the Lord hath not spoken?—when a prophet speaketh in the name of Jahveh, if the thing follow not,

---

[1] *Deut.* xvi. 1-17.

[2] *Deut.* xviii. 1-8; as to the share in the triennial tithe, cf. *Deut.* xiv. 28, 29; xxvi. 12, 13.

nor come to pass, that is the thing which Jahveh hath not spoken: the prophet hath spoken it presumptuously; thou shalt not be afraid of him."[1]

When the reading of the law had ended, Josiah implored the people to make a covenant with Jahveh; that is to say, "to walk after Jahveh, and to keep His commandments, and His testimonies, and His statutes, with all their hearts and all their souls, to confirm the words of this covenant that were written in this book." The final words which lingered in every ear, contained imprecations of even more terrible and gloomy import than those with which the prophets had been wont to threaten Judah. "If thou wilt not hearken unto the voice of Jahveh thy God, to observe to do all His commandments and His statutes which I command thee this day; then all these curses shall come upon thee, and overtake thee. Cursed shalt thou be in the city, and cursed shalt thou be in the field Cursed shall be thy basket and thy kneading-trough Cursed shall be the fruit of thy body, and the fruit of thy ground, the increase of thy kine, and the young of thy flock. . . . Thou shalt betroth a wife, and another man shall lie with her; thou shalt build an house, and shalt not dwell therein: thou shalt plant a vineyard, and shalt not use the fruit thereof. Thine ox shall be slain before thine eyes, and thou shalt not eat thereof. . . . Thy sons and thy daughters shall be given unto another people; and thine eyes shall look, and fail with longing for them all the day: and there shall be naught in the power of thine hand. . . . Jahveh shall bring a nation against thee from

[1] *Deut.* xviii. 9–22.

far, from the end of the earth, as the eagle flieth ; a nation whose tongue thou shalt not understand ; a nation of fierce countenance, which shalt not regard the person of the old, nor show favour to the young." This enemy was to burn and destroy everything : " and he shall besiege thee in all thy gates, throughout all thy land, which Jahveh thy God hath given thee. And thou shalt eat the fruit of thine own body, the flesh of thy sons and of thy daughters . . . in the straitness wherewith thine enemies shall straiten thee." Those who escape must depart into captivity, and there endure for many a long year the tortures of direst slavery; "thy life shall hang in doubt before thee ; and thou shalt fear night and day, and shalt have none assurance of thy life: in the morning thou shalt say, Would God it were even! and at even thou shalt say, Would God it were morning! for the fear of thine heart which thou shalt fear, and for the sight of thine eyes which thou shalt see."[1] The assembly took the oath required of them, and the king at once displayed the utmost zeal in exacting literal performance of the ordinances contained in the Book of the Law. His first step was to purify the temple : Hilkiah and his priests overthrew all the idols contained in it, and all the objects that had been fashioned in honour of strange gods—the Baals, the Asherim, and all the Host of Heaven—and, carrying them out of Jerusalem into the valley of the Kidron, cast

---

[1] *Deut.* xxviii. The two sets of imprecations (xxvii., xxviii.) which terminate the actual work are both of later redaction, but the original MS. undoubtedly ended with some analogous formula. I have quoted above the most characteristic parts of the twenty-eighth chapter.

them into the flames, and scattered the ashes upon the place where all the filth of the city was cast out. The altars and the houses of the Sodomites which defiled the temple courts were demolished, the chariots of the sun broken in pieces, and the horses of the god sent to the stables of the king's chamberlain;* the sanctuaries and high places which had been set up at the gates of the city in the public places, and along the walls were razed to the ground, and the Tophet, where the people made their children pass through the fire, was transformed into a common sewer. The provincial sanctuaries shared the fate of those of the capital; in a short time, from Geba to Beersheba, there remained not one of those "high places at which the ancestors of the nation and their rulers had offered prayers for generations past. The wave of reform passed even across the frontier and was borne into the Assyrian province of Samaria; the temple and image which Jeroboam had set up at Bethel were reduced to ashes, and human bones were burnt upon the altar to desecrate it beyond possibility of purification.[1] The governor offered no objection to these acts; he regarded them, in the first place, as the private affairs of the subjects of the empire, with which he had no need to interfere, so long as the outburst of religious feeling did

* [The Hebrew text admits of this meaning, which is, however, not clea in the English A.V.—Tr.]

[1] 2 *Kings* xxiii. 3-20, 24-27, where several glosses and interpolations are easily recognisable, such as the episode at Bethel (v. 15-20), the authenticity of which is otherwise incontestable. The account in 2 *Chron.* xxxiv. is a defaced reproduction of that of 2 *Kings,* and it places the reform, in part at least, before the discovery of the new law.

not tend towards a revolt: we know, moreover, that Josiah, guided on this point by the prophets, would have believed that he was opposing the divine will had he sought to free himself from the Assyrian yoke by ordinary political methods; besides this, in 621, under Assuretililâni, five years after the Scythian invasion, the prefect of Samaria had possibly not sufficient troops at his disposal to oppose the encroachments of the vassal princes. It was an affair of merely a few months. In the following year, when the work of destruction was over, Josiah commanded that the Passover should be kept in the manner prescribed in the new book; crowds flocked into Jerusalem, from Israel as well as from Judah, and the festival made a deep impression on the minds of the people. Centuries afterwards the Passover of King Josiah was still remembered: "There was not kept such a Passover from the days of the Judges . . . nor in all the days of the Kings of Israel, nor of the Kings of Judah."[1] The first outburst of zeal

[1] 2 *Kings* xxiii. 21-23; cf. 2 *Chron.* xxxv. 1-19. The text of the Septuagint appears to imply that it was the first Passover celebrated in Jerusalem. It also gives in chap. xxii. 3, after the mention of the eighteenth year, a date of the seventh or eighth month, which is not usually accepted, as it is in contradiction with what is affirmed in chap. xxiii. 21-23, viz. that the Passover celebrated at Jerusalem was in the same year as the reform, in the eighteenth year. It is to do away with the contradiction between these two passages that the Hebrew text has suppressed the mention of the month. I think, however, it ought to be considered authentic and be retained, if we are allowed to place the celebration of the Passover in what would be one year after. To do this it would not be needful to correct the regnal date in the text: admitting that the reform took place in 621, the Passover of 620 would still quite well have taken place in the eighteenth year of Josiah, that being dependent on the time of year at which the king had ascended the throne.

having spent itself, a reaction was ere long bound to set in both among the ruling classes and among the people, and the spectacle that Asia at that time presented to their view was truly of a nature to incite doubts in the minds of the faithful. Assyria—that Assyria of which the prophets had spoken as the irresistible emissary of the Most High—had not only failed to recover from the injuries she had received at the hands, first of the Medes, and then of the Scythians but had with each advancing year seen more severe wounds inflicted upon her, and hastening her irretrievably to her ruin. And besides this, Egypt and Chaldæa, the ancient kingdoms which had for a short time bent beneath her yoke, had now once more arisen, and were astonishing the world by their renewed vigour. Psammetichus, it is true after having stretched his arm across the desert and laid hands upon the citadel which secured to him an outlet into Syria for his armies, had proceeded no further, and thus showed that he was not inclined to reassert the ancient rights of Egypt over the countries of the Jordan and the Orontes; but he had died in 611, and his son, Necho II., who succeeded him, did not manifest the same peaceful intentions.[1] If he decided to try his fortune in Syria supported by his Greek and Egyptian battalions, what would be the attitude that Judah would assume between moribund Assyria and the kingdom of the Pharaohs in its renewed vigour?

[1] The last dated stele of Psammetichus I. is the official epitaph of the Apis which died in his fifty-second year. On the other hand, an Apis, born in the fifty-third year of Psammetichus, died in the sixteenth year of Necho after having lived 16 years, 7 months, 17 days. A very simple calculation

It was in the spring of 608 that the crisis occurred. Nineveh, besieged by the Medes, was on the point of capitulating, and it was easy to foresee that the question as to who should rule there would shortly be an open one: should Egypt hesitate longer in seizing what she believed to be her rightful heritage, she would run the risk of finding the question settled and another in possession. Necho quitted Memphis and made his way towards the Asiatic frontier with the army which his father had left to him. It was no longer composed of the ill-organised bands of the Ethiopian kings or the princes of the Delta, temporarily united under the rule of a single leader, but all the while divided by reciprocal hatreds and suspicions which doomed it to failure. All the troops which constituted it—Egyptians, Libyans, and Greeks alike—were thoroughly under the control of their chief, and advanced in a compact and irresistible mass "like the Nile: like a river its volume rolls onward. It said: I arise, I inundate the earth, I will drown cities and people! Charge, horses! Chariots, fly forward at a gallop! Let the warriors march, the Ethiopian and the Libyan under the shelter of his buckler, the fellah bending the bow!"[1] As soon as Josiah heard the news, he called together his troops and prepared to resist the attack.

shows that Psammetichus I. reigned fifty-four years, as stated by Herodotus and Manetho, according to Julius Africanus.

[1] *Jer.* xlvi. 7–9, where the prophet describes, not the army which marched against Josiah, but that which was beaten at Carchemish. With a difference of date of only three or four years, the constituent elements of the army were certainly the same, so that the description of one would apply to the other.

Necho affected not to take his demonstrations seriously and sent a disdainful message recommending him to remain neutral: "What have I to do with thee, thou King of Judah? I come not against thee this day, but against the house wherewith I have war: and God hath commanded me to make haste: forbear thee from meddling with God who is with me, that He destroy thee not!"[1] Having despatched the message, probably at the moment of entering the Shephelah, he continued in a northerly direction, nothing doubting that his warning had met a friendly reception; but however low Nineveh had fallen Josiah could not feel that he was loosed from the oaths which bound him to her, and, trusting in the help of Jahveh, he threw himself resolutely into the struggle The Egyptian generals were well acquainted with the route as far as the further borders of Philistia, having passed along it a few years previously, at the time of the campaign of Psammetichus; but they had no experience of the country beyond Ashdod, and were solely dependent for guidance on the information of merchants or the triumphant records of the old Theban Pharaohs These monuments followed the traditional road which had led their ancestors from Gaza to Megiddo, from Megiddo to Qodshu, from Qodshu to Carchemish, and they were reckoning on passing through the valley of the Jordan, and then that of the Orontes, without encountering any resistance, when, at the entrance to the gorges of Carmel they were met by the advance guard of the Judæan army

---

[1] The message of Necho to Josiah is known to us from 2 *Chron.* xxxv 20–22.

Josiah, not having been warned in time to meet them as they left the desert, had followed a road parallel to their line of march, and had taken up his position in advance of them on the plain of Megiddo, on the very spot where Thutmosis III. had vanquished the Syrian confederates nearly ten centuries before. The King of Judah was defeated and killed in the confusion of the battle, and the conqueror pushed on northwards without, at that moment, giving the fate of the scattered Jews a further thought.[1] He rapidly crossed the plain of the Orontes by the ancient caravan track, and having reached the Euphrates, he halted under the walls of Carchemish. Perhaps he may have heard there of the fall of Nineveh, and the fear of drawing down upon himself the Medes or the Babylonians prevented him from crossing the river and raiding the country of the Balikh, which, from the force of custom, the royal scribes still persisted in designating by the disused name of Mitanni.[2] He returned

---

[1] 2 Kings xxiii. 29; cf. 2 Chron. xxxv. 22, 23. It is probably to this battle that Herodotus alludes when he says that Necho overcame the Syrians at Magdôlos. The identity of Magdôlos and Megiddo, accepted by almost all historians, was disputed by Gutschmid, who sees in the Magdôlos of Herodotus the Migdol of the Syro-Egyptian frontier, and in the engagement itself, an engagement of Necho with the Assyrians and their Philistine allies; also by Th. Reinach, who prefers to identify Magdôlos with one of the Migdols near Ascalon, and considers this combat as fought against the Assyrian army of occupation. If the information in Herodotus were indeed borrowed from Hecatæus of Miletus, and by the latter from the inscription placed by Necho in the temple of Branchidæ, it appears to me impossible to admit that Magdôlos does not here represent Megiddo.

[2] The text of 2 Kings xxiii. 29 says positively that Necho was marching towards the Euphrates. The name Mitanni is found even in Ptolemaic times.

southwards, after having collected the usual tributes and posted a few garrisons at strategic points; at Riblah he held a kind of *Durbar* to receive the homage of the independent Phœnicians[1] and of the old vassals of Assyria, who, owing to the rapidity of his movements, had not been able to tender their offerings on his outward march. The Jews had rescued the body of their king and had brought it back in his chariot to Jerusalem; they proclaimed in his stead, not his eldest son Eliakim, but the youngest, Shallum, who adopted the name of Jehoahaz on ascending the throne. He was a young man, twenty-three years of age, light and persumptuous of disposition, opposed to the reform movement, and had doubtless been unwise enough to display his hostile feelings towards the conqueror.

VICTORIOUS NECHO.[2]

Necho summoned him to Riblah, deposed him after a reign of three months, condemned him to prison, and replaced him by Eliakim, who changed his name to that of Jehoiakim—" he whom Jahveh exalts;" and after laying Judah under a tribute of one hundred talents of silver and one of gold, the Egyptian monarch returned to his own country.[3] Certain indications lead us to believe that he

[1] The submission of the Phœnicians to Necho is gathered from a passage in Berosus, where he says that the Egyptian army beaten at Carchemish comprised *Phœnicians*, besides Syrians and Arabs.

[2] Drawn by Faucher-Gudin, from a photograph published in Mariette. This scarab, now in the Gizeh Museum, is the only Egyptian monument which alludes to the victories of Necho. Above, the king stands between Nit and Isis; below, the vanquished are stretched on the ground.

[3] 2 *Kings* xxiii. 30-55; cf. 2 *Chron.* xxxvi. 1-4, and for the name of Shallum, *Jer.* xxii. 11.

was obliged to undertake other punitive expeditions. The Philistines, probably deceived by false rumours of his defeat, revolted against him about the time that he was engaged in hostilities in Northern Syria, and on receiving news not only of his safety, but of the victory he had gained, their alarm was at once aroused. Judah forgot her own sorrows on seeing the peril in which they stood, and Jeremiah pronounced against them a prophecy full of menace. "Behold," he cried, "waters rise up out of the north, and shall become an overflowing stream, and shall overflow the land and all that is therein, the city and them that dwell therein; and the men shall cry, and all the inhabitants of the land shall howl . . . for the Lord will spoil the Philistines, the remnant of the Isle of Caphtor. Baldness is come upon Gaza; Ascalon is dumb with terror, and you, all that are left of the giants, how long will ye tear your faces in your mourning?"* Ascalon was sacked and then Gaza,[1] and Necho at length was able to re-enter his domains, doubtless by the bridge of Zalu, following in this his models, his heroic ancestors of the great Theban

---

* [R.V., "Ashkelon is brought to nought, the remnant of their valley: how long wilt thou cut thyself?"—Tr.]

[1] *Jer.* xlvii., which is usually attributed to a period subsequent to the defeat at Carchemish or even later; the title, which alone mentions the Egyptians, is wanting in the LXX. If we admit that the enemy coming from the north is the Egyptian and not the Chaldæan, as do most writers, the only time that danger could have threatened Philistia from the Egyptians coming from the north, was when Necho, victorious, was returning from his first campaign. In this case, the Kadytis of Herodotus, which has caused so much trouble to commentators, would certainly be Gaza, and there would be no difficulty in explaining how the tradition preserved by the Greek historian placed the taking of this town after the battle of Megiddo.

dynasties. He wished thereupon to perpetuate the memory of the Greeks who had served him so bravely, and as soon as the division of the spoil had been made, he sent as an offering to the temple of Apollo at Miletus, the cuirass which he had worn throughout the campaign.

We can picture the reception which his subjects gave him, and how the deputations of priests and nobles in white robes flocked out to meet him with garlands of flowers in their hands, and with acclamations similar to those which of old had heralded the return of Seti I. or Ramses II. National pride, no doubt, was flattered by this revival of military glory, but other motives than those of vanity lay at the root of the delight exhibited by the whole country at the news of the success of the expedition. The history of the century which was drawing to its close, had demonstrated more than once how disadvantageous it was to Egypt to be separated from a great power merely by the breadth of the isthmus. If Taharqa, instead of awaiting the attack on the banks of the Nile, had met the Assyrians at the foot of Carmel, or even before Gaza, it would have been impossible for Esarhaddon to turn the glorious kingdom of the Pharaohs into an Assyrian province after merely a few weeks of fighting. The dictates of prudence, more than those of ambition, rendered, therefore, the conquest of Syria a necessity, and Necho showed his wisdom in undertaking it at the moment when the downfall of Nineveh reduced all risk of opposition to a minimum; it remained to be seen whether the conquerors of Sin-shar-ishkun would tolerate for long the interference of a third robber, and would consent to share the spoil with these Africans, who, having had none of the trouble, had hastened to secure the profit. All the Mediterranean dependencies of Assyria, such as Mesopotamia, Syria, and Judæa, fell naturally within the sphere of Babylon rather than that of Media, and, indeed, Cyaxares never troubled himself about them ; and Nabopolassar, who considered them his own by right, had for the moment too much in hand to permit of his reclaiming them. The Aramæans of the Khabur and the Balikh, the nomads of the Mesopotamian plain, had not done homage to him, and the country districts were infested with numerous bands of Cimmerians and Scythians, who had quite recently pillaged the sacred city of Harrân and violated the temple of the god Sin.[1] Nabopolassar, who was too old to command his troops in person, probably entrusted the conduct of them to Nebuchadrezzar, who was the son he had appointed to succeed him, and who had also married the Median princess. Three years sufficed this prince to carry the frontier of the new Chaldæan empire as far as the Syrian fords of the Euphrates, within sight of Thapsacus and Carchemish. Harrân remained in the hands of the barbarians,[2] probably on condition of their paying a tribute, but the district of the Subaru was laid waste, its cities reduced to ashes, and the Babylonian suzerainty established on the southern slopes of the Masios.

---

[1] *Inscrip. of the Cylinder of Nabonidus* mentions the pillage of Harrân as having taken place fifty-four years before the date of its restoration by Nabonidus. This was begun, as we know, in the third year of that king, possibly in 554–3. The date of the destruction is, therefore, 608–7, that is to say, a few months before the destruction of Nineveh.

[2] The passage in the *Cylinder of Nabonidus* shows that the barbarians remained in possession of the town.

Having brought these preliminary operations to a successful issue, Nabopolassar, considering himself protected on the north and north-east by his friendship with Cyaxares, no longer hesitated to make an effort to recover the regions dominated by Egyptian influence, and, if the occasion presented itself, to reduce to submission the Pharaoh who was in his eyes merely a rebellious satrap. Nebuchadrezzar again placed himself at the head of his troops; Necho warned of his projects, hastened to meet him with all the forces at his disposal, and, owing probably to the resistance offered by the garrisons which he possessed in the Hittite fortresses, he had time to continue his march as far as the Euphrates. The two armies encountered each other at Carchemish; the Egyptians were completely defeated in spite of their bravery and the skilful tactics of their Greek auxiliaries, and the Asiatic nations, who had once more begun to rely on Egypt, were obliged to acknowledge that they were as unequal to the task of overcoming Chaldæa as they had been of sustaining a struggle with Assyria.[1] The religious party in Judah, whose hopes had been disappointed by the victory of Pharaoh at Megiddo now rejoiced at his defeat, and when the remains of his legions made their way back across the Philistine plain closely pressed by the enemy, Jeremiah hailed them as they passed with cutting irony. Two or three brief, vivid sentences depicting the spirit that had fired them a few

---

[1] *Jer.* xlvi. 2; cf. 2 *Kings* xxiv. 7, where the editor, without mentioning the battle of Carchemish, recalls in passing that " the King of Babylon had taken, from the brook of Egypt unto the river Euphrates, all that pertained to the King of Egypt."

months before, and then the picture of their disorderly flight: "Order ye the buckler and shield, and draw near to battle. Harness the horses; and get up, ye horsemen, and stand forth with your helmets; furbish the spears, put on the coats of mail. Wherefore have I seen it? They are dismayed and turn backward; and their mighty ones are beaten down, and are fled apace, and look not back; terror is on every side, saith the Lord. Let not the swift flee away, nor the mighty man escape; in the north by the river Euphrates have they stumbled and fallen. . . . Go up into Gilead, and take balm, O virgin daughter of Egypt; in vain dost thou use many medicines; there is no healing for thee. The nations have heard of thy shame, and the earth is full of thy cry: for the mighty man hath stumbled against the mighty, they are fallen both of them together."[1] Nebuchadrezzar received by the way the submission of Jehoiakim and of the princes of Ammon, Moab, and the Philistines;[2] he was nearing Pelusium on his way into Egypt, when a messenger brought him the news of his father's death. He feared lest a competitor should dispute his throne—perhaps his younger brother, that Nabu-shum-lishir who had figured at his side at the dedication of a temple to Marduk. He therefore concluded an armistice with Necho, by the terms of which he remained master of the whole of Syria between the Euphrates and the Wady el-Arish, and then hastily turned

---

[1] *Jer.* xlvi. 3–6, 11, 12.

[2] The submission of all these peoples is implied by the passage already cited in 2 *Kings* xxiv. 7; Berosus speaks of the Phœnician, Jewish, and Syrian prisoners whom Nebuchadrezzar left to his generals, when he resolved to return to Babylon by the shortest route.

homewards. But his impatience could not brook the delay occasioned by the slow march of a large force, nor the ordinary circuitous route by Carchemish and through Mesopotamia. He hurried across the Arabian desert accompanied by a small escort of light troops, and presented himself unexpectedly at the gates of Babylon He found all in order. His Chaldæan ministers had assumed the direction of affairs, and had reserved the throne for the rightful heir; he had only to appear to be acclaimed and obeyed (B.C. 605).

His reign was long, prosperous, and on the whole peaceful. The recent changes in Asiatic politics had shut out the Chaldæans from the majority of the battle-fields on which the Assyrians had been wont to wage warfare with the tribes on their eastern and northern frontiers We no longer see stirring on the border-land those confused masses of tribes and communities of whose tumultuous life the Ninevite annals make such frequent record: Elam as an independent state no longer existed neither did Ellipi and Namri, nor the Cossæans, nor Parsua, nor the Medes with their perpetual divisions nor the Urartians and the Mannai in a constant state of ferment within their mountain territory; all that remained of that turbulent world now constituted a single empire, united under the hegemony of the Medes, and the rule of successful conqueror. The greater part of Elam was already subject to those Achæmenides who called themselves sovereigns of Anshân as well as of Persia, and whose fief was dependent on the kingdom of Ecbatana:[1] it is

[1] "The king and the princes of Elam" mentioned in *Jer.* xxv. 25, xlix

probable that Chaldæa received as her share of the ancient Susian territory the low countries of the Uknu and the Ulai, occupied by the Aramæan tribes of the Puqudu, the Rutu, and the Gambulu;[1] but Susa fell outside her portion, and was soon transformed into a flourishing Iranian town. The plains bordering the right bank of the Tigris, from the Uknu to the Turnat or the Radanu, which had belonged to Babylon from the very earliest times, were no doubt still retained by her;[2] but the mountain district which commanded them certainly remained in the hands of Cyaxares, as well as the greater part of Assyria proper, and there is every reason to believe that from the Radanu northwards the Tigris formed the boundary between the two allies, as far as the confluence of the Zab. The entire basin of the Upper Tigris and its Assyrian colonies, Amidi and Tushkân were now comprised

35–39, and in *Ezek.* xxxii. 24, 25, in the time of Nebuchadrezzar, are probably the Persian kings of Anshân and their Elamite vassals—not only, as is usually believed, the kings and native princes conquered by Assur-banipal; the same probably holds good of the Elam which an anonymous prophet associates with the Medes under Nabonidus, in the destruction of Babylon (*Isa.* xxi. 2). The princes of Malamir appear to me to belong to an anterior epoch.

[1] The enumeration given in *Ezek.* xxiii. 23, "the Babylonians and all the Chaldæans, *Pekôd*, and Shoa, and Koa," shows us probably that the Aramæans of the Lower Tigris represented by Pekôd, as those of the Lower Euphrates are by the Chaldæans, belonged to the Babylonian empire in the time of the prophet. They are also considered as belonging to Babylon in the passage of an anonymous prophet (*Jer.* l. 21), who wrote in the last days of the Chaldæan empire: "Go up against the land of Merathaim, even against it and the inhabitants of Pekod." Translators and commentators have until quite recently mistaken the import of the name Pekôd.

[2] This is what appears to me to follow from the account of the conquest of Babylon by Cyrus, as related by Herodotus.

VOL. VIII.      2 c

in the sphere of Medic influence, and the settlement of the Scythians at Harrân, around one of the most venerated the Semitic sanctuaries, shows to what restrictions the new authority of Chaldæa was subjected, even in the districts of Mesopotamia, which were formerly among the most faithful possessions of Nineveh. If these barbarians had been isolated, they would not long have defied the King of Babylon, but being akin to the peoples who were subject to Cyaxares, they probably claimed his protection, and regarded themselves as his liege men; it was necessary to treat them with consideration, and tolerate the arrogance of their presence upon the only convenient road which connected the eastern with the western provinces of the kingdom. It is therefore evident that there was no opening on this side for those ever recurring struggles in which Assyria had exhausted her best powers; one war was alone possible, that with Media but it was fraught with such danger that the dictates of prudence demanded that it should be avoided at all costs, even should the alliance between the two couts cease to be cemented by a royal marriage. However great the confidence which he justly placed in the valour of his Chaldæans, Nebuchadrezzar could not hide from himself the fact that for two centuries they had always been beaten by the Assyrians, and that therefore he would run too great a risk in provoking hostilities with an army which had got the better of the conquerors of his people. Besides this, Cyaxares was fully engaged in subjecting the region which he had allotted to himself and had no special desire to break with his ally. Nothing is known of his history during the years which followed the downfall of Nineveh, but it is not difficult to guess what were the obstacles he had to surmount, and the result of the efforts which he made to overcome them. The country which extends between the Caspian and the Black Sea—the mountain block of Armenia, the basins of the Araxes and the Kur, the valleys of the Halys, the Iris, and the Thermodon, and the forests of the Anti-Taurus and the Taurus itself—had been thrown into utter confusion by the Cimmerians and the Scythians. Nothing remained of the previous order of things which had so long prevailed there, and the barbarians who for a century and a half had destroyed everything in the country seemed incapable of organising anything in its place. Urartu had shrunk within its ancient limits around Ararat, and it is not known who ruled her; the civilisation of Argistis and Menuas had almost disappeared with the dynasty which had opposed the power of Assyria, and the people, who had never been much impregnated by it, soon fell back into their native rude habits of life. Confused masses of European barbarians were stirring in Etiaus and the regions of the Araxes, seeking a country in which to settle themselves, and did not succeed in establishing themselves firmly till a much later period in the district of Sakasênê, to which was attached the name of one of their tribes.[1] Such of the Mushku and the Tabal as had not perished had taken refuge in the north, among

[1] Strabo states that Armenia and the maritime regions of Cappadocia suffered greatly from the invasion of the Scythians.

the mountains bordering the Black Sea, where they were ere long known to the Greeks as the Moschi and the Tibarenians. The remains of the Cimmerian hordes had taken their place in Cappadocia, and the Phrygian population which had followed in their wake had spread themselves over the basin of the Upper Halys and over the ancient Milidu, which before long took from them the name of Armenia.[1] All these elements constituted a seething, struggling, restless mass of people, actuated by no plan or method, and subject merely to the caprice of its chiefs; it was, indeed, the "seething cauldron" of which the Hebrew prophets had had a vision, which at times overflowed over the neighbouring nations, and at others was consumed within and wasted itself in fruitless ebullition.[2]

It took Cyaxares years to achieve his conquests; he finally succeeded, however, in reducing the various elements to subjection—Urartians, Scythians, Cimmerians, Chaldæi, and the industrious tribes of the Chalybes and the White Syrians—and, always victorious, appeared at last on the right bank of the Halys; but having reached it, he found himself face to face with foes of quite a different calibre from those with whom he had hitherto to deal. Lydia had increased both in wealth and in vigour since the days when her king Ardys informed his ally Assur-bani pal that he had avenged the death of his father and driven the Cimmerians from the valley of the Mæander

---

[1] The Phrygian origin of the Armenians is pointed out by Herodotus and by Eudoxius.

[2] *Jer.* i. 13.

He had by so doing averted all immediate danger; but as long as the principal horde remained unexterminated, another invasion was always to be feared; besides which, the barbarian inroad, although of short duration, had wrought such havoc in the country that no native power in Asia Minor appeared, nor in reality was, able to make the effort needful to destroy them. Their king Dugdamis, it will be remembered, met his death in Cilicia at the hands of the Assyrians about the year 640, and Kôbos, his successor, was defeated and killed by the Scythians under Madyes about 633. The repeated repulses they had suffered had the effect of quickly relieving Lydia, Phrygia, and the remaining states of the Ægean and the Black Sea from their inroads; the Milesians wrested Sinope from them about 630, and the few bands left behind when the main body set out for the countries of the Euphrates were so harried and decimated by the people over whom they had terrorised for nearly a century, that they had soon no refuge except round the fortress of Antandros, in the mountains of the Troad. Most of the kingdoms whose downfall they had caused never recovered from their reverses; but Lydia, which had not laid down its arms since the death of Gyges, became possessed by degrees of the whole of their territory; Phrygia proper came back to her in the general redistribution, and with it most of the countries which had been under the rule of the dynasty of Midas, from the mountains of Lycia to the shores of the Black Sea. The transfer was effected, apparently, with very slight opposition and with little loss of time, since in the four or five years which followed the death of Kôbos, Ardys had risen in the estimation of the Greeks to the position enjoyed by Gyges; and when, in 628, Aristomenes, the hero of the Messenian wars, arrived at Rhodes, it is said that he contemplated proceeding from thence, first to Sardes and

A VIEW IN THE MOUNTAINS OF THE MESSOGIS.[1]

then to Ecbatana, for the purpose of gaining the adherence of Lydia and Media to his cause. Death put an end to his projects, but he would not for a moment have entertained them had not Ardys been at that time at the head of a renowned and flourishing kingdom The renewal of international commerce followed closely on the re-establishment of peace, and even if the long

[1] Drawn by Boudier, from the heliogravure of Rayet and Thomas.

period of Scythian invasion, followed by the destruction of Nineveh, rendered the overland route less available for regular traffic than before, at all events relations between the inhabitants of the Euphrates valley and those of the Ægean littoral were resumed to such good purpose that

THE SITE OF PRIÊNÊ.[1]

before long several fresh marts were opened in Lydia. Kymê and Ephesus put the region of the Messogis and the Tmolus into communication with the sea, but the lower valleys of the Hermos and the Mæander were closed by the existence of Greek colonies at Smyrna, Clazomenæ, Colophon, Priênê, and Miletus—all hostile to the Mermnadæ—which it would be necessary to overcome if these countries were to enjoy the prosperity shared

[1] Drawn by Boudier, from the heliogravure of Rayet and Thomas.

by other parts of the kingdom; hence the principal effort made by the Lydians was either directly to annex these towns, or to impose such treaties on them as would make them their dependencies. Ardys seized Priênê towards 620, and after having thus established himself on the northern shore of the Latmic Gulf,[1] he proceeded to besiege Miletus in 616, at the very close of his career. Hostilities were wearily prolonged all through the reign of Sadyattes (615-610), and down to the sixth year of Alyattes.[2] The position of Miletus was too strong to permit of its being carried by a *coup de main*; besides which, the Lydians were unwilling to destroy at one blow a town whose colonies, skilfully planted at the seaports from the coasts of the Black Sea to those of Egypt, would one day furnish them with so many outlets for their industrial products. Their method attacking it resolved itself into a series of exhausting raids. "Every year, as soon as the fruit crops and the harvests began to ripen, Alyattes set out at the head of his troops, whom he caused to march and encamp to the sound of instruments. Having arrived in the Milesian territory, he completely destroyed the crops and the orchards, and then again withdrew." In these expeditions

[1] The well-known story that Priênê was saved under Alyattes by a stratagem of the philosopher Bias is merely a fable, of which several other examples are found. It would not be possible to conclude from it, as Grote did, that Ardys' rule over the town was but ephemeral.

[2] The periods of duration assigned here to the reigns of these princes are those of Eusebius—that is to say, 15 years for Crœsus, 37 for Alyattes, 5 for Sadyattes, 37 for Ardys; Julius Africanus gives 15 for Sadyattes and 38 for Ardys, while Herodotus suggests 14 for Crœsus, 57 for Alyattes, 12 for Sadyattes, and 59 for Ardys.

he was careful to avoid any excesses which would have made the injury inflicted appear irretrievable ; his troops were forbidden to destroy dwelling-houses or buildings dedicated to the gods ; indeed, on one occasion, when the conflagration' which consumed the lands accidentally spread to the temple of Athena near Assêsos, he rebuilt two temples for the goddess at his own expense. The Milesians sustained the struggle courageously, until two reverses at Limeneion and in the plain of the Mæander at length induced them to make terms. Their tyrant, Thrasybulus, acting on the advice of the Delphic Apollo and by the mediation of Periander of Corinth, concluded a treaty with Alyattes in which the two princes, declaring themselves the guest and the ally one of the other, very probably conceded extensive commercial privileges to one another both by land and sea (604).[1] Alyattes rewarded the oracle by the gift of a magnificent bowl, the work of Glaucus of Chios, which continued to be shown to travellers of the Roman period as one of the most remarkable curiosities of Delphi. Alyattes continued his expeditions against the other Greek colonies, but directed them prudently and leisurely, so as not to alarm his European friends, and provoke the formation against himself of a coalition of the Hellenic communities shattered over the isles or along the littoral of the Ægean. We know that towards the end of his

---

[1] Thrasybulus stratagem is said to have taken place at Priênê by Diogenes Laërtes and by Polyænus. The war begins under Ardys lasts for five years under Sadyattes, instead of the six years which Herodotus attributes to it, and five years under Alyattes

reign he recovered Colophon, which had been previously acquired by Gyges, but had regained its independence during the Cimmerian crisis;[1] he razed Smyrna to the ground, and forced its inhabitants to occupy unfortified towns, where his suzerainty could not be disputed;[2] he half devastated Clazomenæ, whose citizens saved it by a despairing effort, and he renewed the ancient alliances with Ephesus, Kymê, and the cities of the region of the Caicus and the Hellespont,[3] though it is impossible to attribute an accurate date to each of these particular events. Most of them had already taken place or were still proceeding when the irruption of the Medes across the Halys obliged him to concentrate all his energies on the eastern portion of his kingdom.

The current tradition in Lydia of a century later attributed the conflict of the two peoples to a romantic

[1] Polyænus tells the story of the trick by which Alyattes, after he had treated with the people of Colophon, destroyed their cavalry and seized on their town. The fact that a treaty was made seems to be confirmed by a fragment of Phylarchus, and the surrender of the town to the Lydians by a fragment of Xenophanes, quoted in Athenæus. Schubert does not seem to believe that the town was taken by Alyattes; I have adopted the opinion of Radet on this point.

[2] Herodotus and Nicolas of Damascus confine themselves to relating the capture of the city; adds that the Lydians compelled the inhabitants to dwell in unfortified towns. Schubert thinks that the passage in Strabo refers, not to the time of Alyattes, but to a subsequent event in the fifth century; he relies for this opinion on a fragment of Pindar, which represents Smyrna as still flourishing in his time. But, as Busolt has pointed out, the intention of the text of Pindar is to represent the state of the city at about the time of Homer's birth, and not in the fifth century.

[3] The peace between Ephesus and Lydia must have been troubled for a little while in the reign of Sadyattes, but it was confirmed under Alyattes by the marriage of Melas II. with one of the king's daughters.

## THE WAR BETWEEN ALYATTES AND CYAXARES

cause. It elated that Cyaxares had bestowed his favour on the bands of Scythians who had become his mercenaries on the death of Madyes, and that he had entrusted to them the children of some of the noblest Medic families, that they might train them to hunt and also teach them the use of the bow. One day, on their returning from the chase without any game, Cyaxares reproached them for their want of skill in such angry and insulting terms, that they resolved on immediate revenge. They cut one of the children in pieces, which they dressed after the same manner as that in which they were accustomed to prepare the game they had killed, and served up the dish to the king; then, while he was feasting upon it with his courtiers, they fled in haste and took refuge with Alyattes. The latter welcomed them, and refused to send them back to Cyaxares; hence the outbreak of hostilities. It is, of course, possible that the emigration of a nomad horde may have been the cause of the war,[1] but graver reasons than this had set the two nations at variance. The hardworking inhabitants of the valleys of the Iris and the Halys were still possessed of considerable riches, in spite of the losses they had suffered from the avaricious Cimmerians, and their chief towns Comana, Pteria and Teiria, continued to enjoy prosperity under the rule of their priest kings. Pteria particularly had developed in the course of the century thanks to her favourable situation, which had

[1] Grote has collected a certain number of examples in late times to show that the journeying of a nomad horde from one state to another may provoke wars, and he concludes therefrom that at least the basis of Herodotus account may be considered as true.

enabled her to offer a secure refuge to the neighbouring population during the late disasters. The town itself was crowded into a confined plain, on the left bank of a torrent which flowed into the Halys, and the city walls may still be clearly traced upon the soil; the outline of the houses, the silos, cisterns, and rock-cut staircases are still visible

THE RUINS OF PTERIA.[1]

in places, besides the remains of a palace built of enormous blocks of almost rough-hewn limestone. The town was defended by wide ramparts, and also by two fortresses perched upon enormous masses of rock, while a few thousand yards to the east of the city, on the right bank of the torrent, three converging ravines concealed the sanctuary of one of those mysterious oracles whose fame attracted worshippers from far and wide during the annual

[1] Drawn by Boudier, from Charles Texier.

THE ENTRANCE TO THE SANCTUARY OF PTERIA.[1]

fairs. The bas-reliefs which decorate them belong to that semi-barbarous art which we have already met with in the

[1] Drawn by **Boudier,** from a photograph by **Chantre.**

monuments attributed to the Khâti, near the Orontes and Euphrates, on both slopes of the Amanus, in Cilicia, and in the ravines of the Taurus. Long processions of priests and votaries defile before figures of the gods and goddesses standing erect upon their sacred animals; in one scene, a tall goddess, a Cybele or an Anaitis, leans affectionately

ONE OF THE PROCESSIONS IN THE RAVINE OF PTERIA.[1]

upon her chosen lover, and seems to draw him with her towards an image with a lion's body and the head of a youth.[2] Pteria and its surrounding hills formed a kind of natural fortress which overlooked the whole bend of the

[1] Drawn by Faucher-Gudin, from a photograph by Chantre.

[2] These bas-reliefs seem to me to have been executed at about the time with which we are dealing, or perhaps a few years later—in any case, before the Persian conquest.

Halys; it constituted, in the hands of the Lydians, an outpost which effectually protected their possessions in Phrygia and Paphlagonia against an attack from the East; in the hands of the Medes it would be a dominant position which would counteract the defensive features of the Halys, and from it they might penetrate into the heart of Asia Minor without encountering any serious obstacles. The struggle between the two sovereigns was not so unequal as might at first appear. No doubt the army of Alyattes was inferior in numbers, but the bravery of its component forces and the ability of its leaders compensated for its numerical inferiority, and Cyaxares had no troop to be compared with the Carian lancers, with the hoplites of Ionia, or with the heavy Mæonian cavalry. During six years the two armies met again and again—fate, sometimes favouring one and sometimes the other—and were about to try their fortune once more, after several indecisive engagements, when an eclipse of the sun suspended operations (585). The Iranian peoples would fight only in full daylight, and their adversaries, although warned, so it is said, by the Milesian philosopher Thales of the phenomenon about to take place in the heavens, were perhaps not completely reassured as to its significance, and the two hosts accordingly separated without coming to blows.[1] Nebuchadrezzar had followed, not without some misgivings, the vicissitudes of the campaign, and his

---

[1] This eclipse was identified at one time with that of Sept. 30, 610, at another with that of May 28, 585. The latter of these two dates appears to me to be the correct one, and is the only one which agrees with what we know of the general history of the sixth century.

anxiety was shared by the independent princes of Asia Minor, who were allies of the Lydians; he and they alike awaited with dread a decisive action, which, by crushing one of the belligerents beyond hope of recovery, would leave the onlookers at the mercy of the victor in the full flush of his success. Tradition relates that Syennesis of Cilicia and the Babylonian Nabonidus had taken advantage of the alarm produced by the eclipse to negotiate an armistice, and that they were soon successful in bringing the rival powers to an agreement.[1] The Halys remained the recognised frontier of the two kingdoms, but the Lydians probably obtained advantages for their commerce, which they regarded as compensatory for the abandonment of their claim to the district of Pteria. To strengthen the alliance, it was agreed that Alyattes should give his daughter Aryenis in marriage to Ishtuvigu, or, as the Greeks called him, Astyages, the son of Cyaxares.[2] According to the custom of the times, the two contracting parties, after taking the vow of fidelity, sealed the compact by pricking each other's arms and sucking the few drops of blood which oozed from the puncture.[3] Cyaxares died in

[1] The name Labynetos given by Herodotus is a transcript of Nabonidus, but cannot here designate the Babylonian king of that name, for the latter reigned more than thirty years after the peace was concluded between the Lydians and the Medes. If Herodotus has not made the mistake of putting Labynetos for Nebuchadrezzar, we may admit that this Labynetos was a prince of the royal family, or simply a general who was commanding the Chaldæan auxiliaries of Cyaxares.

[2] The form Ishtuvigu is given us by the Chaldæan documents. Its exact transcript was Astuigas, Astyigas, according to Ctesias; in fact, this coincides so remarkably with the Babylonian mode of spelling, that we may believe that it faithfully reproduces the original pronunciation.

[3] Many ancient authors have spoken of this war, or at least of the

the following year (584), full of days and renown, and was at once succeeded by Astyages. Few princes could boast of having had such a successful career as his, even in that century of unprecedented fortunes and boundless ambitions. Inheriting a disorganised army, proclaimed king in the midst of mourning, on the morrow of a defeat in which the fate of his kingdom had hung in the balance, he succeeded within a quarter of a century in overthrowing his enemies and substituting his supremacy for theirs throughout the whole of Western Asia. At his accession Media had occupied only a small portion of the Iranian table-land; at his death, the Median empire extended to the banks of the Halys. It is now not difficult to understand why Nebuchadrezzar abstained from all expeditions in the regions of the Taurus, as well as in those of the Upper Tigris. He would inevitably have come into contact with the allies of the Lydians, perchance with the Lydians themselves, or with the Medes, as the case might be; and he would have been drawn on to take an active part in their dangerous quarrels, from which, after all, he could not hope to reap any personal advantage. In reality,

---

eclipse which brought it to an end. Several of them place the conclusion of peace not in the reign of Cyaxares, but in that of Astyages—Cicero, Solinus, and the Armenian Eusebius—and their view has been adopted by some modern historians. The two versions of the account can be reconciled by saying that Astyages was commanding the Median army instead of his father, who was too old to do so, but such an explanation is unnecessary, and Cyaxares, though over seventy, might still have had sufficient vigour to wage war. The substitution of Astyages for Cyaxares by the authors of Roman times was probably effected with the object of making the date of the eclipse agree with a different system of chronology from that followed by Herodotus.

there was one field of action only open to him, and that was Southern Syria, with Egypt in her rear. He found himself, at this extreme limit of his dominions, in a political situation almost identical with that of his Assyrian predecessors, and consequently more or less under the obligation of repeating their policy. The Saites, like the Ethiopians before them, could enjoy no assured sense of security in the Delta, when they knew that they had a great military state as their nearest neighbour on the other side of the isthmus ; they felt with reason that the thirty leagues of desert which separated Pelusium from Gaza was an insufficient protection from invasion, and they desired to have between themselves and their adversary a tract of country sufficiently extensive to ward off the first blows in the case of hostilities. If such a buffer territory could be composed of feudal provinces or tributary states Egyptian pride would be flattered, while at the same time the security of the kingdom would be increased, and indeed the victorious progress of Necho had for the moment changed their most ambitious dreams into realities. Driven back into the Nile valley after the battle of Carchemish their pretensions had immediately shrunk within more modest limits ; their aspirations were now confined to gaining the confidence of the few surviving states which had preserved some sort of independence in spite of the Assyrian conquest, to detaching them from Chaldæan interests and making them into a protecting zone against the ambition of a new Esarhaddon. To this work Necho applied himself as soon as Nebuchadrezzar had left him in order to hasten back to Babylon. The Egyptian monarch belonged to a persevering race, who were never cast down by reverses, and had not once allowed themselves to be discouraged during the whole of the century in which they had laboured to secure the crown for themselves; his defeat had not lessened his tenacity, nor, it would seem, his certainty of final success. Besides organising his Egyptian and Libyan troops, he enrolled a still larger number of Hellenic mercenaries, correctly anticipating that the restless spirits of the Phœnicians and Jews would soon furnish him with an opportunity of distinguishing himself upon the scene of action.

It was perhaps at this juncture that he decided to strengthen his position by the co-operation of a fleet. The superiority of the Chaldæan battalions had been so clearly manifested, that he could scarcely hope for a decisive victory if he persisted in seeking it on land; but if he could succeed in securing the command of the sea, his galleys, by continually cruising along the Syrian coast, and conveying troops, provisions, arms, and money to the Phœnician towns, would so successfully foster and maintain a spirit of rebellion, that the Chaldæans would not dare to venture into Egypt until they had dealt with this source of danger in their rear. He therefore set to work to increase the number of his war-vessels on the Red Sea, but more especially on the Mediterranean, and as he had drawn upon Greece for his troops, he now applied to her for ship-builders.[1] The trireme, which had been invented by either

---

[1] Herodotus tells us that in his time the ruins of the docks which Necho had made for the building of his triremes could still be seen on the shore of the Red Sea as well as on that of the Mediterranean. He

the Samian or Corinthian naval constructors, had as yet been little used, and possibly Herodotus is attributing an event of his own time to this earlier period when he affirms that Necho filled a dockyard with a whole fleet of these vessels; he possessed, at any rate, a considerable number of them, and along with them other vessels of various build in which the blunt stem and curved poop of the Greeks were combined with the square-cabined barque of the Egyptians. At the same time in order to transport the squadron from one sea to another when occasion demanded, he endeavoured to reopen the ancient canal of Seti I., which had been silted up ever since the last years of the XX$^{th}$ dynasty. He improved its course and widened it so as to permit of two triremes sailing abreast or easily clearing each other in passing. The canal started from the Pelusiac branch of the Nile, not far from Patumos, and skirted the foot of the Arabian hills from west to east; it then plunged into the Wady Tumilat, and finally entered the head of the bay which now forms the Lake of Ismaïlia The narrow channel by which this sheet of water was anciently connected with the Gulf of Suez was probably obstructed in places, and required clearing out at several points, if not along its entire extent. A later tradition

AN EGYPTIAN VESSEL OF THE SAITE PERIOD.

seems also to say that the building of the fleet was anterior to the fi st Syrian expedition.

[1] Drawn by Faucher-Gudin, from a photograph sent by G. Bénédite.

states that after having lost 100,000 men in attempting this task, the king abandoned the project on the advice of an oracle, a god having been supposed to have predicted to him that he was working for the barbarians.[1] Another of Necho's enterprises excited the admiration of his con-

THE ANCIENT HEAD OF THE RED SEA, NOW THE NORTHERN EXTREMITY OF THE BITTER LAKES.[2]

temporaries, and remained for ever in the memory of the people. The Carthaginians had discovered on the ocean coast of Libya, a country rich in gold, ivory, precious woods, pepper, and spices, but their political jealousy prevented other nations from following in their wake in the

[1] The figures, 100,000 men, are evidently exaggerated, for in a similar undertaking, the digging of the Mahmudiyeh canal, Mehemet-Ali lost only 10,000 men, though the work was greater.

[2] Drawn by Boudier, from a photograph taken from the railway between Ismailia and Suez, on the eastern shore of the lake.

interests of trade. The Egyptians possibly may have undertaken to dispute their monopoly, or the Phœnicians may have desired to reach their colony by a less frequented highway than the Mediterranean. The merchants of the Saïd and the Delta had never entirely lost touch with the people dwelling on the shores of the Red Sea, and though the royal fleets no longer pursued their course down it on their way to Puṅt as in the days of Hâtshopsîtu and Ramses III., private individuals ventured from time to time to open trade communications with the ancient "Ladders of Incense." Necho despatched the Phœnician captains of his fleet in search of new lands, and they started from the neighbourhood of Suez, probably accompanied by native pilots accustomed to navigate in those waters. The undertaking, fraught with difficulty even in the last century, was, indeed, a formidable one for the small vessels of the Saïte period. They sailed south for months with the east to the left of them, and on their right the continent which seemed to extend indefinitely before them. Towards the autumn they disembarked on some convenient shore, sowed the wheat with which they were provided, and waited till the crop was ripe; having reaped the harvest they again took to the sea. Any accurate remembrance of what they saw was soon effaced; they could merely recollect that, having reached a certain point, they observed with astonishment that the sun appeared to have reversed its course and now rose on their right hand. This meant that they had turned the southern extremity of Africa and were unconsciously sailing northwards. In the third year they passed through the pillars of Hercules and reached Egypt in safety. The very limited knowledge of navigation possessed by the mariners of that day rendered this voyage fruitless; the dangerous route thus opened up to commerce remained unused, and its discovery was remembered only as a curious feat devoid of any practical use.[1] In order to obtain any practical results from the arduous voyage, it would have been necessary for Egypt to devote a considerable part of its resources to the making of such expeditions, whereas the country preferred to concentrate all its energies on its Tyrian policy. Necho certainly possessed the sympathies of the Tyrians, who had transferred their traditional hatred of the Assyrians to the Chaldæans. He could also count with equal certainty on the support of a considerable party in Moab, Ammon, and Edom, as well as among the **Nabatæans** and the Arabs of Kedar; but the key of the whole position lay with Judah— that ally without whom none of Necho's other partisans would venture to declare openly against their master. The death of Josiah had dealt a fatal blow to the hopes of the prophets, and even long after the event they could not recall it without lamenting the fate of this king after their own heart. "And like unto him," exclaims their

[1] The Greek writers after Herodotus denied the possibility of such a voyage, and they thought that it could not be decided whether Africa was entirely surrounded by water, and that certainly no traveller had ever journeyed above 5000 stadia beyond the entrance to the Red Sea. Modern writers are divided on the point, some denying and others maintaining the authenticity of the account. The observation made by the navigators of the apparent change in the course of the sun, which Herodotus has recorded and which neither he nor his authorities understood, seems to me to be so weighty an argument for its authenticity, that it is impossible to reject the tradition until we have more decided grounds for so doing

chronicler, "was there no king before him, that turned to the Lord with all his heart and with all his soul and with all his might, according to all the law of Moses; neither after him arose there any like him."[1] The events which followed his violent death—the deposition of Jehoahaz, the establishment and fall of the Egyptian supremacy, the proclamation of the Chaldæan suzerainty, the degradation of the king and the misery of the people brought about by the tribute exacted from them by their foreign masters,— all these revolutions which had succeeded each other without break or respite had all but ruined the belief in the efficacy of the reform due to Hilkiah's discovery, and preached by Jeremiah and his followers. The people saw in these calamities the vengeance of Jahveh against the presumptuous faction which had overthrown His various sanctuaries and had attempted to confine His worship to a single temple; they therefore restored the banished attractions, and set themselves to sacrifice to strange gods with greater zest than ever.

A like crisis occurred and like party divisions had broken out around Jehoiakim similar to those at the court of Ahaz and Hezekiah a century earlier. The populace, the soldiery, and most of the court officials, in short all who adhered to the old popular form of religion or were attracted to strange devotions, hoped to rid themselves of the Chaldæans by earthly means, and since Necho declared himself an implacable enemy of their foe, their principal aim was to come to terms with Egypt. Jeremiah, on the contrary, and those who remained

[1] 2 *Kings* xxiii. 25.

faithful to the teaching of the prophets, saw in all that was passing around them cogent reasons for rejecting worldly wisdom and advice, and for yielding themselves unreservedly to the Divine will in bowing before the Chaldæan of whom Jahveh made use, as of the Assyrian of old, to chastise the sins of Judah. The struggle between the two factions constantly disturbed the public peace, and it needed little to cause the preaching of the prophets to degenerate into an incitement to revolt. On a feast-day which occurred in the early months of Jehoiakim's reign, Jeremiah took up his station on the pavement of the temple and loudly apostrophised the crowd of worshippers. "Thus saith the Lord: If ye will not hearken unto Me, to walk in My law, which I have set before you, to hearken to the words of My servants the prophets, whom I send unto you, even rising up early and sending them, but ye have not hearkened; then will I make this house like Shiloh, and will make this city a curse to all the nations of the earth." Such a speech, boldly addressed to an audience the majority of whom were already moved by hostile feelings, brought their animosity to a climax; the officiating priests, the prophets, and the pilgrims gathered round Jeremiah, crying "Thou shalt surely die." The people thronged into the temple, the princes of Judah went up to the king's house and to the house of the Lord, and sat in council in the entry of the new gate. They decreed that Jeremiah, having spoken in the name of the Lord, did not merit death, and some of their number, recalling the precedent of Micaiah the Morasthite, who in his time had predicted the ruin of Jerusalem, added,

'Did Hezekiah King of Judah and all Judah put him at all to death?" Ahikam, the son of Shaphan, one of those who had helped in restoring the law, took the prophet under his protection and prevented the crowd from injuring him, but some others were not able to escape the popular fury. The prophet Uriah of Kirjath-jearim, who unweariedly prophesied against the city and country after the manner of Jeremiah, fled to Egypt, but in vain Jehoiakim despatched Elnathan, the son of Achbor, "and certain men with him," who brought him back to Judah "Slew him with the sword, and cast his dead body into the graves of the common people."¹ If popular feeling had reached such a pitch before the battle of Carchemish to what height must it have risen when the news of Nebuchadrezzar's victory had given the death-blow to the hopes of the Egyptian faction! Jeremiah believed the moment ripe for forcibly arresting the popular imagination while it was swayed by the panic of anticipated invasion He dictated to his disciple Baruch the prophecies he had pronounced since the appearance of the Scythians under Josiah and on the day of the solemn fast proclaimed throughout Judah during the winter of the fifth year of the reign a few months after the defeat of the Egyptians he caused the writing to be read to the assembled people at the entry of the new gate² Micaiah the son of

---

¹ *Jer.* xxvi, where the scene takes place at the beginning of Jehoiakim's reign *i.e.* under the Egyptian domination

² The date given in *Jer.* xxxvi 9 makes the year begin in spring since the ninth month occurs in winter; this date belongs therefore to the late recensions of the text It is nevertheless probably authentic representing the exact equivalent of the original date according to the old calendar.

Gemariah, was among those who listened, and noting that the audience were moved by the denunciations which revived the memory of their recent misfortunes, he hastened to inform the ministers sitting in council within the palace of what was passing. They at once sent for Baruch, and begged him to repeat to them what he had read. They were so much alarmed at its recital, that they advised him to hide himself in company with Jeremiah, while they informed the king of the matter. Jehoiakim was sitting in a chamber with a brazier burning before him on account of the severe cold: scarcely had they read three or four pages before him when his anger broke forth; he seized the roll, slashed it with the scribe's penknife, and threw the fragments into the fire. Jeremiah recomposed the text from memory, and inserted in it a malediction against the king. "Thus saith the Lord concerning Jehoiakim, King of Judah: He shall have none to sit upon the throne of David: and his dead body shall be cast out in the day to the heat, and in the night to the frost. And I will punish him and his seed and his servants for their iniquity: and I will bring upon them, and upon the inhabitants of Jerusalem, and upon the men of Judah, all the evil that I have pronounced against them; but they hearkened not."[1] The Egyptian tendencies evinced at court, at first

---

[1] *Jer.* xxxvi. Attempts have been made to reconstruct the contents of Jeremiah's roll, and most of the authors who have dealt with this subject think that the roll contained the greater part of the fragments which, in the book of the prophet, occupy chaps. i. 4-19, ii, iii. 1-5, 19-25, iv.-vi, vii, viii, ix. 1-21, x. 17-25, xi, xii. 1-6, xvii. 19-27, xviii, xix. 1-13, which it must be admitted have not in every case been preserved in their original form, but have been abridged or rearranged after the

discreetly veiled, were now accentuated to such a degree that Nebuchadrezzar became alarmed, and came in person to Jerusalem in the year **601**. His presence frustrated the intrigues of Pharaoh. **Jehoiakim** was reduced to order for a time, but three years later he **revolted** afresh at the instigation of Necho, and this time the Chaldæan satraps opened hostilities in earnest. They assembled their troops, which were reinforced by Syrian, Moabite, and Ammonite contingents, and laid siege to **Jerusalem**.[1] **Jehoiakim,** left to himself, resisted with such determination that Nebuchadrezzar was obliged to bring up his Chaldæan forces to assist in the attack. Judah trembled with fear at the mere description which her prophet Habakkuk gave of this fierce and sturdy people, "which march through the breadth of the earth to possess dwelling-places which are not theirs. They are terrible and dreadful: their judgment and their dignity proceed from themselves. Their horses

---

exile. Other chapters evidently belong to the years previous to the fifth year of Jehoiakim, as well as part of the prophecies against the barbarians, but they could not have been included in the original roll, as the latter would then have been too long to have been read three times in one day.

[1] 2 *Kings* xxiv. **1–4.** The passage is not easy to be understood as it stands, and it has been differently interpreted by historians. Some have supposed that it refers to events immediately following the battle of Carchemish, and that Jehoiakim defended Jerusalem against Nebuchadrezzar in **605.** Others think that, after the battle of Carchemish, Jehoiakim took advantage of Nebuchadrezzar's being obliged to return at once to Babylon, and would not recognise the authority of the Chaldæans; that Nebuchadrezzar returned later, towards **601,** and took Jerusalem, and that it is to this second war that allusion is made in the *Book of Kings.* It is more simple to consider that which occurred about **600** as a first attempt at rebellion which was punished lightly by the Chaldæans.

also are swifter than leopards, and are more fierce than the evening wolves; and their horsemen spread themselves; yea, their horsemen come from far; they fly as an eagle that hasteneth to devour. They come all of them for violence; their faces are set eagerly as the east wind, and they gather captives as the sand. Yea, he scoffeth at kings, and princes are a derision unto him: he derideth every stronghold: for he heapeth up dust and taketh it. Then shall he sweep by as a wind, and shall pass over the guilty, even he whose might is his god."[1] Nebuchadrezzar's army must have presented a spectacle as strange as did that of Necho. It contained, besides its nucleus of Chaldæan and Babylonian infantry, squadrons of Scythian and Median cavalry, whose cruelty it was, no doubt, that had alarmed the prophet, and certainly bands of Greek hoplites, for the poet Alcæus had had a brother, Antimenidas by name, in the Chaldæan monarch's service. Jehoiakim died before the enemy appeared beneath the walls of Jerusalem, and was at once succeeded by his son Jeconiah,* a youth of eighteen years, who assumed the name of Jehoiachin.[2] The new king continued the struggle at first courageously, but the advent of Nebuchadrezzar so clearly convinced him of the futility of the defence, that he suddenly decided to lay down his arms. He came forth from the city with his mother Nehushta, the officers of

---

[1] *Hab.* i. 6–11.

* [Jehoiachin is called Coniah in *Jer.* xxii. 24 and xxiv. 1, and Jeconiah in 1 *Chron.* iii. 16.—Tr.]

[2] 2 *Kings* xxiv. 5–10; cf. 2 *Chron.* xxxvi. 6–9, where the writer says that Nebuchadrezzar bound Jehoiakim "in fetters, to carry him to Babylon."

his house, his ministers, and his eunuchs, and prostrated himself at the feet of his suzerain. The Chaldæan monarch was not inclined to proceed to extremities; he therefore exiled to Babylon Jehoiachin and the whole of his seditious court who had so ill-advised the young king, the best of his officers, and the most skilful artisans, in all 3023 persons, but the priests and the bulk of the people remained at Jerusalem. The conqueror appointed Mattaniah the youngest son of Josiah, to be their ruler, who, on succeeding to the crown, changed his name, after the example of his predecessors, adopting that of Zedekiah Jehoiachin had reigned exactly three months over his besieged city (596).[1]

The Egyptians made no attempt to save their ally but if they felt themselves not in a condition to defy the Chaldæans on Syrian territory, the Chaldæans on their side feared to carry hostilities into the heart of the Delta Necho died two years after the disaster at Jerusalem without having been called to account by, or having found an opportunity of further annoying, his rival, and his son Psammetichus II. succeeded peacefully to the throne He was a youth at this time,[3] and his father's ministers

[1] 2 *Kings* xxiv. 11–17; cf. 2 *Chron.* xxxvi. 10.

[2] The length of Necho's reign is fixed at sixteen years by Herodotus and at six or at nine years by the various abbreviators of Manetho. The contemporaneous monuments have confirmed the testimony of Herodotus on this point as against that of Manetho, and the stelæ of the Florentine Museum, of the Leyden Museum, and of the Louvre have furnished certain proof that Necho died in the sixteenth year, after fifteen and a half years' reign

[3] His sarcophagus, discovered in 1883, and now preserved in the Gizeh Museum, is of such small dimensions that it can have been used only for a youth.

conducted the affairs of State on his behalf, and it was they who directed one of his early campaigns, if not the very first, against Ethiopia.¹ They organised a small army for him composed of Egyptians, Greeks, and Asiatic mercenaries, which, while the king was taking up his residence at Elephantinê, was borne up the Nile in a fleet of large vessels.² It probably went as far south as the northern point of the second cataract, and not having encountered any Ethiopian force,³ it retraced its course and came to anchor at Abu-Simbel. The officers in

¹ The graffiti of Abu-Simbel have been most frequently attributed to Psammetichus I., and until recently I had thought it possible to maintain this opinion. A. von Gutschmid was the first to restore them to Psammetichus II., and his opinion has gained ground since Wiedemann's vigorous defence of it. The Ialysian mercenary's graffito contains the Greek translation of the current Egyptian phrase "when his Majesty came on his first military expedition into this country," which seems to point to no very early date in a reign for a first campaign. Moreover, one of the generals in command of the expedition is a Psammetichus, son of Theocles, that is, a Greek with an Egyptian name. A considerable lapse of time must have taken place since Psammetichus' first dealings with the Greeks, for otherwise the person named after the king would not have been of sufficiently mature age to be put at the head of a body of troops.

² The chief graffito at Abu-Simbel says, in fact, that the king came to Elephantinê, and that only the troops accompanying the General Psammetichus, the son of Theocles, went beyond Kerkis. It was probably during his stay at Elephantinê, while awaiting the return of the expedition, that Psammetichus II. had the inscriptions containing his cartouches engraved upon the rocks of Bigga, Abaton, Philæ, and Konosso, or among the ruins of Elephantinê and of Philæ.

³ The Greek inscription says *above Kerkis*. Wiedemann has corrected *Kerkis* into *Kortis*, the Korte of the first cataract, but the reading Kerkis is too well established for there to be any reason for change. The simplest explanation is to acknowledge that the inscription refers to a place situated a few miles above Abu-Simbel, towards Wady-Halfa.

command, after having admired the rock-cut chapel of Ramses II., left in it a memento of their visit in a fine inscription cut on the right leg of one of the colossi. This inscription informs us that "King Psammatikhos having come to Elephantinê, the people who were with Psammatikhos, son of Theocles, wrote this. They ascended above Kerkis, to where the river ceases; Potasimto commanded the foreigners, Amasis the Egyptians. At the same time also wrote Arkhôn, son of Amoibikhos, and Peleqos, son of Ulamos." Following the example of their officers, the soldiers also wrote their names here and there, each in his own language—Ionians, Rhodians Carians, Phœnicians, and perhaps even Jews; *e.g.* Elesibios of Teos, Pabis of Colophon, Telephos of Ialysos, Abdsakon son of Petiehvê, Gerhekal son of Hallum. The whole of this part of the country, brought to ruin in the gradual dismemberment of Greater Egypt, could not have differed much from the Nubia of to-day; there were the same narrow strips of cultivation along the river banks, gigantic temples half buried by their own ruins, scattered towns and villages, and everywhere the yellow sand creeping insensibly down towards the Nile. The northern part of this province remained in the hands of the Saite Pharaohs and the districts situated further south just beyond Abu Simbel formed at that period a sort of neutral ground between their domain and that of the Pharaohs of Napata. While all this was going on, Syria continued to plot in secret, and the faction which sought security in a foreign alliance was endeavouring to shake off the depression caused by the reverses of Jehoiakim and his son; and the tide of popular feeling setting in the direction of Egypt became so strong, that even Zedekiah, the creature of Nebuchadrezzar, was unable to stem it. The prophets who were inimical to religious reform, persisted in their

THE FAÇADE OF THE GREAT TEMPLE OF ABU-SIMBEL.[1]

belief that the humiliation of the country was merely temporary. Those of them who still remained in Jerusalem repeated at every turn, "Ye shall not serve the King of Babylon ... the vessels of the Lord's house shall now shortly be brought again from Babylon."[2] Jeremiah endeavoured to counteract the effect of their words, but in vain; the people, instead of listening to the prophet, waxed wroth with him, and gave themselves more and more recklessly up to their former sins. Incense was

[1] Drawn by **Boudier,** from a photograph by Daniel Héron.
[2] *Jer.* xxvii 9, 16.

burnt every morning on the roofs of the houses and at the corners of the streets in honour of Baal, lamentations for Tammuz again rent the air at the season of his festival;[1] the temple was invaded by uncircumcised priests and their idols,[2] and the king permitted the priests of Moloch to raise their pyres in the valley of Hinnom.[3] The exiled Jews, surrounded on all sides by heathen peoples presented a no less grievous spectacle than their brethren at Jerusalem; some openly renounced the God of their fathers,[4] others worshipped their chosen idols in secret, while those who did not actually become traitors to their faith, would only listen to such prophets as promised them a speedy revenge—Ahab, Zedekiah, son of Maaseiah, and Shemaiah. There was one man, however, who appeared in their midst, a priest, brought up from his youth in the temple and imbued with the ideas of reform—Ezekiel son of Buzi, whose words might have brought them to a more just appreciation of their position, had they not drowned his voice by their clamour; alarmed at their threats, he refrained from speech in public, but gathered round him a few faithful adherents at his house in Tel-Abîb, where the spirit of the Lord first came upon him in their presence about the year 592.[6] This little band of exiles was in constant communication with the mother-country, and the echo of the religious quarrels and of the

[1] *Ezek.* viii. 14, 15. [Cf. vol. iv. p. 260.—Tr.]
[2] *Jer.* xxxii. 34; *Ezek.* viii. 7-13, 16.
[3] *Jer.* xxxii. 35; *Ezek.* xvi. 21, xxiii. 37.
[4] *Jer.* xxix. 21-32.   [5] *Ezek.* xiv. 1-8.
[6] *Ezek.* i. 1, 2. We see him receiving the elders in his house in chaps. viii. 1, xiv. 1, xx. 1, et. seq.

controversies provoked between the various factions by the events of the political world, was promptly borne to them by merchants, travelling scribes, or the king's legates who were sent regularly to Babylon with the tribute [1] They learnt, about the year 590, that grave events were at hand, and that the moment had come when Judah recovering at length from her trials, should once more occupy, in the sight of the sun, that place for which Jahveh had destined her. The kings of Moab, Ammon, Edom Tyre, and Sidon had sent envoys to Jerusalem, and there probably at the dictation of Egypt, they had agreed on what measures to take to stir up a general insurrection against Chaldæa.[2] The report of their resolutions had revived the courage of the national party, and of its prophets Hananiah, son of Azzur, had gone through the city announcing the good news to all.[3] "Thus speaketh the Lord of hosts, the God of Israel, saying, I have broken the yoke of the King of Babylon. Within two full years will I bring again into this place all the vessels of the Lord's house . . . and Jeconiah the son of Jehoiakim King of Judah, with all the captives of Judah that went to Babylon!" But Jeremiah had made wooden yokes and had sent them to the confederate princes, threatening

---

[1] *Jer.* xxix. 3 gives the names of two of these transmitters of the tribute—Elasah the son of Shaphan, and Gemariah the son of Hilkiah to whom Jeremiah had entrusted a message for those of the captivity.

[2] *Jer.* xxvii. 1–3. The statement at the beginning of this chapter: *In the beginning of the reign of Jehoiakim*, contains a copyist's error; the reading should be: *In the beginning of the reign of Zedekiah* ( ver. 12).

[3] *Jer.* xxvii., xxviii.

them with divine punishment if they did **not bow** their necks to Nebuchadrezzar; the prophet himself bore **one on** his **own** neck, and showed himself **in** the streets on all occasions thus accoutred, as a living emblem **of** the slavery in which Jahveh permitted His people to remain for their spiritual good. Hananiah, meeting the prophet by chance, wrested the yoke from him and broke **it,** exclaiming, "Thus saith the Lord: Even so will I break the yoke **of** Nebuchadrezzar, King **of** Babylon, within two full years from **off** the neck **of** all the nations." The mirth **of** the bystanders was roused, but **on** the morrow Jeremiah appeared with a yoke **of** iron, which Jahveh had put "upon the neck **of** all the nations, that they may serve Nebuchadrezzar, King **of** Babylon." Moreover to destroy in the minds **of** the exiled Jews **any** hope **of** speedy deliverance, he wrote to them: "Let not your prophets that be in the midst **of** you, and your diviners deceive you, neither hearken ye to your dreams which ye cause to be dreamed. **For** they prophesy falsely unto **you** in My name: I have not sent them, saith the Lord."[1] The prophet exhorted them to resign themselves to their fate, at all events for the time, that the unity **of** their nation might be preserved until the time when it might indeed please Jahveh to restore it: "Build ye houses and dwell in them, and plant gardens and eat the fruit **of** them: take ye wives and beget sons and daughters and take wives for your sons, and give your daughters to husbands, that they may bear sons and daughters; and multiply ye there and be not diminished. **And** seek the

[1] *Jer.* xxix. 8, 9.

peace of the city whither I have caused you to be carried away captive, and pray unto the Lord for it : for in the peace thereof shall ye have peace." [1]

Psammetichus II. died in 589,[2] and his reign, though short, was distinguished by the activity shown in rebuilding and embellishing the temples. His name is met with everywhere on the banks of the Nile—at Karnak, where he completed the decoration of the great columns of Taharqa, at Abydos, at Heliopolis, and on the monuments that have come from that town, such as the obelisk set up in the Campus Martius at Rome. The personal influence of the young sovereign did not count for much in the zeal thus displayed; but the impulse that had been growing during three or four generations, since the time of the expulsion of the Assyrians, now began to have its full effect. Egypt, well armed, well governed by able ministers, and more and more closely bound to Greece by both mercantile and friendly ties, had risen to a very high position in the estimation of its contemporaries; the inhabitants of Elis had deferred to her decision in the question whether they should take part in the Olympic games in which they were the judges, and following the advice she had given on the matter, they had excluded their own citizens from the sports so as to avoid the least suspicion of partiality in

---

[1] *Jer.* xxix. 5-7.

[2] Herodotus reckoned the length of the reign of Psammetichus II. at six years, in which he agrees with the Syncellus, while the abbreviators of Manetho fix it at seventeen years. The results given by the reading of a stele of the Louvre enable us to settle that the figure 6 is to be preferred to the other, and to reckon the length of the reign at five years and a half.

the distribution of the prizes.[1] The new king, probably the brother of the late Pharaoh, had his prenomen of Uahibri from his grandfather Psammetichus I., and it was this sovereign that the Greeks called indifferently Uaphres and Apries.[2] He was young, ambitious, greedy of fame and military glory, and longed to use the weapon that his predecessors had for some fifteen years past been carefully whetting; his emissaries, arriving at Jerusalem at the moment when the popular excitement was at its height, had little difficulty in overcoming Zedekiah's scruples Edom, Moab, and the Philistines who had all taken their share in the conferences of the rebel party, hesitated at the last moment, and refused to sever their relations with Babylon. Tyre and the Ammonites alone persisted in

AFRIES, FROM A SPHINX IN THE LOUVRE.[3]

[1] Diodorus Siculus has transferred the anecdote to Amasis, and the decision given is elsewhere attributed to one of the seven sages. The sto y is a popular romance, of which Herodotus gives the version current among the Greeks in Egypt.

[2] According to Herodotus, Apries was the son of Psammis. The size of the sarcophagus of Psammetichus II., suitable only for a youth, makes this filiation improbable. Psammetichus, who came to the throne when he was hardly more than a child, could have left behind him only children of tender age, and Apries appears from the outset as a prince of full mental and physical development.

[3] Drawn by Boudier, from the bronze statuette in the Louvre Museum

their determination, and allied themselves with Egypt on the same terms as Judah. Nebuchadrezzar, thus defied by

STELE OF NEBUCHADREZZAR.[1]

three enemies, was at a loss to decide upon which to make

[1] Drawn by **Boudier,** from a photograph by Pognon. The figures have been carefully defaced with the hammer, but the outline of the king can still be discerned on the left; he seizes the rampant lion by the right paw, and while it raises its left paw against him, he plunges his dagger into the body of the beast.

his first attack. Ezekiel, whose place of exile put him in a favourable position for learning what was passing, shows him to us as he "stood at the parting of the way, at the head of the two ways, to use divination: he shook the arrows to and fro, he consulted the teraphim, he looked in the liver."[1] Judah formed as it were the bridge by which the Egyptians could safely enter Syria, and if Nebuchadrezzar could succeed in occupying it before their arrival he could at once break up the coalition into three separate parts incapable of rejoining one another—Ammon in the desert to the east, Tyre and Sidon on the seaboard, and Pharaoh beyond his isthmus to the south-west. He therefore established himself in a central position at Riblah on the Orontes, from whence he could observe the progress of the operations, and hasten with his reserve force to a threatened point in the case of unforeseen difficulties having done this, he despatched the two divisions of his army against his two principal adversaries. One of these divisions crossed the Lebanon, seized its fortresses, and leaving a record of its victories on the rocks of the Wady Brissa, made its way southwards along the coast to blockade Tyre.[2] The other force bore down upon Zedekiah

---

[1] *Ezek.* xxi. 21.

[2] The account of this Phœnician campaign is contained in one of the inscriptions discovered and commented on by Pognon. Winckler, the only one to my knowledge who has tried to give a precise chronological position to the events recorded in the inscription, places them at the very beginning of the reign, after the victory of Carchemish, about the time when Nebuchadrezzar heard that his father had just died. I think that this date is not justified by the study of the inscription, for the king speaks therein of the great works that he had accomplished, the restoration of the temples, the rebuilding of the walls of Babylon, and the digging

and made war upon him ruthlessly. It burnt the villages and unwalled towns, gave the rural districts over as a prey to the Philistines and the Edomites, surrounded the two fortresses of Lachish and Azekah, and only after completely exhausting the provinces, appeared before the walls of the capital. Jerusalem was closely beset when the news reached the Chaldæans that Apries was approaching Gaza; Zedekiah, in his distress, appealed to him for help, and the promised succour at length came upon the scene.[1] The Chaldæans at once raised the siege with the object of arresting the advancing enemy, and the popular party, reckoning already on a Chaldæan defeat, gave way to insolent rejoicing over the prophets of evil. Jeremiah, however, had no hope of final success. "Deceive not yourselves, saying, The Chaldæans shall surely depart from us; for they shall not depart. For though ye had smitten the whole army of the Chaldæans that fight against you, and there remained but wounded men among them, yet should they rise up every man in his tent, and burn this city with fire."[2] What actually took place is not known; according to one account, Apries accepted battle and was

---

of canals, all of which take us to the middle or the end of his reign. We are therefore left to choose between one of two dates, namely, that of 590–587, during the Jewish war, and that from the King's thirty-seventh year to 568 B.C., during the war against Amasis which will be treated below. I have chosen the first, because of Nebuchadrezzar's long sojourn at Riblah, which gave him sufficient time for the engraving of the stelæ on Lebanon: the bas-reliefs of Wady Brissa could have been cut before the taking of Jerusalem, for no allusion to the war against the Jews is found in them. The enemy mentioned in the opening lines is perhaps Apries, whose fleet was scouring the Phœnician coasts.

[1] *Ezek.* xvii. 15.        [2] *Jer.* xxxvii. 5–10.

defeated; according to another, he refused to be drawn into an engagement, and returned haughtily to Egypt.[1] His fleet probably made some effective raiding on the Phœnician coast. It is easy to believe that the sight of the Chaldæan camp inspired him with prudence, and that he thought twice before compromising the effects of his naval campaign and risking the loss of his fine army—the only one which Egypt possessed—in a conflict in which his own safety was not directly concerned. Nebuchadrezzar, on his side, was not anxious to pursue so strongly equipped an adversary too hotly, and deeming himself fortunate in having escaped the ordeal of a trial of strength with him, he returned to his position before the walls of Jerusalem.

The city receiving no further succour, its fall was merely a question of time, and resistance served merely to irritate the besiegers. The Jews nevertheless continued to defend it with the heroic obstinacy and, at the same time, with the frenzied discord of which they have so often shown themselves capable. During the respite which the diversion caused by Apries afforded them, Jeremiah had attempted to flee from Jerusalem and seek refuge in Benjamin, to which tribe he belonged. Arrested at the city gate on the pretext of treason, he was unmercifully beaten, thrown into prison, and the king, who had begun to believe in him, did not venture to deliver

---

[1] That, at least, is what Jeremiah seems to say (xxxvii. 7): "Behold, Pharaoh's army, which is come forth to help you, shall return to Egypt into their own land." There is no hint here of defeat or even of a battle.

him He was confined in the court of the palace which served as a gaol and allowed a ration of a loaf of bread for his daily food [1] The courtyard was a public place to which all comers had access who desired to speak to the prisoners and even here the prophet did not cease to preach and exhort the people to repentance "He that abideth in this city shall die by the sword by the famine and by the pestilence but he that goeth forth

PRISONERS UNDER TORTURE HAVING THEIR TONGUES TORN OUT.[2]

to the Chaldæans shall live and his life shall be unto him for a prey and he shall live Thus saith the Lord This city shall surely be given into the hand of the army of the King of Babylon and he shall take it" The princes and officers of the king however complained to Zedekiah of him "Let this man we pray thee be put to death forasmuch as he weakeneth the hands of the men of war and the hands of all the people in

[1] *Jer.* xxxvii. 11-21.

Drawn by Boudier, from a photograph of the original in the British Museum

speaking such words." Given up to his accusers and plunged in a muddy cistern, he escaped by the connivance of a eunuch of the royal household, only to renew his denunciations with greater force than ever. The king sent for him secretly and asked his advice, but could draw from him nothing but threats: "If thou wilt go forth unto the King of Babylon's princes, then thy soul shall live, and this city shall not be burned with fire, and thou shalt live and thine house: but if thou wilt not go forth to the King of Babylon's princes, then shall this city be given into the hand of the Chaldæans, and they shall burn it with fire, and thou shalt not escape out of their hand."[2] Zedekiah would have asked no better than to follow his advice, but he had gone too far to draw back now. To the miseries of war and sickness

A KING PUTTING OUT THE EYES OF A PRISONER.[1]

[1] Drawn by Fancher-Gudin, from several engravings in Botta. The mutilated remains of several bas-reliefs have been combined so as to form a tolerably correct scene; the prisoners have a ring passed through their lips, and the king holds them by a cord attached to it.

[2] *Jer.* xxxviii.

the horrors of famine were added, but the determination of the besieged was unshaken; bread was failing, and yet they would not hear of surrender.[1] At length, after a year and a half of sufferings heroically borne, in the eleventh year of Zedekiah, the eleventh month, and the fourth day of the month, a portion of the city wall fell before the attacks of the battering-rams, and the Chaldæan army entered by the breach. Zedekiah assembled his remaining soldiers, and took counsel as to the possibility of cutting his way through the enemy to beyond the Jordan; escaping by night through the gateway opposite the Pool of Siloam, he was taken prisoner near Jericho, and carried off to Riblah, where Nebuchadrezzar was awaiting with impatience the result of the operations. The Chaldæans were accustomed to torture their prisoners in the fashion we frequently see represented on the monuments of Nineveh, and whenever an unexpected stroke of good fortune brings to light any decorative bas-relief from their palaces, we shall see represented on it the impaling stake, rebels being flayed alive, and chiefs having their tongues torn out. Nebuchadrezzar, whose patience was exhausted, caused the sons of Zedekiah to be slain in the presence of their father, together with all the prisoners of noble birth, and then, having put out his eyes, sent the king of Babylon loaded with chains. As for the city which had so long defied his wrath, he gave it over to Nebuzaradan, one of the great officers of the crown, with orders to demolish it and give it up systematically to the flames. The temple was

[1] *Jer.* xxxviii. 2, 9, 24–27, and 2 *Kings* xxv. 3.

despoiled of its precious wall-coverings, the pillars and brazen ornaments of the time of Solomon which still remained were broken up, and the pieces carried off to Chaldæa in sacks, the masonry was overthrown and the blocks of stone rolled down the hill into the ravine of the Kedron. The survivors among the garrison, the priests, scribes, and members of the upper classes, were sent off into exile, but the mortality during the siege had been so great that the convoy barely numbered eight hundred and thirty-two persons. Some of the poorer population were allowed to remain in the environs, and the fields and vineyards of the exiles were divided among them.[1] Having accomplished the work of destruction, the Chaldæans retired, leaving the government in the hands of Gedaliah, son of Ahikam,[2] a friend of Jeremiah. Gedaliah established himself at Mizpah, where he endeavoured to gather around him the remnant of the nation, and fugitives poured in from Moab, Ammon, and Edom. It seemed

[1] 2 *Kings* xxv. 4–21, in *Jer.* lii. 6–27, 29; cf. *Jer.* xxxix. 2–10, and 2 *Chron.* xxxvi. 17–20. The following is the table of the kings of Judah from the death of Solomon to the destruction of Jerusalem:—

| | | |
|---|---|---|
| I. Rehoboam. | VIII. Joash. | XV. Amon. |
| II. Abijah. | IX. Amaziah. | XVI. Josiah. |
| III. Asa. | X. Uzziah (Azariah). | XVII. Jehoahaz. |
| IV. Jehoshaphat. | XI. Jotham. | XVIII. Jehoiakim. |
| V. Jehoram. | XII. Ahaz. | XIX. Jehoiachin. |
| VI. Ahaziah. | XIII. Hezekiah. | XX. Zedekiah. |
| VII. Athaliah. | XIV. Manasseh. | |

[2] 2 *Kings* xxv. 22; *Jer.* xl. 5–7.

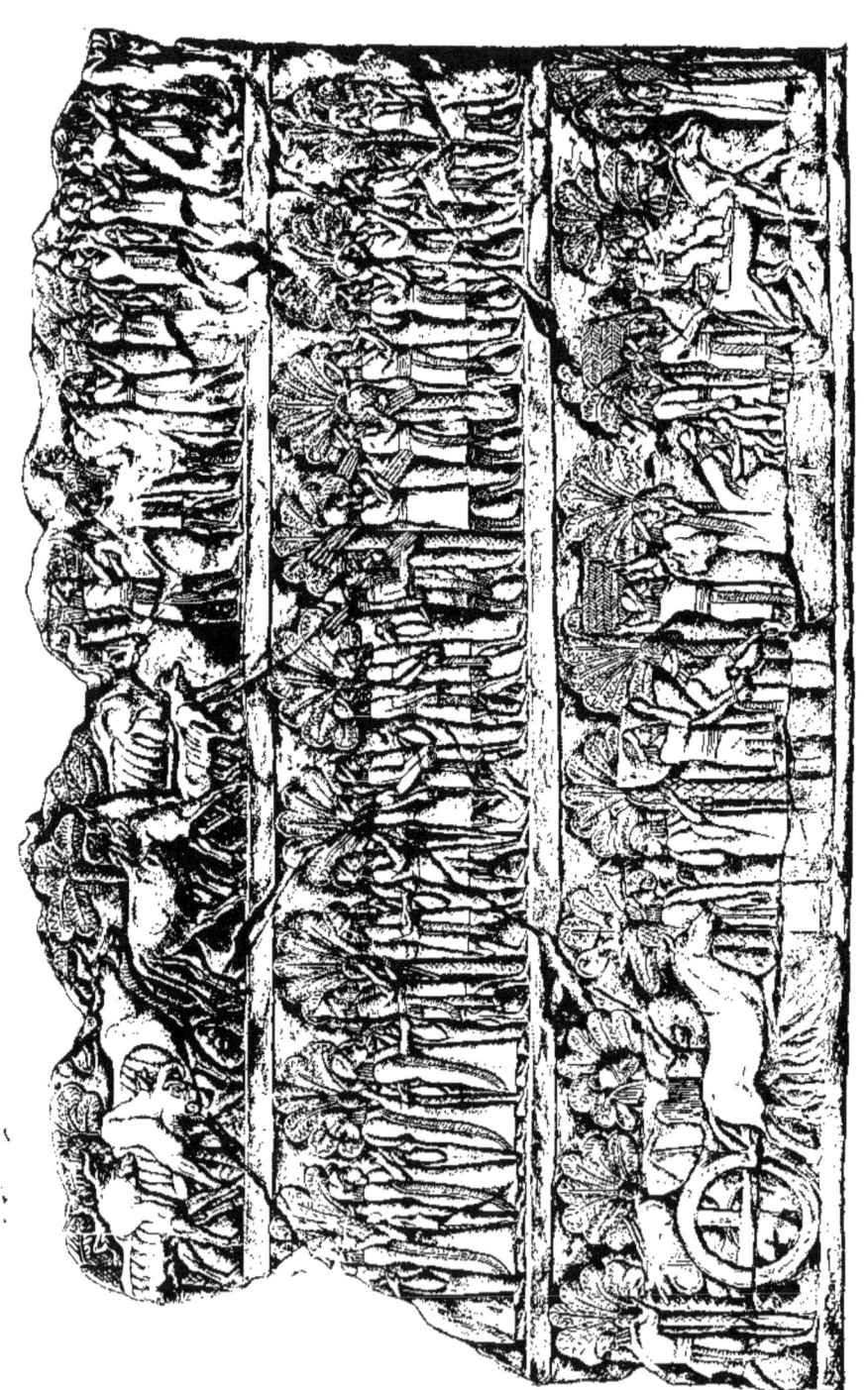

A PEOPLE CARRIED AWAY INTO CAPTIVITY WITH THEIR HOUSEHOLD GOODS AND CATTLE.

Drawn by Faucher-Gudin, from LAYARD, *The Monuments of Nineveh*, vol. ii. pl. 35.

that a Jewish principality was about to rise again from the ruins of the kingdom. Jeremiah was its accredited counsellor, but his influence could not establish harmony among these turbulent spirits, still smarting from their recent misfortunes.[1] The captains of the bands which had been roaming over the country after the fall of Jerusalem refused, moreover, to act in concert with Gedaliah, and one of them, Ishmael by name, who was of the royal blood, assassinated him, but, being attacked in Gibeon by Johanan, the son of Kareah, was forced to escape almost alone and take refuge with the Ammonites.[2] These acts of violence aroused the vigilance of the Chaldæans; Johanan feared reprisals, and retired into Egypt, taking with him Jeremiah, Baruch, and the bulk of the people.[3] Apries gave the refugees a welcome, and assigned them certain villages near to his military colony at Daphnæ, whence they soon spread into the neighbouring nomes as far as Migdol, Memphis, and even as far as the Thebaid.[4] Even after all these catastrophes Judah's woes were not yet at an end. In 581, the few remaining Jews in Palestine allied themselves with the Moabites and made a last wild effort for independence; a final defeat, followed by a final exile, brought them to

[1] For the manner in which Jeremiah was separated from the rest of the captives, set at liberty and sent back to Gedaliah, see *Jer.* xxxix. 11-18, xl. 1-6.

[2] 2 *Kings* xxv. 23-25, and *Jer.* xl. 7-16, xli. 1-15, where these events are recorded at length.

[3] 2 *Kings* xxv. 26; *Jer.* xli. 16-18, xlii., xliii. 1-7.

[4] *Jer.* xliv. 1, where the word of the Lord is spoken to "all the Jews . . . which dwelt at Migdol, and at Tahpanhes (Daphnæ), and at Noph (corr. *Moph*, Memphis), and in the country of Pathros."

irretrievable ruin.[1] The earlier captives had entertained no hope of advantage from these despairing efforts, and Ezekiel from afar condemned them without pity: "They that inherit those waste places in the land of Israel speak, saying, Abraham was one, and he inherited the land: but we are many; the land is given us for inheritance. . . . Ye lift up your eyes unto your idols and shed blood: and shall ye possess the land? Ye stand upon your sword, ye work abomination, and ye defile every one his neighbour's wife: and shall ye possess the land? . . . Thus saith the Lord God: As I live, surely they that are in the waste places shall fall by the sword, and him that is in the open field will I give to the beasts to be devoured, and they that be in the strongholds and in the caves shall die of the pestilence."[2] The first act of the revolution foreseen by the prophets was over; the day of the Lord, so persistently announced by them, had at length come, and it had seen not only the sack of Jerusalem, but the destruction of the earthly kingdom of Judah. Many of the survivors, refusing still to acknowledge the justice of the chastisement, persisted in throwing the blame of the disaster on the reformers of the old worship, and saw no hope of salvation except in their idolatrous practices. "As

[1] Josephus, following Berosus, speaks of a war against the Moabites and the Ammonites, followed by the conquest of Egypt in the twenty-third year of Nebuchadrezzar. To this must be added a Jewish revolt if we are to connect with these events the mention of the third captivity, carried out in the twenty-third year of Nebuchadrezzar by Nebuzaradan (*Jer.* lii. 30).

[2] *Ezek.* xxxiii. 23–27.

for the word that thou hast spoken unto us in the name of the Lord, we will not hearken unto thee. But we will certainly perform every word that is gone forth out of our mouth, to burn incense unto the queen of heaven, and to pour out drink offerings unto her, as we have done, we and our fathers, our kings and our princes, in the cities of Judah and in the streets of Jerusalem: for then had we plenty of victuals, and were well and saw no evil. But since we left off to burn incense to the queen of heaven and to pour out drink offerings unto her, we have wanted all things, and have been consumed by the sword and by the famine."[1]

There still remained to these misguided Jews one consolation which they shared in common with the prophets—the certainty of seeing the hereditary foes of Israel involved in the common overthrow: Ammon had been already severely chastised; Tyre, cut off from the neighbouring mainland, seemed on the point of succumbing, and the turn of Egypt must surely soon arrive in which she would have to expiate in bitter sufferings the wrongs her evil counsels had brought upon Jerusalem. Their anticipated joy, however, of witnessing such chastisements was not realised. Tyre defied for thirteen years the blockade of Nebuchadrezzar, and when the city at length decided to capitulate, it was on condition that its king, Ethbaal III., should continue to reign under the almost nominal suzerainty of the Chaldæans (574 B.C.).[2] Egypt

---

[1] *Jer.* xliv. 16–18.

[2] The majority of Christian writers have imagined, contrary to the testimony of the Phœnician annals, that the island of Tyre was taken

436 THE MEDES AND THE SECOND CHALDÆAN EMPIRE

continued not only to preserve her independence, but seemed to increase in prosperity in proportion to the intensity of the hatred which she had stirred up against her. Apries set about repairing the monuments and embellishing the temples : he erected throughout the country stelæ, tables of offerings, statues and obelisks, some of which, though of small size, like that which adorns the Piazza della Minerva at Rome,* erected incongruously on the back of modern elephant, are unequalled for purity of form and delicacy of cutting. The high pitch artistic excellence to which the schools of the reign of Psammetichus II. had attained was maintained at the same exalted level. If the granite sphinxes[1] and bronze lions of this period lack somewhat in grace of form, it must be acknowledged that they display greater refinement and elegance in the

BRONZE LION OF BOHBAÎT.[2]

by Nebuchadrezzar; they say that the Chaldæans united the island to the mainland by a causeway similar to that constructed subsequently by Alexander. It is worthy of notice that a local tradition, still existi g in the eleventh century of our era, asserted that the besiegers were not successful in their enterprise.

* [One of the two obelisks of the Campus Martius, on which site the Church of S. Maria Sopra Minerva was built.—Tr.]

[1] Above the summary of the contents of the present chapter, will be found one of these sphinxes which was discovered in Rome.

[2] Drawn by Faucher-Gudin, from an engraving in Mariette.

technique of carving or moulding than had yet been attained. While engaged in these works at home, Apries was not unobservant of the revolutions occurring in Asia, upon which he maintained a constant watch, and in the years which followed the capitulation of Tyre, he found the opportunity, so long looked for, of entering once more upon the scene. The Phœnician navy had suffered much during the lengthy blockade of their country, and had become inferior to the Egyptian, now well organised by the Ionians: Apries therefore took the offensive by sea, and made a direct descent on the Phœnician coasts. Nebuchadrezzar opposed him with the forces of the recently

THE SMALL OBELISK IN THE PIAZZA DELLA MINERVA AT ROME.[1]

[1] Drawn by Boudier, from a photograph.

subjugated Tyrians, and the latter, having cooled in their attachment to Egypt owing to the special favour shown by the Pharaoh to their rivals the Hellenes, summoned their Cypriote vassals to assist them in repelling the attack. The Egyptians dispersed the combined fleets, and taking possession of Sidon, gave it up to pillage. The other maritime cities surrendered of their own accord,[1] including Gebal, which received an Egyptian garrison, and where the officers of Pharaoh founded a temple to the goddess whom they identified with the Egyptian Hâthor. The object at which Necho and Psammetichus II. had aimed for fifteen years was thus attained by Apries at one fortunate blow, and he could legitimately entitle himself "more fortunate than all the kings his predecessors," and imagine, in his pride, that "the gods themselves were unable to injure him." The gods, however, did not allow him long to enjoy the fruits of his victory. Greeks had often visited Libya since the time when Egypt had been thrown open to the trade of the Ægean. Their sailors had discovered that the most convenient course thither was to sail straight to Crete, and then to traverse the sea between this island and the headlands of the Libyan plateau; here they fell in with a strong current setting towards the east, which carried them quickly and easily as far as Rakotis and Canopus, along the Marmarican shore. In these voyages they learned to appreciate the value of the

[1] The war of Apries against the Phœnicians cannot have taken place before the capitulation of Tyre in 574 B.C., because the Tyrians took part in it by order of Nebuchadrezzar, and on the other hand it cannot be put later than 569 B.C., the date of the revolt of Amasis; it must therefore be assigned to about 571 B.C.

country; and about 631 B.C. some Dorians of Thera, who had set out to seek for a new home at the bidding of the Delphic oracle, landed in the small desert island of Platæa, where they built a strongly fortified settlement. Their leader, Battos,[1] soon crossed over to the mainland, where, having reached the high plateau, he built the city of Cyrene on the borders of an extremely fertile region, watered by abundant springs. The tribes of the Labu, who had fought so valiantly against the Pharaohs of old, still formed a kind of loose confederation, and their territory stretched across the deserts from the Egyptian frontier to the shores of the Syrtes. The chief of this confederation assumed the title of king, as in the days of Mînephtah or of Ramses III.[2] The most civilised of these tribes were those which now dwelt nearest to the coast: first the Adyrmakhides, who were settled beyond Marea, and had been semi-Egyptianised by constant intercourse with the inhabitants of the Delta; then the Giligammes, who dwelt between the port of Plynus and the island of Aphrodisias; and beyond these, again, the Asbystes, famed for their skill in chariot-driving, the Cabales, and the Auschises. The oases of the hinterland were in the hands of the Nasamones and of the Mashauasha, whom the Greeks called Maxyes.

[1] Herodotus seems to have been ignorant of the real name of the founder of Cyrene, which has been preserved for us by Pindar, by Callimachus, by the spurious Heraclides of Pontus, and by the chronologists of the Christian epoch. Herodotus says that *Battos* signifies *king* in the language of Libya.

[2] The description given by Herodotus of these Libyan tribes agrees with the slight amount of information furnished by the Egyptian monuments for the thirteenth century B.C.

One of the revolutions so frequent among the desert tribes had compelled the latter to remove from their home near the Nile valley, to a district far to the west, on the banks of the river Triton. There they had settled down in a permanent fashion, dwelling in houses of stone, and giving themselves up to the cultivation of the soil. They continued, however, to preserve in their new life some of their ancient customs, such as that of painting their bodies

THE OASIS OF AMON AND THE SPRING OF THE SUN.[1]

with vermilion, and of shaving off the hair from their heads, with the exception of one lock which hung over the right ear. The Theban Pharaohs had formerly placed garrisons in the most important oases, and had consecrated temples there to their god Amon. One of these sanctuaries, built close to an intermittent spring, which gave forth alter nately hot and cold water, had risen to great eminence and the oracle of these Ammonians was a centre of pilgrimage from far and near. The first Libyans who came into contact with the Greeks, the Asbystes and the Giligammes, received the new-comers kindly, giving them

[1] Drawn by Boudier, from Minutoli.

A PORTION OF THE RUINS OF CYRENE, THE NECROPOLIS.
Drawn by Boudier, from PACHO, *Voyage dans la Marmarique.*

their daughters in marriage; from the fusion of the two races thus brought about sprang, first under Battos and then under his son Arkesilas I., an industrious and valiant race. The main part of their revenues was derived from commerce in silphium and woollen goods, and even the kings themselves did not deem it beneath their dignity to preside in person at the weighing of the crop, and the storing of the trusses in their magazines. The rapid increase in the wealth of 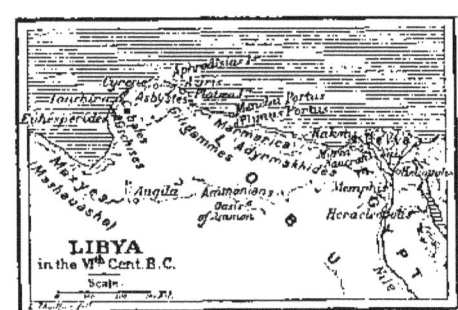 the city having shortly brought about a breach in the friendly relations hitherto maintained between it and its neighbours, Battos the Fortunate, the son of Arkesilas I., sent for colonists from Greece: numbers answered to his call, on the faith of a second oracular prediction, and in order to provide them with the necessary land, Battos did not hesitate to dispossess his native allies. The latter appealed to Adikrân, king of the confederacy, and this prince, persuaded that this irregular militia would not be able to withstand the charge of the hoplites, thereupon applied in his turn to Apries for assistance.

THE SILPHIUM PLANT.[1]

There was much tempting spoil to be had in Cyrene, and Apries was fully aware of the fact, from the accounts of the Libyans and the Greeks. His covetousness must

[1] Drawn by Faucher-Gudin, from the cast of a coin of Cyrene.

444 THE MEDES AND THE SECOND CHALDÆAN EMPIRE

have been aroused at the prospect of such rich booty and perhaps he would have thought of appropriating it sooner had he not been deterred from the attempt by his know ledge of the superiority of the Greek fleets and of the

WEIGHING SILPHIUM IN PRESENCE OF KING ARKESILAS.[1]

dangers attendant on a long and painful march over an almost desert country through disaffected tribes Now that he could rely on the support of the Libyans he hesitated no longer to run these risks Deeming it

[1] Drawn by Faucher-Gudin from a photograph of the original in the oin Room in the Bibliothèque Nationale at Paris The king here represented is Arkesilas II. the Bad.

imprudent, with good reason, to employ his mercenary troops against their own compatriots, Apries mobilised for his encounter with Battos an army exclusively recruited from among his native reserves. The troops set out full of confidence in themselves and of disdain for the enemy, delighted moreover at an opportunity for at length convincing their kings of their error in preferring barbarian to native forces. But the engagement brought to nought all their boastings. The Egyptians were defeated in the first encounter near Irasa, hard by the fountain of Thestê, near the spot where the high plateaus of Cyrene proper terminate in the low cliffs of Marmarica: and the troops suffered so severely during the subsequent retreat that only a small remnant of the army regained in safety the frontier of the Delta.[1] This unexpected reverse was the occasion of the outbreak of a revolution which had been in preparation for years. The emigration to Ethiopia of some contingents of the military class had temporarily weakened the factions hostile to foreign influence; these factions had felt themselves powerless under the rule of Psammetichus I., and had bowed to his will, prepared all the while to reassert themselves when they felt strong enough to do so successfully. The reorganisation of the native army furnished them at once with the means of insurrection, of which they had temporarily been deprived. Although

[1] The interpretation I have given to the sentiments of the Egyptian army follows clearly enough from the observation of Herodotus, that "the Egyptians, having never experienced themselves the power of the Greeks, had felt for them nothing but contempt." The site of Irasa and the fountain of Thestê has been fixed with much probability in the fertile district watered still by the fountain of Ersen, Erazem, or Erasân.

Pharaoh had lavished privileges on the Hermotybies and Calasiries, she had not removed the causes for discontent which had little by little alienated the good will of the Mashauasha: to do so would have rendered necessary the disbanding of the Ionian guard, the object of their jealousy and to take this step neither he nor his successors could submit themselves. The hatred of these mercenaries, and the irritation against the sovereigns who employed them grew fiercer from reign to reign, and now wanted nothing but a pretext to break forth openly : such a pretext was furnished by the defeat at Irasa. When the fugitives arrived at the entrenched camp of Marea, exasperated by their defeat, and alleging doubtless that it was due to treachery, they found others who affected to share their belief that Pharaoh had despatched his Egyptian troops against Cyrene with the view of consigning to certain death those whose loyalty to him was suspected, and it was not difficult to stir up the disaffected soldiers to open revolt. It was not the first time that a military tumul had threatened the sovereignty of Apries. Some time previous to this, in an opposite quarter of the Nile valley the troops stationed at Elephantinê, composed partly of Egyptians, partly of Asiatic and Greek mercenaries— possibly the same who had fought in the Ethiopian campaign under Psammetichus II.—had risen in rebellion owing to some neglect in the payment of their wages having devastated the Thebaid, they had marched straight across the desert to the port of Shashirît, in the hope of there seizing ships to enable them to reach the havens of Idumæa or Nabatæa. The governor of Elephantinê,

Nsihor, had at first held them back with specious promises; but on learning that Apries was approaching with reinforcements, he attacked them boldly, and driving them before him, hemmed them in between his own force and that of the king and massacred them all. Apries thought that the revolt at Marea would have a similar issue, and that he might succeed in baffling the rebels by fair words; he sent to them as his representative Amasis, one of his generals, distantly connected probably with the royal house. What took place in the camp is not clearly known, for the actual events have been transformed in the course of popular transmission into romantic legends. The story soon took shape that Amasis was born of humble parentage in the village of Siuph, not far from Sais; he was fond, it was narrated, of wine, the pleasures of the table, and women, and replenished his empty purse by stealing what he could lay his hands on from his neighbours or comrades—a gay boon-companion all the while, with an easy disposition and sarcastic tongue. According to some accounts, he conciliated the favour of Apries by his invariable affability and good humour; according to others, he won the king's confidence by presenting him with a crown of flowers on his birthday.[1] The story goes on to say that while he was haranguing the rebels, one of them, slipping behind him, suddenly placed on his head the rounded helmet of the Pharaohs: the bystanders immediately proclaimed him

---

[1] The king to whom Amasis made this offering is called Patarmis, and the similarity of this name with the Patarbemis of Herodotus seems to indicate a variant of the legend in which Patarmis or Patarbemis took the place of Apries.

king, and after a slight show of resistance he accepted the dignity. As soon as the rumour of these events had reached Sais, Apries despatched Patarbemis, one of his chief officers, with orders to bring back the rebel chief alive. The latter was seated on his horse, on the point of breaking up his camp and marching against his former patron, when the envoy arrived. On learning the nature of his mission, Amasis charged him to carry back a reply to the effect that he had already been making preparation to submit, and besought the sovereign to grant him patiently a few days longer, so that he might bring with him the Egyptian subjects of Pharaoh. Tradition adds that, on receiving this insolent defiance, Apries fell into a violent passion, and without listening to remonstrance ordered the nose and ears of Patarbemis to be cut off, whereupon the indignant people, it is alleged, deserted his cause and ranged themselves on the side of Amasis. The mercenaries, however, did not betray the confidence reposed in them by their Egyptian lords. Although only thirty thousand against a whole people, they unflinchingly awaited the attack at Momemphis (569 B.C.); but, being overwhelmed by the numbers of their assailants, disbanded and fled, after a conflict lasting one day. Apries, taken prisoner in the rout, was at first well treated by the conqueror, and seems even to have retained for a time the external pomp of royalty; but the populace of Sais demanding his execution with vehemence, Amasis was at length constrained to deliver him up to their vengeance and Apries was strangled by the mob. He was honourably interred between the royal palace and the temple of Nît, not far from the spot where his predecessors reposed in their glory,[1] and the usurper made himself sole master of the country. It was equivalent to a change of dynasty, and Amasis had recourse to the methods usual in such cases to consolidate his power. He entered into a marriage alliance with princesses of the Saite line, and thus legitimatised his usurpation as far as the north was concerned.[2] In the south, the "divine worshippers" had continued to administer the extensive heritage of Amon, and Nitocris, heiress of Shapenuapît, had adopted in her old age a daughter of her great-nephew, Psammetichus II., named Ankhnasnofiribrî: this princess was at this time in possession of Thebes, and Amasis appears to have entered into a fictitious marriage with her in order to assume to himself her rights to the crown. He had hardly succeeded in establishing his authority on a firm basis when he was called upon to repel the Chaldæan invasion. The Hebrew prophets had been threatening Egypt with this invasion for a long time, and Ezekiel, discounting the future, had already described the entrance of Pharaoh into Hades, to dwell among the chiefs of the nations—Assur, Elam, Meshech, Tubal, Edom, and Philistia—who, having incurred the vengeance of Jahveh, had descended into the grave one after the other: "Pharaoh and all his army shall be slain by the sword, saith the Lord God! For I have put this terror in the land of the living: and

---

[1] It was probably from this necropolis that the coffin of **Psammetichus** II. came.

[2] The wife of Amasis, who mother of **Psammetichus** III., **the** queen **Tintkhîti,** daughter of **Petenît,** prophet of Phtah, was probably connected with the royal family of Sais.

he shall be laid in the midst of the uncircumcised, with them that are slain by the sword, even Pharaoh and all his multitude, saith the Lord God!"[1] Nebuchadrezzar had some hesitation in hazarding his fortune in a campaign on the banks of the Nile: he realised tolerably clearly that Babylon was not in command of such resources as had been at the disposal of Nineveh under Esarhaddon or Assur-bani-pal, and that Egypt in the hands of a Saite dynasty was a more formidable foe than when ruled by the Ethiopians. The report of the revolution of which Apries had become a victim at length determined him to act; the annihilation of the Hellenic troops, and the dismay which the defeat at Irasa had occasioned in the hearts of the Egyptians, seemed to offer an opportunity too favourable to be neglected. The campaign was opened by Nebuchadrezzar about 568, in the thirty-seventh year of his reign,[2] but we have no certain information as to the issue of his enterprise. According to Chaldæan tradition, Nebuchadrezzar actually invaded the valley of the Nile and converted Egypt into a Babylonian province,

---

[1] *Ezek.* xxxii. 31, 32.

[2] A fragment of his *Annals*, discovered by Pinches, mentions in the thirty-seventh year of his reign a campaign against [Ah]masu, King of Egypt; and Wiedemann, from the evidence of this document combined with the information derived from one of the monuments in the Louvre, thought that the fact of a conquest of Egypt as far as Syenê might be admitted; at that point the Egyptian general Nsihor would have defeated the Chaldæans and repelled the invasion, and this event would have taken place during the joint reign of Apries and Amasis. A more attentive examination of the Egyptian monument shows that it refers not to a Chaldæan war, but to a rebellion of the garrisons in the south of Egypt, including the Greek and Semitic auxiliaries.

with Amasis as its satrap.[1] We may well believe that Amasis lost the conquests won by his predecessor in Phœnicia, if, indeed, they still belonged to Egypt at his accession: but there is nothing to indicate that the Chaldæans ever entered Egypt itself and repeated the Assyrian exploit of a century before.

This was Nebuchadrezzar's last war, the last at least of which history makes any mention. As a fact, the kings of the second Babylonian empire do not seem to have been the impetuous conquerors which we have fancied them to be. We see them as they are depicted to us in the visions of the Hebrew prophets, who, regarding them and their nation as a scourge in the hands of God, had no colours vivid enough or images sufficiently terrible to portray them. They had blotted out Nineveh from the list of cities, humiliated Pharaoh, and subjugated Syria, and they had done all this almost at their first appearance in the field—such a feat as Assyria and Egypt in the plenitude of their strength had been unable to accomplish: they had, moreover, destroyed Jerusalem and carried Judah into captivity. There is nothing astonishing in the fact that this Nebuchadrezzar, whose history is known to us almost entirely from Jewish sources, should appear as a fated force let loose upon the world. " O thou sword of the Lord, how long will it be ere thou be quiet? put up thyself into the scabbard; rest and be still! How canst thou be quiet, seeing the Lord

---

[1] These events would have taken place in the twenty-third year of Nebuchadrezzar; the reigning king **(Apries)** being killed and his place taken by one of his generals **(Amasis),** who remained a satrap of the Babylonian empire.

hath given thee a charge?"[1] But his campaigns in Syria and Africa, of which the echoes transmitted to us still seem so formidable, were not nearly so terrible in reality as those in which Elam had perished a century previously; they were, moreover, the only conflicts which troubled the peace of his reign. The Arabian chroniclers affirm, indeed, that the fabulous wealth of Yemen had incited him to invade that region. Nebuchadrezzar, they relate, routed, not far from the town of Dhât-îrk, the Joctanides of Jorhom, who had barred his road to the Kaabah, and after seizing Mecca reached the borders of the children of Himyrâ: the exhausted condition of his soldiers having prevented him from pressing further forward in his career of conquest, he retraced his steps and returned to Babylon with a great number of prisoners, including two entire tribes, those Hadhurâ and Uabar, whom he established as colonists in Chaldæa.[2] He never passed in this direction beyond the limits reached by Assur-bani-pal, and his exploits were restricted to some successful raids against the tribes Kedar and Nabatæa.[3] The same reasons which at the commencement of his reign had restrained his ambition to extend his dominions towards the east and north, were operative up to the end of his life. Astyages had not inherited the martial spirit of his father Cyaxares, and only

[1] *Jer.* xlvii. 6, 7.

[2] Most of the Arabic legends relating to these conquests of Nebuchadrezzar are indirectly derived from the biblical story; but it is possible that the history of the expeditions against Central Arabia is founded on fact.

[3] This seems to follow from Jeremiah's imprecations upon Keda (*Jer.* xlix. 28–33).

one warlike expedition, that against the Cadusians, is ascribed to him.[1] Naturally indolent, lacking in decision, superstitious and cruel, he passed a life of idleness amid the luxury of a corrupt court, surrounded by pages, women, and eunuchs, with no more serious pastime than the chase, pursued within the limits of his own parks or on the confines of the desert. But if the king was weak, his empire was vigorous, and Nebuchadrezzar, brought up from his youth to dread the armies of Media, retained his respect for them up to the end of his life, even when there was no longer any occasion to do so. Nebuchadrezzar was, after all, not so much a warrior as a man of peace, whether so constituted by nature or rendered so by political necessity in its proper sense, and he took advantage of the long intervals of quiet between his campaigns to complete the extensive works which more than anything else have won for him his renown. During the century which had preceded the fall of Nineveh, Babylonia had had several bitter experiences; it had suffered almost entire destruction at the hands of Sennacherib; it had been given up to pillage by Assur-bani-pal, not to mention the sieges and ravages it had sustained in the course of continual revolts. The other cities of Babylonia, Sippara, Borsippa, Kutha, Nipur, Uruk, and Uru, had been subjected to capture and recapture, while the surrounding districts, abandoned in turn to Elamites, Assyrians, and the Kaldâ, had lain uncultivated for many years. The canals at the same time had become choked with mud, the banks had fallen in, and the

---

[1] Moses of Chorene attributes to him long wars against an Armenian king named Tigranes; but this is a fiction of a later age.

waters, no longer kept under control, had overflowed the land, and the plains long since reclaimed for cultivation had returned to their original condition of morasses and reed beds; at Babylon itself the Arakhtu, still encumbered with the *débris* cast into it by Sennacherib, was no longer navigable, and was productive of more injury than profit to the city: in some parts the aspect of the country must have been desolate and neglected as at the present day, and the work accomplished by twenty generations had to be begun entirely afresh. Nabopolassar had already applied himself to the task in spite of the anxieties of his Assyrian campaigns, and had raised many earthworks in both the capital and the provinces. But a great deal more still remained to be done, and Nebuchadrezzar pushed forward the work planned by his father, and carried it to completion undeterred and undismayed by any difficulties.[1] The combined system of irrigation and navigation introduced by the kings of the first Babylonian empire twenty centuries previously, was ingeniously repaired; the beds of the principal canals, the Royal river and the Arakhtu, were straightened and deepened; the drainage of the country between the Tigris and the Euphrates was regulated by means subsidiary canals and a network of dykes; the canals surrounding Babylon or intersecting in the middle of the city were cleaned out, and a waterway was secured for navigation from one river to the other, and from the plateau Mesopotamia to the Nar-Marratum.[2] We may well believe

[1] The only long inscriptions of Nebuchadrezzar which we possess, are those commemorating the great works he designed and executed.

[2] The irrigation works of Nebuchadrezzar are described at leng

that all Nebuchadrezzar's undertakings were carried out in accordance with a carefully prepared scheme for perfecting the defences of the kingdom while completing the system of internal communication. The riches of Karduniash, now restored to vigour by continued peace, and become the centre of a considerable empire, could not fail to excite the jealousy of its neighbours, and particularly that of the most powerful among them, the Medes of Ecbatana. It is true that the relations between Nebuchadrezzar and Astyages continued to be cordial, and as yet there were no indications of a rupture; but it was always possible that under their successors the good understanding between the two courts might come to an end, and it was needful to provide against the possibility of the barbarous tribes of Iran being let loose upon Babylon, and attempting to inflict on her the fate they had brought upon Nineveh. Nebuchadrezzar, therefore, was anxious to interpose, between himself and these possible foes, such a series of fortifications that the most persevering enemy would be worn out by the prolonged task of forcing them one after another, provided that they were efficiently garrisoned. He erected across the northern side of the isthmus between the two rivers a great embankment, faced with bricks cemented together with bitumen, called the *Wall of Media;* this wall, starting from Sippara, stretched from the confluence of the Saklauiyeh with the Euphrates to the site of the modern village of Jibbara on

and perhaps exaggerated, by Abydenus, who merely quotes Berosus more or less inaccurately. The completion of the quays along the Arakhtu, begun by Nabopolassar, is noticed in the *East India Company's Inscription.* A special inscription, publ. by H. Rawlinson, gives an account of the repairing of the canal Libil-khigallu, which crossed Babylon.

the Tigris; on both sides of it four or five deep trenches were excavated, which were passable on raised causeways or by bridges of boats, so arranged as to be easily broken up in case of invasion. The eastern frontier was furnished with a rampart protected by a wide moat, following, between Jibbara and Nipur, the contours of a low-lying district which could be readily flooded. The western

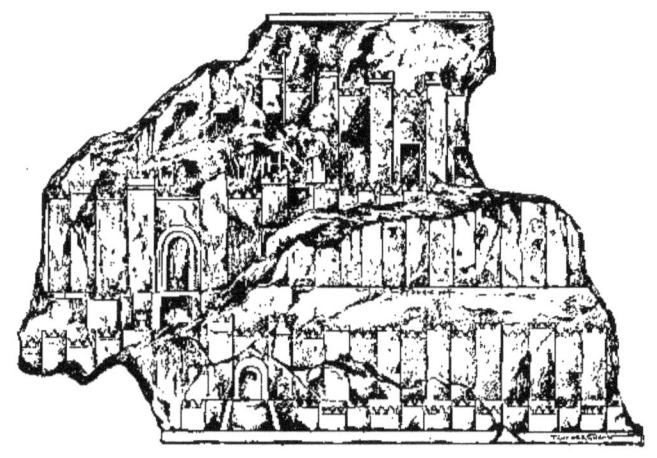

CITY DEFENDED BY A TRIPLE WALL.[1]

boundary was already protected by the Pallakottas, and the lakes or marshes of Bahr-î-Nejîf: Nebuchadrezzar multiplied the number of the dikes, and so arranged them that the whole country between the suburbs of Borsippa and Babylon could be inundated at will. Babylon itself formed as it were the citadel in the midst of these enormous outlying fortifications, and the engineers both of Nabopolassar and of his son expended all the resources of their

[1] Drawn by Faucher-Gudin, from a bas-relief of the time of Sargon in the Museum of the Louvre.

art on rendering it impregnable. A triple rampart surrounded it and united it to Borsippa, built on the model of those whose outline is so frequently found on the lowest tier of an Assyrian bas-relief. A moat of great width, with banks of masonry, communicating with the Euphrates, washed the foot of the outer wall, which retained the traditional name of Imgur-bel: behind this wall rose Nimitti-bel, the true city wall, to a height of more than ninety feet above the level of the plain, appearing from

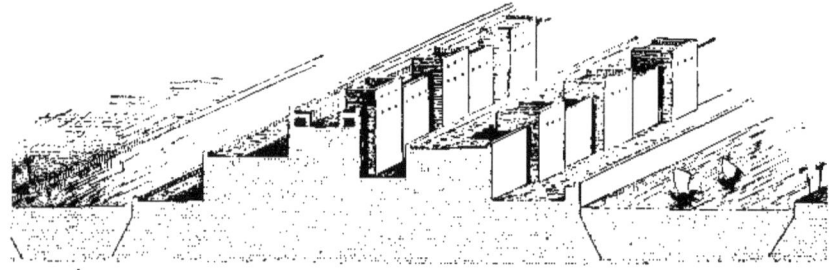

PROBABLE SECTION OF THE TRIPLE WALL OF BABYLON.[1]

a distance, with its battlements and towers, more like a mountain chain than a rampart built by the hand of man; finally, behind Nimitti-bel ran a platform on the same level as the curtain of Imgur-bel, forming a last barrier behind which the garrison could rally before finally owning itself defeated and surrendering the city. Large square towers rose at intervals along the face of the walls, to the height of some eighteen feet above the battlements: a hundred gates fitted with bronze-plated doors, which could be securely shut at need, gave access to the city.[2]

[1] Reproduced by Faucher-Gudin, from the restoration by Dieulafoy.
[2] The description of the fortifications of the city is furnished by Herodotus, who himself saw them still partially standing; the account

458 THE MEDES AND THE SECOND CHALDÆAN EMPIRE

The space within the walls was by no means completely covered by houses, but contained gardens, farms, fields, and, here and there, the ruins of deserted buildings. As in older Babylon, the city proper clustered round the temple of Merodach, with its narrow winding streets, its crowded bazaars, its noisy and dirty squares, its hostelries and warehouses of foreign merchandise. The pyramid of Esarhaddon and Assur-bani-pal, too hastily built, had fallen into ruins: Nebuchadrezzar reconstructed its seven stages, and erected on the topmost platform a shrine furnished with a table of massive gold, and a couch on which the priestess chosen to be the spouse of the god might sleep at night. Other small temples were erected here and there on both banks of the river, and the royal palace, built in the marvellously short space of fifteen days, was celebrated for its hanging gardens, where the ladies of the harem might walk unveiled, secure from vulgar observation. No trace of all these extensive works

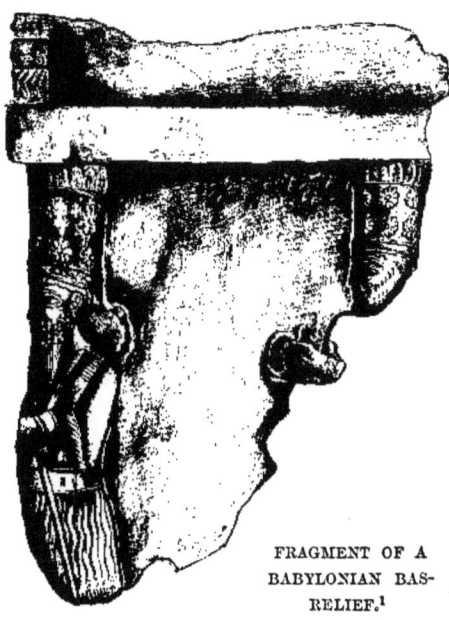

FRAGMENT OF A BABYLONIAN BAS-RELIEF.[1]

of their construction has been given by Nebuchadrezzar himself, in the *East India Company's Inscription.*

[1] Drawn by Faucher-Gudin, from a sketch in Layard.

remains at the present day. Some scattered fragments of crumbling walls alone betray the site of the great ziggurât, a few bas-reliefs are strewn over the surface of the ground, and a lion of timeworn stone, lying on its back in a depression of the soil, is perhaps the last survivor of those

RUINS OF THE ZIGGURÂT OF THE TEMPLE OF BEL.[1]

which kept watch, according to custom, at the gates of the palace. But the whole of this vast work of reconstruction and ornamentation must not be attributed to Nebuchadrezzar alone. The plans had been designed by Nabopolassar under the influence of one of his wives, who by a strange chance bears in classic tradition the very Egyptian name of Nitocris; but his work was insignificant

[1] Drawn by Faucher-Gudin, from a sketch in Layard.

compared with that accomplished by his son, and the name of Nebuchadrezzar was justly connected with the marvels of Babylon by all ancient writers. But even his reign of fifty-five years did not suffice for the completion of all his undertakings, and many details still remained imperfect at his death in the beginning of 562 B.C. Though of Kaldu origin, and consequently exposed to the suspicions and secret enmity of the native Babylonians, as all of his race, even Merodach - Baladan himself, had been before him, he had yet succeeded throughout the whole of his reign in making himself respected by the turbulent inhabitants of his capital, and in curbing the ambitious pretensions of the priests of Merodach. As soon as his master-hand was withdrawn, the passions so long repressed broke forth, and proved utterly beyond the control of his less able or less fortunate successors.[2] As far as we are able

THE STONE LION OF BABYLON.[1]

[1] Drawn by Faucher-Gudin, from a photograph furnished by Fathe Scheil.
[2] The sequel of this history is known from the narrative of Berosus. Its authenticity is proved by passages on the *Cylinder of Nabonidus*. Messe schmidt considers that Amil-marduk and Labashi-marduk were overthrown by the priestly faction, but a passage on the *Cylinder,* in which Nabonidus

to judge by the documents which have come down to us, two factions had arisen in the city since the fall of Nineveh, both of which aspired to power and strove to gain a controlling influence with the sovereign. The one comprised the descendants of the Kaldâ who had delivered the city from the Assyrian yoke, together with those of the ancient military nobility. The other was composed of the great priestly families and their adherents, who claimed for the gods or their representatives the right to control the affairs of the state, and to impose the will of heaven on the rulers of the kingdom. The latter faction seems to have prevailed at first at the court of Amil-marduk, the sole surviving son and successor of Nebuchadrezzar. This prince on his accession embraced a policy contrary to that pursued by his father: and one of his first acts was to release Jehoiachin, King of Judah, who had been languishing in chains for twenty-seven years, and to ameliorate the condition of the other expatriated Jews.[1] The official history of a later date represented him as having been an unjust sovereign, but we have no information as to his

represents himself as inheriting the political views of Nebuchadrezzar and Nergal-sharuzur, leads me to take the opposite view. We know what hatred Nabonidus roused in the minds of the priests of Merodach because his principles of government were opposed to theirs: the severe judgment he passed on the rule of Amil-marduk and Labashi-marduk seems to prove that he considered them as belonging to the rival party in the state, that is, to the priestly faction. The forms of the names and the lengths of the several reigns have been confirmed by contemporary monuments, especially by the numerous contract tablets. The principal inscriptions belonging to the reign of Nergal-sharuzur deal only with public works and the restoration of monuments.

[1] 2 *Kings* xxv. 27–30; cf. *Jer.* lii. 31–34.

misdeeds, and know only that after two years a conspiracy broke out against him, led by his own brother-in-law Nergal-sharuzur, who assassinated him and seized the vacant throne (560 B.C.). Nergal-sharuzur endeavoured to revive the policy of Nebuchadrezzar, and was probably supported by the military party, but his reign was a short one; he died in 556 B.C., leaving as sole heir a youth dissipated character named Labashi-marduk, whose name is stigmatised by the chroniclers as that of a prince who knew not how to rule. He was murdered at the end nine months, and his place taken by a native Babylonian a certain Nabonâîd (Nabonidus), son of Nabo-balatsu-ikbi who was not connected by birth with his immediate prede cessors on the throne (556–555 B.C.).

No Oriental empire could escape from the effects of frequent and abrupt changes in its rulers: like so many previous dynasties, that of Nabopolassar became enfeebled as if from exhaustion immediately after the death of its most illustrious scion, and foundered in imbecility and decrepitude. Popular imagination, awe-struck by such a sudden downfall from exalted prosperity, recognised the hand of God in the events which brought about the catastrophe. A Chaldæan legend, current not long after related how Nebuchadrezzar, being seized towards the end of his life with the spirit of prophecy, mounted to the roof of his palace, and was constrained, as a punishment for his pride, to predict to his people, with his own lips, the approaching ruin of their city; thereupon the glory of its monarch suffered an eclipse from which there was no emerging. The Jews, nourishing undying hatred for the conqueror who had overthrown Jerusalem and destroyed the Temple of Solomon, were not satisfied with a punishment so inadequate. According to them, Nebuchadrezzar, after his victorious career, was so intoxicated with his own glory that he proclaimed himself the equal of God. "Is not this great Babylon," he cried, "which I have built for the royal dwelling-place, by the might of my power, and for the glory of my majesty!" and while he thus spake, there came a voice from heaven, decreeing his metamorphosis into the form of a beast. "He was driven from men, and did eat grass as oxen, and his body was wet with the dew of heaven, till his hair was grown like eagles' feathers, and his nails like birds' claws." For seven years the king remained in this state, to resume his former shape at the end of this period, and recover his kingdom after having magnified the God of Israel.[1] The founder of the dynasty which replaced that of Nebuchadrezzar, Nabonidus, was certainly ill fitted to brave the storms already threatening to break over his kingdom. It has not been ascertained whether he had any natural right to the throne, or by what means he attained supreme power, but the way in which he dwells on the names of Nebuchadrezzar and Nergalsharuzur renders it probable that he was raised to the throne by the military faction. He did not prove, as events turned turned out, a good general, nor even a soldier of moderate ability, and it is even possible that he also lacked that fierce courage of which none of his predecessors was ever destitute. He allowed his army to dwindle away and his fortresses to fall into ruins; the foreign

---

[1] *Dan.* iv.

alliances existing at his accession, together with those which he himself had concluded, were not turned to the best advantage; his provinces were badly administered, and his subjects rendered discontented: his most salient characteristic was an insatiable curiosity concerning historical and religious antiquities, which stimulated him to undertake excavations in all the temples, in order to bring to light monuments of ages long gone by. He was a monarch of peaceful disposition, who might have reigned with some measure of success in a century of unbroken peace, or one troubled only by petty wars with surrounding inferior states; but, unfortunately, the times were ill suited to such mild sovereignty. The ancient Eastern world worn out by an existence reckoned by thousands of years as well as by its incessant conflicts, would have desired, indeed, no better fate than to enjoy some years of repose in the condition in which recent events had left it; but other nations, the Greeks and the Persians, by no means anxious for tranquillity, were entering the lists. For the moment the efforts of the Greeks were concentrated on Egypt where Pharaoh manifested for them inexhaustible good will, and on Cyprus, two-thirds of which belonged to them the danger for Chaldæa lay in the Persians, kinsfolk and vassals of the Medes, whose semi-barbarous chieftains had issued from their mountain homes some eighty years previously to occupy the eastern districts of Elam.

END OF VOL. VIII.

# INDEX

## A

Abdimilkôt, 124
Abu-Simbel, Graffito at, 415
Abu-Simbel, Temple of, 417
Achæmenes, 281
Achæmenides, 384
Adrammelech (Adarmalik), 117
Adyattes. *See* Meles
Æolians, The, 103
Africa, Egyptian fleet sails round, 406, 407
Ahaz, 20
Ahura-mazdâ, 274
Ahura-mazdâ, Map of the lands created by, 274
Altaku (Eltekeh), 27, 29, 36
Alyattes, 393, 394
Amadai (Madai) *See* Medes
Amasis, 447, 448
Amenertas, Queen, 338, 358, 359
Ammon (*or* Ammonites), 422
Ammon, Oasis of, 440
Amon (of Judah), 311, 316
Amon, Priestesses of, 337
Andaria, 151, 201
Anshân, *or* Anzan (*see also* Persia), 282
Apries (Uaphres), 422, 425, 436
Apries, Head of a sphinx of, 263
Apries, Sphinx of, 422
Apries, Vase in form of helmed head of, 262
Arabia, Submission of, to Assur-bani-pal, 243
Arabians, 288, 289
Arabs (*see also* Aramæans), 131, 146, 153, 243
Arabs, Submission of, to Esarhaddon, 135
Aramæan sheikhs, 192
Aramæans, The, 56, 63
Arbela, 204, 215
Ardys, 108, 177
Argistis II., 150
Armenia, 119
Arpad, 37
Arvad, 148, 171, 175
Aryans, The, 275

Ashdod, 360
Asia Minor, 177, 389
Asmakh, 353
Assur-bani-pal (Kandalanu), 162, 165-168, 175, 185, 228, 239, 260, 288, 293, 294, 323, 338
    Babylon captured by, 232
    Bas-relief of, 299
    Head of, 187
    Library of, 293
    Submission of Arabia to, 243
Assur-bani-pal and his queen, 216
Assur-etililâni, 323-325
Assur-nadin-shumu, 41
Assyria (or Assur)
    Art of, 68
    Egyptian influence on art, 162, 289
    Elam conquered by, 217
    Ezekiel's description of, 79
    Prisoners of, 427
    Revolt of Egypt against, 163
Assyrian cavalry raid, 73
Assyrian helmet, 195
Assyrian king, 428
Assyrian lion-hunts, 197
Assyrian soldiers, Raid by, 43
Assyrian triangle (map of), 300
Assyrians carrying away captives, 431
Astyages (Ishtuvigu), 400, 451
Athribis, 155, 174
Atyadæ, The, 101

## B

Baal (god), 314
Bâal L, King of Tyre, 148, 150, 158, 175
Babylon, 454, 463
    Capture of, by Assur-bani-pal, 231
    Destruction of, by Sennacherib, 61
    Fortifications of, 455, 456
    Kings of, 40
    Lion of, 460
    Rebuilding of, 133
    Revolt of, under Merodach-baladan, 5
Babylonian bas-relief, 458
Bartutua, 128, 129, 307
Bavian, Bas-reliefs at, 66
Bavian, Stele at, 69

# INDEX

"Bel, Taking the hands of," 169, 232
Belibni (King of Babylon), 6, 41
Bel-marduk, 61
Bel-marduk, Temple of, at Babylon, 168, 170, 221, 459
Benhadad II. (Adadidri *or* Hadadezer), Death of, 13
Bît-Adini (in Bît-Dakkuri), 56
Bît-Amukkâni, 56, 220
Bît-Dakkuri (*or* Bît-Dakuri), 56, 220
Bît-Dayaukku, The, 88
Bît-Imbi, 247, 257
Bît-Yakin, 40, 64, 325
Bohbaït, Lion of, 436
Bubastis, 10

## C

Calah, 160, 324
Calah, Palace of, 160, 161
Carchemish, 148, 377
Carchemish, Battle of, 381
Carian inscription, 348
Carian mercenaries, 178, 349
Carians, The, 178, 179, 334, 339, 345
Carthage (Qart-hadshat), 14
Chaldæa, 267. *See also* Karduniash
Chaldæan empire, The new, 378
Chalybes, 103
Cilicia, 124, 176
Cimmerians, The, 111, 112, 113, 119, 122, 125, 307
  Attacked by Gyges, 182, 183
  Battle against the Greeks, 240
  In Syria, 319
Colophon, 236
Comana, 97
Cossæans, The, 9
Cyaxares (Huvakshatara), 268, 295, 307, 322, 326, 381, 388, 395
Cyaxares attacks Nineveh, 299
Cyaxares drives back the Scythians, 323
Cyprus, 148, 160
Cyrene, 439, 443
Cyrene, Ruins of, 441

## D

Damascus, 159
Daphnæ, 350, 433
Daphnæ, Fortress of, 347
Dascylus (Daskylos), 108, 177
Deiokes, 85, 87, 268
Dido (Elissa), 14
Dur-Sharrukin, 63, 324

## E

Eastern World, Map of the, 229, 331
Ecbatana (Agbatana), (*see also* Hamadân), 86
Ecbatana, Kingdom of, 85, 132

Edom, 422
Egypt
  Assyrian province, 155, 173, 175
  Brook of (Wady-el-Arish), 123
  Esarhaddon's invasion of, 153
  Ethiopians withdraw from, 339
  Greater Egypt, End of, 343
  Revolt against Assyria, 163
  Tanuatamanu reconquers, 191
Egyptian army, 403
Egyptian fleet, 403–407
Egyptian head, Saite period, 81
Egyptian influence on Assyrian art, 160, 289
Egyptian torso at Turin, 265
Egyptian vessel, 404
Ekron, 23, 27, 28
Elam, 330
  Disabled by discord, 225
  Final ruin of, 259, 261
  First subject to Assyria, 217
  Revolutions in, 247
  Sennacherib's expedition against, 45, 53
Elisa. *See* Dido.
Ellipi, 56, 88
Elulai, 19, 26, 148
Ephesus, 234, 240
Esarhaddon (Assur-akhê-iddin), 83, 115, 167
Esarhaddon as King of Egypt, 158
Esarhaddon takes Memphis, 155, 159
Esarhaddon's campaigns against the Kalda, 121
Esarhaddon's invasion of Egypt, 153
Eth-baal (of Sidon), 13, 26
Ethiopia, 138
Ethiopians withdraw from Egypt, 339
Etius (Etiaus), 387
Ezekiel (the prophet), 418, 449
Ezekiel's description of Assyria, 79

## G

Gambulâ (*or* Gambulu), The, 56, 202
Gebel-Barkal, Hemispeos of, 143, 144
Greek, Egyptian, 348
Greeks, Battle of the Cimmerians against the, 240
Gyges, 109, 177–181, 234–239, 340

## H

Habakkuk (the prophet), 412
Hadadezer (*or* Adadidri). *See* Benhadad II.
Halys, Banks of, 104
  Battle of the, 399
  Caves on the banks of, 115

# INDEX

Hamadân *(See also* Ecbatana), 89
Hamadân, View of, 88
Hazor, 27
Heraclidæ, The, 101, 102, 109, 177, 179
Hezekiah, 5, 21, 29, 33, 37, 149
Hezekiah, Reforms of, 20
Hiram II., 15
Hittite syllabary, 104
Hoplites, Greek, 413
Hoplites in action, 335
Horses as tribute, 176
Huldah, the prophetess, 363

## I

Indabigash, 245, 247
Ionian mercenaries, 350
Ionians, The, 103, 347, 437
Iran, 277
Iranian soldiers, 311
Iranian tableland, 84
Ishtar (of Arbela), 203
Israel, Kingdom of, 159

## J

Jeconiah. *See* Jehoiakim
Jehoahaz *or* Shallum (of Judah), 378
Jehoiakim (Jeconiah), 378, 408-411, 461
Jeremiah (the prophet), 316, 363, 379, 408, 409, 426
Jerusalem
  Destruction of, 428, 429
  Fortified by Hezekiah, 29
  Siege of, by Nebuchadrezzar, 412
  Siege of, by Sennacherib, 36
  Temple of, 20, 371, 417
Jews submit to Sennacherib, 31
Joppa, 27
Josiah, 362, 363, 373, 377
Josiah's religious reforms, 371
Judæa, Map of, 23
Judah, Kingdom of, 12, 311, 362
Judah, Kings of, 430

## K

Kalakh. *See* Calah
Kaldâ, The (*or* Aramæans), 52, 63, 201, 220
Kalda, Esarhaddon's campaigns against, 118
Karduniash invaded by Tammaritu, 194
Kedar, Sheikhs of, 135, 192, 243, 257, 407
Khalludush, 46, 53, 252
Khalludush invades Karduniash, 53
Khalule, Battle of, 57
Kharkhar, 89, 131
Khâti, The, 148, 160

Khumbân-igash, 212, 213, 221, 223, 225
Khumbân-Khaldash II., 147
Kition, *or* Citium (Amathus), 19
Kouyunjik, 292
Kouyunjik, Palace of, 69
Kui, The, 64
Kutur-nakhunta, 54, 55

## L

Lachish (Tell-el-Hesy), 29, 33
Libya (Lubim), 196
  Greeks in, 438
  Map of, 443
Limir-patesi-assur, 174
Lubdi, 150, 201
Lycians, The, 239
Lydia, 93, 237, 267
Lydia, Kingdom of, 101, 103, 177, 183
Lydian horsemen, 181
Lydians, 400

## M

Madyes, 306, 310, 322, 395
Magan, 47
Magnesia (of Sipylos), 236
Manasseh (of Judah), 149, 311, 316
Mannai, The (the Minni), 64, 126, 185, 196, 201
Mannai, Incursions of, under Esarhaddon, 126
Mantumibâit *(see* Montumihâit) 163
Marduk-ushezib, 40
Mashauasha, The (Maxyes), 335, 439, 446
Mashauasha, Flight of the, 351
Medes, The, 84, 89, 90, 201, 271, 324, 380, 455
  Attacked by Sennacherib, 9
Media, 267
  Flora and fauna, 277
  *Wall of*, 456
Median Empire, The, 401
Medic horseman, 298
Mediterranean, 173
Mediterranean vessels, 48
Megiddo, 376
Megiddo, Battle of, 376, 377
Meles, 109
Melukhkha, 48
Memphis, 10, 160, 190, 339, 433
Memphis taken by Esarhaddon, 155, 160
Memphite bas-relief, 359
Mermnadæ, The, 109, 177, 391
Merodach-baladan *or* Mardukabalidinna (King of Babylon), 5
Messogis, Mountains of, 390
Midas, 94, 96, 101
Midas, Monument of, 95

# INDEX

Milesians, Fort of the, 347
Miletus, 237
Mitanni, 148
Moab, 422
Montumihâit, 173, 189, 337–341, 359
Montumihâit, Head of, 174
Mugallu (of Milid), 151
Mushezib-marduk, 53–58
Mushku (*or* Mushki), The, 387
Mutton I., 13
Mutton II. (*or* Mattan), 15

## N

Nabo-bel-shumi, 248
Nabonidus, 460, 461
Nabopolassar (Nabu-bal-uzur), 325, 326, 381, 454, 459
Nagitu, 52
Nahr-el-Kelb, 156
  Mouth of, 156
  Stele of, 157
Nahum, the prophet, 196, 304, 305
Nana
  Image of, 252
  Statue of, 221, 249
*Nâr-marratum*, Map of the, 48
*Nâr*, The fleet of Sennacherib on the, 49
Nebuchadrezzar (Nebuchadnezzar), 381, 402, 423, 426, 450, 451, 462
  Besieges Jerusalem, 412
  Stele of, 424
Nebuchadrezzar and Media, 386
Necho, 164, 189, 403, 408, 412
Necho II., 374, 377
  Invasion of Syria by, 375
  Scarab of, 378
Nergal-ushezib, 53
Nergal-ushezib in battle, 54
Nineveh, 48, 323
  Attacked by Cyaxares, 299
  Destruction of, 328
  Fosse at, 302
  Map of, 301
  Mounds of, 63
Nisæan horses, 279
Nisaya, 273
Nubians, The (Put), 196

## O

Obelisks at Rome, 421, 437

## P

Pakruru, 336
Pasargadæ, The, 281
Pasargadæ (city) 285
Pelusium, Sennacherib's disaster at, 38

Persia, 282
Persia, Scene in, 283
Persian, A, 287
Persian archer, 285
Persian foot-soldiers, 297
Persian Gulf, 41, 47
Persian intaglio, 82
Persian realm, Map of the, 280
Persians, The, 280
Philistines, The, 64, 422
Phœnicians, The, 159, 257, 378
Phraortes (Fravartish), 268, 280, 287, 294, 295
Phrygian gods, 96, 99
Phrygians, 96, 104
Platæa, 439
Priene, Site of, 391
Psammetichus I., 174, 175, 333, 340, 344, 345, 348
  Buildings of, 355
  Revolt of, 233
  Statue of, 235
  Syrian policy of, 361
Psammetichus II., 414, 421, 422
Pteria, 103, 114, 395, 398
  Ruins of, 396
Pukudu (*or* Puqudu), The (Pekod), 56, 221
Pygmalion, 14

## R

Rabshakeh, The, of 2 Kings, 30
Rabshakeh, under Esarhaddon and Assurbani-pal, 172
Raphia, 153, 154
Red Sea, The, 405
Rusas II., 151, 152
Rusas III., 212

## S

Sabaco (Shabaka), 163
  Cartouche of, 11
Sadyattes, 177–180
Sais, 163
  Ruins of, 361
Sardanapalus, 267
Sardes (Sardis), 102, 105, 108, 236
  View of, 105
Sardis. *See* Sardes
Scythian invasion, The, 390
Scythian soldiers, 311
Scythians, The, 111, 112, 122, 125–128, 306, 324, 362
  Driven back by Cyaxares, 323
  Incursions of, under Esarhaddon, 127
  Tending their wounded, 308
Sennacherib (Sin-akhê-irba), 72
  Bas-relief of, 65
  Besieges Jerusalem, 37

# INDEX

Buildings of, 71
Head of, 79
Impression of seal of on clay, 80
Invades Elam, 53
Jews submit to, 33
Murder of, 117
Sennacherib's disaster at Pelusium, 39
Sennacherib's expedition against Elam, 45
Sepharvaim (*or* Sibraîm), 37
Shabaka. *See* Sabaco
Shabaku. *See* Sabaco
Shabarain. *See* Sepharvaim
Shabitoku, 11, 27, 137
Shamash-shumukîn, 162–170, 218, 219, 231, 340
Shapenuapit II., 337–341
Sharezer, 117–119
Shupria, 150, 151
Sidon (*see also* Tyre), 15, 17, 22, 124
Silphium, 443
Silphium, Weighing, 445
Sinai, Desert of, 153
Sin-shar-ishkun, 324, 325
Sion, Mount, 314
Susa, 385
Destruction of, 249
Gods carried off from, 249
Tumulus of, 253
Syria, 171, 330
Coalition against, 221
Invaded by Necho II., 375
Syrian shipwrights, 48
Syrians, The white, 103, 109, 113, 177

## T

Tabal, The, 151, 176, 184, 309, 387
Taharqa (Tirhakah) 138, 139, 145, 153, 158, 165, 189, 337
Buildings of, in Ethiopia, 142
Bronze statuette of, 83
Column of, at Karnak, 141
Head of, 145
Second defeat of, 171
Tabarqa and his queen, 139
Tammaritu, 210, 226, 248
Tammaritu invades Karduniash, 194
Tanuatamanu, 138, 189, 339.
Bas-relief of, 191
Reconquers Egypt, 191
Tartan, The, of 2 Kings xviii., 34 ; of Isaiah xx., under Esarhaddon, 171, 172
Teiria, 107
Theban queen, Statue of a, 338
Thebes, pillaged by the Assyrians, 190
Thracians, The, 90
Tirhakah. *See* Taharqa
Tiummân, 201–216, 246
Treres, The, 113
Tul-Barsip (capital of Bît-Adini), 48
Tulliz, 205
Battle of, 207, 209, 212, 213
Tyre, 12, 146, 423, 435
Map of, 18
Ruin of its kingdom, 27
Trade of, 16
Tyrseni, The, 101, 103

## U

Uaté, 257, 258
Ummân-minânu, 56–59
Urartu, *or* Kingdom of Van (Armenia), 150, 185, 389
Urtaku, 193, 209

## Z

Zedekiah (Mattaniah) of Judah, 417, 418, 422, 427, 428
Zephaniah (the prophet), 317
Zeus Labraundos (on coin), 106
Zinjîrli (*or* Sinjîrli), Stele at, 154–158

www.ingramcontent.com/pod-product-compliance
Lightning Source LLC
Chambersburg PA
CBHW042226010526
44113CB00043B/2669